SURVIVING THE
CONFEDERACY

Also by John C. Waugh

The Class of 1846:
From West Point to Appomattox—
Stonewall Jackson, George McClellan,
and Their Brothers

Reelecting Lincoln:
The Battle for the 1864 Presidency

Sam Bell Maxey
and the Confederate Indians

Last Stand at Mobile

SURVIVING THE
CONFEDERACY

Rebellion, Ruin, and Recovery—
Roger and Sara Pryor During the Civil War

JOHN C. WAUGH

HARCOURT, INC.

New York   San Diego   London

Copyright © 2002 by John C. Waugh

All rights reserved. No part of this publication may be reproduced or
transmitted in any form or by any means, electronic or mechanical,
including photocopy, recording, or any information storage and retrieval
system, without permission in writing from the publisher.

Requests for permission to make copies of any part of the work
should be mailed to the following address: Permissions Department,
Harcourt, Inc., 6277 Sea Harbor Drive, Orlando, Florida 32887-6777.

www.HarcourtBooks.com

Library of Congress Cataloging-in-Publication Data
Waugh, John C.
Surviving the Confederacy: rebellion, ruin, and recovery:
Roger and Sara Pryor during the Civil War/John C. Waugh.—1st ed.
p.   cm.
Includes bibliographical references and index.
ISBN 0-15-100389-0
1. Pryor, Roger A. (Roger Atkinson), 1828–1919.   2. Pryor, Sara Agnes Rice,
1830–1912.   3. Confederate States of America—Biography.   4. Married
people—Confederate States of America—Biography.   5. United States—
History—Civil War, 1861–1865—Social aspects.   6. Virginia—History—Civil
War, 1861–1865—Social aspects.   7. United States—History—Civil War,
1861–1865—Campaigns.   8. Virginia—History—Civil War, 1861–1865—
Campaigns.   9. United States—History—Civil War, 1861–1865—Biography.
10. Virginia—History—Civil War, 1861–1865—Biography.   I. Title.
E467 .W36 2002
973.7'13'092—dc21   2002008982

Text set in Fournier MT
Designed by Cathy Riggs

Printed in the United States of America

First edition
A C E G I K J H F D B

For my angel mother,
who always hoped her son would write a book

Contents

Roger and Sara Pryor's Virginia

George Skoch

SURVIVING THE
CONFEDERACY

Introduction

*W*ashington was having one of its first events of the new social season, on a Thursday afternoon December 20, 1860. The daughter of a wealthy Washington grocer was marrying a congressman from Louisiana. It was a very Southern and very high-society affair. The bride's father's large house had been converted into a conservatory redolent with masses of blooming roses and lilies. There were lit fountains, magnificent wedding gifts, and a stunning bride in a stunning bridal dress.

At the reception President James Buchanan was seated in an armchair at one end of the drawing room. Sara Pryor stood behind him, thinking how much he had aged during the summer that she had been away in Virginia, when the president glanced back over his shoulder at her and said, "Madam, do you suppose the house is on fire? I hear an unusual commotion in the hall."

"I will inquire the cause, Mr. President," Sara said.

Out in the entrance hall Sara found Congressman Lawrence Keitt of South Carolina leaping into the air, shaking a paper over his head, and exclaiming, "Thank God! Oh, thank God!"

One of Roger Pryor's closest friends and colleagues, Keitt had been in Congress since 1852, elected as a radical states' rights Democrat. He was one of the South's most outspoken, defiant defenders in Congress and in South Carolina had been actively promoting secession for a decade, appearing intent on rending the Union "from turret to foundation stone."[1]

Sara took hold of him and said, "Mr. Keitt, are you crazy? The president hears you and wants to know what's the matter."

"Oh!" Keitt cried. "South Carolina has seceded! Here's the telegram. I feel like a boy let out from school."

Sara returned to the drawing room, bent over Buchanan's chair, and said in a low voice, "It appears, Mr. President, that South Carolina has seceded from the Union. Mr. Keitt has a telegram."

Buchanan stared at her, stunned. Falling back and grasping the arms of his chair, he whispered, "Madam, might I beg you to have my carriage called?"

Out in the hallway again, Sara found Buchanan's secretary, sent him without explanation for the president's carriage, and remained waiting there herself until it pulled up at the door.

Without pausing or stopping to be questioned, Buchanan left and drove immediately to the White House to await official word of this long-dreaded national catastrophe. The news would not become known, except in official circles, until late evening.

Back at the wedding reception, Sara searched for Roger and found him in a corner with Keitt. The Pryors called their own carriage and drove to Stephen and Addie Douglas's house. There were no more thoughts of bride or bridegroom, wedding cake or wedding breakfast—the wedding celebration had been ruined. Sara's spirit was mired in foreboding and regret, and the night mirrored her mood; it was dark, a drizzling rain was falling, and the streets were mired in mud.[2]

ROGER AND SARA PRYOR were Virginians herein cast as the pivotal figures to portray the agony of the South and its people—a particular class of its people—in the crucible of the Civil War.

Roger and Sara moved in the highest levels of politics and society, in both the North and South before the war, and in the South during it. But there was nothing in their backgrounds to prepare them for their plunge into the maelstrom, hardship, and heartbreak of a brother's war. That they dealt with it as they did is in itself heroic.

I found them, as many such things are found, by serendipity, while looking for a Confederate couple who could carry the story. I had met Roger—a longhaired, angry-eyed, fire-eating secessionist—at Fort Sumter, when writing *The Class of 1846*, but thought nothing further of him until I was sifting through anthologies of Confederate women's writings on the Civil War, searching for the right woman, and ran repeatedly into Sara Pryor. When I discovered Sara was Roger's wife and that she had written two delightful books of memoirs *and* looked like an angel, I knew I had found my couple.

They did not disappoint me. There could not have been a more appropriate pair. As Sara said, they "lived in the last two-thirds of the splendid nineteenth century," and knew some—indeed, most—of the men and women "who made that century notable."[3] From the beginning of their long life together, to its end, they were "in touch with the prominent shapers of events," North and South.[4]

When the country was splitting in the turbulent 1850s, they were there—in Washington, intimates of two presidents. When the split came, Roger was there—on the floor of Congress, helping to drive the wedge. When President Buchanan heard that the first Southern state had seceded, Sara was there—whispering the news in his ear. When Confederate guns opened on Fort Sumter and plunged the country into the bloody Civil War, Roger was there—in the delegation demanding the fort's surrender. When the fighting began, Roger was there—a colonel, then a brigadier, and finally, a private, in the Confederate army. When the South became a nation of refugees, Sara was there—homeless with the rest. When the war finally came down to the siege of Petersburg,

Sara was there—living the terror. When Ulysses S. Grant's army finally broke Robert E. Lee's lines in the Petersburg trenches and marched into their city and ended the war, both Sara and Roger were there—sharing the agony. Throughout, when "sunshine and shadow chased one another across the entire panorama of the war," they were there—amid all the suffering and dying.[5] And when it was over, they were still there—working to reknit the severed Union. From beginning to end they were there, and their story is well worth telling.

Now that I know them, they have become family. I hope you will feel the same way.

CHAPTER 1

———••◆••———

Roger

𝓝ottoway Court House was a serene, prosperous little southside Virginia village and county seat. It was cocooned in a deep and placid nineteenth-century tranquility that was disordered only on court days or by political meetings on the town square. Any new mechanical wonder imported by a local planter was a bugle blast in an otherwise church-quiet existence.[6]

It lay on the banks of the Nottoway River in Nottoway County 67 miles southwest of Richmond and 189 miles from the Federal capital in Washington. The stage from Petersburg bound for North Carolina rolled through daily. The village counted fifteen dwellings, one mercantile house, one hotel, a saddler, a tailor, a blacksmith shop, and a population of seventy people, including a physician and a lawyer. Supplementing the courthouse was a clerk's office and a jail for debtors and criminals, and there was a flour mill on the river. The town, the river, and the county were named alike for a tribe of Virginia Indians long since displaced.[7]

There, in the town where his father was the Presbyterian pastor at Shiloh Church, Roger Atkinson Pryor grew up.

On his father's side Roger descended from two long and upstanding ancestral lines, the Blands and the Pryors, both deep-rooted in the old Virginia gentry and with strong pedigrees in revolution and politics.[8] The Blands could look back on nearly two centuries as landed gentry in young America, to the year Theodorick Bland purchased an estate on the James River in 1654. In both fortune and understanding this first Bland was said to be inferior to no man of his time in the country, that "with his personal graces, his literary accomplishments, and his distinguished career," he was "a brilliant star set in the early skies of Virginia history," a star that gleamed brightly as one of the King's Council for the colonial commonwealth.[9]

As the Bland line eddied and branched down through succeeding generations, it produced an abundance of Theodoricks and Richards, many of them estimable men in their time and place. One of the Richards was a member of the Virginia House of Delegates and a political writer and thinker of the first rank. It was said of him that "his intellectual calibre was capacious, his education finished, his habits of application indefatigable." His distinguished contemporary Thomas Jefferson thought him "the wisest man south of James River."[10] He was seen as "staunch and tough as whitleather" with "something the look of old parchments, which he handleth and studieth much."[11]

That "whitleather" Richard had a nephew named Theodorick, another brilliant star in the Bland line, one of the first patriots to rouse the colonies to resistance against the British in the Revolution. Born about 1742, the only son among several daughters and delicate in health from birth, he was sent at age eleven to England for an education. He returned to Virginia more than a decade later as a physician, one of the first Virginians to devote himself to the study of medicine. By 1771 his frail constitution had turned his aspirations into longings for the rural life of a planter, with its quiet, peaceful seclusion and studious repose—a "sighing for some sequestered Abyssinian happy valley."[12] But Revolution loomed, and that did not lend itself to tranquility. So he went to war instead, a captain of the first troop of Virginia cavalry and then a colonel of the First Continental Dragoons. He fought at Brandywine and later commanded the post at Charlottesville. George Washington thought well of him, and he was a friend of Thomas Jefferson, of the Marquis de Lafayette, and of Patrick Henry.

That same Theodorick became a member of the Virginia convention that met in June 1788, after the Revolution, to ratify a new constitution for the confederation of states. He voted against the Constitution, believing it repugnant to the interests of his country. But when it was adopted over his opposition, he was elected by his district in Virginia to the first Congress that convened under it. He was never for long permitted to live the life of leisure and serenity he so prized, but was occupied to the end of his forty-eight-year lifetime with unrelieved public service, civil and military. He was described as tall, somewhat corpulent in his later days, and of a noble countenance, his manners being "marked by ease, dignity and well-bred repose." He was seen as "virtuous and enlightened" in character and "estimable for his private worth and respectable for his public services."[13] Much the same might be said of other Blands. And as the line branched, it interconnected with other pedigrees of merit in Virginia, such gold-plated names as the Lees and the Randolphs.

The Pryor line was no less blue-blooded than that of the Blands. Pryors had come to Britain from Normandy, with William the Conqueror in 1066. The first Pryor in the New World was John, who came from England in the early 1700s and also became a friend of Patrick Henry. Roger's grandparents, Richard Pryor and Anne Bland, merged the two lines in 1805 and produced yet another Theodorick, the oldest of six sons, who was to become Roger's father.[14]

Theodorick Pryor's early education was at academies in Dinwiddie and Brunswick Counties. In 1823, when he was eighteen years old, he entered Hampden-Sydney College, a southside Virginia institution of high repute. Patrick Henry had sent seven sons to the college and had been on its board with James Madison. Theodorick graduated in three years with the highest distinction and as a member of that school's elite Union Society. He matriculated to the University of Virginia in Charlottesville, studied law for a year, and became a lawyer.

He then married Lucy Atkinson, who brought to the union yet a third line rich in church, law, literature, and education, and which would give Roger his middle name when he entered the world on July 19, 1828. He was followed soon by a sister, Lucy. But in 1830, when Roger was less than two years old, their mother died.

Too grief stricken to continue in the law, Theodorick entered the Union Theological Seminary at Hampden-Sydney, in 1831, and a year later became an ordained Presbyterian minister and was installed at Shiloh Church. In December that same year, he eased his sorrow with a second wife, Frances Epes, giving Roger and Lucy a new mother, and eventually two stepsisters and a stepbrother.

Theodorick's God-serving life was in the Bland tradition. He said, "To me it is a source of much comfort and of praise, that, in looking up the long line of my forefathers, I find so many Ministers of the Most High God."[15] It was true. There had been nearly as many pastors and ministers in his accumulated ancestry as there had been Theodoricks.

One admirer said of Roger's father that he was "a man cast in the mould of which martyrs were made in the olden time, and whether roasted, broiled, or boiled, he would never have yielded one iota in the confession of that faith which he so long held and so strongly defended."[16] As a pastor he was considered "eminent for piety, eloquence, and usefulness."[17] He was a man of sturdy common sense, who had a strong mind and a way with words. Another admirer said of him that he "fulfills my idea of a model pastor."[18]

He also fulfilled his family's idea of a model father; they believed that "his life stood for all that was true and fine." Young people confided to him both their joys and sorrows. He made of his home, one of them later wrote, an "atmosphere of culture and true religion," and "there was no excuse for being late for family prayers morning or night." The one noteworthy fault they found in him was his impatient, quickly excited, blunt-speaking nature, a trait he was to hand down to his son.[19]

Roger was later to say that the Pryors got their brains from the Blands. His father said, however, that he thought they had some brains even before they merged with the Blands.[20] Wherever the brains came from and however much of them he had inherited, Roger planned to put them to optimum use. When he was only twelve years old he vowed, "I am going to make my mark at whatever I do; if it is blacksmithing, I will be a good blacksmith."[21]

But blacksmithing was not his ambition. He began his education at the Classical Academy of Ephraim Dodd Saunders, in Petersburg, near where he was born, an institution not noted for producing blacksmiths. Then in 1843, following the precise path pioneered twenty years before by the father he admired, he entered Hampden-Sydney College, became a member of the elite Union Society, and fell in love with books. He had early read *Boswell's Johnson*, later confessing to his own son that it had given him a taste for literature and the habit of reading. Those were his signature traits at Hampden-Sydney.[22]

Hampden-Sydney College was made to order for the love of reading, rural serenity, and studious repose that Roger had inherited from the Bland line. It was a little all-male academy housed in a building on a hill among the chinquapins, a tree-shrub of the chestnut family common throughout the South, particularly southside Virginia. A well-armed student at Hampden-Sydney was obliged to carry a pocketful of chinquapin nuts, not just for munching but as weaponry. The country about the little college was also a kingdom of pine barrens and scrub oak groves, rooted in red clay soil. The open field around the academy building was scarred by gullies, weed filled, and teeming with cows and hogs belonging to professors, who raised them to supplement their meager incomes. The cows, with bells clanging, working their cuds, grazed up to the windows of the academic building, creating a discord that often challenged study. It was a cow-pasture college. But in its time it had sent out into the workaday world many useful, even great, men.[23]

By the summer of 1845 Roger, almost seventeen years old, was nearly the man he had been growing up to be. He was a lanky six feet tall and "erect as a shaft," with the elastic step of an Indian, and he walked with "a restless, rapid gait." He had a striking and graceful presence, an ingratiating manner, and irresistibly charming speech. His hair, raven and glistening, hung long, loose, and straight to his shoulders, framing a classic face. There was a fire in his eyes, which were steel gray, but there was also in him a moderating strain of gentleness. He had a high forehead, a pronounced nose, and prominent cheeks. His face was innocent of hair and always would be. His features were mobile and expressive. His mouth was strong, large, and "strangely nervous." He was restless by nature and ruled by an "impetuous temperament," but he bore himself as if born to distinction, which indeed he was. He was ambitious, with a bulldog passion to master thoroughly whatever he undertook.

His salient characteristic was his voice, well-pitched and penetrating and capable of torrents of eloquence when deeply stirred. At such times the words came cartwheeling out so rapid-fire that they defied stenographic report, and his voice vibrated "like a trumpet." Few who heard or saw him, even at this early age, forgot him.[24]

THERE WAS A MEETING of Presbyterian divines in Charlottesville in the summer of 1845, and Theodorick attended with Roger. To see Charlottesville was to understand why Thomas Jefferson chose to live there and only reluctantly ever left. Its setting blended mountains, fields, woodlands, and running streams into "a landscape of quiet, but uncommon beauty." To the west of the little village soared the Blue Ridge Mountains, one of the boldest and most beautiful horizons in the world. Theodorick and Roger approached Charlottesville from the east over a level landscape where, one writer has written, "nature seems to sleep in eternal repose." Another wrote that "there was almost a sense of pain at the stillness which seemed to reign." It was a place, yet another writer said, "where earth herself seemed struggling heavenward."[25]

Cradled in this scenic grandeur, Charlottesville was a village of "simple belfries" piercing the mists of surrounding green, and dominated by the classic pantheon and tall colonnades of the University of Virginia, Thomas Jefferson's legacy to his beloved state. There were four churches in the village, two bookstores, several dry-goods establishments, and a female seminary.[26]

There was also in Charlottesville at that time hospitality to spare. It was, in fact, an age in Virginia when visiting and being visited had been elevated to an art form, and when hospitality was considered "the chief of virtues."[27] It was said that all Virginia houses were "built of elastic material capable of sheltering any number of guests, many of whom remained all summer." Indeed, that was rather expected when a visit was promised.[28]

It was said also that "the Virginia gentleman of those days was hospitable, as men are truthful, for his own sake first. His hospitality was spontaneous, unconscious, and free as heaven itself with its favors. All it asked in return was that you should come when you pleased, go when you pleased, stay as long as you pleased, and enjoy yourself to the top of your bent."[29]

Whenever large conventions of clergymen came to Charlottesville—and they came often—the visiting divines were taken into the town's elastic and hospitable homes. No man's house in the village was more elastic or more valued for its hospitality than the warm and welcoming home of Dr. Samuel Pleasants Hargrave, a physician. Any large religious or literary meeting coming to town caused the doctor to send the chairman a note asking how many guests he might be permitted to host. He had done this in advance of that summer's meeting of Presbyterian clergymen, and he had drawn Theodorick Pryor. So the Pryors, father and son, made their way out to the Hargrave house, which sat on one of the terraced hills overlooking the Blue Ridge.

After they entered the house, Roger, ever exuberant, bounded up toward his assigned room two stair steps at a time, and for the first time, saw Sara Agnes Rice. She was fifteen years old. She was brown eyed, with auburn hair plaited into long braids—and she was beautiful.

CHAPTER 2

— •◦• —

Sara

$\mathscr{S}$ara Agnes Rice, born in Halifax County, Virginia, on February 19, 1830, was not quite two years younger than Roger Pryor. At age three, she remembered, she ceased being "merely an inert absorber of light and warmth and comfort," and became aware of "the pain in the world," which she would spend the rest of her life passionately longing to ease in herself and others. The pain that triggered this passion at such an early age was the pitiable sight of a colony of doomed ants rushing madly about on a stick of wood as it was being laid over a bed of red-hot coals.[30] Her distress was profound and heartfelt.

Like Roger, Sara was descended from a preeminent Virginia line. The first Rice in her lineage in America was a Welshman, Thomas Rice, who arrived in Hanover in the Virginia colonies in about 1680. Her great-grandfather David Rice was a clergyman— there were many clerics in her ancestry, as in Roger's—and a pioneer in the dissenting movements of his time. He was a founding trustee of Hampden-Sydney College and the father of Presbyterianism in Kentucky. Sara came to believe that in Virginia "everybody's great-grandfather knew my great-grandfather."[31] This widely known David Rice married Mary Blair, the daughter of a Pennsylvania clergyman, and their son William grew up to be respected in Virginia as "a man of dignified bearing and classical culture." He was also a friend and neighbor of Patrick Henry—as many in that day seemed to be.[32]

Samuel Blair Rice, William's son, a physician turned Baptist minister, was a tall, lean, straight-figured cleric with an earnest look, a sympathetic nature, and a rapid-fire preaching style.[33] In the 1820s he married Lucinda Walton Leftwich, who bore him Sara.

There were more children under Pastor Rice's roof than could be well cared for, and Sara's mother, though fertile, was frail and sickly. When a childless but much loved Aunt Mary and Uncle Samuel Hargrave from Hanover took a shine to the little three-and-a-half-year-old, Sara went, though not without tears, to live with them. It was not an uncommon practice in that time—to relieve the pressure on a too ample household—to let a loved child go temporarily to live with another loving relative.

There were no railway lines in Virginia in the early 1830s. Travel in those days was in a carriage pulled by a pair of horses, with a goatskin-hair trunk strapped on behind or, if the journey was long, with a light wagon for baggage. Sara set out for Hanover in one of these carriages, creaking and rocking, pitching and jolting on high springs over rutted roads, tossing and lurching like a ship at sea. Twenty-five miles of this was quite enough in one day for a pair of horses and their passengers, so each night they put in at a country tavern, where Sara, homesick and weeping for her mother, sank into a deep feather bed and tearful sleep. Late one night, weary from the journey, they finally turned up an avenue of cedars lining the lane leading to the house in Hanover. With the next morning's sun, Sara ran out in her bare feet onto a veranda shaded by roses, and from that hour her homesickness was transformed into "perfect contentment," soon blossoming into a childhood "of absolute serenity and happiness."[34]

Little Sara could not have been gathered into abler or more loving arms. Aunt Mary was tall, graceful, and very beautiful, with large gray eyes, and dark curls framing a face of delicate features lit by a sunburst smile. She was a woman far in advance of her times—an accomplished English scholar of strong mind, independent thought, and large tolerance—with a father who was yet another friend and neighbor of Patrick Henry. Aunt Mary possessed "a discriminating love of literature," which she would pass on to Sara. Although childless, she possessed "a rare skill in the management of youth." A mixture of "tenderness and firmness . . . unfailing tact and sympathy," Mary became passionately devoted to this young and only charge, who already was showing rich natural gifts, which a perceptive aunt could readily recognize.[35]

Sara's general impression of her growing-up years was of gardens—gardens everywhere, abloom with roses, lilies, violets, jonquils, flowering almond and double-flowering peach trees innocent of fruit but "cherished for the beauty of their blossoms." Her recollection was of orange and lemon and flowering pomegranate trees planted in tubs on the conservatory floor; of cacti, jasmine— the "queen of flowers"—abutilon, golden lantana, and snowy camellias, the "most poetic and elegant of all flowers—so pure and sensitive, resenting the profanation of the slightest touch." There were cool, crisp white violets in the February snows, and in the early hot summer there were tall lilacs, snowballs, myrtles and syringas, glowing beds of tulips, purple iris, and lily of the valley— "a paradise of sweets." There were passion vines dropping golden globes of fruit, and cool figs "bursting with scarlet sweetness."[36]

For Sara it was as if fairies, mounted on butterflies, visited each flower and painted it in the night. She was a dreamer. It was a time when living rooms were called parlors, and when the grown-ups gathered there and talked of politics or religion or slavery. At such times Sara retired into the inner chambers of her imagination.[37]

Aunt Mary's husband, Dr. Hargrave, was a distinguished physician and an ardent Presbyterian, also ahead of his time, who against the common practice had emancipated his inherited slaves.[38] After the Bible and the Westminster Catechism, Uncle Samuel pinned his faith on the *Richmond Whig* and Henry Clay, the great Whig statesman. To make Henry Clay president of the United States, he believed, was "something to live for." When the great Kentuckian passed through Richmond in Sara's early childhood, virtually all of Hanover made the twenty-five-mile ride to see and hear him, the Hargraves among them. Sara's uncle was resolved that she should see "the next President."

A procession of citizens was to escort Clay to the banquet hall, and Uncle Samuel had found a vacant doorway on the line of march, and there they awaited his coming. "Ah, there he comes!" he finally exclaimed. "Look well, little girl! You may never again see the greatest man in the world." Sara could see nothing but knees from her vantage point so close to the floor, so the uncle hoisted her to his shoulders. Then all she could see was "a tumbling sea of hats." But presently a space momentarily cleared, much as the Red Sea must have parted for Moses, and the great man, passing by, looked and saw her on her uncle's shoulders. He smiled, lifted his hat, and gallantly bowed to her.[39]

When Sara was nine, her aunt and uncle moved from Hanover to Charlottesville to solicit for her the best education and social life available. Aunt Mary was intent on properly developing that impressive natural talent she had early seen in her young niece. So they moved to the house with the terraced grounds on the hill overlooking the Blue Ridge and enrolled Sara in the seminary, a school for girls run by a much loved Presbyterian clergyman. In this "great brick hive for girls," as Sara called it, she began her formal schooling.

After several months, however, Aunt Mary reluctantly realized that a seminary education wasn't working for Sara. However admirable the school, it was not doing what the Hargraves had hoped it would. So they set out to educate Sara themselves as best they could at home. With help from master tutors, Sara studied history, essays, poetry, the best fiction of the time, French, philosophy, and music. She was delighted, happy to escape the prison of the seminary classroom.

She set up a summer desk in the apple tree in the garden, among the flowers, and a winter desk beside the blazing fire in her uncle's office. She studied hard—"worked," she said, "as never maiden worked before." By her thirteenth year she had learned to read French from a square-shouldered German with an upright shock of coarse black hair, who stared sternly at her through his spectacles. With a grammar held aloft in his left fist, he punctuated every rule with his right, "coming down hard on my aunt's mahogany." The pounding appeared to be necessary, Sara confessed, for she believed the gift for "divers kinds of tongues" was not part of her natural equipment.

What she passionately loved was music, especially the genius outpourings of Beethoven and Liszt. This *was* part of her natural equipment; she had a special gift for it. Aunt Mary put her in the hands of a brilliant German pianist, a pupil of Liszt himself. This maestro was an itinerant eccentric, but brilliant, virtuoso who was "the incarnation of music." But he was also the incarnation of thriftlessness and in a chronic state of flight from creditors. His teaching hours were controlled by his debts. He often arrived toward midnight, pounding on the doors of his students, rousing them from bed for their lessons, then disappearing before the dawn to elude his hoard of creditors, whom he had "not the faintest intention of ever paying."

Under this bizarre music master, Sara learned "a large rendering of noble music." Thirteen years old, her hair hanging down her back in matching braids, her feet barely reaching the foot pedals, she played the organ for a convention of clerics in the little Episcopal church across the street from their house. The lyrics were sung by a choir of manly student voices from the university, supplemented by two or three female voices from the town, and Sara's "own little pipe."[40]

There was no circulating library in Charlottesville, but the current periodicals of the day arrived through the mails—*Graham's Magazine* from Philadelphia, the *Home Journal* from New York, and the *Southern Literary Messenger* from Richmond. The serialized novels of the wildly popular Charles Dickens came from London in monthly installments in the newspapers and were impatiently awaited, and greatly preferred over Scott and Thackeray.[41]

There was not much talk in the Hargrave parlor of the "four d's" that dominated most polite discussion in most parlors of the day—"dress, domestics, diseases, and disasters." The conversation in the house in Charlottesville rather turned on "things of character and mind." And Sara was old enough now to be part of it. She became "one of her aunt's thoughtful circle."[42]

When Sara entered her teenage years, dancing was in deep eclipse as a form of social release. A religious crusade against card playing and dancing had shut down much of the gaiety of more freewheeling times. To have a regular dancing party, with violins and cotillion, was, Sara said, like "driving a coach-and-six straight through the Ten Commandments."[43]

So there was romantic letter-writing instead. It was a time when letters were written with quill pens, without erasure, blotted with sand from a perforated box, sealed with wax, without envelope, and sent with sighs. Fanciful seals and motto wafers were in high favor among romantic young people. *L'amitié c'est l'amour sans ailes* (Friendship is love without wings) was a great favorite among the motto wafers affixed to letters. Also popular was a maiden in a shallop (a small open boat) gazing upward to a star, with the legend *Si je te perds je suis perdu* (If I lose you I am lost) elegantly imprinted. The most delicate refusal of a lover was a lady's card embossed "With thanks," sealed with a bird in flight and the legend, "Liberty is sweet!"[44] Thanks, but good-bye; I know you will understand.

By age fifteen Sara was ever more lovely and desirable. Boys from the university were coming to call. It was a tender time, when a seeker of a beautiful, genteel young girl's favor discoursed poetry with her rather than sports and gave her a volume of a British poet rather than a box of bonbons.[45]

Sara, however, had other things on her agenda than beaux. She had her own horse—named Phil Duval—which she rode through the woods and hills of Charlottesville, dressed in her fashionable riding habit of green cloth, with green velvet turban, and long green feather fastened with a "diamond" buckle.[46]

It was about this time that Powhatan Starke, a neighbor's guest from Maryland's Eastern Shore, visited for a year and added a stimulating new dimension to Sara's young life. He was a delightful addition, witty and joy inducing, joining in and enhancing every scheme for pleasure, serenading her and her friends with his gift of music. Powhatan taught Sara piano waltzes not to be found in music books, and the polka—to further outrage the sensibilities of polite society and send the carriage-and-six straight through the Ten Commandments. The popular songs of their years were "Oft in the Stilly Night," "The Last Rose of Summer," "Eileen Aroon," "Flow Gently, Sweet Afton," and "Vive l'Amour"—and Powhatan sang them all.[47]

THE NEWS THAT the large convention of Presbyterian clergymen was coming to town and that the Hargraves had offered their home put Sara and her most intimate friend, Lizzie Gilmer, "as much on the *qui-vive* as if we had bought numbers in a lottery." Lizzie had just returned from a two-month absence, and the girls had their hearts set on spending a week together—just the two of them—catching up. But here was this convention, and a clergyman guest, coming to spoil the fun. However eager the aunt and uncle were to receive their guests, when the girls learned that the reverend gentleman was bringing his son, they were plunged into despair. "Ruined," they complained. "A dreadful small boy to be amused and kept out of mischief."

When the front door opened and the "dreadful small boy" turned out to be a slender longhaired youth even older than they, bounding toward them up the stairs two steps at a time, Sara moaned, "Mercy! Worse and worse! There's no hope for us!" Now, instead of a snot-nosed kid to be entertained in the little private parlor that had been fitted out for the girls at the far end of the hall, there was *this* annoyance.

But Roger Pryor was nothing if not charming. Sara had not yet shed her girlhood braids, but he treated her as if she were a queen. He was so alert and sensitive, so witty, so amiable, that he was, by a unanimous vote of two, soon awarded the full freedom of their private sanctuary.

For Sara the week "passed like a dream." And when the stage drew up out front to take their guests to the rail station, it was a melancholy parting. When the winding horn of the stage had faded entirely away in the distance, Sara, who had been taught to "entreat the Father of all" to watch over departing friends and see them safely on their way, thought there would be no great harm in including the slender boy by name.

Take care of him, she petitioned, and added—*"for me!"*[48]

This gentle stirring in her heart caused Sara, after Roger left, to write a love story, "The Birthnight Ball," in which, among other things, she wrote, "the stars, with vain ambition, emulate her eyes," words at the time she thought "quite delicate and suggestive." Later she came to believe the entire work was "inane foolishness" and "sad trash." Her proud uncle nonetheless sent the piece to the *Saturday Evening Post,* and the editor proposed, because of her youth, that she waive payment. It hardly mattered to Sara. She was in love. That's what mattered.[49]

CHAPTER 3

Harry Hotspur
and the Washington Belle

The charmer from Hampden-Sydney returned to the academy on the hill among the chinquapins and livestock and graduated the following spring, 1846, at the head of his class, valedictorian, and the pride of the Union Society.

Still following precisely in the career path of his father before him, Roger matriculated to the University of Virginia, the school of choice in the South for sons of planters and aristocrats reaching college age.[50] There, beginning in the 1846–47 school year, he studied modern languages under Professor Maximilian Schele de Vere, the refined and celebrated Swedish linguist who, some believed, never met a language he couldn't speak; moral philosophy under Professor William H. McGuffey, a scholar with a prodigious memory who, some believed, never read a book he couldn't memorize, and whose *Eclectic Readers* for elementary schools had already made him a household name; and mathematics under Professor Edward H. Courtenay, a West Pointer who never met a theorem he couldn't master.

In his second year Roger began reading law under John Barbee Minor, an untiring, dignified, gifted, and eloquent young teacher who loved the common law and who, some believed, never met a mind he couldn't stimulate.[51]

Roger didn't neglect the brown-eyed girl in auburn braids at the hospitable Hargrave house on the hill overlooking the Blue Ridge. She had become ever more beautiful, desirable, and accomplished. She delighted in putting on an apron and helping her uncle in his practice, gravely assuming "the airs of a physician's assistant." She lived the life privileged young girls lived in a university town, associating with professors' families, absorbing "the literary atmosphere"—and thinking of Roger.[52]

He began courting her when he returned to Charlottesville. True to the requirement of the times, he romanced her with prose and poetry. He sent her "no end of books"—a "gorgeous" Shakespeare, Macauley's *Essays*, Hazlitt's *Age of Elizabeth*, and Leigh Hunt's *Fancy and Imagination*. He followed them up the hill to read them all aloud to her, together with the poetry of Shelley, Keats, Byron, and Coleridge.[53]

He wooed and won her in this fashion, and from the start she was a more-than-willing conquest. When Roger was finished at the university and had his law degree, a wedding date was set, and Aunt Mary, delighted with the match, sent out invitations inscribed on paper embossed with orange blossoms and tied with white satin ribbons.[54] They were married in Halifax, Virginia, by Roger's father, in the parlor of Sara's father's house, on November 8, 1848. Sara wore a wedding dress of India muslin with flounces of handsome thread lace, a silver comb from Tiffany's, and a long white veil held in place by a wreath of white roses. Lizzie Gilmer was a bridesmaid. It was a small wedding, for Sara's mother was still ill and frail.[55]

The day of the wedding Roger left his bride briefly, to vote for the first time for a president—decidedly against the Whig, Zachary Taylor, and emphatically for the Democrat, Lewis Cass.[56] The country was now gripped in a quickening sectional conflict over slavery. Democrats, particularly Southern Democrats— Roger was ardently one of those—favored Cass, who was considered friendly to the South. Taylor, a Southerner and a slaveholder, was the preferred candidate of both Southern proslavery and Northern antislavery Whigs.

Sara, who couldn't vote because she was too young and because she was a woman, awaited her wedding night, perhaps reflecting that she had begun her acquaintance with her handsome young groom by beseeching God to take care of him—for her. According to her Presbyterian upbringing, she was taught, further, that "every prayer must be followed by efforts for its fulfilment." She therefore saw that she must now "take care of him." She believed—as young wives in love ardently do—that he needed caring for.[57]

Roger opened a law office on a corner off the court green in Charlottesville. In a short time, however, he came down with a throat infection, a serious drawback for a lawyer, who must talk. A Philadelphia specialist ordered him to give his voice a rest, move to a more congenial climate, and stop speaking in court, or out, until he was cured.[58] It was a career-ending edict, for as the *New York Evening Post* was later to write, "In those days a Virginia lawyer without speaking was no lawyer at all."[59]

Roger and Sara, with their little infant daughter, Marie Gordon, born in 1850 and named for George Loyal Gordon, the best man at their wedding, moved to Petersburg, where Roger could become a journalist, a calling in which he could talk without speaking.[60] Roger had a way with words and was the sort who would have his say, one way or the other.

On October 3, 1850, he purchased a newspaper in Petersburg, Drinkard's *Republican,* for twelve hundred dollars with all of its attachments—fixtures, type, forms, presses, printing materials, six inherited employees, and its goodwill. He renamed it something more in keeping with its place and his politics, the *Southside Democrat.* With it he set out to wage war with the city's anti-Democratic Whig newspaper, the *Intelligencer,* representing the political majority in Petersburg and the surrounding area. Roger, a vigorous advocate of Southern rights, seemed a fitting instrument for pounding a party linked to the twin Northern doctrines so abhorred in the South—free soil and abolition.[61]

Petersburg was a homecoming for Roger. He had been born and raised in its shadow. In 1850 the city was one hundred years old and claimed Pocahontas, far older than that, as its first noteworthy resident.[62] It began as a colonial town at the falls of the Appomattox River, along the line that separates the Tidewater from the Piedmont, in 1748. It was enlarged with expanded powers in 1784 and proclaimed a city in 1850. When Roger and Sara moved there that same year, it still had no gaslights—they would follow the Pryors into town a year later. Its unpaved main street was muck in the rainy season, and local livestock still grazed at the street's edge and drank from its gutters.[63] The city had a population just over fourteen thousand, only some six thousand of them white. It was about half the size of Richmond, but still one of the larger cities of the South, and it welcomed character and cultivation in its newcomers. Money with its "meretricious adornments and its vulgar display" opened few of its doors.[64] It was perfect for the Pryors.

Petersburg was both a production center and a market for local cotton. With a weather pattern that inexplicably matched Atlanta's, it was something of an extension of the cotton South.[65] Tobacco, however, not cotton, was the main staple and money crop in the country surrounding the town, and the prime manufacturing industry in the city itself—the true source of its wealth and prosperity.[66]

Roger began one morning soliciting subscribers for his newspaper, and before the week was up, he had enough to justify putting it out. He was only twenty-two years old, but, Sara said with pride, he sailed the little craft, a paper of "pluck and spirit," boldly out into "the troubled sea of politics."[67] Roger was by nature, one who knew him said, "talented, studious, ambitious, bold to contempt of consequences."[68] In the beginning, however, he was a careful helmsman, closeting himself in his little office, studying and writing. The editorials spinning from his pen were soon, one reader noted, "a revelation of strength and purity in classic English."[69] For Roger the English had to be classic. He believed throughout his lifetime that an error in grammar was a crime. He was equally intolerant of mispronounced and misspelled words.[70] He believed that a "copious and elegant vocabulary" was "not only the fit and felicitous vehicle of worthy thought, but is in itself a beauty and a power."[71]

His blunt style and incisive editorial opinions began attracting attention, and his star was soon rapidly on the rise. The Compromise of 1850, an attempt to dampen the rising fires of disunion, had been passed in Congress. But it had not put down the South's conviction that Northern antislavery free-soil sentiment was blocking the South's expansion into the western territories and threatening to tip the delicate balance of political power in the country disastrously to the Northern advantage. Roger was cogently expressing his views on this subject and other political issues of the day, and although his journal was but a small country paper and he was hardly more than a boy, he was being seen as a Southern editor to be reckoned with.

He was attracting the kind of attention that such standing invites. Sara kept their little house as elastically hospitable as possible for the quality of the company that began passing through. As she explained to a visiting Englishman when her front door mysteriously stuck as he was trying to leave, "The American door opened of itself to an incoming guest, but positively refused, without coaxing, to let him out."[72]

One of the first celebrities to come courting the favor of the young Southern editor was the acclaimed Hungarian patriot Louis Kossuth. Kossuth was five feet eight inches tall and wore a military uniform with a sword in a steel scabbard that bounced along the ground behind him as he walked. His shoulders rounded over a slight frame. His bluish gray eyes were set in an oval face, under his high broad deeply wrinkled forehead and straight dark hair. With his heavy beard and mustache, he appeared more a visionary and political theorist than a soldier and the leader of a revolution.

Winfield Scott, the general in chief of the U.S. Army, regarded him as "a gigantic humbug."[73]

When Kossuth stopped in Petersburg on a swing through southern and western cities to drum up support for his freedom crusade in Hungary, he gave Roger a revolutionary-sized cigar. But after he left, Roger came out editorially for American non-intervention in Hungarian affairs. When Kossuth read Roger's article he must have regretted the waste of a good cigar. "*So young, and yet so depraved!*" he exclaimed. Thinking better of what he had just said, he added with tact, "I mean, of course, politically!"[74]

Also among those passing through was a rising American politician, Stephen A. Douglas, the stumpy, brash, powerful, and precocious Democratic U.S. senator from Illinois, who had recently returned from a tour of Europe. He was with his wife, Martha, and since he was aspiring to the presidency in 1852, he was more than pleased to talk with the young editor of Petersburg's fiery Democratic newspaper. Douglas was himself only thirty-nine years old, with a massive head, a resolute face, and a demeanor and carriage that, despite his short stature, discouraged thinking him insignificant. People called him "the Little Giant." He was charmed by Sara, as everybody was. He told her she resembled the dazzling Empress Eugénie of France, whom he had also just recently met.[75]

With visitors such as these, politics on a national and international level came knocking on Roger's office door. It was a natural development, for as one observer said, it was "impossible . . . for a man of his tastes and force not to drift into politics outside of the sanctum of his paper." His voice had returned to full volume, and the public was soon seeing him not just as an emerging editor but as one of the ablest and most eloquent stump speakers in the state.[76] In the summer of 1852 he was named a delegate from Virginia to the Democratic National Convention in Baltimore. Douglas was a candidate, together with several other front-runners, all at odds with one another. Roger liked Douglas, but in the end he preferred the dark horse that emerged, Franklin Pierce. So did the rest of the Virginia delegation, which swung its fifteen votes to him on the thirty-fifth ballot, broke a deadlocked convention, and gave the handsome New Englander the nomination fourteen ballots later.

Roger's subsequent friendship with Pierce was a major turning point in his already galloping career. The president-elect liked this impetuous and brash Virginia editor with the shoulder-length hair who wrote in classic English and had a penchant for strong statements. Pierce liked what he wrote, the editorials that supported both old-line Whig and new-line Democratic principles.[77] So when the new administration made the *Washington Union* its party organ and wanted two coeditors to run it—one from the North, one from the South—Roger got the call as its Southern voice. He sold his *Southside Democrat,* and he and Sara, their daughter, Marie Gordon, and their infant son, born in July 1851—another Theodorick—moved to Washington.

In Washington, Roger was an instant insider at the highest levels of the new administration. Sara said she was "a proud woman" when Pierce sent for "my young editor" in early 1853 to consult with him on his inaugural address. She felt from that moment that she belonged not to the little boardinghouse world in which they lodged in Washington, "nor to any other small world." She felt that she "belonged to the nation."[78]

The capital city of that nation in the early 1850s struck Sara as "a garden of delights." Spring brought to it "an early robe of green, thickly embroidered with gems of amethyst and ruby, pearl and sapphire." Sara, ever a lover of flowers, watched as the crocuses, hyacinths, tulips, and snowdrops "made haste to bloom before the snows had fairly melted." The trees on the White House grounds, on the lawn fronting the Smithsonian Institution, and on the slopes around the Capitol donned their "diaphanous veils of green" earlier than anywhere else. "To walk through these incense-laden grounds, to traverse the avenue of blossoming crab-apples," Sara exclaimed, "was pure pleasure."[79]

Washington was like a great vibrating village. The Capitol itself rose, Sara thought, "like a white cloud above the smoke and
mists." In evenings there was often a passing moment, as the sun
was setting, when the Capitol's unfinished dome was bathed by the
lingering late-afternoon light and glowed like "a great blazing
star"—"the star of our country," Sara said, "the star of our hearts
and hopes."[80]

If Washington had its pleasures, Sara also saw that it had its
drawbacks: cold ice-laced streets in winter, whirlpools of dust and
driving rain turning the streets to mud in the spring, the onslaught
of fierce heat and humidity in the summer. Rapid climatic changes
often brought all of these extremes "in one week, or even one
day." As one wag said, "It has the climates of all parts of the habitable globe. It rains, hails, snows, blows, freezes, and melts in
Washington, all in the space of twenty-four hours." Prudence dic-
tated that one not go out on any given day without "a fan, an overcoat, and an umbrella"—a versatile arsenal against the inconstant
elements.[81]

Politics and the turns in political fortune every four years gave
Washington a "floating population" with "a new central jewel [a
new president] and new colors and combinations in the setting"
that made social life almost as variable as the weather. But under-
girding the political changes in the 1850s was an unchanging world
of "old residents" that didn't shift with the political kaleidoscope.
This steady social core never sought the new, but did accept it occasionally, "with discretion, reservations, and much discriminating
care."[82]

A bleak ever-blackening political cloud was hovering over the
Union by the early fifties, darkening the horizon and confounding
legislation with sectional division, bitter partisanship, and attempts
at "impossible compromises." It was a time in the House and Senate chambers of "interminable speeches, not clearly understood,
but heard with reverent conviction that all was coming out right in

the end." "Alas!" Sara was to say in retrospect, "our eyes were holden so we could not see."[83]

The day of Pierce's inaugural, March 4, 1853, was perhaps a harbinger of coming sorrow. The sun was blocked by lowering clouds, from which snow was thickly falling, driven by an angry northeast wind. Sara watched from a balcony above Pennsylvania Avenue as the snow escorted the president-elect to his swearing in. The Democrats were returning after four years of Whig rule, a new central jewel was being inlaid, and despite the weather the crowd was immense, the largest ever gathered for an inaugural. From the White House to the Capitol, windows, balconies, and roofs were thronged. The sidewalks bordering the avenue were packed. Most of the crowd, Sara believed, were of "the mighty army" of eager office-seekers of the party newly come to power. The South was content. For them the new central jewel glittered. Pierce was known as a Northern Democrat with pro-Southern sentiments.

At forty-eight, he was the youngest president the country had yet elected, of slender, almost boyish figure, called "Purse" by his friends. He spoke his inaugural address from memory, and it should have been an hour of luminous exultation and glory for him. Instead, he was nearly overwhelmed by a weary overburdening melancholy. Only two months before, his only son, Bennie, a beautiful boy of thirteen, had been killed in a railroad collision, before the eyes of his horrified parents. It had darkened their lives and everything around them, much as the clouds were darkening the city on Inauguration Day. The White House was to be "shrouded in gloom," an unhappy and somber social center for a new administration.[84]

The times were no more upbeat than the circumstances. The nation was not only threatened with disunion, but there was talk of annexing Cuba, and the filibustering that went with it. A war with Spain loomed, and there was a land treaty with Mexico to be negotiated, as well as fishery questions with England to be settled.

Young America had a Monroe Doctrine to protect and a Manifest Destiny to pursue. And Europe stood on the brink of war, between England and Russia.

Pierce was a gentleman, with a kind, courteous, and considerate temper and an outgoing nature, cordial and hospitable to enemies and friends alike—and "one of the most striking men that ever sat in a saddle."[85] He was tenacious in his views, but inexperienced and indecisive in action. A village innkeeper in his native New Hampshire, when asked for an estimate of him, said, "Waal, up here, where everybody knows Frank Pierce, and where Frank Pierce knows everybody, he's a pretty considerable fellow, I tell you. But come to spread him out over this whole country, I'm afraid that he'll be dreadful thin in some places."[86]

The *Washington Union* was Pierce's mouthpiece in the capital—every administration had one. Roger's job, with his Northern coeditor, John W. Forney, was to write favorably of the administration and the party, reflect their thinking, and defend them from editorial attack.

From their base in the boardinghouse run by Mrs. Tully Wise, a fellow Virginian, the Pryors stood on the upper rung of Washington's social, political, and literary ladder.[87] They were friends to the president, cabinet members, and other great and famous men, living, working, or visiting in the capital. For, as Sara said, they now belonged to the nation. The couple were intimates of Winfield Scott, general in chief of the army and the military genius who had masterminded the spectacular American victories in the Mexican War; of Senator Sam Houston, the hero of Texas independence; and of Washington Irving, the most popular and celebrated of American writers.

Scott was physically enormous, six feet five inches tall, massive, imposing, heroic, and ceremonious—with an appetite to match. Like Roger, the great general was a native of Dinwiddie County and former Petersburg resident. He never failed to tell everybody present that he had been a groomsman at Roger's father's wedding. And as he did with every other young Washington beauty, Scott addressed Sara as "fair lady." In her case it was not a misnomer.[88]

Houston, nearly as tall and as imposing as Scott, was a figure who in Sara's eyes "had had romance enough in his past life for a dozen heroes." He had lived among the Indians and fought and won the war of independence for Texas. "What," Sara wondered, "had he not done?" He was a western exotic, with hanging eyebrows and iron-gray whiskers. He was a formidable stump speaker but preferred to sit quietly in the Senate chamber, following the flow of debate while relentlessly whittling soft pine sticks into miniature crosses, hearts, and amulets. He was known now and then to pull an exquisitely carved pine heart from the pocket of his tiger-skin vest and present it to some young lady whose beauty had attracted his notice.[89]

Washington Irving, dark-eyed, with a winning smile, and now in his dotage with only a few years to live, was apt to fall asleep in the middle of a conversation, whereupon a whisper would pass among his auditors, "*Shhh*, Mr. Irving is asleep." After a while he would abruptly awaken, rub his hands, and exclaim in his sweet, husky voice, "Well, as we were saying," and take up the conversation just where he had left it.[90] Sara said that scholarly atmosphere and melancholy romance "always circled him like the fragrance of lavender in an old casket."[91]

It was an era in Washington of "political and social brilliance," a time, one of Sara's friends said, when "eloquent men still thundered forth heroic sentiments in classic periods, and lovely women had . . . sloping shoulders and oval faces."[92] Although storm clouds of sectional division were gathering and oratorical wars were erupting daily on the floors of Congress, social life in the capital seemed, on its surface, smiling and peaceful. Pierce's Washington was noteworthy for its handsome men and lovely women. Old-fashioned quadrilles and cotillions, with an occasional waltz number, ruled the dance floors of the city. It was a time when fashion and mirth, beauty and wit, were prized and Washington was a center of continuous novelty, perpetual changes, and new faces.

The fashions of the times, always of intense interest to Sara, were graceful, rich, and picturesque. The belles of the city wore their hair *à la Grecque*, wreathed in flowers, or with a simple golden dagger or arrow holding it in place. Gowns were festooned with blossoms that trailed over bodice and skirt, and the most fashionable materials were imported from abroad. Gloves, fans, handkerchiefs, bonnets, accessories, and the most beautiful of the gown patterns were shipped in from Europe. Scarcely a steamer tied up at the wharf on the Potomac that didn't bring to the capital dainty boxes of Parisian flowers, bonnets, and other compelling adornments.[93]

Just as Roger was starring in his sphere, Sara was excelling in hers, ranked high on the list of Washington beauties. One of her admirers called her "the beautiful and brilliant Mrs. Pryor."[94] Virginia Clay, wife of Alabama senator Clement C. Clay, called her "the beautiful *brune*," with the "soft-brown hair and eyes," who "wore a distinctive coiffure and carried her head charmingly," and was admired for her intellectuality.[95]

The stable core of Washington society, the one that viewed new faces with discrimination and reservations, embraced this "beautiful *brune*" and offered her advice. It was permissible and proper, she was told, for young matrons to attend morning and afternoon receptions with a sister when one was available and her husband wasn't. But if the husband was too busy to take her to evening balls, she simply could not go. Another piece of advice to her from the start was never, under any circumstances, ride in men's carriages—particularly if they were foreigners.[96]

While Sara was trying to avoid riding in carriages with foreign men, Roger was commenting on foreign affairs and was soon in editorial hot water for it—not a new environment for him. There was a war looming between England and Russia, in the Crimea. Roger had reviewed a book and, in his blunt way, set off a commotion. In the review he praised Russia, whose vigorous expansionism was being just as vigorously opposed by a quartet of allied powers led by England. Roger wrote, "In every element of national strength and happiness Russia is great and prosperous beyond any other country in Europe." He predicted that instead of going to war, these nations "will consolidate and perpetuate their friendly relations by the same just and pacific policy which has regulated their intercourse in times past." Many readers of the *Union*, who had already sided with England in the dispute and were calling for war against Russia, didn't want to hear this.[97]

About the same time, Roger wrote an editorial in the *Union* on the relations of the United States, Great Britain, and Russia in light of the impending war. Its tone was strongly anti-British. Appearing in the administration newspaper, the article suggested that Pierce was sympathetic to Russia.[98] The owner of the newspaper, Robert Armstrong, advised Roger to disavow the editorial "upon further consideration." Upon further consideration, Roger refused. Armstrong then advised him to "think twice before giving up a large salary," and Roger said, "*Damn* the money!" and either resigned or was fired.[99] He clearly held independent opinions, wrote them, and was then not one to back down or recant, whatever anybody thought or did. As Roger's Northern coeditor on the *Union*, John Forney, rightly said, Roger was a man of "impetuous and dazzling temperament."[100]

This hothead and his wife and two children returned to Richmond in 1853, where Roger acquired an interest in the *Richmond Enquirer* and became one of its editors. The *Enquirer* was a storied journal, for half a century the leading newspaper of the South, founded by Thomas R. Ritchie when Thomas Jefferson was president, and run in partnership with Ritchie's two sons, William and Thomas Jr. The elder Ritchie, now in his seventies and called "Father Ritchie," was considered one of the great editors of his day and the delight of all for "his chronic Virginia peculiarities." He was earnestly serious-minded, fond of gardens, poetry, and children, and always "intensely Virginian," with an unshakeable faith in states' rights. It was said that his efforts to make peace between contending rivals generally resulted in the renewal of strife, and his defense of a cause generally awakened "new storms of ridicule." But one fellow editor described him as "the kindest and most genteel old fogy who ever wore nankeen pantaloons, high shirt-collars, and broad-brimmed straw hats." Completing the wardrobe of this kindly curmudgeon was generally a white Marseilles vest, thin pumps, and silk stockings, winter or summer. He was a power in the Democratic party in all seasons, and his paper was widely viewed as the "Democratic Bible."[101] Virginia Clay confessed that from earliest girlhood she had been taught three essentials, amounting to commandments: "To be proud alike of my name and blood and section; to read my Bible; and, last, to know my *Richmond Enquirer*."[102] It was a good fit for the intensely Democratic Roger Pryor.

Roger appeared not to have lost Pierce's favor for his Crimean opinions. The president still thought enough of the young editor to ask him to take on a special diplomatic mission to Greece in 1855. His assignment was to settle a long-standing dispute involving the property of a U.S. citizen. So at age twenty-seven, somewhat callow for diplomacy, Roger sailed to Athens to negotiate a settlement. Not only did he successfully do that, but he also engineered a diplomatic triumph with Greece's Queen Mathilde, whom he charmed with a discussion of the night-blooming cereus, a plant of the cactus family with a large white flower that opens only in the dark.[103] He then extended his time abroad, on Secretary of State William Marcy's instructions, to gather all the intelligence he could about conditions in Greece. Sara had been unable to share his mission or join in his botanical discussions with the queen because she had pediatric responsibilities at home.[104]

Roger lingered on following the diplomacy and his scouting for the state department and visited Venice, Rome, Constantinople, and Egypt before booking passage home on a vessel called the *Pa-*

cific. At Marseilles he was the victim of a lapse in protocol. He discovered his baggage had been opened, something one nation doesn't do to another nation's executive agent. So he let the *Pacific* sail without him while he remained a few days more seeking redress. It may have been the most providential taking of umbrage of his life, for the ship never reached America, was never heard from again, and very likely lies somewhere yet on the bottom of the Atlantic. Safely arriving home again on a later, luckier vessel, Roger declined another diplomatic mission, this one to Persia, and returned instead to his editorial duties on the *Enquirer.*[105]

The unhappy Pierce administration was in its twilight days, and Pierce, weary, harassed, and overmatched—"so tired of the shackles of Presidential life that I can scarcely endure it!"—would soon be out of office.[106] But before he left, the president had one last favor to bestow on the Pryors, this one on Sara, whom he liked at least as much as he liked Roger. Pierce brought her two books, sumptuously bound in green morocco and inscribed in his own hand, from her "friend Franklin Pierce." When Roger was still on his mission, the president traveled to Charlottesville for a day, to visit Jefferson's tomb and home. There he gave Sara the books, and she played the piano for him, Thalberg's "La Stanièra," Henselt's "Gondola," and "L'Elisir d'Amour." The ill-starred young president left her with an impression she would never lose of "his kindness of heart, his captivating voice and manner."[107]

After Roger returned from Greece, he settled into his editorial seat at the *Enquirer.* There was much to write about—the continuing North-South split over slavery in the territories and an important gubernatorial election in Virginia. Sara turned her attention to keeping a pleasant house always open to guests and to busying herself with her beloved flowers.

Roger's political vistas were far more turbulent than Sara's peaceable gardens. What he and many others in the Democratic Party considered to be a virus in American politics was infecting the

South. The new American Party, popularly called the Know-Nothings, was marshaling a strong run at seizing control of the Virginia state government. It was a serious threat, seriously regarded.

The Know-Nothing movement was a third-party phenomenon that began as a secret political organization, the Order of the Star-Spangled Banner. It had exploded almost without warning on the American political scene, "like a clap of thunder from a brilliant sky," exulted one of its adherents, "remarkable for the suddenness of its birth."[108] It had "come over the old parties like an avalanche from the Alps," another, not an adherent, said of it, "whelming rider and horse, captain and cattle, in a common ruin" and making "strange havoc . . . among the political parties."[109]

Surfacing first in New York, it spread like a fanned fire through local and state campaigns in the North in 1854 and invaded Virginia that same year. Its popular name, the Know-Nothings, stemmed from the practice of its fraternally bound members to answer all questions about the organization with, "I know nothing." It was nativist, anti-immigrant, and anti-Catholic. It represented a growing frustration and antagonism in the country against foreigners and the movement was spreading southward, where such sentiment was strong.

The Know-Nothings had become a haven for old-line Whigs, whose own party was splitting and collapsing all around the country in the struggle over slavery in the territories and who were being left politically homeless. The new party had swept the entire ticket in Massachusetts and carried Delaware in October. It had come up big in the voting in Pennsylvania, Ohio, and Indiana. It had become a force to be dreaded; it was winning elections. With a foothold already in the South, the party was eager to score big in Virginia, that region's key state. Their speakers had "waked up thousands" already in other Southern state and local elections. Their numbers and intensity reminded one critic of "Kilkenny cats, always devouring each other."[110]

The Southern Know-Nothings seized on immigration. It was an issue that resonated well in the South, which saw an unchecked flood of foreign migrants padding the North's power in Congress. There was a natural anti-immigrant strain running throughout the South, anyhow, and there had been for a long time. Many Southerners considered immigrants criminals, paupers, and troublemakers—the Catholic Germans and Irish in particular. Worse, in the Southern view, most immigrants pouring into the North were intensely antislavery.

The new party had become known—affectionately by its members and scornfully by its critics—as "Sam." And nobody was more scornful of "Sam" than Henry A. Wise, the Democratic candidate for governor in Virginia in 1855, unless it was Roger Pryor, who threw himself and his newspaper unrestrainedly into Wise's campaign.

Of Know-Nothingism, Wise demanded, "What?" Then answered: "*Nobody knows.* To do what? *Nobody knows.* How organized? *Nobody knows.* Governed by whom? *Nobody knows.* How bound? By what rites? By what test oaths? With what limitations and restraints? Nobody, Nobody knows!!! All we know is that persons of *foreign birth,* and of *Catholic faith,* are proscribed, and so are all others who don't proscribe them at the polls."[11]

Wise was a piece of work in any time and place. One reporter described him as "pale and thin [and] dress[ed] like an old man." His face above his white cravat, the reporter noted, gave off a "livid pallor." But he had "a dark and brilliant eye," which seemed "sometimes to flash almost unearthly rays of light over his whole countenance." He walked in "long Indian strides," and on the stump he was a terror, tall, lean, and cadaverous, staring down his foes with piercing eyes and soaring "into the regions of commanding eloquence." A stranger seeing him for the first time compared him to "a corpse galvanized." His voice "had the compass of an organ pipe, and ranged from the persuasive softness of a lute to the metallic ring of the bugle note." His specialty was fierce sarcasm and invective that could gather into a frightening hurricane of rhetoric. He was virulently anti-Know-Nothing and "in every way fitted to strike terror to the hearts of the members of the new secret order."[112] Driving this political cyclone was "a steel-spring energy" that "never bent or broke."[113]

Wise believed, as Roger and most Democrats did, that the Know-Nothings were "an oath-bound, dark-lantern, clap-trap, hypocritical, truth-stretching, abolition-hatched party," led by "broken down party hacks" and "political bankrupts."[114] He believed if the party was not stopped in Virginia, it would continue to insinuate itself, injecting its venom throughout the rest of the South. A relentless chewer and picturesque swearer, sins he attempted to atone for with religious orthodoxy and abstention from mint juleps,[115] Wise opened his campaign in Norfolk in January 1855, figuratively spitting and cussing, with a slashing attack on the Know-Nothings. One Democratic newspaper said "his words 'were as fire that ran.'"[116] He kept the fire running, with Roger stoking it with editorial support, in an exhaustive, relentless personal four-month campaign. Wise traveled over three thousand miles, to every county in the state, all the way to the Ohio border, giving fifty speeches consuming two hundred hours of stump time.[117]

The editor of the *Richmond Whig* called him "Gizzard-foot," after a description of blacks in one of Wise's own speeches.[118] The rabidly pro-Know-Nothing Richmond *Penny Post* called him "a ranting demagogue, an unprincipled renegade, a truculent bully whose manners and conversation denoted that he was a brawler, and a foul-mouthed slanderer who unblushingly used the very scrapings and refuse of political style." It was nothing for Wise to flay the Know-Nothings without mercy or letup in three-and-a-half-hour speeches.[119]

Nobody marched more militantly beside Wise throughout his crusade than Roger Pryor. His editorials in the *Enquirer* against the Know-Nothings were pure thunder. So offensive was he at times, writing or speaking, that he became involved in two duels during the campaign—not an unusual thing for outspoken Southern editors, and even more common for Roger.[120] They were not his first duels, nor would they be his last. Wise won the election by ten thousand votes and was generally credited with single-handedly halting the Know-Nothing crawl southward. He crowed that "I have met the Black Knight with his visor down, and his shield and lance are broken."[121]

"The Black Knight's" later defeat in the presidential election the following year sealed the party's doom nationally and ended its short but spectacular run in American politics. A transparency—a backlighted projection—in a victory celebration in Murfreesboro, Tennessee, after the national election read:

> SAMUEL, infant son of Abolitionism,
> was wounded by Henry A. Wise of Va., in 1855,
> and died of public opinion, in the North, 1856.
> Here lies Sam,
> As great a sham,
> As ever gulled a nation;
> He lived and lied,
> Blasphemed and died
> And now his doom's damnation.[122]

Wise wrote that he owed Roger more than any man in Virginia, and the state Democratic Party presented the young editor with a silver service in appreciation, which Sara took into custody.[123]

The Know-Nothing campaign had made Roger a modest national reputation. And by 1857 he decided he must make a change. The country was changing, and had been for more than a decade, and not to his liking. The United States were becoming much more of a consolidated Union than the South originally intended, straying from the Southern idea of a federation of sovereign states. A powerful North-driven antislavery impulse was in crescendo. What Roger and many Southerners were seeing was a continuing, desperate need to preserve the South's rights and protect its balance of political power in the Union in the face of these changes. The Compromise of 1850 and the Kansas-Nebraska debates in 1854 had deepened his fears. The threat to the South's basic social-economic system—the Southern way of life—and the danger of the South being reduced to an impotent and imperiled minority in the national government was now palpable. South Carolina's John C. Calhoun had long seen this threat and had railed and struggled against it through most of his political lifetime. Roger was seeing it as well and had been for some time. He believed if the tide could not be stayed or reversed, secession might become necessary, indeed desirable.[124]

To fight the Northern tide, Roger founded another daily newspaper, *The South,* intended as a unifying voice for the Southern point of view—an organ to air the extreme states' rights views of the Virginia Democracy. *Frank Leslie's Illustrated Newspaper* described Roger, not yet twenty-nine years old, as "a bold writer" who "unfolds his designs without fear and asks for no favors." It predicted that *The South* "will undoubtedly be the acknowledged organ of the extremists of the South."[125] Indeed, it immediately took its place with the *Charleston Mercury* and the *New Orleans Delta* in the ranks of the bitter-enders pushing Southern claims.[126] But it did not prosper, and Roger cut it back to a semiweekly. In late 1858 he shut it down altogether and became an editor instead of the Washington *States,* a newspaper viewed as Stephen Douglas's mouthpiece in the national capital.

This venture lasted less than a year. Roger, independent-minded as always, but hired for his talent and friendship with Douglas despite their sometimes differing opinions, wrote a series of articles examining the heated question of slavery in the territories. In them he generally assumed the position of the James Buchanan administration and the Dred Scott decision that territorial legislatures did not have the power to keep slavery from their territories. This ran uncomfortably counter to Douglas's position that the territories ought to be able to decide that for themselves on the basis of popular sovereignty. Douglas and Buchanan, by this time, although of the same party, were bitterly not of the same mind. Probably because of this, Roger left the paper in June 1859, but with no hard feelings toward Douglas, who continued to be his friend.[127]

Roger had decided to enter politics himself. A seat in the U.S. House had opened in Virginia's Fourth District, the seat once held by the celebrated John Randolph of Roanoke. William O. Goode had held it for the three most recent congresses, but he had died of consumption in July 1859, and Roger aspired to replace him.

The now-seasoned editor was more than ready. He had honed his oratorical skills in debates at the Southern Commercial Conventions of 1856, 1857, and 1858. He had matched rhetoric with the ablest Southern orator of the day, William Loundes Yancey.

Yancey was an Alabama lawyer, sometime politician, full-time fire-eater, and a sleepless advocate of Southern unity, secession, and independence long before it became fashionable. He was "a compact, middle-sized man, straight limbed, with a square built head and face, and an eye full of expression." He looked on the world with "an air of perfect sincerity." On the surface Yancey was seen as "a very mild and gentlemanly man, always wearing a genuinely good-humored smile and looking as if nothing in the world could disturb the equanimity of his spirits." But his calm exterior masked a fire of holocaust dimension within.[128]

Few, even in that time of great public speakers, could sway an audience as Yancey could. He was captivating on a podium, a born orator who had no equal in the South before a popular audience. In his oratory he was said to stand out "like Saul of old above all others who spoke," uttering "silvery music" with "grace and polish." "He simply swept his audiences off their feet," one who had heard him said. "Nobody compared with him."[129]

The Southern Commercial Convention first met in Augusta, in 1837, when Roger was only nine years old. It was designed to air major economic and political problems particular to the South, and sixteen of such conventions would be held before the final one in Vicksburg, in 1859. The earliest ones had centered on purely economic issues. But by the mid-1850s, politicians had seized control and the conventions had become launchpads for protest against Northern political aggression and seedbeds of Southern secessionist sentiment. When the convention met in Savannah in December 1856, the *Louisville* (Kentucky) *Journal* charged that most of its members were "brazen faced disunionist," "blazing fire-eaters" deadly hostile to the national existence, "as thoroughly treasonable as the vilest conclave that ever polluted the soil of South Carolina," a "scandalous body."[130]

At Savannah the matter of the African slave trade, outlawed by the Constitution after 1808, abruptly resurfaced. For half a century no large body of Southerners had seriously proposed to reopen it. But it was suddenly reincarnated at the Savannah convention, in the form of a resolution in favor of it. The resolution was defeated, but the subject returned stronger than ever the next year at Knoxville, when a committee was formed, with Roger and Yancey both on it, to study the matter and report to the convention that was to meet in Montgomery in May 1858.

In Montgomery it would dominate all other issues. The convention met in an unfinished cotton warehouse with four thick brick walls but with no roof and no floor. Some four hundred delegates from ten states packed into the quasi-building under an Alabama spring sky. The meeting's temporary chairman was William Yancey. The chairman of the slave-trade committee, L. W. Spratt of South Carolina, proposed that the convention adopt resolutions that slavery was right, and being right, there could be no wrong in reopening the slave trade; that, indeed, reopening it was "an expedient and proper policy"; and that a committee be named to explore ways of doing so.[131]

Neither Yancey nor Roger, though members of Spratt's committee, had figured in shaping these resolutions. Indeed, they had not heard them until Spratt read them on the floor. Yancey, however, rose to champion them. He did not favor reopening the slave trade per se. On the contrary, he condemned it. In a straight vote he said he would condemn it forever. But Yancey wanted secession, and he therefore favored reopening the slave trade to that end. He argued that reviving the trade would strengthen the South in what had become an unequal political contest with the North. He would have Congress legalize the slave trade and then leave the matter of embracing it to the individual states.[132]

Turning up his siren voice, expanding it to fit the size of the warehouse, Yancey electrified the audience. One delegate to the convention said, "I remember nothing but Yancey for two days. He began with such a torrent of eloquence—such a Niagara."[133] Yancey argued that a quickened flow of new imported slaves into the South would make more of them available to a larger number of masters and scale down the prohibitively high prices of slaves, which was holding back Southern expansion into the territories. He insisted that the law prohibiting the slave trade was unconstitutional and fatally discriminated against Southern interests. The North could import unlimited free immigrant labor, while the labor supply of the South was shut off and stunted. Population in the North was therefore outstripping the South and unbalancing the political and economic equality of the sections. This quickening imbalance, coupled with rampant Northern abolitionism, was seen as a deadly threat to the South.[134]

Southern fire-eaters were split over the issue. Roger, at first sympathetic to the idea, was now emphatically against it.[135] He rushed immediately to the front of the fight, challenging the South's preeminent orator in a two-hour speech in the floorless, roofless warehouse. Roger argued that the resolutions were designed to destroy the Union. This proposal to reopen the African slave trade, he said, was "utterly repugnant to grave and sensible men," that it was "purely and simply a proposition to dissolve the Union, because it cannot be carried out while the Union lasts." He said the resolutions would only confirm the worst Northern suspicions of Southern

secessionist designs. As long as the South was in the Union, a resolution to reopen the slave trade was ill-advised, impractical, and unconstitutional. It could only drive a wedge deeper between North
and South.[136]

Roger, like many Southern leaders, was caught between two
powerful magnets pulling in opposite directions—love for the
Union on one hand, fear for Southern rights on the other. His heart
was with the Union, but not if it meant sacrificing Southern political equality and the Southern way of life. He said Virginia would
follow cotton states, such as Yancey's Alabama, into secession only
if they would select some honorable issue that would unite the
South. But, he argued, this wasn't it. "Give me a case of oppression
and tyranny sufficient to justify a dissolution of the Union," he
said, "and give me a united South, and then I am willing to go out
of the Union."[137]

He said, "I affirm that neither history nor posterity would ap-
plaud us in staking the Union on the revival of the slave trade. . . .
It is an unworthy issue . . . a painful proposition . . . repugnant to
the instincts of Southern chivalry. . . . If you intend to dissolve the
Union, say so in manly and in explicit language . . . and we of Virginia will be prepared to back, or to give reason for abiding in the
Union."[138]

So, what case of oppression and tyranny would be enough to
take Virginia out? Yancey demanded. And Roger said, "Should a
Black Republican president be installed in the executive chair in
Washington, and the power of the government be palpably in his
hands," that would be case enough.[139]

Despite Yancey's eloquence and perhaps partly because of
Roger's, the slave-trade resolutions were not adopted at Montgomery. Similar resolutions introduced the next year, however,
would be, following another contentious convention in Vicksburg.
Spratt, whom the New York editor Horace Greeley derisively
christened the "philosopher of the new African slave trade," finally
got his way.[140]

Roger had gone head-to-head with the South's best orator and proved he could handle himself at that level. He was now viewed as one of the ablest of the Southern orators, thought of as a "Harry Hotspur" in Virginia.[141] It was a time when oratory counted in the South—perhaps as much as in any society anywhere. And Southern oratory's main aim—an urgent one—as Roger entered the canvass, was to protect, defend, and preserve states' rights, the slave economy, Southern culture, and the South's agrarian way of life against the Northern menace. It had come down to that by 1859.[142]

Roger was thirty-one years old now, still as lean as in his youth. The long lank dark hair still fell straight down to the collar of his coat. One admirer thought he might have passed for a divinity student or a young professor of moral philosophy, rather than the duel-prone, fiery, and impetuous editor he had become. His figure was erect as ever, finely chiseled, his gestures "easy and graceful, his features mobile and expressive across every shade of emotion."[143]

With a carefully crafted campaign speech, he began stumping the district. His rhetoric drew crowds, and his silver tongue attracted connoisseurs. In Roger's second run for the seat a year later, a renowned Whig orator, on a busman's holiday, rode sixty miles to hear him speak. That orator said, "You think I didn't stand up in a hot sun three mortal hours just to hear him abuse my party? He is wonderful, with the finest vocabulary I have ever known."

Another student of incendiary rhetoric wrote some years later, "Of all the men I ever heard speak, Pryor made the strongest impression on me.... He was a born orator; thorough master of those rare persuasive powers that captivate and lead multitudes" with a "wonderfully organized vocal apparatus, which he played upon with the skill of a musical expert. No speaker of the present time can claim to rival him in the easy flow of rhetoric that sparkled through his harmoniously balanced periods."

Yet another observer was to say, "He had a poetic imagination, which is the basis of all true oratory. His vocabulary, though florid, was superb, and kept company with the airy creatures of his exuberant imagination." He combined, that critic said, "a logical mind with his poetic fancy" and had "the face, the figure, the dramatic air, the attitude, and the vocabulary." He was everything a Southern orator ought to be—inflammatory, impassioned, and convincing.[144]

While Roger mounted the stump, "delighting our Democratic friends" with his oratory, Sara waited in Charlottesville with the children, who now numbered five, including two more sons, Roger Atkinson and William Rice, born in 1854 and 1858, and a second daughter, Mary Blair, born in 1856. One observer thought the three Pryor boys so beautiful and noble-looking that "they might serve as models for infant Apollos." Sara's heart swelled with pride. "They *were* lovely," she agreed, "my boys—my three little boys!"[145]

From Charlottesville the proud mother and wife wrote a friend for a recipe for "brandy-peaches," explaining that Roger was speaking all over the country, trying to win votes for a seat in Congress. "I'm not sure he will be elected," she wrote, "but I *am* sure he will like some brandy-peaches! If he is successful, they will enhance the glory of victory—if he is defeated, they will help to console him."

After he was elected to fill out the vacated term, and then reelected the following year, Sara saw no further need for brandy-peaches either to exult or console him. "I was pretty sure by this time," she later wrote, "that he would always be elected."[146]

So Roger and Sara returned to Washington. Roger was sworn into the Thirty-sixth Congress on December 5, 1859. Only three days earlier John Brown had been executed at Charlestown in western Virginia for attempting to agitate a slave insurrection at Harpers Ferry in October. No state was more tightly strung at the moment over the issues of slavery, abolitionism, and states' rights than Virginia. And no congressman sworn in that day in Washington was more tightly strung than Roger Pryor.

CHAPTER 4

───•◦•───

The Fire-Eater

*R*oger and Sara moved into a large house on New York Avenue in Washington with servants brought with them from Virginia—the couple had never owned slaves. For transportation they bought horses and a coach and hired a coachman.

"We had come to stay!" Sara exulted. "My husband represented the old district of his kinsman, John Randolph of Roanoke, and his constituents were devoted to him. They would never supplant him with another. Of that we could be sure. God granting life and health, we were going to be happy young people."[147]

It was a time, she noted, when "there was still plenty of room in the world." Houses were built "broad and low" and carriages were slung wide and close to the ground. Furniture was outsized. Drawing rooms were filled with sturdy square-built armchairs, sofas, and tables. Pianos were solid and stump-legged, built with both an ear for music and an eye for the demands of fashion. The furnishings, architecture, and decor were designed to harmonize with the enormous hoops the women wore, so the belles of Sara's day might sail "fearlessly about, with no danger of jostling a neighbor or overturning the furniture." Rooms were not yet furnished with spindly spider-legged chairs and tables. Nor had the tabletops become display surfaces for delicate, breakable china, glass, and bric-a-brac. There was no need, Sara said, for milady to "reef her sails."[148]

Sara was finely tuned to changing styles in coiffure and dress, and she could see how they had changed in Washington since Franklin Pierce's day. It was now the administration of James Buchanan. The beauties of the capital no longer wore their hair *à la Grecque* but in heavy braids coiled coronetlike and crowned by an occasional tiara of velvet and pearls, or jet or coral. Ruffled dresses had given place to paneled skirts combining plain and embossed or brocaded fabrics. Close-fitting bodices were the fashion of the time. Low necks and lace berthas had become de rigueur, with half-length evening gloves of kid or silk, embroidered or bejeweled on the backs.

Jewels and embroidery were conspicuous, worn now even by men. Gentlemen of fashion in Washington society appeared in sparkling studs and cravat pins. Bright varicolored vests of the richest brocade and embroidered satins and velvets accented male evening attire, which was swallow-tailed and embellished with broad cravats of bright soft silk.[149]

Southern women continued to dominate the capital's social world. The *New York Herald* was to say that "with their natural and acquired graces, with their inherited taste and ability in social affairs, it was natural that the reins had fallen to them."[150] By the late 1850s Southern hospitality imported to Washington from below the Mason-Dixon line had lent charm to government circles and lifted the capital "to the very apex of its social glory."[151]

Washington society of the fifties prized office, position, talent, beauty, wit, and charm in both men and women. Few esteemed wealth, or if they did, they did not speak of it.[152] But Virginia Clay wrote that "people are mad with rivalry and vanity."[153] Sara believed that nearly every man present at one of Washington's glittering soirees was *Somebody* and every woman *Somebody's* wife. Evening parties were the rage, scheduled and arranged so that pleasant people might meet distinguished strangers and one another—to delightful but never blatant music.[154] The galop, however, was introduced to Washington's dance floors with Buchanan's administration and was wildly popular.[155]

Early in their return to Washington, Roger and Sara recemented a warm friendship with one of the capital's power couples, Stephen and Adele Douglas. Sara encountered Senator Douglas for the first time at a crowded ball. She had retreated to a chair outside the crush, when Douglas approached her carrying a glass and a bottle of champagne.

He said to her, "I need no introduction, madam. I am sure you cannot have forgotten the man who met you a few years ago in the little Petersburg hotel and told you how like you are to the Empress Eugénie. No? I thought not."

Douglas bent down and spoke gravely. "Now, I shall send Mrs. Douglas to see you," he said. "I wish you to be friends. Not pasteboard friends, with only a bit of cardboard passing between you now and then, but real good friends, meeting often and being much together."

Just then, as he poised the bottle to fill her glass and drink to that intention, his elbow was bumped and a cataract of foaming champagne cascaded over Sara's neck and shoulders and the front of her gown. An icy flood down her bosom had rechristened their friendship. Sara gasped. Douglas said, "Don't worry about the gown! You have excuse now to buy another."[156] Easy for him to say.

Adele Douglas was the senator's second wife. Martha, his first, whom the Pryors had met in Petersburg, had since died and he had remarried a stunning beauty with a rich ancestry. Adele's maiden name was Cutts, and she was the great-niece of Dolly Madison, Washington's social lioness in the days of the War of 1812. This second Mrs. Douglas was one of the most statuesque of women—of "truly magnificent appearance," one of her admirers said.[157] "Beautiful as a pearl," Sara thought, "sunny-tempered, unselfish, warm-hearted, unaffected, sincere."[158]

Adele was tall, stately, gracious, and unassuming, with a sweet oval face, large brown eyes, a small Grecian forehead topped with braids of glossy chestnut hair, and hands, Virginia Clay said, "which might have been chiseled by Phidias." She was called Addie by her friends, and one admirer described her as "a most lively and queenly apparition." She was a devout Catholic and the capital's reigning belle—a style setter for Washington society— "conspicuous for her beauty wherever she passed." But there was more to Addie Douglas than just dazzling presence. She was also an irrepressible reader and a gifted linguist. Douglas's brother-in-law, who should know, thought her "as good as she is handsome," and one of her principal charms was a generous disposition and a gracious ability to make the awkward feel at ease and the discomfited comfortable. She and Sara did meet often, as Douglas had hoped, and became more than pasteboard friends.[159]

Despite the glamorous sheen, there was a sharper, more troubled edge to the Washington that Roger and Sara had returned to in 1859. By the winter of 1859–60, the gaiety in Washington was waning. Public receptions were becoming frosty and perfunctory. Ordinary "at homes" were being abandoned. Only an occasional society wedding gave social zest now to the rapidly sobering times. The women of Washington, thoroughly alarmed by the clamor of a rising national rage on the House and Senate floors, went daily now to the galleries to listen, appalled by the contention and the "lurid picture of disunion and war" being drawn there by members Northern and Southern. When belles met they no longer spoke of "furbelows and flounces, but talked of forts and fusillades." There was a grim foreboding that terrible trouble was brewing and that they were witnessing the "closing days of Washington's splendour."[160]

Washington society was becoming as divided socially as the Congress was split politically—strictly along North-South lines. Conversations at dinner parties were edgy and embarrassing. Names were dropping from visiting lists. One didn't always know his neighbor's biases, so must tread softly. Republicans were largely ostracized in Democratic circles, and Northerners in Southern circles.[161] One young Washington matron confessed she had "seriously canvassed the propriety of getting ill to avoid unpleasant *contretemps.*"[162] Sara Pryor sadly tried to straddle both camps, "perfectly well knowing that both were in the wrong."[163]

We are "dancing over a powder magazine!" Virginia Clay had written her father-in-law. Everything, she told him, was excitement and confusion. "Southern blood," she wrote, "is at a boiling temperature all over the city." She deplored the Northern radicals who were daily insulting all whom they dared. She saw "Black Republicans" at "every corner of our political fence," and "hot taunts of defiance" being hurled into the teeth of Northerners by goaded Southerners.[164] One Southern wife thought some of the Northern men looked "as if born to be the natural enemies of mankind."[165]

The Congress that convened in December 1859 was a body in which the democratic process had virtually stopped working. "The halls of Congress," a noted journalist later wrote, "steamed with vituperative, invective malignity."[166] Wild charge and counter-charge thundered on the House floor. Uproar succeeded uproar. Members crowded into the aisles in hot temper. One member feared that "a few more such scenes and we shall hear the crack of the revolver and see the gleam of brandished blade."[167] Senator James Hammond of South Carolina admitted to a friend, "I keep a pistol now in my drawer in the Senate as a matter of *duty* to my section & to enforce it in either House."[168] Senator James Grimes of Iowa wrote that "the members on both sides are mostly armed with deadly weapons, and it is said that the friends of each are armed in the galleries."[169]

When the Congress convened, Sara saw that it was "evident from the first hour that the atmosphere was heavily charged. The House resolved itself into an angry debating society, in which the only questions were: 'Is slavery right or wrong? Shall it, or shall it not, be allowed in the territories?'" She clearly saw that the breech between North and South, which had been only "a rift in the rock" four years before, had become "a yawning chasm." "What," she wondered, "might it not become in four years more?"[170]

Alexander H. Stephens, a former Whig congressman from Georgia, was watching events with a furrowed brow and beginning to fear a far shorter time frame than that. "Men will be cutting one another's throats in a little while," he would soon predict. "In less than twelve months we shall be in a war, and that the bloodiest in history. Men seem to be utterly blinded to the future."[171]

All of the acrimony, chaos, and gridlock centered immediately in the new Congress on the election of a Speaker in the House. It was a replay of a prolonged fight to pick a Speaker in 1856, when Southerners, after a two-month multivote standoff, grudgingly settled for Massachusetts Republican Nathaniel Banks. But this time, three years later, it was a far more bitter, passion-charged impasse, driven by a far less courteous and conciliatory Southern contingent.

No party appeared to have certain control of the House. There were 237 members from thirty-three states, and it would take 119 votes if all members were present to elect a Speaker. Democrats held 101 seats. But 13 of those couldn't be counted on to be faithful. That left them with but 88 secure votes. Republicans had 109 members, 10 short of being enough to organize the House. The balance of power was lodged in the votes of 26 Know-Nothings and 1 holdover Whig. Negotiations had been going on all summer, and the Republicans thought they had enough votes by December to elect John Sherman of Ohio. The Democrats, seeking to quash that prospect, were scrambling for support for their candidate, Thomas S. Bocock of Virginia, another Hampden-Sydney graduate and a twelve-year House veteran.

The balloting quickly froze into a standoff, with Sherman consistently polling more than a hundred votes, virtually all of them Republican, in roll call after roll call—but never quite enough for election. The Democrats, prodded by their belligerent Southern bloc, fought an angry rearguard action to keep Sherman from the speakership at all costs. Sherman had come to embody all that the Southerners detested about what they called the Black Republicans. He had been one of sixty-eight Republicans who had endorsed a book called *The Impending Crisis of the South,* by Hinton Rowan Helper, which agitated for a revolution of lower-class whites in the South. The book's seditious doctrines were viewed by many Southerners as the direct trigger of John Brown's raid at Harpers Ferry in October. Sherman had signed the offending book, without having read it—a not uncommon practice—and in retrospect, as a friend later wrote, "would as soon have recommended rattlesnakes as nursery companions."[172]

But the Southern Democrats were unbending and unforgiving. Any Black Republican who endorsed the book, whether he had read it or not, must never be Speaker of the House. They waged the fight, bitter from the start, to keep Sherman from the seat, leading first with Bocock. When that didn't work, they rallied behind a kaleidoscopic procession of other candidates, thrown up day after day to thwart the Republican bid.

Only two days into the session, when most freshmen congressmen are still awed and reticent, Roger Pryor had waded brazenly into the thick of the fight, firing a furious fusillade at the Republicans and their candidate. Roger, according to a correspondent for a Wisconsin newspaper, "belongs to the long-haired gentry. But men of his quaint and crotchety nature must be singular, if not *outre,* in some one or more external features." He wore gray clothes, the reporter wrote, had sharp eyes, put on airs, and looked generally "rather scowling and defiant." In argument he was "logical, connected, and forcible," vehement in utterance and gesture, with a voice and body that fairly shook with mingled earnestness and excitement. He wasn't "a whit stronger man," the reporter said, "than he thinks he is, though a stronger man than he generally has the credit of being. Is most naturally inclined to be a fire-eater, though he can be something else if it is gratifying to his ambition, is nothing from profound and sincere conviction, and is altogether delighted if he can create a sensation."[173]

Roger, as Sara had learned and the Congress was about to, was never one to hold back. And when he took up a cudgel, he wielded it without fear and with little thought for the consequences. "The gentleman from Virginia," one of his colleagues was to say before this session ended, "should be more guarded and circumspect in his language."[174]

But guarded and circumspect were not in Roger's makeup. Seizing the floor, on December 7, he opened with a broadside against a Know-Nothing congressman from Tennessee who had just delivered a speech that rubbed Roger the wrong way. Roger said he would not have "ventured to thrust myself into the presence of this august body" if not "impelled...by a feeling of surprise and indignation" at a position assumed in a speech by the Tennesseean, Thomas A. R. Nelson.

"I am not to be deterred," Roger began, "from a free and fearless declaration of my sentiments touching that gentleman by anything he can say, much less by anything he dare do"—an undiplomatic introductory that stirred a commotion and brought a shower of hisses from the Republican benches. It would not be the last commotion Roger would stir, nor his last shower of hisses.

He then waded into the speakership fight. "Allow me here to protest most emphatically that I am no disunionist," he said, but "as warm an admirer of the Union, in the spirit of the Constitution, as the gentleman from Tennessee." But that, said Roger, was the problem—that spirit had flown. And "when that spirit has departed, when the divinity has been dethroned from the altar," he said, "I no longer pay my homage there...when the spirit of the Constitution has been exorcised and outraged; when there is no longer in it that equity and justice which our fathers intended to breathe into it wherewith to animate the inert mass, then I am a disunionist."

He blamed the Republicans for this dethroning, charging them with "essaying to force the South to disunion," with principles "destructive of the Federal Union and of the sanctity of the Constitution." He accused them and their candidate of violating that Constitution and the integrity of the Union, and pronounced Sherman therefore "unfit to fill the office of Speaker." With this unfit candidate, Roger insisted, the Republicans are attempting to usurp the government, "to the end of perverting it to the oppression of our [Southern] liberties and the destruction of our rights."[175]

By Christmas every member's nerves were as frayed as Roger's. The Republicans, unmoved and unyielding, were sticking like adhesive to Sherman. Thaddeus Stevens, the irascible, ironic, sardonic, slavery-hating Republican radical from Pennsylvania, said he intended to vote for Sherman until "the crack of doom."[176] There was very little holiday cheer on the House floor and much talk of doom. The government, without an organized appropriating arm, was broke and at a standstill.

On December 29, after the twenty-third ballot had brought yet more deadlock, Roger was again on his feet, baiting the Republicans. "Greater than any individual wrong," he said, "greater than any private calamity, do we [Democrats] regard the wrong and the calamity of aiding Black Republicanism a single step in the consummation of its mischievous schemes." He called the nomination of Sherman itself "a proclamation of war" that "gave the signal of hostilities" against the South. Sherman's mere candidacy, Roger charged, is "an affront to Southern feeling and a challenge to Southern resistance." The Republican motive, he said, "is as transparent as their conduct is detestable;" it is "the artifice of ambition working with the resources of hypocrisy."

He said, "The entire history of this sectional struggle exhibits the South in a uniform attitude of defense; and exhibits the North pursuing an invariable policy of insult and encroachment." Nonetheless, he said, the South will exercise restraint—to a point: "The people of the South . . . are resolved, in the first instance, to vindicate their rights *in the Union*, peaceably if possible, by force if necessary." He said, however, "it is possible, if need be, to organize a confederacy out of our own resources, and to rear a fabric of government which shall survive the lapse of ages, and renew with brighter illustration the republican glories of antiquity."[177] He was talking secession.

On January 11, the thirty-fourth ballot still showed no movement. Voting stopped and negotiation began anew. During the hiatus, Roger took the floor once more and said to the Republicans, in effect, for God's sake, put somebody up whom Democrats can live with. He named Thomas Corwin of Ohio and William Pennington of New Jersey as moderate Republicans whom Democrats could at least tolerate. The Republican purpose in throwing Sherman up ballot after ballot, he charged, was not just to elect a Republican, but "to vanquish us . . . to degrade us"—"to impart the sting of personal insult to our defeat"—"to dishonor [our] section."

"And you profess to be Union men too!" he raged, you "whose policy and conduct are the origin and instigation of all the perils to the Union." He challenged them to withdraw Sherman. "No, gentlemen of the Opposition," he said, "if you are lovers of the Union, you must take down this candidate of yours; for I tell you, in all candor, that [his] election . . . will intensify and inflame and propagate that extraordinary state of agitation and resentment that now prevails everywhere through the slaveholding States."[178]

A fortnight of bargaining was followed by another week of more fruitless voting. Finally, on January 30, just before the fortieth ballot, Sherman did as Roger wished—although not because he wished it—by pulling out of the race, in favor of William Pennington. Thaddeus Stevens, reminded that he had said he would stick with Sherman until the crack of doom, said he thought he "heard it cracking."[179] Pennington was elected Speaker four ballots later—the forty-fourth—on February 1, with 117 votes, the exact number required that day. After eight bitter weeks of deadlock, the House was organized—barely, but at last.

One observer described Pennington as "a kind-hearted, placid, amiable, negative old gentleman... accepted as oil upon the waters."[180] He was sixty-four years old, a relic born in another century, and like Roger, only a freshman. But he was highly seasoned politically. He had been governor of New Jersey and had built a reputation for moderation. He had reluctantly left a comfortable law practice to run for Congress, from the Newark district. Now he had another job he didn't really want. But he assumed the chair and made a conciliatory speech, pledging "to do my duty with impartiality and justice to all," and praying "that by wise and prudent counsels peace and order may yet reign in our midst...." He said, "I feel I have a national heart, embracing all parts of our blessed Union."[181] But despite his "national heart," sectional hatred and antagonism would continue to boil over on the House floor.[182]

Indeed, the House under Pennington became what young Charles Francis Adams Jr., a scion of the famed Adamses of Massachusetts, described as "a national beer-garden." Sectional feeling ran high, and bad manners were conspicuously evident. Whiskey, expectoration, and bowie knives, Adams noted, were the order of the day. They seemed to him to be the only kind of "order" observed on the floor. When nothing was going on, the House was "simply a general hubbub." When something was, confusion became confounded. Pennington, Adams said, could only ride "upon the storm; not, indeed, directing, but, with uplifted voice and gavel, acting rather as *maestro*, or grand conductor, to this thundering song of the nation."[183]

The cool pure white marble and Greek Corinthian architecture of the Capitol gave no true hint of the heat within, even if its still-unfinished exterior did suggest chaos. "The times," Cox of Ohio said, were "sadly out of joint," and "for vituperative philippic, there was Roger A. Pryor."[184]

Charles Francis Adams Jr. remembered seeing Roger at one of Buchanan's receptions, "a rather tall and lank Virginian . . . in shabby black . . . and ugly as a stone fence, with tallowy, close-shaven features, and prominent high cheek-bones." Adams remembered that his eyes had "a hard, venomous look" that he thought seemed representative "of a large class—men who were just spoiling for a fight."[185]

As Roger was spoiling for a fight and winning celebrity—or notoriety, depending on the observer's North-South orientation—for his belligerent states' rights thrusts and counterthrusts on the floor, Sara was becoming known in society as one of Washington's most lovely, kindly, and gracious hostesses, in "peace-making contrast to her war-whooping husband."[186] Sara believed her "war-whooping husband" was the first congressman to wear "the gray," a suit cut from cloth presented to him by his constituents. A Northern congressman observing him wearing it on the floor for the first time said archly, "Virginia, instead of clothing herself in sheep's wool, had better don her appropriate garb of sackcloth and ashes."[187]

Sackcloth and ashes weren't Roger's style. He was into confrontation—and worse. Sara's Harry Hotspur of a husband had an affinity for evoking the Code of Honor. And it was about to get him into trouble again. He and the code seemed made for each other—and were often linked. Roger had a natural bent for inviting duels and surviving them. He practiced two professions most prone to them, journalism and politics, in the only section of the country—the South—that still condoned them. Indeed it was the heyday for affairs of honor in the South in the most angry of times.

His aggressiveness, passionate tongue, acid pen, and intense opinions, delivered unalloyed in sledgehammer blows had pitched him into duels—and into national prominence as a notorious duelist. He was never unwilling to back up at twenty paces anything he ever wrote or said. And the things he wrote or said were often open invitations to step off those paces.

His son's affinity for the dueling ground greatly distressed Roger's minister father—gave him "great trouble," he said—although in the South it was not unknown for men of the cloth to march off those twenty paces themselves.[188] What greatly troubled Roger's father horrified Sara. She empathized with the new bride in a story she remembered reading, who witnesses her husband's duel and the sound of the pistol shot "echoes ever after through her brain, filling it with insistent foreboding."[189]

In Roger's first duel no shots were exchanged, and in the next he fired into the ground intentionally. Then there was the son of John Minor Botts, a noted Southern Whig, whom Roger also declined to shoot. He later challenged Thomas F. Goode, his opponent in his first run for Congress. And that by no means exhausted the list.[190]

In one of his more celebrated duels, in 1858, Roger was challenged by Dr. Oswald Finney, one of the Eastern Shore's wealthiest and most influential citizens, a Whig member of the Virginia State Senate. Something Finney had said caused Roger to deliver one of his editorial sledgehammer blows. Finney sent him a challenge, and they met on a dueling field in Manchester near the Free Bridge one morning. At the first shot Finney fell, badly wounded, a bullet to his rib, which had deflected toward his spine. He would recover, however, and live on for another forty years.[191]

Nobody was ever killed in one of Roger's duels. And either because he was a sure shot, or lucky, or both, he was never winged or injured himself. But he had ample opportunities. His insult-laden language readily lent itself to somebody taking serious offense. What he said on the floor of the House on January 20, soon after arriving in Congress, about *New York Herald* editor James Gordon Bennett was typical of his unexpurgated invective. Roger called Bennett "that notorious individual . . . conspicuous by the persistent and flagrant violation of all the rights and virtuous instincts of humanity," "a wretch," "a miscreant," "a foul and filthy creature, whose name is the execration of both continents," "a fiend" of "a guilty and miserable existence," "an individual whose unutterable and unapproachable infamy distinguishes and stigmatizes him as the shame and the opprobrium of humanity."[192]

Unvarnished duel-inducing words. But for Bennett to take much offense at such vicious name-calling would have been the pot calling the kettle black, because he had often written and published such, or worse, about others. The day before, in an editorial Bennett had called Roger "a mental shoulder-hitter, a philological pugilist, a moral bully. These traits marked him as an editor, when he always assailed his political opponents with the vilest personal abuse." He had simply "transferred his brutality and violence," Bennett charged, "from the columns of the newspapers to the floor of Congress."[193] There was some truth in that. But Roger didn't see it that way.

For the most part, dueling was a ritual conducted wholly in the South. Every state in the Union had outlawed it by the 1830s, but the *code duello* would not die quietly. In the South it was considered an indispensable recourse for an honorable and offended man. Benjamin Franklin had described it as perhaps the most flagrant and ridiculous violation of separation of powers in existence. He said that anyone appealing to it "makes himself judge in his own cause, condemns the offender without a jury, and undertakes himself to be the executioner."[194] Henry Adams spoke of the South as a semibarbarous region of "barbecues and stump harangues, gouging and pistol shooting."[195] But Franklin and Adams were both Yankees.

Although dueling was mainly a male pastime in the South, generally setting the Southern man apart from the women and children, women had been known to participate. It was also a practice exclusively reserved to the upper classes. Only the social elite dueled—and only with social equals. Everyone else—"crackers," "peckerwoods," and "piney woods folk" (euphemisms for poor whites)—brawled, which was an activity beneath the dignity of a Southern gentleman.[196]

Dueling had a positive function of sorts. It tended to make brash men more careful to watch their words—except in Roger's case. The threat of a challenge and possible death often enforced more civilized behavior. It was something beyond the law, however, that often appeared necessary or unavoidable, and could erupt over anything—reputations, opinions, politics, money, or women. There was no thought that a duel would change anything or anybody's mind. And its purpose was not to kill anybody—indeed, generally when the gunplay began "everybody missed everybody."[197] It was a social institution in the South, and its purpose was to resolve a point of honor, which for most educated professional Southern men of the time was more precious than life itself.[198]

Virtually all professions were represented on the dueling fields of the South, not only preachers now and then, but doctors as well. In no profession, however, one lawyer argued, was the *code duello* of "more primal force than with lawyers, the army not excepted."[199] Southern editors and publishers might have challenged that claim, for they seemed frequently called to the field of honor. The famous often dueled. Andrew Jackson did it more than once. Army generals and navy captains did it. Dozens of congressmen, several governors and U.S. senators, and a host of prominent planters also did it.[200]

All the Southern states had laws against it, but as Lewis F. Linn, a Missouri senator, said, it was like getting married: "The more barriers erected against it, the surer are the interested parties to come together."[201] And the tenor of the publicity a duel received depended on the reporting editor's opinion of it or of the duelists involved. If an editor favored dueling or if the victor in the duel was a friend, his headline might be a mild, "Unfortunate Affair," "Unhappy Transaction," or "Lamentable Affray." If the editor was against dueling or if a friend of his had been the unhappy—or worse, dead—victim, the headline would likely be an angry, "Horrid Murder," "Cowardly Assault," or "Dastardly Assassination."[202]

Roger took his predisposition for dueling with him to Congress. As Charles Francis Adams Jr. had noted, he seemed of a class of men who appeared always spoiling for a fight. He was not the only one. It was generally assumed that whenever a member was seen handing a note or card to a colleague, in the charged atmosphere on the floor, he was issuing a challenge.[203] Indeed, as one alarmed observer noted, "The very atmosphere was quivering with challenge."[204]

A fight, if not a challenge, was stewing in Roger's head on April 5, 1860, as he listened to Owen Lovejoy of Illinois giving a speech on the House floor. Lovejoy was about as "Black" as Republicans got in most Southern congressmen's minds. He was, worse, a Congregational minister with a reputation for helping runaway slaves escape their masters. He was "a man of considerable brains and a good deal of body," with a big bushy mane of hair and a tremendous cannonlike voice.[205] He never feared to turn that firepower publicly on any of slavery's champions. Samuel Cox of Ohio said that it seemed as if Lovejoy "cultivated an ignorance of parliamentary law, in order to say the most indecorous things."[206]

On this day Lovejoy was delivering a vicious screed against slaveholding and slaveholders. "Sir, than robbery, than piracy, than polygamy," he was shouting, "slaveholding is worse—more criminal, more injurious to man, and consequently more offensive to God.... The sum of all villainy. Put every crime perpetrated among men into a moral crucible, and dissolve and combine them all, and the resultant amalgam is slaveholding."

As if this wasn't gall and wormwood enough for the outraged Southerners, Lovejoy had drifted, in an unparliamentary way, into the area fronting the Democratic benches. This was too much for Roger. Advancing menacingly from the Democratic side of the House toward Lovejoy, he hissed, "The gentleman from Illinois shall not approach this side of the House, shaking his fists and talking in the way he has talked. It is bad enough to be compelled to sit here and hear him utter his treasonable and insulting language; but he *shall not,* sir, come upon this side of the House, shaking his fist in our faces."

Seats emptied as members on both sides of the aisle instantly leaped to their feet. John F. Potter, a Republican from Wisconsin, his mustache bristling, shouted, "We listened to gentlemen upon the other side for eight weeks, when they denounced the members upon this side with violent and offensive language. We listened to them quietly, and heard them through. And now, sir, this side *shall* be heard, let the consequences be what they may."

"Let the gentleman speak from his seat, and say all under the rules he is entitled to say," Roger countered, "but sir, he *shall not* come upon this side, shaking his fist in our faces and talking in the style he has talked. He shall not come here gesticulating in a menacing and ruffianly manner."

A pounding gavel from the chair was doing little to quell the tempest. Thirty or forty members from both sides were now bunched around Roger and Lovejoy. The Speaker was summoned and began begging the members to return to their seats.

"Order that black-hearted scoundrel and nigger-stealing thief to take his seat," snarled William Barksdale of Mississippi, a slave owner, "and this side of the House will do it." Barksdale was the paradigm of Southern resistance. He was known to wear a wig and atop it a hat pulled down over his right eye. He was thickset, broadshouldered, and stub-legged, with small fierce eyes and a way of throwing his head to the side, turning up his chin, and talking in a short, sharp way, "like a New York B'hoy."[207]

Martin J. Crawford of Georgia, of milder disposition, with a reputation for keen practical wisdom, later wrote, "I never said a word to anybody, but quietly cocked my revolver in my pocket and took my position in the midst of the mob. . . . I had made up my mind to sell out my blood at the highest possible price." Crawford believed that not a dozen overseers in Georgia would submit to such language as Lovejoy was using.[208]

The Speaker eventually restored order without any gunfire, and the congressmen drifted grudgingly back to their seats. Lovejoy was permitted to resume his philippic, which basically branded slaveholding as unchristian barbarism, from the neutral ground of the clerk's desk. His language hadn't mellowed a wit, however, nor had Barksdale's. As Lovejoy rammed his points home, Barksdale shouted further interjections from his seat over a pounding gavel from the podium, adding such embellishment to his description of Lovejoy as "infamous, perjured villain," and "the meanest slave in the South is your superior." Other Southerners added amens of their own. "The man is crazy," said Lucius J. Gartrell of Georgia. Elbert S. Martin of Virginia threatened, "If you come among us we will do with you as we did with John Brown—hang you up as high as Haman."[209]

The *New York Times* was appalled: "If any person had been taken into the House, on that day, blindfolded, and had merely listened to what was going on around him, he would naturally have supposed himself to have been inveigled into some dismal den of ruffianism...and to be surrounded by the brutal scoundrelism which festers in the moral cesspools of a great city." The evident antagonisms on the floor reminded the editor of "the hates of rival factions at an Irish fair."[210]

Roger said nothing further that day, but "hanging higher than Haman" in his mind was something Potter of Wisconsin had done in the wake of the brouhaha. On April 11 Roger took the floor and accused Potter of doctoring the report in the *Congressional Globe*, the record of debates and proceedings in the Congress, inserting things in it Potter didn't say. Potter retorted that he had simply put back in some things that had been left out or incorrectly reported. He then accused Roger of editing his own remarks. Roger admitted he did in two instances substitute one word for another, which in no sense changed the meaning, "certainly not making the language stronger, or putting me in any more heroic attitude"—as he intimated Potter had himself done in his changes to his own words.

Potter then accused Roger of erasing one of Potter's edits without consulting him.[211]

All of this, to Roger's way of thinking, called for a duel. So he sent Potter one of those cards or notes that was generally construed as a challenge. Potter could scarcely decline, since Mrs. Potter was reported to have told him to "do whatever is necessary to preserve your honor—even if I go home to Wisconsin alone."[212]

As a newspaper editorial suggested, it was to be Potter, "a large, brawny Hercules of a man," against the "narrow-breasted" Pryor.[213] Having the choice of weapons and circumstance, Potter picked the bowie knife—sometimes called an Arkansas toothpick or the American sword—in a closed room until one of the principals fell, and he went immediately into training with it.[214] Roger's seconds refused to allow their man to duel in "this vulgar, barbarous, and inhuman mode." It was not only contrary to the code—one of Roger's friends called it "tom-cat terms"—but was offensive to Southern chivalry.[215]

Thaddeus Stevens, with his ever-sardonic sense of humor, suggested they duel with dung forks instead.[216] The duel was called off, but for the rest of his life Potter would be known as "Bowie Knife" Potter.[217] Roger would continue to be known as one of a class of men who appeared always spoiling for a fight. Potter was a hero back in Wisconsin and assured of reelection. A friend wrote him, "Defeat John Potter, you might as well smother the fires of a volcano with your foot—it can't be did."[218] The Missouri delegation to the Republican National Convention in Chicago, in May, would carry in a huge bowie knife, eight to ten feet long, labeled, "The knife that John F. Potter intended to use in his engagement with Roger A. Prior [*sic*] had the affair not been called off." A curtain with a full-length picture of Potter was dropped from the ceiling with the inscription: "He always meets a Pryor engagement."[219]

Senator James Hammond commented on the affair in the House, in a letter to a friend: "As everybody has a revolver and the

South does not intend again to be surprised into hearing another Lovejoy speech, a general fight in one or the other House with great slaughter is always on the tapis. There are no relations, not absolutely indispensable in the conduct of joint business, between the North and South in either House. No two nations on earth are or ever were more distinctly separate and hostile than we are here."[220]

This bomb waiting to blow was mercifully defused at midnight on June 25, when the two houses by concurrent resolution adjourned until December. Speaker Pennington, perhaps happier than anybody to see it end, brought his much-abused gavel down one more time and wished all "an affectionate farewell."[221] It had been a long, wearing, angry session.

Meanwhile important political lines had been drawn. The Black Republicans had nominated a dark horse from Illinois, Abraham Lincoln, for president over the front-runner and expected nominee, New York senator William H. Seward. Democrats had split into two parts. The regular party had nominated Stephen Douglas, and breakaway Southern Democrats had nominated John C. Breckinridge, of Kentucky, Buchanan's vice president. A fourth ticket of worried men—a pickup fusion of old-time Whigs, Know-Nothings, and assorted others that Sara called "the ruffled-shirt gentry"[222]—had formed the Constitutional Union Party, in hopes of saving the Union, and nominated John Bell, an ex–Speaker of the House and U.S. senator from Tennessee.

The bitter fighting on the floors of Congress was simply transferred for the rest of this critical election year to the national canvass. And Roger Pryor was still in the middle of things. Although his friend Douglas was running on one rail of the split Democracy, Roger was backing John C. Breckinridge to the end. That is where every good fire-eating, faithful, secession-minded Southern man was lining up.

Virtually nobody in the South was lining up for Abraham Lincoln, whom one fire-eating Southern congressman's wife described as "this low fellow."[223] "I cannot believe that we will ever have such a man as Abraham Lincoln President of the U.S.," another wrote in her diary in North Carolina. "No! It cannot be."[224] If it can be, Robert Toombs, a volcanic U.S. senator from Georgia, wrote a friend, "I see no safety for us, our property and our firesides, except in breaking up the concern."[225] He was striking a common chord in the unhappy South.

Roger left Washington and mounted the stump in Virginia. He was up for reelection to his own House seat, but had no opposition. He ratcheted up his incendiary oratory full fire in behalf of the Breckinridge ticket. He spoke from stumps everywhere, a "stormy petrel" preaching the doctrines of "organized resistance," conditioned on the assumption that Lincoln, a Black Republican, would be elected. The one thing he had told Yancey that would cause him to agree to secession was about to happen. It was said that nobody on the stump excited the public mind of southside Virginia as Roger Pryor did.[226]

Despite his hypnotic eloquence, however, Virginia went to the polls as "the bright tints of autumn were just appearing" on its forest-crowned western hills, and cast its fifteen electoral votes for Bell's Constitutional Union ticket.[227] And Lincoln was elected— "State after State going for rail-splitting abolitionism and Lincoln," one Southern wife wrote.[228] As Northerners were saying, Lincoln would soon "swing that long body into the White House."[229]

There was a quickening sense that with the government about to fall into the hands of the Black Republican Party and its long-bodied president-elect, Southern institutions were doomed. The South's leading statesmen—men such as the Georgians Robert Toombs and Alexander Stephens—had predicted this might happen if Northern sectionalism succeeded in winning control of national affairs. It had never happened before, but now it had. With Lincoln's election, as they saw it, Northern abolitionism, under the black banner of Republicanism, had triumphed, and the South was in deadly danger.[230] Augusta Jane Evans, an angry Southern novelist, wrote that she believed secession was now "the only door of escape from the worse than Egyptian bondage of Black-Republicanism."[231]

Also believing this, Roger returned to Washington in December 1860 for the second session of the Thirty-sixth Congress.

CHAPTER 5

——•·•·•——

Coming Untied

a wit said of Washington in late 1860 that it might have been called a city "if it were not alternately populous and uninhabited." It was, he wrote, a deserted village in the summer, and when inhabited, in the fall, winter, and spring, it was "the hibernating-place of fashion, of intelligence, of vice—a resort without the attractions of waters either mineral or salt, where there is no bathing and no springs, but drinking in abundance and gambling in any quantity." It was, in short, he thought, "a great, little, splendid, mean, extravagant, poverty-stricken barrack for soldiers of fortune and votaries of folly"—a "strange, lop-sided city-village."[232]

Everybody in this "city-village" of a capital was worried about something in the first year of this new and troubled decade, and most of them, about the way the Union seemed thundering toward disunion. "The people slept," the novelist Augusta Jane Evans wrote, "upon the thin heaving crust of a volcano," which seemed inevitably about to burst.[233] Margaret Sumner McLean, a Northern-born socialite wife of a Southern army officer, was hearing disunion openly avowed for the first time and feeling "as much shocked as if the existence of a God were denied."[234]

An old-time politician, visiting in Roger's library, spoke sadly of the looming dissolution of the country, and little Marie Gordon, the Pryors' eldest child, only eight years old, slipped her hand into his and said, "Never mind! *United* will spell *Untied* just as well."[235]

That would be more than just a clever child's "little *mot*" to President James Buchanan, probably the most worried man in the country. "A nation untied," to him, had a dreaded ring.

Buchanan wasn't cut out for this kind of out-of-control crisis. Augusta Jane Evans was to write of him, quoting Tacitus, "'He was regarded as greater than a private man whilst he remained in privacy, and would have been deemed worthy of governing if he had never governed.'"[236] The president was crowding seventy. He was, in his golden years, tall and stout, with a still-imposing physique and a flowing mane of snowy hair and beautiful hands. He made a distinguished appearance, enriched by courtly old-world manners. He was fastidious in his dress, always scrupulously neat, and remarkable for his unvarying choice of pure white cravats.[237]

One of his eyes was hazel and the other was blue—"a pair of misfit eyes," one observer said—eyes that ironically mirrored his dual political vision.[238] He was a Northerner, a Pennsylvanian, with Southern sentiments—the South's kind of Yankee, noted for his pro-Southern, antiabolitionist views. He had been elected president in 1856, with strong Southern support, and his cabinet was top-heavy with Southern men, who, it was believed, controlled him. The uncharitable called men like James Buchanan "doughfaces."

He was cautious, fussy, and legalistic, plodding and unimaginative, with a passion for precision. He was a diligent and tireless letter writer, and he enjoyed society and dancing but wasn't comfortable making new friends. With the friends he did have, he relished a good drink, a cigar, and a long evening's conversation. But even in conversation he was timid about venting his own opinions on controversial issues. Disliking confrontation, he isolated himself as much as possible from dissenting points of view.[239]

Now he was faced with the most monstrous of dissents. More than anything else, Buchanan wanted out of this gruesome responsibility. Some Saturday afternoons in those troubled times, Roger and Sara were invited to sit on the White House veranda, and one time Sara, standing silently near the president in a quiet corner, heard him mutter, "Not in my time—not in my time"—not in his time would the Union be severed and the country drowned in blood.[240]

Roger and Sara attended the same church as the president. Every Sunday he entered, it was always at the last moment, just as the bells at Saint John's were beckoning, and walked briskly to his pew near the pulpit. From her pew near the door, Sara watched him as each Sunday he rose immediately as the benediction ended and strode rapidly up the aisle, past a congregation waiting for him to leave first. When Sara came to know him well enough, she spoke to him as he passed. She sometimes said, "A good sermon, Mr. President!" And he unfailingly replied, "Too long, madam, too long."[241]

Much too soon, on December 20, 1860, the distraught president learned from Sara at that Thursday afternoon wedding reception in Washington that South Carolina had seceded. What he greatly dreaded was happening. The Union was coming untied—and in his time.

"One link is missing!" Catherine Edmonston, a North Carolinian who had married a South Carolinian, cried into her diary. "One pearl lost from the glorious string! Pray God that it be not the beginning of Evils."[242] Even the heavens seemed in a fury. The aurora borealis had been seen in the Gulf states—a rare sighting there. The sky glowed as from a great fire and the northern lights danced. One Southerner, sensitive to signs, cried, "Oh, child, it is a terrible omen; such lights never burn, save for kings' and heroes' deaths."[243]

More earthly harbingers of coming dissolution had been painfully plentiful since the presidential election. In early December Buchanan's cabinet had begun to shatter. Secretary of Treasury Howell Cobb of Georgia, its strongest Southern voice, had resigned on December 8, the first to go, saying, "The evil has now passed beyond control."[244] Lewis Cass, the secretary of state from Michigan, followed when Buchanan refused to reinforce the forts in Charleston Harbor. Other Northerners in the schism-ridden cabinet threatened to leave unless the president took a bolder stand against the onrushing rebellion. Nine days after South Carolina seceded, Secretary of War John B. Floyd, a rampant Virginia secessionist and former governor, resigned, under a cloud of scandal, at Buchanan's request. On January 8 in the new year, Secretary of the Interior Jacob Thompson of Mississippi, the last Southern holdout in the cabinet, left.

The thunderous split in the country, moving now so fast, growing so wide, was mirrored on the two clamorous floors of Congress. The air trembled with "gross intemperance of speech in the House, furious criminations and recriminations in the Senate, open declarations in favor of disunion, and excitement which is without parallel in the history of the republic."[245]

The second session of the Thirty-sixth Congress convened on December 3. Buchanan sent a message to Capitol Hill that satisfied nobody. In it he said no state has a right to secede, but if a state chooses to do so, nobody has the power to stop her, either. This fainthearted, enigmatic, issue-straddling position had encouraged secessionists, irritated Republicans, and disheartened everybody else. The House, trying to do something to stop the hemorrhaging, appointed a Committee of Thirty-three—one member from each state—to assess the crisis.

On December 18 Kentucky senator John J. Crittenden introduced a last-ditch compromise package in the Senate in the form of a bundle of amendments to the Constitution. It would make all territory north of the Missouri Compromise line, running to the Pacific, free soil forever, and all territory south of the line, slave soil forever. Congress would be forbidden ever to abolish slavery or interfere with it in the slave states or in the District of Columbia. The national government would reimburse slave owners for slave property lost to violations of the Fugitive Slave Law. That law itself would be vigorously enforced and could never be repealed. It gave the seceded states nearly all they asked for to stay in the Union. The Northern Republicans would not stand for it.

By January 7 the House had turned its back on the Crittenden compromise. Roger wired a friend in Richmond: "The last hope extinguished to-day." The next day he wired a friend in New York: "No chance of compromise. Republicans will not yield."[246]

On the House floor Roger flung himself into the teeth of the storm. Even as many Southern congressmen were leaving, he rose to champion Southern rights. On the last day of the year he offered a resolution: "That any attempt to preserve the Union between the States of this Confederacy by force would be impracticable, and destructive of republican liberty." It was tabled. On January 12 he refused to vote funds for the navy, "when it is to be employed for the inhuman purpose of subjugating sovereign States. . . ." He vowed, "I would sink it in the abyss of ocean before I would grant it a farthing." And he promised, "I will discharge my duty here by opposing every appropriation for the support of an Army and Navy that are to be employed in this unhallowed enterprise."[247]

Other states of the Deep South were leaving. Mississippi was the first to follow South Carolina out of the Union, on January 9. In succeeding waves, before the end of the month, Florida, Alabama, Georgia, and Louisiana left. On the first day of February, Texas followed. A week later even the Choctaw Indian Nation, in what would one day become the state of Oklahoma, went with the rising tide of rebellion.

On January 28 Roger seized the floor in earnest for a long, biting, and bitter speech. His tirade covered seven tightly packed columns in the *Congressional Globe* and was reprinted as a pamphlet.

He said, "The rapid march of events, outstripping the dilatory movements of procrastinating politicians, leaves us no question to consider but the alternative of peace or war. The dispute has become incapable of accommodation." He reminded Congress that six of the thirty-three states had already seceded since the beginning of the session, and others would surely follow. "It is an idle and unmeaning mockery to talk of *preserving* the Union," he said. We are "in the presence of so tremendous a catastrophe" as "the overthrow of Government, the partition of a great empire, and the imminent hazard of civil war."

He ran down the checklist of Southern grievances against the North: equality of the states subverted, the Southern states excluded from equal participation and rights in the common domain; state sovereignty usurped; the South cheated of its constitutional rights and threatened by sectional discrimination; faith violated and engagements broken. It was no different, Roger insisted, from the British domination the Founding Fathers deemed intolerable and seceded from in 1776.

Roger called Lincoln's election "the fatal 6th of November" and interpreted it as a declaration of war by the North upon the South—with "a president pledged to put our rights and our property [meaning slavery] 'in the course of ultimate extinction.' Under that threat," Roger argued, "the rights of the South are no longer secured by constitutional guarantees, but are suspended on the accident of an unfriendly Administration.

"The Constitution of Washington," Roger insisted, "is substituted by the platform of Lincoln." Lincoln and his party have rejected compromise "to push the dispute to the arbitrament of the sword." He charged that "the dominant party in the North have effected that which the world in arms could not have accomplished—the overthrow of this once glorious Confederacy." And "they now propose to consummate their work by afflicting the country with the calamities of civil war." To recover lost liberties, Roger threatened, there is the right of secession, reserved by "express stipulation" to Virginia and other states when assenting to Union in the first place—the right to resume their original sovereignty, "whenever, in their opinion, the conditions of alliance might be violated."

Roger believed emphatically that that time had arrived: "Whensoever occasion shall require—and occasion does now demand it—we are prepared to assert our equality among the sovereigns of the earth, and to make good the claim against all comers."[248]

John Barbee Minor, Roger's law professor from the University of Virginia, was horrified by what was happening in the Union and might have been thinking of his one-time student when he lashed out against "frantic ultraism." Watching the Union unraveling from Charlottesville, he wrote that "madness, literal frenzy, seems to me to possess our Countrymen."[249]

One by one as their states seceded, senators and congressmen rose on the floor to resign their seats, deliver often tearful farewells, and leave for the last time. Apprehension was quickening among those Southerners who remained, fearing that Lincoln's inaugural on March 4 would be disrupted by rioting and violence. They began sending their wives and children across the Potomac to sanctuary in the South.

From the hour of the painful exodus of the Southern lawmakers, all Washington seemed to change. "Imagination," one of Sara's friends wrote, "can scarcely conjure up an atmosphere at once so ominous and so sad. Each step preparatory to our departure was a pang."

Carriages and messengers darted excitedly through the streets. Vehicles lumbered to the wharf and rail station, filled with baggage of departing senators and members and their families. "What can I tell you, but of despair, of broken hearts, of ruined fortunes, the sobs of women, and the sighs of men!" one woman wrote. "For days I saw nothing but despairing women leaving...suddenly, their husbands having resigned and sacrificed their all for their beloved States. You would not know this God-forsaken city, our beautiful capital."[250]

"The journey south in those days," said one who was to make it, "was not a delight. Its components were discomfort, dust and doubt."[251] Roger felt Sara must seek sanctuary with the rest. Sara said sad farewells to her friends, fearing many would be farewells forever. She hastily and tearfully packed their personal and household belongings, tagged them to follow after her, and before Lincoln's inaugural left with her little boys—their sisters were already in Virginia—and their nurse, Eliza Page. They boarded a steamer to Aquia Creek, south of Washington, into that "discomfort, dust, and doubt." Standing out on deck and gazing backward as long as she could see the dome of the Capitol, she began her journey homeward—to who knew what. "We bade adieu to the bright days," she later wrote, "the balls . . . the round of visits, the levees, the charming 'at homes'"—the days, the country, and the city they had treasured. Since Virginia had not seceded, Roger was to remain in Washington until Congress adjourned and Lincoln was inaugurated.[252]

All of Washington arose "red-eyed, unrefreshed, expectant"[253]—Roger with it—on Inauguration Day. The night before, one who was there wrote, "was a restless and trying one to every man in Washington. Nervous men heard signal for bloody outbreak in every unfamiliar sound. Thoughtful ones peered beyond the mist and saw the boiling of the mad breakers." Washington on Inauguration Day resembled "more the capital of Mexico than that of these United States." Daybreak found a light battery drawn up on G Street, facing the treasury building; infantry held both approaches to the Long Bridge spanning the Potomac; squadrons of cavalry guarded the crossings of key avenues—all ready to quell any sign of riot or uprising. And bands had come to the capital from all over the country "to drown bad blood in the blare of brass."[254]

To this blast of trumpet and drum, Lincoln assumed the office—to James Buchanan's vast relief—and the expected trouble didn't happen. But Roger told Sara that "o'er all there hung a shadow and a fear."[255] The public mind, another wrote, "was feverish and unquiet."[256] The country seemed "plunging into a pathless future."[257] The newly formed Confederate provisional government in Montgomery, Alabama, hoping the predominant Northern sentiment would be to let the errant sisters go in peace, sent three ministers to seek recognition and make treaties of amity and goodwill with the newly installed Lincoln administration. The three, Martin J. Crawford, the former U.S. congressman from Georgia, John Forsyth, a noted Southern editor and former U.S. minister to Mexico, and André B. Roman, a distinguished ex-governor of Louisiana, arrived in Washington and were rebuffed—neither officially recognized nor received, not even corresponded with by the new president.

Crawford—who in the near-brawl on the House floor in the Pryor-Lovejoy brouhaha the year before had quietly cocked the revolver in his pocket, ready to sell out his blood at the highest price—met with four Southern lawmakers still in Washington: Roger, two of his fellow Virginia congressman—Daniel C. de Jarnette and Muscoe Russell Hunter Garnett, both planters, ardent secessionists, and ferocious defenders of slavery—and Louis T. Wigfall, the pugnacious senator from Texas who, like Roger, was a notorious duelist always spoiling for a fight. They read Lincoln's inaugural address together and agreed it was hostile and that the new president intended to attempt to collect the revenues and reinforce and hold Forts Sumter, in Charleston Harbor, and Pickens, at Pensacola, and retake other places already lost. They had heard that six Union vessels waited in New York Harbor fully provisioned and ready to sail. They saw Lincoln as a man of firmness and believed his cabinet would yield to his will. The prospects for a diplomatic solution and recognition were dim for the new Southern Confederacy.[258]

IF VIRGINIA'S SON, Roger Pryor, was ready now to secede, the mother wasn't. No state suffered greater agony over a shattering Union than Virginia. None loved the Union more than she. None had given so much to it in talent and skill. To see it destroyed seemed unthinkable. Yet no state was more important to the newborn Confederacy. A Southern Confederacy without Virginia seemed to Annie Harper in Natchez, Mississippi, "like a body without its head, a cripple indeed."[259] Without Virginia, the already seceded states of the Deep South could not sustain their bold departure. They had to have Virginia for her men, her resources, her geographical position, and her moral leverage with the other border states. If she could be forced into secession, the rest of the upper South would inevitably follow. The seceded states were bending every effort to " 'fire the heart' of the conservative old commonwealth," flooding her with delegations armed with speeches to convince. But such talk raised what one young Virginia belle called the "sudden spectral thought of war." All felt the presence of that dreaded specter, and most Virginians in early 1861 were disposed to wait—to avoid secession and war, if possible, barring some overt act of hostility that would make secession and war impossible to avoid. Virginia wavered unhappily, torn between duty to the Union and loyalty to her Southern sisters.[260]

Almost never had Virginia been counted with the states threatening Southern independence. It was a fact that disgusted fire-eaters everywhere. However there had been an exception to this—when the irrepressible governor of the state, Henry A. Wise, who had halted the march of the Know-Nothings in the South the year before, led a revolt against the prospect of the election of the first Republican candidate for president in 1856. Elect that Black Republican, John C. Frémont, Wise argued in effect, and Virginia would leave the Union.

"If Frémont is elected," he said in his most strident voice, "there will be a revolution. If not, there will be a respite of a few years only unless the North changes its whole tone of society. We will not remain in confederacy with enemies who endanger our peace and safety by means the most insidious and dangerous."[261] It was the same argument that was raised against Lincoln throughout the South four years later.

But Wise's rebellion had been an aberration. He was now no longer governor and Virginia was no longer eating fire. It was, indeed, doing everything it could to intervene on the side of union. On December 19, the day before South Carolina seceded, the Virginia legislature passed resolutions inviting the states to attempt to adjust the sectional differences in a "Peace Convention" in Washington on February 4, 1861. It was an eleventh-hour bid to save the Union, and twenty-one states accepted and sent commissioners. But on the very day it met, delegates from the seven seceded cotton states met in Montgomery to form a Southern Confederacy. The Virginia peace convention was shoveling sand uphill.

There was a limit, however, to how much even Virginia could stand. In early January the state's house of delegates passed a resolution that made this clear. The resolution—adopted 112 to 5—flatly opposed federal coercion of the seceded states, promising that any such force would meet Virginia's resistance. But that time had not come and, God willing, never would. On February 13 the Virginia State Constitutional Convention convened and again voted emphatically not to secede.

Roger attempted to explain his state's schizophrenia to his Northern colleagues on the floor of Congress. In her actions, he said, his state "has declared this, and nothing else: that, so far as she is concerned, she is willing . . . to make one more effort to save the Union; but unless justice and right be rendered her, she will not hesitate a moment to sever the ties which bind her to an iniquitous and oppressive association."[262]

These were difficult times for Roger. Virginia was dragging its feet; he was impatient, now chafing for secession. Congress was getting uglier by the hour, and he was bemoaning "these degenerate days."[263] But the misery was coming to an end in the Congress. On March 2, two days before Lincoln's inaugural, the House adjourned sine die. Roger's days as a U.S congressman were, in effect, over.

On April 4 Virginia still had its foot on the brakes. That day its state convention meeting in Richmond again rejected, eighty-nine to forty-five, a motion to pass an ordinance of secession and have it voted on by the people. It was akin to a test vote on immediate secession, and it showed that a large majority of its delegates—two to one—were still trying to be loyal Unionists. But by now hope had nearly died. There was only the slenderest promise that peace might be patched together between the North and the lower South.

In their hearts many pro-Unionists believed what Virginia House of Delegates member Edward Burks believed, when he said in early January, "I fear the union is *irretrievably* gone." He said, "I am myself for secession, rather *revolution*, if nothing else will do. But I am for exhausting *every other* measure first. Revolution is the last resort."[264]

Like Burks, many Virginians were now calling secession what it really was—revolution. In late January an army colonel, the Virginian Robert E. Lee, wrote his son from his frontier post in San Antonio, Texas. "The South in my opinion," Lee wrote, "has been aggrieved by the acts of the North as you say. I feel the aggression, & am willing to take every proper step for redress." However, he wrote, "As an American citizen I take great pride in my country, her prosperity & institutions & would defend any State if her rights were invaded. But I can anticipate no greater calamity for the country than a dissolution of the Union. It would be an accumulation of all the evils we complain of, & I am willing to sacrifice every thing but honour for its preservation. I hope therefore that all Constitutional means will be exhausted, before there is a resort to force. Secession is nothing but revolution."[265]

The Virginia convention's rejection of secession yet one more time on April 4 exhausted Roger Pryor's patience. It was now clear to him and the other fire-eaters that Virginia was not going to secede unless something drastic happened, and they knew that unless Virginia seceded, the cotton states could not make this revolution hold up. The "something drastic" would have to be an actual outbreak of hostilities somewhere. They knew then that Virginia would have no choice but to side with the South. They had to do something to make it happen.

Convinced of this, Roger in early April, "in those wavering days," left Sara and the children in Petersburg and boarded a train for Charleston, South Carolina, where outbreak now seemed most likely. He intended to help make the something drastic happen and was ready, as one writer has written, to pour "out his heart in fiery words."[266]

CHAPTER 6

Strike a Blow!

Charleston in 1861 was the queen city of the Carolinas, boasting fifty thousand inhabitants and an elegant mix of homes with harbor-fronting piazzas, where, one reporter wrote, "the sea breeze comes up with health on its wings."[267]

This ocean-facing city's sparkling appendage was its harbor, one of the northern hemisphere's most beautiful sheets of water. It was two miles across, and on its seaward end hulked Fort Sumter. Across the harbor from Sumter, inland to the west, were Charleston and its Battery, the flagstone parade facing the water. A mile across the main channel to the north of Fort Sumter, on Sullivan's Island, sat old Fort Moultrie, the Revolutionary War relic built to shield Charleston from invasion by sea. It had been abruptly abandoned during Christmas 1860 when the Union garrison transferred in the night to Fort Sumter. To the south, Cummins Point on Morris Island jutted to within thirteen hundred yards of Sumter. And some fifteen hundred yards southeast of Sumter was Fort Johnson on the north rim of James Island. Two miles from Sumter westward toward the city, on a marshy mudflat called Shute's Folly Island, sat another abandoned Federal fortification, called Castle Pinckney.

At the harbor's entrance the forlorn, newly garrisoned Fort Sumter sat "in the very jaws of the rampant lion of secession."

There had been three months of Confederate "battery-building" on the fingers and promontories jutting into the harbor toward the fort. They now formed a menacing semicircle of nearly fifty cannon and mortars of varying calibers, all with the hapless fort and its understaffed Union garrison in their crosshairs. And overseeing this formidable Confederate firepower was a man who knew how to use it.[268]

Pierre Gustave Toutant Beauregard, a new major general in the service of the Confederate provisional government, was a West Pointer who had distinguished himself in the Mexican War and in all ways before and since. Born in 1818 in Saint Bernard Parish on the outskirts of New Orleans, he would be forty-three years old on May 28. In appearance he was a compact, fastidious Louisiana Creole. His uniforms were tailored to perfection, he was always meticulously neat, and his manners were faultless, French, and deferential. His voice was pleasant and insinuating, with a Gallic lilt. His apprehension was lightning quick, his judgments razor sharp. His speech was terse and vigorous, and like any good Frenchman, he was fond of the society of the gentler sex and at his best in their company. But he was equally comfortable in the far less gentle company of war.[269]

Less than six months before, he had been in the U.S. Army, the newly appointed superintendent of the military academy at West Point, and an officer of uncommon promise. But he had resigned when his native Louisiana seceded, and had been sent to Charleston by the new provisional Confederate government to take command of the ring of fire encircling Fort Sumter, make it ready, and then await further orders about just what to do with it. He had arrived on March 1.

After South Carolina seceded in late December, its new governor, Francis Pickens, began installing the batteries ringing Sumter, with the intention of isolating the fort if that is what it took to acquire it. But this was not an idea or a project newborn. South Carolina had been preparing for this moment for a decade. In 1850 the state legislature had passed an act looking toward defending the state from "the abolition horde which threatens to invade us." The act had earmarked the huge sum of three hundred thousand dollars to create a state ordnance department with an up-to-date arsenal, appoint an ordnance officer, recruit an ordnance company, and buy arms, armament, and ammunition. Since then South Carolina had purchased more than a hundred and ten cannon, including the sixteen stubby ten-inch siege mortars, weapons built primarily to reduce a fortified stationary position and now frowning on Sumter. It was believed to be the largest inventory of heavy ordnance ever purchased by a state government. At the beginning of April much of it was in Charleston Harbor ready to open on Sumter from three points of the compass—west, south, and northeast.[270]

Governor Pickens's military engineers had done good work installing all of that firepower, but Beauregard, with his expert and practiced eye, saw ways to improve it, and he had. On April 1, after a month on the job, he wired Montgomery: "Batteries here ready to open.... What instructions?"[271]

The provisional government in Montgomery had hoped that blasting the Union garrison out of Fort Sumter would not be necessary, that the fort would be evacuated and handed over peaceably. But by early April it had become apparent that was not going to happen. Like the idea that secession itself might be peaceable, this was yet another "cuckoo song" of misguided hope.[272] Indeed, a Union flotilla was even then on its way to attempt to reprovision the fort. Beauregard was instructed on April 10 to demand its evacuation and, if refused, to reduce it.[273]

Roger Pryor arrived in Charleston on the same day that these orders from Montgomery reached Beauregard. Since he was South Carolina's kind of celebrity, a secession-minded Virginian, Roger was serenaded at the Charleston Hotel. From its piazza the young firebrand, whom the New York editor Horace Greeley was now calling "the eloquent tribune of Virginia," began pouring out his heart in fiery words.[274]

One observer saw him, a "pale, frantic man, limber and dark-haired, with uplifted arms and clinched fists," perorating on the balcony.[275] "I thank you especially," he began, tossing his shoulder-length hair as he paced the piazza up and down, "that you have at last annihilated this accursed Union, reeking with corruption and insolent with excess of tyranny. Thank God! it is blasted with the lightning wrath of an outraged and indignant people. Not only is it gone, but gone forever."

He said he was not there to speak for Virginia officially—he wished to God he were, for he would "put her [out of the Union] before twelve o'clock to-night." But, he said, "I bid you dismiss your apprehensions as to the Old Mother of Presidents. Give the old lady time. She cannot move with the agility of her younger daughters. She is a little rheumatic." But he knew the cure for that kind of rheumatism. "As sure as to-morrow's sun will rise upon us," he said, "just so sure will Old Virginia be a member of the Southern Confederation. And I will tell you, gentlemen, what will put her in this Southern Confederation in less than an hour by the Shrewsbury clock. Strike a blow!"[276]

That might indeed happen—and soon. But first, to do this thing right, Beauregard would serve an eviction notice on Fort Sumter. So, on the afternoon of April 11, three of his aides-de-camp piled into a boat, at 2:20 by the Shrewsbury clock, and began rowing across the harbor to deliver the notice to Major Robert Anderson, commanding the Union garrison.

The leader of this delegation of three aides in a rowboat was James Chesnut Jr., a South Carolina patrician both in truth and demeanor, the son of one of the state's wealthiest planters. He had been a U.S. senator from South Carolina in happier days, and he had resigned his seat on December 10, ten days before his state seceded. Indeed, he had resigned so he could go home and help it secede, becoming one of the principal authors of the ordinance of secession. Chesnut was steady, talented, coolheaded, aristo-cratic, self-effacing—too much so, his wife, Mary, sometimes believed—and largely underappreciated. But he had a talent for being available and useful when needed.[277]

Also in the boat were twenty-seven-year-old Captain Stephen Dill Lee, a talented West Pointer who had graduated seventeenth in his class in 1854, and Lieutenant Colonel Alexander Robert Chisolm. Chisolm was in the boat because he owned it. He was an extremely able, versatile, and resourceful planter who was managing his family's four-thousand-acre ancestral estate, a coastal plantation sixty miles south of Charleston, when Governor Pickens called him for help. Pickens needed somebody who could provide slaves (Chisolm owned two hundred) to help construct the batteries on Morris Island, somebody who also knew the water approaches to Charleston intimately and who owned a boat. Chisolm qualified on all three counts. His boat, a large six-oared affair manned by six strong-armed slaves, had been pressed into this high-level courier service by Beauregard.[278]

The three emissaries in Chisolm's boat put in at the Sumter wharf at three forty-five in the afternoon on April 11, carrying a white flag, and met with Anderson in the guard room. Anderson was one of the U.S. Army's most highly regarded artillerists; indeed, he had been Beauregard's gunnery instructor at West Point. He was a native of Kentucky married to a Georgia girl, but he was also a soldier who prized duty and was sternly faithful to the Union. Handed the demand to evacuate by his ex-artillery student, Anderson met with his officers for an hour, then at four thirty told the three Confederate emissaries that regrettably he must decline—he would not evacuate Sumter.

The Confederates, without further conversation, prepared to leave. An ever-gracious host, Anderson saw them to the main gate. As they were about to climb back into their boat and return to Charleston, he asked, "Will General Beauregard open his batteries without further notice to me?"

After a moment's hesitation, Chesnut replied, "I think not," and then, more firmly, "No, I can say to you that he will not, without giving you further notice." Anderson then, in something of an offhanded aside, remarked that he would await the first shot, though he would be starved out anyhow in a few days if Beauregard didn't batter the fort to pieces first. This heavily freighted remark was only indistinctly heard by the messengers, who had now entered the boat.

What did he say? Would the major care to repeat that?

Anderson obliged, and Chesnut asked if he might report that to Beauregard as well. Anderson declined to give it the status of a report but admitted that it was a fact. The boatload of emissaries then pushed off to take Anderson's refusal and this pregnant offhanded addendum back to Charleston.[279]

Beauregard immediately wired Montgomery with Anderson's refusal to be evicted and his side remark. The bombardment was put on hold while all of Charleston awaited the reaction from the Confederate government. Beauregard was now feeling the press of time. Pilots had come in from the sea, reporting that Federal vessels come to reprovision Sumter had appeared outside the bar. He must act soon.

Wired instructions from Confederate Secretary of War, Leroy P. Walker, arrived at eleven o'clock that night. Walker said they did not desire needlessly to bombard Fort Sumter. He directed Beauregard to find out if Anderson would be willing to give up the fort before he was starved out, and if so, what day and at what time. If Anderson still said no, then Beauregard was ordered to open fire.

Chisolm's boat pushed off again, and this time Roger Pryor, now also an aide-de-camp to Beauregard, was aboard, making it a foursome. This second delegation arrived at Fort Sumter at a quarter to one in the morning, April 12. With the new summons in hand, Anderson again met with his officers, and for two hours left the Confederates—minus Roger, who had remained in the boat on grounds that his state had not yet seceded—cooling their heels in a casemate.

At last, at three fifteen, Anderson advised the impatient Confederates that he would evacuate the fort on April 15, if—and here was the rub—if he didn't in the meantime receive contradictory instructions from Washington, or additional supplies. This would not do. At three thirty, Chesnut, Lee, and Chisolm, in the casemate, wrote out a terse rejoinder that the Confederate batteries would open fire on the fort in exactly one hour.

Much moved, Anderson again escorted the emissaries to their boat at the wharf, cordially pressed their hands in farewell, and delivered another addendum: "If we never meet in this world again, God grant that we may meet in the next." Louis Wigfall would later chuckle over that and say to Mary Chesnut, imagine Anderson "giving Chesnut a rendez in the other world."[280]

The boat with the four Confederates rowed directly to Fort Johnson, on nearby James Island. They were met by Captain George S. James, in command of the mortar batteries there, who was also an admirer of Roger Pryor. James roused his command, and seeing Roger in the boat, said to him, "You are the only man to whom I would give up the honor of firing the first gun of the war," and offered him the lanyard. Roger pulled back aghast, and in a husky voice, said, "I could not fire the first gun of the war." Lee thought him almost as much an emotional wreck at that idea as Anderson had been at the idea he was about to be blasted by half a hundred Confederate cannon. Virginia hadn't yet seceded and Roger was still a U.S. congressman.[281] Like many Virginians, he was ambivalent, even now, despite his militant front. Though he was agitating hard for secession, part of him still treasured the Union and regretted its breakup. Pulling a lanyard to start a war on its bloody course was more than he could do.

One of James's officers stepped up and offered to take his place. "No!" said James. "I will fire it myself."[282]

The four men in the boat rowed back out into the harbor, pulled up about a third of the way between Forts Johnson and Sumter, and waited. It was four thirty in the morning. The night was still and clear under bright starlight, and the sea was calm.[283] As they sat silently in the boat, the oarsmen resting on their oars, the shot shattered the utter quiet. The shell rose from the mouth of Captain James's mortar and arched high, hissing into the night sky and bursting directly over Fort Sumter. The echo of its thunder died away across the harbor and all was quiet again for a passing moment.

Shots from other batteries in the ring of Confederate fire followed, and soon the harbor was thundering and crashing with shot and shell.[284] The men in the garrison at Sumter watched awestruck "as battery after battery opened fire and the hissing shot came plowing along leaving wreck and ruin in their path."[285]

The men in the boat started back toward Charleston. The signal shot they had launched had jolted the fitfully sleeping city wide awake. It "woke the echoes from every nook and corner of the harbor," Stephen Lee later wrote, "and in this the dead hour of night, before dawn, that shot was a sound of alarm that brought every soldier in the harbor to his feet, and every man, woman, and child in the city of Charleston from their beds."[286]

On April 4 Mary Chesnut, in a hotel in Charleston, wrote in her diary, "How can one settle down to anything? One's heart is in one's mouth all the time." When the Union vessels—"this show of war outside of the bar"—started arriving, she shuddered. Federal guns might open on them at any moment. She saw her beloved South moving irretrievably "into the black cloud ahead of us."

Mary knew her husband was somewhere out in the harbor, in a boat, demanding Sumter's surrender. At four o'clock in the morning on April 12, she heard the peaceful chimes of Saint Michael's church and began to hope. But at four thirty the signal shot soared into the sky and hope died. She sprang from her bed, "and on my knees—prostrate—I prayed as I never prayed before." Outside her room she heard feet pounding down the corridor—all hurrying toward the rooftop. Mary put on her gown and a shawl and followed them.[287]

Soon the wharves and the Battery were thronged with what another Charleston diarist, twenty-two-year-old Emma Holmes, called "anxious hearts."[288] Yet another observer, watching as white cannon smoke "rose in wreaths upon the soft twilight air," spoke of "palpitating hearts and pallid faces."[289] Emma lived on Sullivan Island not far from Fort Moultrie, and she heard and felt every shot from the guns of Sumter, which began replying to the Confederate fire some two hours after the first signal shot.[290]

The bombardment from the Confederate batteries and the counterfire from Anderson's casemates—belching "iron vengeance"—continued all through the day and evening of April 12. "The curling white smoke," one observer wrote, "hung above the angry pieces of friend and foe, and the jarring boom rolled at regular intervals on the anxious ear. The atmosphere was charged with the smell of villainous saltpetre." It was a "melancholy scene, the sky was covered with heavy clouds, and everything wore a sombre aspect." Through this smoky purgatory Roger spent the day, "during the thickest of the fight, and in the face of a murderous fire from Fort Sumter," carrying dispatches to Beauregard from the batteries on Morris Island, often passing within hailing distance of the besieged fort.[291]

About six o'clock in the evening it began to rain. It stormed for hours, the wind screeching as if to outscream the shrieking shells. The tempest lashed up and down the Atlantic seaboard, wailing and sobbing.[292] Houses along the water rocked in the night, and the windows shook and rattled as if in a storm on a ship at sea.[293]

The firing slacked off as the tempest hammered both the Union and Confederate gunners. But the morning of April 13 broke bright, clear, and brilliantly beautiful under a cloudless sky, and the firing resumed. At eight o'clock, hot shot from an eight-inch Columbiad at Fort Moultrie set the barracks at Sumter afire. As thin smoke curled above the ramparts, growing more and more dense as it rose into the morning air, the cry rose from the Confederate batteries, *Fort Sumter is on fire!* Every Confederate battery opened with renewed vigor. A south wind drove hot smoke and cinders into the casemates of the fort. The Union gunners, nearly suffocating, threw themselves on the ground and covered their faces with wet cloths, or rushed to the embrasures to catch the occasional draft of clear air that made it possible to breathe.[294]

The roaring and crackling flames, the dense clouds of whirling smoke, the bursting enemy shells, the exploding ammunition in the burning rooms, the crashing shot, and the thud of falling masonry in every direction made the fort a pandemonium.[295]

Outside the bar the Union flotilla, which had been visible to all since the day before, was powerless, lying "as idle as a painted ship upon a painted ocean."[296] The men-of-war that would have permitted the fleet to attempt to raise the siege had not yet arrived.

The fire raging in the barracks was moving steadily toward the magazine. All egress to the fort had been cut off except through the lower embrasures. Stored hand grenades and many of the shells being lobbed in from the Confederate batteries that had not detonated were now exploding as the flames reached them. Anderson and his officers and men were smoke-blackened and exhausted, although none had yet been killed or wounded. About one o'clock in the afternoon, under the quickening Confederate fire, the flagstaff at the fort was carried away, and the colors plunged heavily to the parade below.

In Charleston, Beauregard saw them fall. This time he launched two boats. James Chesnut climbed into one, a steamer called the *Osiris*, and went for the city fire department. The other, Chisolm's boat, set out for Sumter, with Chisolm, Stephen Lee, Roger, and a newcomer to the negotiating game, Porcher Miles, aboard. Miles was one of Roger's former congressional colleagues, a South Carolinian who had resigned his seat in December. He was a onetime math professor at the College of Charleston and an ex-mayor of the city, and, like James Chesnut, had been a member of South Carolina's secession convention.

Chisolm's boat was halfway out into the harbor when the colors were hoisted again over Sumter. So the oarsmen turned the boat about and began rowing back toward Charleston. They had gone but a short distance when a white flag went up over the embattled fort. They turned eagerly about and rowed vigorously for Sumter once more.

What was happening at Sumter was more complicated and unreal than they knew. Through the smoke and cinders a strange apparition had appeared abruptly at one of the embrasures, staring in through flaming eyes. Behind this incendiary visage was Louis Wigfall, the senator from Texas, who Mary Chesnut called "the Stormy Petrel," and who, another of his friends said, "chafes at the restraints of civil life [and] likes to be where he can be as rude as he pleases."[297]

Here he was, unaccountably at the smoky embrasure, rudely demanding to see Major Anderson. When the astonished Anderson arrived, Wigfall said he had come in a boat from Beauregard. It was only partly true. Wigfall had come in a boat, all right, rowed by a South Carolina private from Point Cummins. But though he was an aide-de-camp to Beauregard, Wigfall hadn't seen the general in several days. Not only was he unexpected, he was unempowered, unconnected, and unauthorized.

"To what am I indebted for this visit?" Anderson demanded.

Wigfall replied. "For God's sake, Major, let this thing stop. There has been enough bloodshed already."

"There has been none on my side," Anderson replied, "and besides, your batteries are still firing on me."

"I'll soon stop that," Wigfall said. Turning to the Union gunner who was holding the sword with the white handkerchief skewered to its tip that Wigfall had carried into the fort, he said, "Wave that out there." The gunner snapped back with something that passed for "wave it yourself," and Wigfall snatched up the sword and took a few steps toward the open embrasure.

Anderson called him back. "If you desire that to be seen you had better send it to the parapet."

Since the parapet was not a place anybody really wanted to go at that moment, a white hospital sheet was produced and waved from an embrasure by one of the gunners. That was the white flag the boatload of Confederates had seen as they were rowing back toward Charleston that had caused them to turn about one more time.

Wigfall got down to business. "You have defended your flag nobly, sir," he told Anderson. "You have done all that is possible for man to do, and General Beauregard wishes to stop the fight. On what terms, Major Anderson, will you evacuate this fort?"

Anderson said he would consider leaving only on the terms Beauregard proposed on April 11, or die defending his command. The first alternative seemed the more reasonable to Wigfall.

Carrying those terms, mirroring Beauregard's earlier ones, the visitor climbed out of the embrasure and back into his rowboat, and left as he had come. Anderson had agreed to evacuate the fort in exchange for the right to salute the flag and march out with the honors of war and with arms and private baggage.[298]

Shortly after Wigfall left, Chisolm's boat with the four delegates sent by Beauregard arrived. They were directed from an embrasure not to attempt landing at the wharf, which was mined and dangerously near the fire. This second wave of visitors, to what was beginning to look like an afternoon open house, were helped through the embrasure and taken to Anderson. As Beauregard had directed, they offered to help put out the fires. A fireboat was standing by.

Anderson said, "Present my compliments to General Beauregard, and say to him I thank him for his kindness, but need no assistance." He suggested that the worst was over, the fire had settled over the magazine, but since it hadn't yet exploded and blown them all to bits, the real danger had passed.

Anderson was less worried about the fires than he was about what the visit from these new visitors implied about the visitor who had just left. "Gentlemen," he asked, his brow knit with worry, "do I understand you have come direct from General Beauregard?"

When he was assured they had, he exclaimed, "Why, Colonel Wigfall has just been here as an aide to and by authority of General Beauregard, and proposed the same terms of evacuation offered on the 11th instant." The Confederate emissaries said they were not authorized to offer terms, only to offer help, and that probably Wigfall wasn't, either, since he had not seen the general for several days.

Anderson was nonplussed and embarrassed. "There is a misunderstanding on my part," he lamented, "and I will at once run up my flag and open fire again." The Confederates urged him not to do that until the matter was explained to Beauregard. They asked him if he would be willing to put his understanding with Wigfall into writing for them. He agreed.[299]

As Anderson wrote out the terms once more, Roger, who this time had entered the fort with the rest of the delegation, Virginia secession or no, waited in the only habitable gun casemate, which doubled as the surgeon's quarters. It was powerfully hot and stuffy, and Roger was thirsty. Providentially, a large black bottle and a tumbler rested on the table beside him. The place was somewhat dark, having been built up all around with boxes of sand to make it shellproof, and Roger, without attempting to read the label, poured an ample shot into the tumbler and drank it down.

Whatever it was, it didn't taste to him like water, whiskey, or anything else he recognized. It was, in fact, iodide of potassium, not all that thirst-quenching but plenty poisonous. Captain Samuel W. Crawford, the garrison surgeon, was hurriedly sent for. When Roger excitedly explained what he had just done, Crawford said, "If you have taken the amount of that solution that you think you have, you have likely poisoned yourself."

Pale and horrified, Roger gasped, "Do something for me, doctor, right off, for I would not have anything happen to me in this fort for any consideration." Leaning on the doctor, Roger was helped down the line of casemates to the improvised dispensary to have his stomach pumped.

Narrowly saved from being the first casualty of the war, Roger was soon out of trouble. But Crawford's trouble was just starting. His fellow officers in the garrison demanded to know what right he had to interpose in a case of that kind. If any Rebel leader chose to come over to Fort Sumter and poison himself, they reasoned, the doctor had no business interfering with such a laudable intention. Crawford countered with the no less reasonable argument that he was accountable to the U.S. government for the medicine in the hospital and therefore could not permit Roger to carry any of it away.[300]

Meanwhile, Wigfall, carrying away Anderson's terms of evacuation, found Chesnut in the *Osiris*, standing in the harbor with a company of firemen to help put out Sumter's fires. When Beauregard heard Wigfall's report, he launched yet another boat, this one carrying his chief of staff, David R. Jones, and another aide-de-camp, Charles Allston Jr. They were authorized officially to receive any proposition Anderson might wish to make.[301]

When they arrived at Sumter about 2:45 P.M., this new pair of emissaries relayed Beauregard's message to Anderson, who told them of Wigfall and of the second boat, which had just left. Anderson read Jones and Allston the terms, which they carried back to Beauregard, who now had at least three copies. At seven o'clock that evening—April 13—Jones, Roger, Miles, and Navy Captain H. J. Hartstene, yet another aide-de-camp, climbed into the fourth boat of the day and returned to Sumter with the final agreed-upon terms. Anderson would evacuate at nine o'clock the next morning. A steamer would take the garrison to the Union ships lying outside the bar.[302]

Sunday, April 14, was bright, with sunlight slanting across the rooftops of Charleston and sparkling diamondlike on the water. The harbor looked "deep and rich," as it always did under bright sunlight on sunny spring afternoons. The "filmy atmosphere" at that time of year in those latitudes, as one writer has described it, made "the sky above the darkling afternoon sea a pale but luminous turquoise." There was "a wonderfully soft strength in the peaceful brightness of the sun.... The harbor was flecked with brilliantly decked craft of every description, all in a flutter of flags and carrying a host of passengers in gala dress. The city swarmed across the water to witness the ceremony of evacuation."[303]

Anderson evacuated with a final salute to his flag, and by four thirty, some thirty-six hours after the first signal shot was fired, the flag of the new Confederacy was raised over Sumter's shot-battered and fire-charred walls. John Jones, a writer who was about to become a clerk in the Confederate war department, wrote in his diary in Richmond on April 12, "This is the irrevocable blow! Every reflecting mind here should know that the only alternatives now are successful revolution or abject subjugation."[304]

Mary Chesnut wrote from Mulberry Plantation, in South Carolina, after the surrender, "I have been sitting idly today, looking out upon this beautiful lawn, wondering if this can be the same world I was in a few days ago."[305]

Following the evacuation, Beauregard called Roger, handed him a report on the bombardment and evacuation, and sent him to deliver it in person to the Confederate war department in Montgomery. Roger left on April 18. For better or worse the young Virginia fire-eater had had his way. The blow he had worked so long and hard for had been struck. The wait for his state to join the Confederacy was about to end.

John Letcher, the governor of Virginia, hated what was happening. He was a lifelong moderate, who, unlike Roger, had fought his state's drift toward secession, desperately trying to steer his charge between the extremes of "passion and recklessness."[306] But he now saw, to his deep regret, that there would be no stopping it. He was also a practical politician. He would now go with the drift.

On April 15 Abraham Lincoln issued a call for 75,000 militia to put down the rebellion. Letcher was notified that his state's quota would be three regiments of 2,340 men, to rendezvous at Staunton, Wheeling, and Winchester. Letcher's reaction was immediate, angry, and unqualified. "I have only to say," he wrote the president, "that the militia of Virginia will not be furnished to the powers at Washington for any such purpose.... Your object is to subjugate the Southern States, and a requisition made upon me for such an object ... will not be complied with." You have chosen "to inaugurate civil war," Letcher charged, "and having done so, we will meet it in a spirit as determined as the Administration has exhibited toward the South."[307]

Virginia hesitated no longer. On April 17, "in a blaze of excited indignation" and "amid tears, jeers, and cheers," the state constitutional convention, which had tried so hard to work out any solution but this, passed an ordinance of secession by a vote of eighty-eight to fifty-five, to be put before the voters of the state on May 23.[308]

CHAPTER 7

Cradle Days of the Confederacy

*M*ontgomery, Alabama, where the seven states to first secede sent delegates to shape a new government, and where Roger went with Beauregard's report, had the advantage of geography. It was mutually convenient—or inconvenient, depending on the point of view—to every other part of the new Confederacy.

Centrally situated, it was adolescent, as cities went, but forty years removed from the frontier—a mix of the brawling and the sophisticated. It sat among its many gardens on a high bluff of seven hills on the banks of a sweeping bend of the Alabama River, which was a quarter mile wide and flowed toward Mobile at four miles an hour. The country around was well wooded and richly cultivated in broad fields of cotton and Indian corn. Mobile lay some three hundred navigable miles downriver to the south, and Washington, some eight hundred overland miles to the northeast.

The city began as the site of Indian villages and, in the eighteenth century, a landing for traders on the river. It emerged as an incorporated entity in 1819, the year Alabama became the twenty-second state. Founded by an unlikely partnership of Georgians and Northern real estate speculators, it became the capital of Alabama, in 1847. It was the centerpiece of the cotton-rich "Black Belt" country, so named for its rich, dark, loamy soil and its heavy concentration of black slaves.[309]

With its nearly nine thousand permanent residents in 1861, half white and half black, Montgomery was the second-largest city in Alabama, after Mobile, and its main business was politics, sturdily undergirt by cotton, railroads, and the river. The cotton fields that surrounded the town made it, per capita, one of the wealthiest cities south of the Mason-Dixon Line. As befits a community with a political bent, where words and opinion mattered, it supported four newspapers, all solidly secessionist.

The town was short on amenities. It offered but three hotels, and only one of those, the Exchange, had any claim to elegance— and that, not a strong one. Montgomery's food didn't please every palate, either, and the supply of both food and lodging was quickly swamped as the city's population instantly doubled after secession, when all roads seemed to lead to it. That was the situation as Roger headed for Montgomery after Fort Sumter fell. Six people were sleeping in rooms intended for only three. The city, "scarcely more than a great inland village," had become, one visitor noted, the "cradle of the Confederacy," which had "turned a society, provincially content to run in accustomed grooves, quite topsy-turvy."[310]

Montgomery's permanent inhabitants were said to be "a frugal, simple, hog-and-hominy living people, fond of hard work and, occasionally, of hard drinking."[311] William Henry Russell, the celebrated visiting correspondent for the *London Times*, denounced the city, saying it had "little claims to be called a capital." Its streets were too "hot, unpleasant, and uninteresting" for his cosmopolitan taste. "I have rarely seen a more dull, lifeless place," he growled. It looked to him like a small town in the Russian interior. He described its Grecian-style capitol, which gazed from the heights down Montgomery's dusty main street, as an "Athenian Yankee-ized" structure "erected on a site worthy of a better fate and edifice."[312] T. C. De Leon, a visiting American observer, was kinder to the capitol, saying it "stared down the street with quite a Roman rigor."[313]

The city not only housed the new Provisional Confederate Congress but an outsized congress of dogs and of mosquitoes, flies, and other pests notable not only for their numbers but for their size and appetites. In certain seasons lethal fevers prevailed.

In early February into this centrally situated, pest-infested, dog-dominated, underequipped, unready but in some ways charming, city flocked forty-three delegates from six of the seven seceded states. They would be joined in early March by the seventh, Texas, raising the number to an even fifty. Called there at the insistence of South Carolina, they were gavelled to order on February 4, in the Alabama senate chamber, with its "Egyptian" mantelpiece and stately columns. They styled themselves a Convention of Deputies, soon to transmogrify into the first Provisional Confederate Congress, which Russell, the *London Times* correspondent, called "legislators or conspirators."[314]

Lawrence Keitt wrote his wife, Susan, that their goal was "a great one . . . the work of bringing a nation into existence."[315] The nation makers immediately made Howell Cobb of Georgia their leader, an obvious choice to preside over this collection of path hewers. He was a Friar Tuck of a man—big, double chinned, honey eyed, curly headed, jolly, able—and highly seasoned in politics at the highest levels. He was a former Speaker of the U.S. House of Representatives, a former governor of his state, and as Buchanan's secretary of the treasury, the strongest man in that harried and unhappy president's cabinet. He was also the most popular of all the delegates in Montgomery.[316]

The weather in Alabama smiled on the new breakaway enterprise. The "glorious sun" shone out "from silvery parting clouds with undimmed lustre," wrote "Sigma," the correspondent for the *Charleston Courier.* These revolutionary delegates who had "left the Babylon of American politics to seek the far-famed Canaan of

Southern desire" were beginning their new enterprise "under fair and brilliant omens."[317]

The delegates were generally well-known to one another from past political associations. Nine of them had been U.S. senators. Seventeen had been congressmen. Four of them had been both. One had been a secretary of war, another a secretary of the treasury. They were heavily represented by veterans of the bench. Among them were eighteen judges or former judges from various levels, state and federal. Two delegates had been members of state cabinets. Fourteen had been state senators and thirty-three had served in state legislatures. It was a high-octane collection of leading political minds of the South. Thirty-eight of the fifty were college graduates. Forty of them were lawyers. Seventeen were planters.[318] Some believed the congress would "compare favorably with the most gifted and distinguished in any deliberative body that has assembled in this or any other country."[319]

The delegates assumed broad prerogatives and set to work with breathtaking speed. They had to legislate, so they became a temporary one-house congress. They empowered themselves to choose a provisional president and vice president, so they were also kingmakers. Within four days they had hammered out a provisional constitution, patterned liberally on the Constitution of the Union they had just seceded from—with minor changes to fit their states' rights–slaveholder philosophy. A day later they had named the provisional president and vice president of their new government, which would remain provisional for one year, to be replaced then by a permanent entity with its permanent constitution, elected bicameral congress, and elected executive.

The new government sprang, one observer said, "full grown from foam of the angry sea of politics," and from the "disseevered fragments" of "the mother government."[320]

Not only in the constitution it adopted but in the way it all worked, it was "Washington over again, only on a smaller

scale."[321] Montgomery teemed, as Washington teemed, with officials, would-be officials, commission seekers—military and otherwise—office hunters, hangers-on, and political voyeurs. It brimmed
with activity and rocked to cannon-booming salutes for distinguished arrivals—or simply for the arrival of good news. Lawrence
Keitt wrote his wife that the birthing of the new nation was being
accomplished in an atmosphere of "pageantry, cheers, enthusiasm
and waving kerchiefs."[322]

Lobbyists, "those unclean birds," were out in force, reinforcing
the Washington-like ambience.[323] "No point in Montgomery was
remote enough—no assemblage dignified enough," it was said, "to
escape the swoop of the lobby vulture."[324] A joke was going around
Montgomery that the "lobbyists differed from congressmen only in
that they chewed their cigars rather than smoked them."[325]

From the start there was an undercurrent consensus that Jefferson Davis, who had just resigned as U.S. senator from Mississippi,
would be the president of this new nation. The powerful political
triumvirate from Georgia—Howell Cobb, Robert Toombs, and
Alexander Stephens—were also mentioned, but the Georgians
couldn't form a solid front behind any one of their three powerful
leaders. Besides, as Cobb wrote his wife on February 6, "All that I
have seen and learned since I got here has satisfied me that it is a
most undesirable position."[326]

Davis's election was a strangely low-key event by most political standards. There was no obvious electioneering, no wire
pulling, no candidate management, no bargaining, no promises,
and no dissenting votes.[327] There was dissenting sentiment, particularly from South Carolina and Georgia, but nothing strong enough
to matter.

Without seeking the office or being asked, Davis was unanimously elected, and a telegram was sent immediately to his Briar-
field plantation in Mississippi. When it arrived, Davis was in the
garden with Mrs. Davis cutting roses. He read the wire, Mrs. Davis
later reported, and looked so grieved by it that she feared some evil

had befallen the family. After a few moments of painful silence, he broke the news to her "as a man might speak of a sentence of death."[328] If this Mexican War hero and preeminent politician of the South had any druthers in this new venture, it was to be on the battlefield, commanding Mississippi troops—if there were to be any battles and if Mississippi was to have any troops. But Davis was West Point–trained and believed in duty. He boarded a train next day for Montgomery, passing through Chattanooga, Marietta, and Atlanta. At every major rail station on the way, he was greeted and cheered by well-wishers.

Alexander Stephens, one of the Georgians—"Little Aleck," he was called—had been named vice president and was sworn in early, on February 11, his birthday. Little Aleck, who had just turned forty-nine, appeared ages older. He was spare and frail almost to the point of nonexistence. He scaled one hundred pounds, on a heavy day, and seemed nearly bloodless. It was suggested that he was "a refugee from the graveyard."[329] But he was brilliant, an intellectual and political force to be reckoned with. He had been a leading Whig congressman and friend of fellow Whig Abraham Lincoln when they served together in the U.S. Congress in the late 1840s.

Davis arrived in the new Confederate capital on February 16, to a fifteen-gun salute and cheers that "thrilled the inner life with enthusiasm." He was conducted to the Exchange Hotel through brightly lit streets and a cascade of fireworks. At the hotel a large clamorous crowd called him to the balcony. Davis came out accompanied by that fire-spewing Alabama hothead William Lowndes Yancey. Worn out physically and emotionally, Davis greeted the crowd briefly. Yancey reached into his own powerful forensic storehouse and pulled out an unforgettable bon mot that was soon on every lip: "The man and the hour have met."[330]

On the eighteenth the presidential inaugural procession formed on Montgomery Street, with Davis and Little Aleck riding together in a magnificent carriage drawn by six stately grays. It moved up Market Street to the crash of celebrating cannon, lusty cheers, and the quick-time tempo of the new minstrel tune called "Dixie," written by a Northener.[331] A vast crowd, probably the largest ever seen in Montgomery, thronged the doors, windows, and portico of the capitol and spilled out over the ground that sloped away from the front of the building into the town below. Davis stood on the blue marble of the front portico, between two tall white pillars, and looked out on the crowd as the Reverend Basil M. Manly, a venerable Montgomery cleric, opened the ceremonies at noon with a prayer to the clear heavens, urging the Almighty to "turn the counsel of our enemies into foolishness." Howell Cobb administered the oath to the new president, and Davis delivered his address in his usual "calm and forceable manner," hitting "the key-notes of Southern independence." The ladies "wreathed him with flowers" afterward—freshly cut japonica, hyacinths, and spring magnolias. A reporter wrote, "Ten thousand hearts beat high with joy, admiration and hope for the administration of the new President." That night a celebratory levee ended the day. Public buildings and many private homes were brilliantly lit. Rockets and Bengal lights caromed across the night sky to the catchy beat of "Dixie."[332]

The new president wrote home to his wife that "the audience was large and brilliant. Upon my weary heart was showered smiles, plaudits, and flowers; but, beyond them, I saw troubles and thorns innumerable."[333]

Davis's office for the moment, where he took his "weary heart, troubles, and thorns," was one of the parlors of the Exchange Hotel, where he also resided until his wife, Varina, arrived and the first family moved into the white frame mansion, belonging to Colonel Edmund Harrison, on Washington Street. It was but a few convenient steps from Government House, "a great red brick pile" of converted warehouses and counting rooms, where the business of the new Confederacy was soon being conducted, where the executive office and cabinet rooms were, and where Davis worked at least fifteen of every twenty-four hours.[334]

On March 4, the day the new Republican president was being

inaugurated in Washington, a new Confederate flag was unfurled defiantly for the first time over the capitol in Montgomery. "Sigma" of the *Courier* called this new banner of seven stars and stripes, red and white on a blue field, the "emblem of Southern liberty." The busy Confederate congress adjourned for the occasion to the rotunda and joined a concourse of citizens and a detachment of state artillerists pulling a brass howitzer. A few minutes before four o'clock in the afternoon, seven southern belles representing the seven seceded states ascended the ledge encircling the summit of the capitol and arranged the flag on the staff to the stirring strains of the "Marseillaise." As the clock on the building's face finished tolling four, the howitzer boomed, the band played "Dixie," and the emblem of Southern liberty was unfurled over the capitol by Letitia Tyler, "a lady of extraordinary beauty, intelligence and patriotism," the granddaughter of ex–U.S. president John Tyler.[335]

A week later, on March 11, the new Confederate government held its first official reception in the parlors of the Exchange Hotel. Many ladies, "distinguished not more by beauty and grace than the lively interest they exhibited in the stirring events of the times," lent their charms to the evening.[336]

Roger arrived in Montgomery from Charleston soon after Fort Sumter fell, carrying Beauregard's report. When he had left Charleston, the corn was just emerging in the fields and the trees were just beginning to unfold their spring foliage. In Montgomery, farther south in climate and inclination, the corn was already in silk and tassel, blackberries were nearly in season, and strawberries and peas were having their day.[337] Roger reached the Confederate capital nearly simultaneously with the news that Virginia had voted to secede. Davis and Stephens were meeting with Secretary of War Leroy Pope Walker when that news arrived.

"It will probably end the war," Stephens said.[338]

Howell Cobb's younger brother, Thomas, also a member of the provisional congress, was even more optimistic. He had written his wife earlier that he foresaw no war at all—"a little collision perhaps and much confusion, but no bloody or extensive war. The action of Virginia decides the question. Peace is certain on her secession."[339]

When the word of that secession reached the streets of Montgomery, the city erupted in "wild excitement." The new *Courier* correspondent, "Palmetto," reported "the usual salutations from loudmouthed cannon, the accustomed outspreading of flags, and the usual amount of liquoring up." In the evening the largest crowd "Palmetto" had yet seen in Montgomery collected under and around the portals of the Exchange Hotel to hear "honeyed words of eloquence"—huzzahs for his commonwealth's secession—from the newly arrived Roger, whom he called "Virginia's second Patrick Henry."[340]

The Congress eagerly greeted the official delegation arriving from Roger's Virginia. Delegates from the newly seceded border states of Tennessee and Arkansas followed, raising the number of state delegations from seven to ten. In May, North Carolina would make it eleven.

Roger didn't linger long in Montgomery. He delivered Beauregard's report and his honeyed words, and headed back to Richmond. At stops in North Carolina between Wilmington and Weldon, he was called out to speak, and in Richmond on the twenty-fifth he addressed a huge crowd that had come to serenade South Carolina officers who had just arrived in the Virginia capital from Fort Sumter.[341]

It would not be long until the entire Confederate provisional executive department and congress—with all its trappings—would follow both Roger and the South Carolina heroes to Richmond. A bill to remove the seat of government was introduced on the first day of May. When the Confederate Congress adjourned on May 21 it was a fait accompli. The next session would convene in Richmond on July 20. And when it was finally decided, one observer noted, "Montgomery began to wail."[342]

Davis, his staff, and some of his cabinet caught the northbound train from Montgomery and passed through country that looked "like a military camp." The cars teemed with troops, "all as jubilant as if they were going to a frolic, instead of to fight."[343] The presidential entourage pulled into the Petersburg railroad station from Weldon, North Carolina, at five o'clock in the morning on May 29. They were met there by Governor Letcher, Richmond mayor Joseph Mayo, and a turnout of Petersburg dignitaries. Carriages drove them through Roger and Sara's still-sleeping hometown past darkened houses on Sycamore, Bollingbrook, and Second Streets, over the Appomattox River on the old Pocahontas wagon bridge, to a waiting train on the Richmond and Petersburg line.[344] The entourage arrived in Richmond, where nearly every house was flying the stars and bars, to "an outburst of enthusiasm."[345]

From the moment the Virginia State Convention voted to secede, on April 17, Richmond had been girding itself for war—and for the likelihood that it would be in the eye of this hurricane of rebellion. The city council passed an ordinance to issue city notes to raise funds it knew it would need. When it was clear the capital was moving to Richmond, the council earmarked buildings to house the new government.[346] It purchased a "White House" for President Davis and his family for $42,894, with furnishings, at the corner of Twelfth and Clay Streets—the elegant mansion built in 1818 by John Brockenbrough, the president of the Bank of Virginia, and his wife, Gabriella Harvie Randolph Brokenbrough.[347]

The country around Richmond overnight became a sprawling encampment—a staging ground for the war many thought and hoped would never happen—as the provisional government worked to put a command structure together. Richmond College was turned into a camp for artillery instruction. The Central Fair Grounds, a mile and a half north of the city, became a drill field called Camp Lee. Richmond was soon walled in by military tenting grounds, where troops from every state in the new Confederacy were pouring in, reporting to drill and then fight, though nobody then knew quite when or where. The wharfs at Rocketts, the city's riverfront landing, were taken over by a nascent Confederate navy. The Tredegar Iron Works, the biggest foundry in the South, began forging war material exclusively for the new government.[348]

Sallie Putnam wrote that Richmond was waking by morning to "the reveille of the drum" calling the soldiers to duty, and by night, to taps calling them to rest. Martial music and the tramp of marching feet filled the days. "Nothing was seen, nothing talked of, nothing thought of," Sallie wrote, "but the war in which we had become involved."[349] Varina Davis described Richmond as "one great camp—men hurried to and fro with and without uniforms and arms, with that fixed look upon their faces that they acquire when confronted with danger and the necessity for supreme effort."[350]

The *Richmond Dispatch* wrote, "We began to feel as if we were in the Metropolis of the South.... We almost begin to forget the quaint, staid days of 'Auld Lang Syne' when every countenance was as familiar as the curb stones, and we felt like one family." Richmond was suddenly moving at "a pace which she never had before."[351]

One newcomer reported that "the city was thoroughly jammed—its ordinary population of forty thousand swelled to three times that number by the sudden pressure." By early May troops were streaming into the bloated city from every corner of the Confederacy at a rate of five hundred to a thousand a day, thronging the streets "from daylight to dark." Hotels were packed to capacity, their corridors aglitter with "arms, epaulettes, and gold lace." Beds were set up in every room, in parlors, and in hallways. Billiard tables substituted for beds. Houses became barracks. People were shoehorned into every space. Virginia's vaunted hospitality was stretched to the breaking point.[352]

As the new government was aborning in Montgomery, the military arm of the new Confederate states had begun flexing in Pensacola, close to Montgomery and reachable by sea. By April 28 troops were rallying to the colors there, not knowing precisely where they were to fight but aware that they were very likely headed for Virginia, and all "positively fighting among themselves to get there first."[353] Mary Chesnut believed that "every man from every little country precinct wants a place in the picture."[354] Before the government moved from Montgomery to Richmond, 360,000 would-be soldiers had offered their services. Two Confederate armies were, in fact, now forming, one in Pensacola and one in Charleston. But only a small fraction could be immediately armed and equipped. Secretary of War Walker when heading to his office was being waylaid by volunteers offering their lives for the cause.[355] In Montgomery, Henry Hilliard, a former Alabama congressman and U.S. diplomat, reported, "In several districts military organizations are so large that the officers had to draft [men to] stay at home."[356] By July, 194 regiments and 30 batteries had been enlisted into service, and the secretary was recommending 300 more regiments. The Confederate congress called for 400,000 more troops and the issue of $100 million in bonds and a like amount in treasury notes.[357] As one ardent Rebel said, "The speech-making was over forever, and the work of the war had begun."[358]

In Petersburg, Roger was ready to fight. He believed, as many other Southern politicians did, that he had talked for the South—louder than most—and now he must fight for her.[359] Politicians were demanding commands in the new army and, with their political clout, getting them. Roger was one of those, a politician transformed overnight into a colonel, not on military ability, knowledge, or, as far as anybody knew, aptitude. He had had zero military training, unless you wanted to call *dueling* military training.

This neophyte was given a regiment—the Third Virginia Infantry—on May 3, in Norfolk. The Third had been around since Governor Wise's administration, formed as a new voluntary militia command in Norfolk, in late 1856. When war came, its colonel, James G. Hodges, commanding since 1858, was moved to the Fourteenth Virginia to make room for Roger.

Hodges was a thirty-three-year-old Portsmouth native, a highly regarded physician whose fearless devotion to the sick in the yellow fever epidemic of 1855 had won him prominence and election as mayor of Portsmouth in 1856 and reelection in 1857.

So Roger's elevation to this command was not popular with the men of the Third Regiment. The *Richmond Daily Dispatch* took note of it, not kindly. "I am sorry," its editor wrote, "that so noble a fellow [Pryor] should be placed in a position which exposes him to unkind feeling on the part of so many of his regiment. The occasion of this is, that he was made to supersede Colonel Hodges, whose excellence as a soldier and as a man is felt warmly by all under his charge. It is a great blunder to cause such a change when everything was moving with such satisfaction."[360]

Roger was accompanied to Norfolk by Lieutenant Colonel Fletcher H. Archer, his second in command, a Petersburg lawyer, fellow University of Virginia graduate, and Mexican War veteran. Third in command was Joseph Mayo Jr., a Virginia Military Institute graduate, a lawyer, and a journalist, who had been Roger's friend since they had worked together on the *Southside Democrat*.

Roger's appointment, if not a hit with his troops, was highly popular with Sara. She was bursting with pride, though much exercised that her young colonel had no shoulder straps to identify his lofty new military rank. So she undertook, also without any military experience, to embroider something herself. The Rebel army hadn't yet decided on the star for a colonel's insignia and Sara supposed he would wear an eagle, like all the colonels she had ever known in Washington. Since no embroidery bullion could be had, she bought heavy bullion fringe, cut it in lengths, and made eagles—"probably," she thought, "of some extinct species, for the like were unknown in Audubon's time, and have not since been discovered." However, Sara later confessed, "they were accepted, admired, and what is worse, worn."[361]

CHAPTER 8

———•◦•———

Sewing for the Rebellion

𝒥n the unreal hours and days following the Union surrender at
Fort Sumter, business came to a standstill in Richmond.

On the afternoon of April 14, the news of the surrender
reached the city by telegraph and was greeted with wild celebrations. Cannon acclaimed the day, their reverberations rattling windows for miles around. Bonfires were lit and rockets catapulted
into the sky. All that night the bells of Richmond tolled, and
"Dixie," fast becoming the Confederate anthem, rang out over the
seven hills of the city.[362]

People, with their hearts in their throats, prowled the streets to
hear the latest news from the North. Reports filtered in of Southern sympathizers being arrested and thrown into Fort Lafayette,
the political bastille in New York Harbor, and outrage mounted.
Crowds collected throughout the city, and fire-eaters shouted impassioned speeches that audiences cheered with thunderous applause. "We had great firing of cannon," the *Richmond Examiner*
reported, "all sorts of processions, an infinite number of grandilo-
quent, hifaluting speeches, and some drinking of healths, which
has not improved healths."[363]

On April 16 an ad hoc body styled the Spontaneous Southern
Rights Convention met in Richmond's Metropolitan Hall. It was

an intensely emotional gathering packed with four hundred delegates. Its door was kept by a guard with a drawn sword, and the
new Southern flag was raised over the capitol to shouts and applause. The governor had it taken down, for that other Virginia
gathering, the State Constitutional Convention, had not yet passed
an ordinance of secession.

On the seventeenth the Spontaneous Southern Rights Convention, which the press was calling the "Peoples" convention, met to
discuss a new political organization of the state. As it deliberated,
the lieutenant governor rushed into the hall with the news that the
state convention had at last voted for secession. There was a moment of breathless quiet, then a thundering explosion of shouts
and applause, and tears of joy. Former president John Tyler, ex-
governor Henry Wise, and a former U.S. senator from Virginia,
James Mason, all spoke. Governor Letcher entered the hall and
pledged he would support the will of the people. R. M. T. Hunter,
another former U.S. senator from Virginia, said, "You may place
your ... hand against Niagara with more certainty of staying the
torrent than you can oppose this movement. It was written long
ago in the everlasting stars that the South would be driven out of
the Union by the North."[364]

On the nineteenth Richmond formally celebrated secession.
The city glowed. Sallie Putnam, walking about, saw not a single
building without a gleaming light. The biggest torchlight procession in Richmond's memory snaked through the city, swelling in
numbers until it reached Main Street. Rockets soared everywhere,
Roman candles spun out "myriads of stars," and torches lit the
seven hills.[365]

SUSAN LETCHER, WIFE OF the governor of Virginia, was at home
in the stately Governor's Mansion, not wanting to hear or see any
of it. Her guest in this trying time—through the cannon fire at
Sumter and the wild celebrations in the streets—was Sara Pryor.

In "the calm and seclusion of Mrs. Letcher's rooms," Sara said, they were shut off from much of the secession storm raging without. The governor's wife was a motherly, domestic woman and a devout Episcopalian, who had chosen to ignore the rising fury—for the sake, Sara believed, of her "present peace." Believing—hoping—it was a tempest that would surely pass, the two women quietly talked of family matters and sewed on little gowns and pinafores and reminisced about the life they had enjoyed together in Washington in the sweeter times of the 1850s, when the governor had been a U.S. congressman. They spoke little of the trouble boiling in the streets outside.

Still, it was hard to bear. The governor was nervous and sleeping badly. He had a history of fever and rheumatism and bouts of erysipelas—Saint Anthony's fire, a painful inflammation of the skin. But quiet, Mrs. Letcher believed, would surely return, and when it did, she promised Sara, they would all go down to Old Point Comfort to bathe in the sea and get strong and well. As for war, she believed it would never come to that.[366]

Southern womanhood in general, however, was "gushing patriotism"—spewing fire—like Vesuvius.[367] Susan Sparks Keitt, former congressman Lawrence Keitt's tart-tongued wife, vowed, "We women, like those of old, will cut our hair for bowstrings to plague the Enemy as long as possible."[368] Kate Cumming in Mobile believed "that if the men did not fight, the women would."[369]

A poet wrote:

> *Fold away all your bright tinted dresses,*
> *Turn the key on your jewels today*
> *And the wealth of your tendril-like tresses*
> *Braid back in a serious way.*
> *No more delicate gowns—no more laces;*
> *No more loit'ring in boudoir or bower;*
> *But come—with your souls in your faces—*
> *To meet the stern wants of the hour.*[370]

In Petersburg, where Sara soon returned after Sumter—Roger was in Norfolk soldiering—the women organized into sewing societies to fit out the new Confederate volunteers, stitching "love and hope and sentiment into the rough seams and hems of nondescript garments they sent to the camps by bales."[371] The women did not rest from this impulsive labor of love even on Sundays. Sewing machines were carried into churches, which became storehouses for flannel, muslin, linen, and uniform cloth. Sewing classes were summoned by tolling church bells—"signals calling us to labor as sacred as worship," one young woman in Petersburg said. Sara and her friend Agnes, who was visiting from Richmond, instituted a sewing class that met daily at Sara's house on Market Street.[372]

Nothing that needed making was too big or too small—from sewing kits to heavy tents stitched from cumbersome sailcloth. "There was absolutely nothing which a man might possibly use," Sara said, "that we did not make for them. We embroidered cases for razors, for soap and sponge, and cute morocco affairs for needles, thread, and court-plaster, with a little pocket lined with a bank-note"—little touches of refinement, she said, for the soldiers' knapsacks. She wrote, "'How perfectly ridiculous!' do you say? Nothing is ridiculous that helps anxious women to bear their lot—cheats them with the hope that they are doing good."[373]

In Fredericksburg, Betty Herndon Maury was hard at work stitching "six pairs of pantaloons, six jackets, and eight shirts." A week later she met several of her suits on the street and "felt like speaking to them."[374] The same rush to the needle and the loom was being replicated by women "with tearful eyes and saddened hearts" all over the South in the days following the bombardment of Fort Sumter and the beginning of the war. Young, fun-loving, lighthearted girls, whose lives before had been "made up of dance and song and moonlit sails," turned to the sewing needle and loom[375]—to weaving and spinning, what Kate Cumming called "this ancient work."[376]

Margaret Junkin Preston in Lexington, Virginia, who thought as a poet thinks, wrote:

> *They stitch the rough jacket, they shape the coarse shirt,*
> *Unheeding though delicate fingers be hurt;*
> *They bind the strong haversack, knit the gray glove,*
> *Nor falter nor pause in their service of love.*[377]

Mary Chesnut found it difficult to find a woman without knitting in her hand. "Socks for soldiers is the cry," she told her diary. "One poor man said he had dozens of socks and but one shirt.... It gives a quaint look, the twinkling of needles, and the everlasting sock dangling."[378]

"We knitted on the way to and from meetings, and knitted [in] carriages as we drove," an Alabama knitter reported. "Even when we sat on our porches in summer evenings our knitting needles clicked on."[379] A father, hearing the hum of his daughter's loom weaving flannel, considered it sweeter than the music of a piano. Susan Blackford's husband, from Lynchburg, Virginia, gone for a soldier, wrote, "This is the age of heroines and I glory in the fact that my wife and mother are among them."[380]

"The quondam belle of the ball-room," Sallie Putnam marveled, "the accomplished woman of society, the devotee of ease, luxury and idle enjoyment, found herself transformed into the busy sempstress. The click of the sewing-machine was the music which most interested them, and the 'stitch, stitch, stitch,' from morning till night."[381] One of those accomplished women of society who had "taken to knitting socks," confessed, "I have been cramping my fingers and puzzling my brain in 'heeling' and 'toeing,' 'rounding off' and 'taking up,' till I am at times entirely oblivious of the weightier matters of the war."[382]

The wealthiest women in the South were working as hard as the poorest. And they were sharing more than work. "Sad! sad!" young Kate Cumming in Mobile wrote, "were the grief-stricken hearts left behind," as regiment after regiment began mobilizing and leaving for the scene of coming conflict. "But there was not one of those sorrowing mothers, wives, or sisters," she believed, "that did not assist in buckling on the armor of their loved ones, and wishing them godspeed, bade them go forth and battle for the right."[383]

In Winchester, Virginia, where the women worked without stint making lint for dressing wounds, rolling bandages, stitching together jackets and trousers, haversacks, and havelocks, Cornelia McDonald marked new and disturbing sensations. Women now "not infrequently had their flounces caught by a spur, or would run against a carbine. The clashing of sabers and jingling of spurs became a familiar sound."[384]

But many Southern women, if they could, would have been soldiering, too. Sara believed that no soldier enlisted under Virginia's banner could possibly have been more determined, dedicated, or committed than the young women of her state. "They were uncompromising," she said.[385] They were putting engagements on hold wholesale until their lovers had fought the Yankees.[386]

Sara overheard Ben, a love-smitten young man at Petersburg, who had not yet enlisted, say to Helen, his sweetheart, "You promised me my answer to-night."

"Well, you can't have it, Ben," Helen said, "until you have fought the Yankees."

"What heart will I have for fighting," he said, "if you give me no promise?"

"I'll not be engaged to any man," she answered, "until he has fought the Yankees. You distinguish yourself in the war, and then see what I'll have to say to you."

"But suppose I don't come back at all!" exclaimed Ben.

"Oh, then I'll acknowledge an engagement and be good to your mother—and wear mourning all the same—*provided*—your wounds are all in front."[387]

There was a strong general feeling among many of these

young Rebel women that "none but the brave deserve the fair."[388] Mary Chesnut, however, didn't share the feeling. "Those fiery Joan d'Arc damsels who goad up their sweethearts," she complained to her diary, "bode us no good."[389]

For good or no, goaded or not, young Southern men were leaving for the expected seat of war with the departure of every train. And the day finally came, in late April, when the first volunteers from Petersburg—which would one day boast it sent more men to the war than there were voters left behind—were ready to leave.[390] They gathered at the head of Sycamore Street to march down to the lower depot. The entire town turned out to see them off and wish them godspeed.

The reigning beauties of the town were all there, and Agnes told them, "We are not to cry, you know."

"Of *course* not!" said Helen, blinking away tears behind her smile.

The drums beat and a cymbal crashed and the band broke into "Dixie." It was the first time Sara had ever heard it.

"Forward! March!" The order came down and the volunteers moved toward the depot. Young women, old men, boys, matrons, and every family servant surged along beside them on the sidewalk. At the depot mothers, sisters, and sweethearts pressed a last loving kiss on their departing boys and were enfolded in farewell embraces.[391]

The Reverend William H. Platt, rector of Saint Paul's Church, a Mexican War veteran who had been drilling them on the square, pronounced the departing benediction: "Drive back the invaders from our soil, and the deepest and most earnest prayers of mothers, sisters and wives will hourly ascend to the God of battles for your safety and success."[392]

When the young volunteers were aboard the train and its wheels began slowly turning, taking them away, Ben leaned out of his window and whispered to Helen gazing up at him from below.

"Can't I have the promise now, Helen?" he asked.

"Yes!" Helen exclaimed. "Yes, Ben—*dear* Ben, I promise!"

As the cars gathered speed and rolled away, Helen turned and calmly announced to the others, "Girls, I'm engaged to Ben Shepard."

"*I'm* engaged to half a dozen of them," said one.

"That's nothing," said another, "*I'm* engaged to the whole regiment."[393] Engagements were in again.

As it was said of another dazzling Virginia belle in another context, "She rides with the cavalry, drives with the artillery, and walks with the infantry, and . . . flirts equally with all." It was "born in her. . . . She likes them all, and in the sweet joyousness of her temper wants to please them all, and she succeeds."[394]

For many women, however, the parting of their men to war wasn't engagement, it was devastating disengagement. "O My God, and must I write it?" Ethelinda Eagleton wrote in her diary when her husband signed up. "He has enlisted in the service of his country—to war—the most unrighteous war that ever was brought on any nation that ever lived. . . . 'Tis a dark, gloomy day to me. I feel more like I was preparing for Mr. E's funeral than any thing else."[395]

Ella Thomas in Augusta, Georgia, wrote in her diary, "Trusting to the God of Battles, I shall see my husband go, feeling that if one word of mine could keep him at home I would not utter it"—even though he left "for months—perhaps forever!" As she thought of him leaving, tears welled in her eyes and rolled irresistibly down her cheeks. "My darling husband how I love him," she told her diary. "Oh God shield him in the hour of danger." After he left, Ella wrote, "I think of [him] and miss him so much now, what oh God would be my feelings if I should never see him more!"[396]

All through the South they were leaving—and the women were waving them "on to the conflict, shedding their brightest smiles and cheering them to victory with their syren voices."[397] All of them were dying inside and bracing as best they could "to bear," as one of them wrote her daughter, "the cruel trial of the absence of your precious Father . . . the chief of our hearts."[398] Annie Harper in Natchez believed each farewell was "something like . . . closing the coffin lid."[399]

In Petersburg after the soldiers left, Nellie Gray, one of those "loving, light-hearted girls whose feet were set to music and dancing," had watched them go and felt she was "in a city of mourning and dread."[400] Sara, with Roger in Norfolk, also felt a depressing void—they all did. Silence and anxiety fell on the town "like a pall." *What should we do now?* It was a question they were all asking. And one of them said, "We will hold a prayer meeting in each other's houses, at four o'clock every afternoon. We can *pray*, if we cannot fight."[401]

What many of these Southern women did, virtually by reflex as the incomprehensible war began and their men marched away toward it, was to start diaries and journals. They had to give voice—to speak their deepest feelings, even if only to themselves.

"Everyone is sad, not *knowing* what to look for in the future—," Virginia Davis Gray wrote in Arkansas, "even what to *hope* for is questionable." So she wrote:

> *By the parlor fire, one Saturday night*
> *We sat to write our journal*
> *Expecting to write by bright pine light*
> *The events of the past diurnal.*
> *"O give me paper," Roberta cries*
> *"That I a journal may keep*
> *And see with my eyes how fast time flies*
> *Before I lie down to sleep."*[402]

Volunteers swarming in on trains from the Confederate states, passed through Petersburg on the road to war. As each train approached this major rail hub, it cried its coming with a long whistle, and the women rushed to meet it. The hero of Charleston himself, General Beauregard, approached at the head of his troops. The city had been forewarned, and the women sent their servants laden with trays of refreshments for him and his soldiers, and then went themselves bearing flowers. Beauregard stepped down and shook hands around, filling his arms with bouquets before the train moved on, carrying him yet farther northward to what soon might be the seat of war. Other legions coming up from the South followed Beauregard through the city, and Sara says none left without being met and refreshed.[403]

Soldiers seemed to be everywhere along the rail lines leading north. Mary Chesnut, in a train headed north herself, wrote that soldiers seemed to fill the air—certainly to fill all space. "Every woman from every window of every house we passed," she told her diary, "waved a handkerchief, if she had one. This fluttering of white flags from every side never ceased, from Camden to Richmond." Mary watched as parties of girls flocked to every station simply to stare and wave at the troops passing through. She looked at all this with mixed feelings. "No casualties yet, no real mourning, nobody hurt," she wrote in her diary. "So it is all parade, fife, and fine feathers." She despaired that there were but "two or three sensible men who are still left in the world."[404]

The women of the Confederacy in these first early days and weeks couldn't do much about the madness and unreality of it all. "We are leading the lives which women have lead since Troy fell," one of them wrote, "wearing away time with memories, regrets and fears; alternating fits of suppression, with flights, imaginary, to the red fields where great principles are contended for, lost and won; while men, more privileged, are abroad and astir, making name and fortune and helping to make a nation."[405]

But the women of this new nation-in-the-making were bound to be part of it. In western Georgia, Kate Featherston Peddy, whose passionate love for her soldier husband sang though every letter she sent him, wrote in her loneliness that "every thing looks like the grave to me now. It seems to be continually a black cloud of sorrow hanging over me all the time." But she also wrote, "'Tis woman's lot, to be a friend when others fail, to look on death and fear it not, to smile when others' cheeks grow pale.' "[406] That seemed the very least the women of the South, who one of their male admirers called "these queens of love, regnant in the realm of home," were now resolved to do.[407]

And there was very little within their power they were not prepared to do. Some, when the fighting did begin, would even be pressed into the manufacture of gunpowder—a unique service for female natures. Gunpowder can't be made without niter. And before this war would end, the niter would have to be concocted from human urine. Jonathan Haralson, agent in charge of the Selma Nitre and Mining Bureau in Alabama, would soon be sending barrels around town in wagons to collect the contents of ladies' chamber pots—in the early morning hours to avoid embarrassment. This would give rise to this racy doggerel:

> *Jon Haralson! Jon Haralson!*
> *Where did you get the notion*
> *Of sending barrels around our street*
> *To fill them with that lotion?*
> *We thought the women did enough*
> *At sewing shirts and kissing;*
> *But you have put the lovely dears*
> *To patriotic p———g.*[408]

Whatever they were put to, the women were embracing it. "Were we not Confederate soldiers," Mary Gay demanded, "or very near akin to them?"[409] Few were the Southern women who did not believe that of themselves. Sara did.

CHAPTER 9

------◆◆◆------

A Message from the Guns

$\mathcal{S}$ara's heart pounded as she read the telegram from Roger in Norfolk in May. It was short but thrilling. It said: "Suppose you pay me a visit!" After days of watching trainloads of Confederate soldiers moving northward through Petersburg toward an as yet indefinite seat of war, Sara had been called by the soldier who mattered most in her life.

Long before time to leave, she was at the Petersburg depot with her three boys—the girls, Marie Gordon and Mary, were with Aunt Mary—waiting to catch the train that would take them the ten miles to City Point to catch the boat for Norfolk sixty miles downriver. It then seemed a lifetime that she waited at the landing on the James for the boat. Had it already come and passed without stopping for them?

"Oh, Captain," she cried for the third time to the boat-company officer at the landing, "do you think the boat—"

"In a moment, lady," the officer said. "The boat is just coming round the point." And there it was, slowing, to take aboard "the happiest woman in the world."

The James River, on which Sara's boat was now embarked, did not make clear statements. It was not, Sara knew, "a clear stream of silver like the Potomac." It rose in western Virginia, at Iron Gate, between the Alleghenies and the Blue Ridge, and emptied into the sea at Norfolk. The tributaries that flowed into it as it worked its way to the Atlantic were dirt yellow, muddied by the peculiar clay of the Virginia countryside through which they passed. But the James was, Sara knew, *"par excellence,* the romantic river of our country."[410]

Old-time Richmond folk said that the sound of the James, "the voice of that tireless river," haunted them even when they were gone from it, for no matter how long, "like a strain of sweetest music."[411]

On the river's banks in 1779 the aristocracy of Virginia had made Richmond the state capital. Now it was the capital of a new Confederacy. The first wars the English fought with the Indians on the new continent were fought along this river. The first American Revolution ended here. A second was beginning—along these same banks.

What Sara feared was what young Constance Cary, a Virginia belle of "bewitching beauty," living at Vaucluse, the elegant house near Alexandria, also feared.[412] From there Constance could hear the drums of Washington beating across the Potomac, and she worried, as Sara did, that the voice of the tireless James was about to blend with "the tramp of rusty battalions, the short imperious stroke of the alarm-bell, the clash of passing bands, the gallop of eager horsemen, the roar of battle or of flames leaping to devour their prey, the moan of hospitals, the stifled note of sorrow!"[413]

But how serene it now seemed to Sara on her way to meet Roger—"how peacefully the old river glided between its banks." Now and then the soft murmur of voices reached her from the shore, and occasionally the boat put in at a busy landing to drop a mailbag, offload packages and barrels, or lower the gangplank to let off a planter heading home.

As evening approached, the river grew dark. Sara saw "phantom ships" flash briefly out of the darkness around them, to be swallowed up again in the night. The boat passed little skiffs carrying fishermen ending a workday on the water. Overhead, homing birds flapped past on "heavy wings." A sense of peace and calm to match the river stole over Sara. "War?" she thought. "Oh, surely, surely not! Something would prevent it. Surely, blood would not be shed because of those insulting words" she had heard hurled angrily across the House and Senate floors. "If the veil could have been lifted," she thought, "if one had said 'Behold, I shew you a vision—you may yet avert its fulfilment,' how merciful would that have been!"[414]

The boat arrived at the wharf at Norfolk after midnight. By sunrise Sara was up and dressed. Soon she heard the clank of spurs on the deck, the new sound of war. To Sara, however, it had a happy ring. For wearing them and standing before her in his new uniform with her homemade eagles bristling on either shoulder was her husband.[415]

There was to be a dress parade of Roger's regiment that day, and Sara and the other wives were invited. Roger had come with his staff in the afternoon to the hotel where the wives were staying, to escort them to the parade ground personally. A siege gun stood on the swatch of green parade, commanding the waters of the sea glinting blue and silver under the afternoon sun, ready to jack practice rounds at a buoy out in the water.

One of Roger's handsome young artillery officers approached Sara, saluted, and invited her to honor his company by firing their first shot. There, standing at the side of the behemoth, Sara waited with lanyard in hand.

"Wait for the word of command, Madam," the officer said.

"And then what?" Sara asked.

"Oh, then *pull* steadily," he said, stepping back.

"Make ready!" came the command. "Fire!"

Sara yanked the lanyard. The gun, the first fired by the Third Virginia Volunteers, leaped backward and sent a mighty roar out over the water. Congratulated all around, Sara returned to her place and was told that her eyes were congested by the concussion and that she must return home and bathe and bandage them at once.

"Evidently," she mourned, "I was not fit for artillery service."[416]

There was some doubt, too, whether Roger, the hothead who had helped prod the war into existence, was fit for the fighting of it. He was already earning a reputation with some of his men as a martinet. In his first days in command, he got off on the wrong side of his company of Marion Rifles. Virginians on May 23 were voting on secession, and Roger had let the first fifteen men on the Rifles' roll go to the courthouse to vote. When all but one voted against secession, Roger was outraged. Refusing to let any more from the company go into town to vote, he confined in a lower room of the hospital those who already had. Ordered by Governor Letcher to release them, Roger assembled the entire regiment, blasted the Rifles with a scouring speech, charged them with disloyalty to Virginia, and disbanded them.[417] It was an act hardly calculated to win affection. But winning affection, other than Sara's, had never been Roger's strong suit.

At Vaucluse, the Virginia homestead near Alexandria where Constance Cary lived, it was Sunday, and she and her "happy band" of young friends were picking wildflowers. The forest was a "canopy of young leaves on the forest boughs," shading a cornucopia of pink honeysuckles, blue lupine, beds of fairy flax, anemones, and ferns. It was a perfect late-spring day. The air was humming with "the song of birds and the music of running water from a forest stream."

Into this idyllic tableau there suddenly burst the shrill whistle of a locomotive—"an unwonted sound on Sunday," Constance thought.

"Do you know what it means?" one of them asked.

One of them knew. He said, "It is the special train carrying Alexandria volunteers to Manassas, and to-morrow I shall follow with my company."

Quiet fell on the little group. "A cloud," Constance said, "seemed to come between us and the sun."[418]

Mary Chesnut in South Carolina knew what it was. "War cloud lowering," she told her diary.[419]

Judith McGuire, in Winchester, was startled on the evening of July 18 by the sound of "myriads of horses, wheels, and men" on the Shenandoah Turnpike. Joseph E. Johnston's army was passing through, on its way to join Beauregard before Manassas Junction.[420] Cornelia McDonald saw them, too, as they passed her gate in the day, an entire army in motion, "a proud sight ... with the Confederate banners waving, the bands playing and the bayonets gleaming in the noonday sun." The bands trumpeted "Dixie" and the "Bonnie Blue Flag," Cornelia wrote, "almost giving wings to their feet as they moved triumphantly on, keeping time to the joyous music."[421] Eighteen-year-old Kate Sperry saw them, too, but for her the joy was only in the music. "I never felt as sad in all my life," she told her diary. "I am miserably depressed. . . . War appears to have a more demoralizing effect than we would suppose."[422]

All roads now seemed to lead to Manassas. The trains that were running up from the South through Petersburg and Richmond, the armies moving out on the turnpike—all were pointing toward Manassas, the little Virginia village south of Washington.

Sara's stay with Roger in Norfolk had been all too brief. In early June he had sent her on from there, with their three little boys, to The Oaks in Charlotte County, the residence of her uncle, Dr. Izard Bacon Rice. Seventy miles southwest of Richmond and miles from the nearest railroad depot, The Oaks was a large, old-fashioned house on a two-thousand-acre plantation, surrounded by an oak grove "alive with chattering squirrels." Dr. Rice grew tobacco in fields stretching as far as Sara could see—"a vast level sea of green ... covering the low, gently rounded, undulating hills" sloping down to the Staunton River.

Dr. Rice's grandfather, though a slaveholder, had written the first published protest in the country against slavery as "inconsistent with religion and policy." Dr. Rice's father, who had inherited the plantation, its slaves, and the liberal ideas of the grandfather, had added his own special eccentricity to the mix. To punish a slave for some fault, instead of applying the lash, Dr. Rice's father would stand the offender in his presence while he read aloud long passages from Homer or Virgil. For fear of such punishment, the offense was rarely repeated.

Dr. Rice had in his turn inherited the land, the liberalism, and the slaves from his classics-reading father. He stopped subjecting them to the *Iliad*, the *Odyssey*, and the *Aeneid*, and instead assembled them on Sundays to speak a few words to each, praising the women if their children appeared in clean, well-kept garments; rewarding the little ones with new shoes; exchanging a pleasant jest here and there. He presented a cabin to every newly wed slave couple, with timber for the bridegroom to expand it or enclose a garden plot or a poultry yard. To every mother who gave birth, he gave a pig as a celebration gift.

There on that liberally run plantation, Sara had spent most of June and July. On the afternoon of July 21, Dr. Rice, as was his custom on warm summer days, had taken refuge from the sun and the flies, under the oak trees, and had stretched out on the ground for a nap. He suddenly exclaimed, "There's a battle going on—a fierce battle—I can hear the cannonading distinctly."

"Here," he called to Sara, "lie down—you can hear it!"

"Oh, no, no," Sara gasped, her fear for Roger rising in her throat. "I can't! It may be at Norfolk."

With his ear to the ground, Dr. Rice was hearing the thunder of battle at Manassas 150 miles away.[423] The fighting had begun. The war Sara had hoped would surely not happen was irretrievably under way.

CHAPTER 10

·•·•·

Seeing the Elephant

$\mathscr{T}$he news from Manassas at the end of the day of the first big battle of the war electrified the South.

Roger Pryor wasn't in the battle. So Sara, relieved of that worry, wrote that everybody thought it "Glorious News! . . . A glorious triumph for the South—an utter rout of the enemy."[424] In Richmond, John Jones, the Rebel war clerk, exclaimed, "Joy ruled the hour! The city seemed lifted up, and every one appeared to walk on air."[425] Many in the South believed it was a victory that would undoubtedly end the war. "The battle of Manassas . . . has secured our independence," predicted Thomas R. R. Cobb, the brother of Howell Cobb, who was busy raising troops in Georgia.[426]

The battle was fought on July 21, 1861. It was Sunday and an ungodly way to observe the Lord's day. The vanguard of Major General Irwin McDowell's Union army, some thirty-seven thousand strong, had begun moving from Centreville toward Manassas Junction the night before, under a full moon. It was one very green army against another just as green. And both sides, being green, were surprised. McDowell lacked reliable reconnaissance. So he didn't know that Joseph E. Johnston's Confederate Army of the Shenandoah had marched past a watchful Judith McGuire, Cornelia McDonald, and Kate Sperry two days before at Winchester on its way to join the Confederate force already massed at Manassas under P. G. T. Beauregard. The Confederates—numbering thirty-five thousand and intending to hit the Federal left flank— didn't know that McDowell, at about eight thirty in the morning, would strike their left flank first, at Sudley Ford on Bull Run Creek.

The Northern army drove the Confederates back to a battle-torn rise on Henry House Hill. There the Confederates had made a stand with the brigades of Barnard Bee, Francis Bartow, Nathan G. "Shanks" Evans, and Thomas J. Jackson, men little known before but about to become household names in the South. And there Bee, the South Carolina brigadier, had shouted to his men, "Look! There is Jackson standing like a stone wall! Rally behind the Virginians!" Bee would be dead before the day ended and would never know that his words would make Stonewall Jackson and his brigade immortal.

The Confederates held Henry House Hill behind the unmovable Jackson, and just before four o'clock in the afternoon, fresh Confederate troops, many of them Johnston's men from the Shenandoah, launched a crushing counterattack against the Federal right, in flank and rear. The Union army began to give way, at first in good order, then in panic. Soldiers and sightseers from Washington, who had come out with picnic baskets to cheer what they believed would be the one and only rebellion-ending battle of the war, swarmed onto the one bridge across Bull Run that led to the road to Centreville, Washington, and safety. But a Confederate shell disabled a wagon on the bridge, blocking and jamming the road. Hysteria, confusion, and panic mounted, and Union soldiers and civilians alike streamed back in terrified disorder into Washington in a pounding, dispiriting rainstorm that had begun late in the day.

There was no pursuit. The victorious Confederate army was as exhausted and disorganized in victory as the Union army was in defeat. It had been a stunning Confederate triumph, but it had also been a killing field. Nearly three thousand Union soldiers were

dead, wounded, or missing, and nearly two thousand Confederates. "Wild war's deadly blast" had scorched the losers and the
winners alike.[427]

It was the killing—the "deadly blast"—not the victory, that
was stirring the Confederate women's deepest emotions. They
were feeling the hard hand of a war they had not started. Margaret
Johnson Erwin, in Mississippi, called it "irresponsible murder,"
and believed "all our world is becoming a man-made charnel
house."[428] Sara said, "My heart sank within me at the tale of
blood."[429] Cornelia McDonald, in Winchester, wrote in her diary,
"We did not begin to realize the horrors of our victory till Tuesday
evening when the wagons began to come in with their loads of
wounded men; some . . . too, with the dead."[430]

Many with loved ones who had been in the battle—mothers,
fathers, and sisters—hurried to the battlefield and to Richmond,
desperate to learn something, dreading what that something might
be. Nowhere did the dread run deeper than in the Spotswood
Hotel, in Richmond, where the wives of ten Confederate officers
known to be in the battle huddled together in terror as the fighting
raged less than a hundred miles away. For one of them, the wife of
Francis Bartow of Georgia—"sweet and saintly Mrs. Bartow,"
with her "softest, silkiest voice and ways"—the terror became grief
when she learned her husband had been killed.[431] "Among ourselves," Margaret Sumner McLean wrote, "with that poor stricken
woman in the midst of us, there could be nothing like rejoicing,
and one of our number, coming out of her room said, 'God help us
if this is what we have prayed for!' "[432]

Elsewhere, the victory was celebrated with wild cheering. The
Richmond Daily Whig hailed it the "greatest battle since Water-
loo."[433] One woman said, "Men were beside themselves with joy
and pride—drunk with glory."[434] But then the wagons began
rolling in with the wounded, dead, and dying to the melancholy
beat of the "Dead March of Saul." It soon seemed to Mary Chesnut that they were never beyond the reach of that dreadful dirge.

"It comes and it comes," she told her diary, "until I feel inclined to close my ears and scream."[435]

This was something new and shocking, these returning bloody, mangled, dead and wounded bodies. They had gone to war as soldiers and were returning as but "a poor shadow of manhood," a "torn remnant of a man."[436] Few had quite expected that, and all now had to deal with it somehow. Richmond's mayor, Joseph Mayo, called a meeting of citizens to coordinate care for the wounded, and the city council voted an "indefinite appropriation" for medicines.[437] "Ladies who would have shrunk a few days before from the sight of blood," Margaret McLean wrote, "devoted all their time to dressing wounds and caring for the sick."[438] Makeshift hospitals were set up in warehouses, and cushions from church pews substituted as mattresses for hospital beds.[439]

What of those boys she had watched board the train and roll away to war? Sara thought. What would life hold now for some of their wives, mothers, and sweethearts at home—for the beautiful girls they had become engaged to? Could glory dry a widow's tears or console an aged mother? It was all so strange, even unreal, to Sara. Could it be true? Had these things actually happened in Virginia?[440]

THE DAY BEFORE MANASSAS, the Provisional Confederate Congress met in Richmond for its third session. On July 24 Roger reported there for his other duty in this war, having been appointed by the Virginia Convention as a delegate. Two days after he was seated, he cast his first vote. Then he left. He would not cast his second vote for three months. His heart wasn't where the votes were. It was where the action was.

And Sara's heart was where Roger was. She had to be near him, wherever that was going to be. She resolved, without consulting him, to follow his regiment through the war, wherever it was going and however long the war was going to last. She thought, "I would give no trouble. I should be only a help to his sick men and his wounded." Despite every entreaty from her friends, she began collecting her camp equipment: a field stove with a rotary chimney, ticks for bedding, to be filled with straw or hay or leaves—whatever was available—a camp chest packed with tin utensils, blankets, and other gear for soldiering. A tent could be requisitioned, she thought, from the regimental quartermaster.

News reached her that Roger's Third Virginia Infantry had moved to a new camp, across the James River from Newport News, about six miles from Smithfield. This was her opportunity. Her father-in-law called it her "wild-goose chase." But she left, anyhow, with her little boys, through a countryside teeming with soldiers. The train they were riding was repeatedly sidetracked to let more urgent troop trains pass through. The little boys loved it. They cheered the soldiers and picnicked throughout the day.

When she reached Smithfield, Sara found that she would not be permitted to be a soldier. The people in town took her camping outfit, boxed it, stored it in a warehouse, and put her up instead in a private home. Soon, as it looked to her as if she might be in Smithfield "the rest of my natural life," she rented a small furnished house, bought a cow for milk for her boys, and opened an account with the grocer and with a fisherman who went out nightly on Pagan Creek to catch mullets for breakfast. She also found in Smithfield that she was not *"la fille du régiment"* (the daughter of the regiment) she had thought she would be, but *"la mère"* (the mother). Daily she went to the sick men in their winter quarters and ministered to them according to her young motherly ability. She believed she had "enlisted for the war."[441]

To Roger it also looked as if he was "buried in Smithfield" for the war, while the fighting would be elsewhere. He wrote the war department, begging for a transfer to a more immediate seat of action. "Above all things," he wrote, "it is my wish to get into a position which will afford me some promise of active service. In my present situation, I foresee no possible chance of meeting the enemy."[442]

Meanwhile he was boning up. He knew absolutely nothing about how to command troops and wage war. Nothing in his education had prepared him for it. He had never been in any army, much less commanded a regiment. He set about reading the two bibles of warfare, Confederate General William Joseph Hardee's *Rifle and Light Infantry Tactics* and the works of the interpreter of Napoleon's campaigns, Baron Antoine Henri Jomini.[443]

His study was interrupted in November when he was called to Richmond for the provisional congress's fifth session. On January 8 he was appointed to the committee on military affairs, and for the next two months, he went about working to help cobble together as large a Confederate army as possible. This was the provisional congress's last hurrah. It was to be disbanded in February and replaced by a new elected bicameral congress. Roger had been elected to sit in the new congress's House of Representatives from Virginia's Fourth District. As Sara had predicted in an earlier time, he could probably be elected forever.

His election had been without an opponent, but it was not without critics, or without complications. Edmund Ruffin, a fellow Virginia firebrand whose relationship with Roger had blown hot and cold over the years—and was now blowing cold—regretted he had no opposition in his district. "I have strong objections to him, besides that of his being now in service as Colonel of a regiment," Ruffin wrote in his diary. "If such plurality of offices is not illegal, it is extremely objectionable. No man can fill both places at the same time. The higher the military office, the greater is the objection. An officer of a high grade cannot be spared from his command, if he is good for anything. Again, he will be tempted & induced to seek popularity with his soldiers to secure votes for his election to Congress, & so prostitute his service & duties to advance his self-interest."[444]

Roger obviously didn't agree with Ruffin. The Congress, however, did. It ruled in late March that no man could hold an army commission and sit in Congress, too. Roger had campaigned for election on the promise to defeat any such prohibition. Failing to do that, he had to choose between lawmaking and fighting. He chose fighting.[445]

Edward A. Pollard, the editor of the *Richmond Examiner*, also disagreeing with Ruffin, thought the prohibition rendered Congress "the most inane, unimportant, incompetent, and barren of public assemblies." Its most distinguished members also held military commissions. Like Roger, most of them took their commissions and left their seats. The decision, Pollard protested, stripped the Congress of "nearly all it had of worth and talents, and in a day reduced it to an inane body of mediocrities."[446]

If Roger couldn't hold two offices, neither could Jefferson Davis. So he had to settle for the one he wanted least. He took the oath as the first president of the Confederacy for a six-year term and delivered a twenty-minute inaugural address on February 22, 1862, on George Washington's birthday, beside Washington's statue in Richmond's public square. Inauguration Day was bleak with rain and snow, and the new president took his oath, one eyewitness said, "in the heaviest burst of the storm."[447] Sara would one day remember that "it was a black day of rain and snow; the new government, destined never to flourish in sunshine, was born in storm and tempest."[448]

Two days after this storm-tossed inaugural, the new Confederate Congress unanimously adopted a resolution declaring that the people of the Confederate states were unalterably determined never again to affiliate politically with the people of the United States.[449] It was to be a war to the knife.

"It is no pastime," Roger said in one of his last speeches in the provisional congress, "it is no tournament, it is no holiday rehearsal of war; but it is war indeed, red, wrathful and consuming war in which we are engaged—a war of which the issue must be

victory or death." He promised, "The way to liberty is no prim-
rose path of dalliance. By forty years of agony in the wilderness,
and by the passage of the Red Sea, the people of old escaped from
the house of bondage to the land of freedom. By many blows, by
many wounds, by much blood, is the South destined to achieve its
independence."[450]

In Washington, Abraham Lincoln was working on delivering a
blow. On the day Davis was inaugurated, he had ordered a forward
movement on all fronts for the Union armies. The army in the east,
now under the command of Major General George B. McClellan,
had been maddeningly slow to move. And, indeed, despite the
president's order, this forward movement would not begin until
mid-March. Then McClellan at last embarked his command, now
known as the Army of the Potomac, the largest military force ever
assembled on the American continent, and shipped it toward the
Virginia Peninsula.

Anne Frobel had gone into Alexandria about that time and
there found "the *whole world* moving toward Richmond."[451] Richmond city councilman Thomas H. Wynne saw it, too, and warned
that Virginia was to be "the outpost, the bulwark against which our
invaders were directing their force, and her soil was the theatre
which had been chosen for the issue."[452] A Confederate officer in
Yorktown, awaiting the Union juggernaut, wrote of "the thick
clouds" of coming trouble gathering around the Confederate
capital.[453]

In the capital Joseph Mayo, in his late sixties, mayor of Richmond since 1853 and a descendent of the city's founder, was steeling his resolve to be Horatio at the bridge. "If the city of Richmond
was ever surrendered to our enemies," he vowed, "it should not be
by a descendent of its founder. He would sooner die than surrender
our city; and if they wished a mayor who would surrender [it] they
must elect another in his place."[454]

Roger returned to Smithfield to resume his military persona.
But the first Sara knew of it was when an orderly knocked on her

door at the rented house, carrying an order from the colonel—her husband—commanding her to change her base immediately to Richmond. She was ordered to leave Smithfield, which was in the path of the invading army, by daybreak next morning.

She protested. "Tell the colonel it is impossible!" she told the messenger. "I can't get ready by tomorrow morning to leave."

The messenger took exception to such rank insubordination. "Madam," he gravely counseled, "it is none of my business, but when Colonel Pryor gives an order, it is best to be a strict constructionist."

Mr. Britt, the grocer, closed his store for the day and mobilized his employees to help Sara comply with the orders. The cow was presented, with Sara's compliments, to a neighbor. Her camp equipment was retrieved from the warehouse and her belongings packed.

As the sun rose next morning Sara found herself seated atop a trunk in an open wagon, on her way to Zuni, the rail station fifteen miles inland. She had rarely seen a lovelier morning. Cattle were grazing in the fields, and thin lines of smoke curled into a cloudless sky from the cottages along the road. But behind her she could hear the discordant thunder of the guns on the Union warships in the harbor at Newport News—a thunder to which her ears were reluctantly growing accustomed. But now, as she retreated along this quiet and picturesque road, the thunder was taking on a new and more ominous meaning. At Zuni she entrained for Richmond, and when she arrived, she checked into the Exchange Hotel, as near to Roger, to headquarters, to news from the Peninsula, as she possibly could be.[455]

On the Peninsula, on April 5, 1862, McClellan laid siege to Yorktown, where nearly eighty years before, George Washington had forced a British surrender and the new nation had been born. For a month McClellan bombarded the little town and its fifteen thousand Confederate defenders.

Roger was in the Yorktown lines with his regiment, in Lieutenant General James Longstreet's division, and under siege by some of his own soldiers—the Portsmouth National Grays—who believed him too overbearing and arrogant. The Grays was a Virginia militia company of railroad men, navy-yard workers, artisans, shopkeepers, and clerks, organized in Portsmouth in 1856. Their one-year enlistments for the war were about up and most of them wanted to reenlist, but not under Roger. So they began reenlisting into other commands. Roger mustered them and, at his insolent best, said he understood some of them wanted to go home. One of the company assured him that that wasn't the case; they only wanted to go to the companies where they had reenlisted. This enraged Roger nearly as much as the Marion Rifles' vote against secession. He accused the Grays of shirking in the face of impending battle. John Lingo, a corporal speaking for the company, said bluntly, "Colonel Pryor, we are not leaving on account of the enemy or approaching battle, but we do not desire to serve any longer under *your* command." Roger threw them all in jail on a charge of mutiny. Since their reenlistments into different companies were illegal under a new law, the Grays, though released after only three hours in the slammer, remained with the Third Virginia, and Roger later apologized to them for his harsh language and hard treatment. But the Grays were in no mood to forgive. "I never will forget how he served the company at Yorktown…as long as I live," one of them later wrote.[456]

If Roger's star was setting with some of his own men, it was rising elsewhere. The war on the Peninsula was just beginning when his name was sent up by Jefferson Davis for promotion to brigadier general. Several Confederate senators in Richmond had initiated a move to promote him in late 1861. The nomination had gone up to the Congress on All Fools' Day, before the siege of Yorktown—a day for it that many of his unhappy soldiers might have considered appropriate—and was approved by the Senate on April 16.

Richmond in the spring of 1862 was not without its receptions and parties, even in the midst of impending war, with the enemy thundering at its gates and "every morning's paper enough to kill a well woman [or] age a strong and hearty one."[457] Varina Davis had planned a presidential reception at the Spotswood Hotel the evening following the announcement of Roger's promotion in the newspapers. At the Exchange Hotel, where Roger and Sara were staying, a crowd gathered to serenade and congratulate the new brigadier. Learning he had gone to the Spotswood for the reception, they followed, and with shouts and cheers called for him to come out.

But Roger, for one of the few times in his life, was backward, bashful, and embarrassed. He fled into a corner of the drawing room and ducked behind a screen of plants. Sara was standing near President Davis, attempting to hold his attention with talk about the weather, when the voices called out: "Pryor! *General* Pryor!"

Sara was unable any longer to endure the suspense. Trembling, she asked Davis, "Is this true, Mr. President?"

Davis looked at her with what she took to be a benevolent smile and said, "I have no reason, madam, to doubt it, except that I saw it this morning in the papers." Davis wasn't given to believing much that he read in the Richmond press. Mrs. Davis, meanwhile, was prying the reluctant Roger from his sanctuary behind the plants. "What are you doing lying there *perdu* [lost] behind the geraniums?" she demanded. "Come out and take your honors."

Sara was ecstatic. The next day, the bristling bullion-fringed eagles she had stitched for Roger, and which had "faithfully held guard on the Colonel's uniform," were retired "before the risen stars of the Brigadier-General."[458] When he marched from Yorktown to Williamsburg, it was at the head of his own brigade.

Although this new-risen star in the Confederate military firmament was not hailed as a point of light by everybody, the senators who had lobbied for his promotion in December had said he "possesses in a high degree the confidence and esteem of all the officers and men of the brigade, and his appointment would give entire satisfaction."[459]

However, two prominent Alabamans, the renowned firebrand orator and Roger's onetime forensic foe, William Yancey, and Confederate Senator Clement C. Clay, were no more satisfied than some of Roger's soldiers. They assailed his appointment as misdirected patronage. They were unhappy that there were more than forty Alabama regiments in the field and only five Alabama brigadiers. They knew Davis believed that any civilian colonel "must win his spurs before he could secure such an appointment." The two men wrote Davis, charging him with violating his own axiom by appointing Roger, and compounding the sin by giving him Alabama troops. They considered Roger's spurs modest at best, certainly not glittering enough to make him more worthy of promotion than their Alabamans.[460]

On Saturday, May 3, Joseph E. Johnston, commander of the besieged Confederate army on the Peninsula, whom one critic called "this arch retreater," ordered Yorktown evacuated.[461] He began a measured withdrawal toward Richmond, over two roads saturated with rain and hub-deep in mud, planting torpedoes (as mines were called) as he went. The next morning, McClellan found the Confederates gone and launched his army over the mined and waterlogged roads in pursuit. In the afternoon, McClellan's advance skirmished with Johnston's rear near Williamsburg, halfway to Richmond, on the narrowest neck of land between the York and James Rivers. Filing into the town, the Confederates entrenched behind a four-mile line of thirteen defensive redoubts anchored in the center by a bastion called Fort Magruder.

The fighting the next day, Monday, May 5, was sharp and heavy and in a "pitiless" rainstorm. It was "a battle fought without a plan" by two armies on the move toward Richmond.[462] The fighting, south of the fort in the morning, north of it in the afternoon, was along a ravine in terrain so broken and tangled with natural obstacles and trees felled to make an abatis (sharpened branches pointed outward toward the enemy) that it was impossible to keep up a unified front or mount a coordinated attack. It was a case of desperate fighting from stump to stump and log to log in rain-soaked woods. Artillery shells tore into the abatis, and the smoke of battle mixed with the rain to make seeing in any direction difficult.

"Pandemonium broke loose," one Confederate soldier said. "It seemed to me as if the brass pieces fairly howled while the roll of the small arms was something indescribable. Ordinarily heavy musketry rises and falls like the sound of the sea, but here it was one deep, incessant, prolonged, deafening roar."[463]

For a time under these conditions the Confederates held the huge Federal force at bay. But as the day wore on and McClellan fed more and more of his troops into the fight, Major General Winfield Scott Hancock's Union division outflanked the Confederates and occupied a part of the line. In the evening the Confederates gave it up, pulled out altogether, and continued their retreat westward toward Richmond. It had been but a delaying action, and the toll was heavy again—another seventeen hundred Confederate dead, wounded, and missing to trouble Sara's spirit. It was said that the dead "lay in every direction, like a rail fence thrown down."[464]

Roger lost nearly a third of his brigade but distinguished himself in the fighting at Williamsburg. General Longstreet mentioned him favorably in his official report, saying that, "Brig. Gen. Roger A. Pryor had but a portion of his brigade engaged. He used his small force with effect in making a successful attack, and, toward the close of the conflict, in repelling a vigorous assault of the enemy."[465] Those with him spoke of Roger's "great coolness and judgment."[466] He praised his men, saying, "I owe it to the officers and soldiers of my command to declare that their valor and devotion realized my highest conception of patriotic duty."[467]

McClellan pushed slowly on through Williamsburg after Johnston's army and moved his juggernaut to the outskirts of Richmond, then dividing it in half—three of his corps on the north side of the Chickahominy River, and two isolated on the south side.

Seeing this division, Johnston also saw an opportunity. On Saturday, May 31, he attacked the two Union corps south of the river, at Fair Oaks, or Seven Pines, a flat, swampy, forested crossroads just east of Richmond.

It was to be another ruined weekend, another two days of what a correspondent with the Army of the Potomac called "bloody work." The Confederate attack was late being delivered—not until about one o'clock in the afternoon. The first Rebel assault made headway, but McClellan called for help from across the Chickahominy to reinforce the "beaten and disorganized relic" isolated at Seven Pines. By the next day the momentum had changed.[468] At the end of the two-day battle, nothing had been decided. Johnston had been severely wounded but had failed to destroy the two isolated Union corps, and now the reinforced Federal line was too strong to attack again.

Roger's brigade had been in the middle of it all, fighting beside the brigades of George E. Pickett and Cadmus Wilcox. Longstreet praised Roger again in his report—for his "usual gallantry and ability."[469]

The enemy also praised him. General McClellan later reported that when the Confederates were in possession of a part of the Union line, Roger had gone among the Federal wounded giving them whiskey and water, and telling them it was "repayment of the kindness" with which Confederate wounded were treated at Williamsburg. In a log house filled with dead and wounded Union soldiers, Roger assisted in amputating the limb of a member of the 104th Pennsylvania Regiment.[470] There was nothing of cowardice, and a liberal vein of compassion, in Roger's makeup.

SPRING WAS COVERING Richmond's "amphitheatric hills" as the Union army thundered to its gates.[471] The season of renewal had opened, as it always did, "with a sudden glory of green leaves, magnolia blooms, and flowers among the grass."[472] But it had also come with something entirely new—this massing of troops for battle on Richmond's outskirts. In nearby Gordonsville, where a Confederate army was gathering, Sallie Bird wrote that "troops are pouring in by the carloads." She wrote in wonder of sentinels "pacing up and down before every church door, the churches being filled with powder, cartridges, cannon balls, etc."[473]

The streets of Richmond were filled with what Constance Cary called "a continually moving panorama of war." Richmond's women were full-time "greeting, cheering, choking with sudden emotion, and quivering in anticipation of what was yet to follow." The citizens of the city had begun to feel, Constance noted, "like the prisoner of the Inquisition in [Edgar Allan] Poe's story, cast into a dungeon with slowly contracting walls."[474]

The war was indeed "at the very gates now."[475] There was hardly a family in the city whose father, son, sweetheart, friend, or brother was not marching and fighting with the defending army. And on May 31, when the fighting reached the city gates, at Seven Pines, Richmond was for the first time baptized in fire. "It was so near," Constance Cary wrote, "that the first guns sent our hearts into our mouths, like a sudden loud knocking at one's door at night."[476]

"The booming of the cannon," Nellie Gray wrote, "sounded in our ears and thundered at our hearts. Friends gathered at each other's houses and looked into each other's faces and held each other's hands, and listened for news from the field." When "the sullen boom of the cannon broke in upon us . . . we would start and shiver as if it had shot *us*, and sometimes the tears would come. But the bravest of us got so we could not weep."[477]

Sallie Putnam felt the seven hills of the city tremble with "the rush and shock of battle . . . as though an earthquake were undermining the foundations." The "whir and whiz of the musketry" fell on her ears "like the sound of a mighty rushing wind, with furious showers of hail."[478]

When night fell and brought a pause in the cannonading,

people in Richmond lay down fully dressed on their beds. But few slept. The soldiers on the battlefield slept on their arms in a warm pouring rain. Early the next morning as the fighting resumed, the entire city was out on the streets.

Ambulances, litters, carts—every vehicle that could be commandeered—now came and went "with a ghastly burden." Those wounded who could walk, Constance Cary said, "limped painfully home, in some cases so black with gunpowder they passed unrecognized." Pallid women "flitted bareheaded through the streets, searching for their dead or wounded." The churches were thrown open for communion services or for prayer. Women in the city swarmed to places of worship to sew—"as fast as fingers and machines could fly." Rough beds were fashioned from the pews for the wounded. Men too old or infirm to fight rode out on horseback or went afoot to meet the returning ambulances. In some ghastly cases they met and escorted their own dead or dying sons back to Richmond. "There is always woe for some house," Mary Chesnut told her diary. By the afternoon the day after the battle, the streets were one vast hospital. Unused buildings had been thrown open to shelter the wounded.[479]

Constance Cary could scarcely believe the agony she was seeing as she walked through the streets, past "one scene of horror to another." At the Saint Charles Hotel she saw the worst of it: "Men in every stage of mutilation, lying waiting for the surgeons upon bare boards, with haversacks or army blankets, or nothing, beneath their heads. Some gave up the weary ghost as we passed them by."[480]

The way many Confederate soldiers were going to their graves tore at the heartstrings of Ada Bacot. Ada was a nurse at Monticello Hospital in Charlottesville. It was early June and oppressively warm, and the wounded and the sick were crowding in from the Virginia battlefields, not only from around Richmond, but from Stonewall Jackson's army in the Shenandoah Valley. Ada saw the narrow graves where the dead were to be laid, all jammed together, and her dread deepened. Many of the names had already been defaced from the rude slabs of wood identifying them. "A dreadful sickning feeling comes over me," she told her diary, "when I think how they are hurryed to their last resting place without one friendly eye to see where they are laid or one loved one to shed a tear over their lonely graves."[481]

Day after day wailing dirges were crying dead Confederate soldiers to graves, perhaps more friendly but no less sorrowful in Hollywood Cemetery in Richmond. "One could not number those sad pageants in our leafy streets," Constance Cary wrote. As the dead passed, under "crape-shrouded banners," mourners stood on the sidewalks or at windows "with bare, bent heads."[482]

Despite its melancholy function, Hollywood Cemetery was "a picturesquely beautiful spot."[483] A longtime Richmond resident called it "one of the most beautiful cities of the dead anywhere."[484] Its hills were deep-shaded by holly, pine, and cedar and deciduous trees, now fresh in their new green spring foliage. As always in the spring the banks of the river that ran past in the valley below were "enameled with wild flowers." The thickets were alive with May blossoms and dogwood. From a summit on a bluff overlooking the city, under the ample shade of a large oak tree, Constance could see the spires and roofs of the city and the white colonnade of the Confederate capitol. Richmond itself, despite all that was happening, was richly green and verdant, "upon hills, girdled by hills."[485]

The city, Sara knew, had "waked up to a keen realization of the horrors of war." And the horror presented "a strange scene." Ambulances carrying the wounded, the dead, and the dying from the battlefield passed down one side of the street as fresh companies marched by on the other side on the way to the front, each cheering the other. Batteries of artillery pounded through the streets, and couriers galloped in and out of the tableau. Hurrying crowds, blacks running messages, newsboys hawking "extras" printed on short sheets of yellow paper, were everywhere. Every house had been opened for the wounded. They lay on verandas, in hallways, and in drawing rooms of Richmond's mansions. Young belles and not-so-young matrons stood in their doorways, offering food and fruit to the marching soldiers, then turning, after they had passed, to minister to the desperately wounded men inside. Sara calculated that some five thousand wounded were taken in and cared for in private homes and hospitals. The city, she said, "had 'no language but a cry!' "[486]

Above that cry, word reached Sara that Roger had fallen ill with malaria and lay fevered and sick in his tent a few miles from the city. She found him there, his tent pitched in a field of daisies. Sara moved him at once to the Spotswood Hotel, in Richmond, where the doctor told her, "He wants nothing now except some buttermilk and good nursing."[487] Buttermilk could be bought; good nursing of her husband was Sara's specialty.

THE BATTLE AT Seven Pines lasted two days. When Joe Johnston fell on the first day, command of the Confederate army on the Peninsula passed for a few hours to Gustavus W. Smith, but then, the next day, to Robert E. Lee. Lee, one of the most promising officers in the Old Army before the war, had sadly left that army with the outbreak of the Civil War because he could not raise his sword against the people of his own state of Virginia. Governor Letcher had immediately offered him command of the state's land and sea forces with the rank of major general, which Lee accepted. When the Confederate government had moved to Richmond and taken over all operations of the war, Lee had become a high-level military adviser to Jefferson Davis. Now, for the first time, he assumed direct command of a major army, which he would call the Army of Northern Virginia. His intention was to throw that army against McClellan's invaders, drive them from Richmond's gates, and, if possible, destroy them.

The heat in Richmond on June 26 was intense. Sara greatly feared it because of its debilitating effect on her recuperating husband, still lying weak and listless in the room in the Spotswood Hotel. She was reading the morning papers aloud to him, fanning him as she read, when a peremptory knock on the door brought her to her feet. A note to "Brigadier-General Pryor" that looked ominous to Sara was handed in. Roger read it and slipped to the side of the bed and reached for his boots. The note was from General Longstreet. It read: "Dear General, put yourself *at once* at the head of your brigade. In thirty-six hours it will be over." Before Sara could grasp its meaning and consequences, Roger was gone.[488]

She ran out into the hall, searching for other wives of officers in Roger's brigade also in the hotel, hoping to learn more from them. On the stairway she met Lieutenant Colonel Joseph V. Scott, of Roger's brigade. As he passed her, he exclaimed—to her anxious inquiry—"No time until I come back, madam!" Turning, he paused, raised his hand, and added, "If I ever come back."

Fanny Poindexter, wife of a captain in Roger's brigade, came weeping and wringing her hands. She cried, "Do you think that we could drive out to camp and see them once more before they march?"

Sara and Fanny hurried into the street, found a carriage, and, prodding the driver to utmost speed, were soon within sight of the camp. It was a scene of chaos, hurry, and confusion. Ambulance wagons were hitching up, troops were falling in line, servants were shuttling back and forth, horses were standing to be saddled, light wagons were being loaded. A captain from Roger's staff met Sara and said, as he led her to her husband's tent, "The General will be so glad to see you, madam! He is lying down to rest a few minutes before we move."

Roger enfolded Sara in his arms as she entered his tent, but there were no words of sadness. They spoke to cheer one another. Unable to curb her anxiety, Sara ran out to find John, Roger's manservant, to see that he had brandy and cold tea—in the event good water was not to be had in the field. Flies were everywhere, a swarming host. Sara had never seen so many. They "blackened the land," tainting the food and tormenting the horses.

When Sara returned to Roger's tent, Fanny was standing outside waiting for her. "I can see my husband only at the head of his company," Fanny cried. "Look! They are forming the line."

The two wives stood aside as the brigade formed. Shouts of "Fall in! Fall in!" ran through company after company. Roger mounted his horse, drew his sabre, and gave the order to march. With a steady tramp the brigade filed past them, the only two women, Sara realized—of the many who loved them—who knew of their going and had come out to cheer them, bless them, and wave them farewell.[489]

CHAPTER 11

---•·◆·•---

Somebody's Darling

For nearly three months beleaguered Richmond had heard what Sallie Putnam called "the dread music of artillery."[490] Distant at first, its thunder was coming ever closer.

About sunset the day before Roger climbed from his sickbed at the Spotswood Hotel to ready his brigade for battle, Sallie had climbed to the roof of the capitol in Richmond and had seen, "as far as the eye could reach, the encampments of the soldiery, in waiting for the most furious contest of arms ever then expected on this continent." The white tents of the armies dotted the landscape "like snowflakes in winter."[491]

McClellan had pushed the bulk of his great army forward into the fields east of Richmond after the battle of Seven Pines, intending to drive on into the city. He had positioned another part of his army out of reach on the southwest bank of the Chickahominy.

Having said farewell to Sara, Roger was now marching toward that host, in Longstreet's division. It was not a long march from where they had started—only a few miles—to the Union line.

Lee was taking the battle directly to the Federal army. Four Confederate divisions were on the march. Lee's plan was to send A. P. Hill's division across the Chickahominy near Mechanicsville in advance of the divisions of D. H. Hill and Longstreet. A fourth command under Stonewall Jackson was coming up, and in consort, they were all to strike the Union right wing under Fitz-John Porter and power it back, away from Richmond.

By three o'clock in the afternoon on June 26, the generally prompt Jackson inexplicably had not yet appeared. It was not like him. The impetuous and impatient A. P. Hill would wait no longer. He attacked without Jackson, which was not Lee's intention. The guns opened, and the mighty battle began. The trigger had been pulled, and now it was to be a fight to the finish, however long it took.

SARA PRYOR AND FANNY Poindexter, left alone in the deserted camp, could not bear to remain there after the men had marched away. They were about to climb into their carriage when the driver pointed back with his whip toward puffs of blue smoke rising from McClellan's guns.

Sara thought, "So near, so near!"

Riding homeward the two women were too numbed even for tears, and yet unable, either of them, to comfort the other. Presently the carriage stopped, and the driver appeared at the carriage door.

"Lady," he said, "there's a man lying on the roadside. We just passed him. Maybe he's drunk, but he 'pears to me to look mighty sick."

The two women leaped from the carriage in an instant. Here was an opportunity to do something—anything—to relieve their tense, pent-up feelings. The man beside the road wore the uniform of a Confederate soldier. His eyes were closed, and a thin thread of blood trickled slowly from a wound in his throat, staining his shirt.

They knelt beside him and Fanny took out her handkerchief and gently pressed it against the wound to stop the flow of blood. Sara saw then that Fanny was "one of those nervous, teary little women who could rise to an occasion."

The soldier opened his eyes but was unable to speak.

"What in the world are we to do?" Fanny said. "We can't possibly leave him here!"

The driver spoke: "I can tote him to the carriage. He ain' no heavy-weight, an' we can carry 'im to that hospital jus' at the edge of town." The driver reached to pick the soldier up. "Come now, sir!" he said as he cradled him in his arms. "Don't you be feared. I'll tote you like a baby."

The driver drove slowly to the hospital and Sara and Fanny were terrified lest their patient die before they reached help. There a surgeon ordered a stretcher and had the soldier carried inside.

The women waited in the little reception room until the surgeon reappeared and said, "It is well for him, poor fellow, that you found him when you did. His wound is not serious, but he was slowly bleeding to death! Which of you pressed that handkerchief to it?"

Sara told him Fanny did.

The doctor said, "He had probably been sent to the rear after he was wounded, and had tried to find General Pryor's camp." There had been minor preliminary engagements along the front the day before. "He missed his way," the surgeon guessed, "and went farther than necessary. It has all turned out right. He is able now to write his name—'Ernstorff'—so you see he is doing well. When you pass this way, you must call and see him."[492]

On the battlefield, a few miles distant, the Confederate push had driven the Union force back through Mechanicsville. Porter fell in behind a strongly prepared position at Beaver Dam Creek and Ellerson's Mill, regrouped, and turned to make a stand. A. P. Hill, still unsupported by Stonewall Jackson, threw his men against the Union line and met a stone wall of his own. His brash charge failed, and the day's fighting was done. It had been an appallingly bloody beginning to Lee's offensive —fourteen hundred Confederates killed, wounded, or missing, starkly disproportionate to Federal losses of less than four hundred.

All through the afternoon and into the evening the dread music of the cannon thundered across the hills of Richmond. Back in the Spotswood Hotel, Sara shut herself in her darkened room and later wrote that it "thrilled our souls with horror."[493] At twilight a note came from Governor Letcher telling her a fierce battle was raging—as if she didn't know it—and inviting her to the governor's mansion, where from the roof one might see the flash of musket fire and the smoke of artillery.

"No!" Sara protested. "I did not wish to see the infernal fires." She preferred to wait alone in her darkened room, feeling what many Confederate wives were feeling at that hour, a nearly wild, "almost insupportable" fear that her husband would be wounded or killed.[494]

Richmond was strangely quiet in counterpoint to the thunder rolling in from Mechanicsville. Nearly everyone in the city had gone to one of its seven hills to witness what Sara called "the aurora of death." As it grew dark a servant entered her room to light her candles, but Sara forbade it. The servant asked if she did not mean to go to supper. Sara didn't wish to do that, either. So she had coffee brought to her. She must keep up her strength. God knows, she thought, what news she might hear before morning.

Night came on, hot and close. Flashes from the guns glimmered on the horizon along the battle line. Their deep thundering echoed from hill to hill and reverberated throughout the valley.[495] Sara sat at an open window, watching for couriers in the street. About nine o'clock the firing stopped. Surely, she thought, somebody would remember the wives and bring them news. As she leaned on the windowsill with her head resting on her arms, she saw two young men walking slowly down the deserted street. They paused at a closed door opposite her window and sat down on a low step. They began chanting a mournful strain in what Sara, her ear ever tuned to music, recognized as a minor key, much, she thought, like one of the occasional interludes of Chopin, which "reveal so much of dignity in sorrow." She was strongly moved—as she always was by such music—and began to weep, "not for my own changed life, not for my own sorrows, but for the dear city; the dear . . . city, so loved, so loved!"

A full moon had risen above the trees in the capitol square. Soon the city would be flooded with light. Would a dark invading host come in with the light, Sara asked herself, to desecrate and destroy?

She remembered another such night in Richmond, a long time ago, when she was a little girl. She had come to Richmond with her aunt and uncle, and coming as she did from the quiet countryside, the splendor and immensity of the big city had so oppressed her that she couldn't sleep. Hot, fevered, and afraid, she had risen from her bed and stolen to the window to look out. As on this present night of waiting and watching, there had been a full moon and the same awful stillness. Below her that night in the street, a watchman had called out, *"All's well!"* Soon the cry was repeated at a distance: "All's well!" Fainter and fainter the echo grew until it became a distant whisper. The watchmen, she thought then, were telling her, telling all the helpless little babies and children, all the sick and old, that God was watching over them, that "All's well, All's Well." Watching again this evening, with Richmond at war and the sounds of battle rumbling in the night, Sara thought that the watchman was forever gone, his cry forever stilled.[496]

Just before dawn a hurried footstep came at last to her door, bringing her a message from the battlefield. "The General, madam," its bearer told her, "is safe and well. Colonel Scott has been killed. The General has placed a guard around his body, and he will be sent here early to-morrow.[497] The General bids me say he will not return. The fight will be renewed, and will continue until the enemy is driven away."

It was heart-relieving good news clothed in heartrending bad news. And it spread quickly. The courier had been making the rounds. Presently, Fanny Poindexter was knocking at Sara's door. She was in tears.

"She is bearing it like a brave, Christian woman," Fanny sobbed. "*She!* Who?" Sara exclaimed. "Tell me quick."

"Mrs. Scott," Fanny replied. "I had to tell her. She simply said, 'I shall see him once more.' The General wrote to her from the battle-field and told her how nobly her husband died—leading his men in the thick of the fight—and how he had helped to save the city."

Sara, remembering Colonel Scott's last words to her on the stairway that first day, was herself distraught. Alas, that the city should have needed saving! What had Mrs. Scott and her children done to deserve this? Why should they suffer? Who was to blame for it all?[498] Sara could have resonated with the anguished cry of a Northern mother, who was writing a letter to her daughter, the wife of a Southern soldier, that same morning: "Oh! This melancholy war, how it drags upon the heart strings."[499]

The wounded and dying began streaming into town at twilight, as Sara stood vigil at her window. That night she was not the only sleepless one in the city. Sallie Putnam later wrote, "There were none of us who had not friends, the nearest and dearest, exposed to the dreadful hazards of battle." There could be no sleep "when our hearts were torn with apprehensions for their safety."[500]

SARA NOW KNEW what she must do. The children were safe with their grandmother. She would write and ask that every particle of her household linen, except a change, be rolled into bandages, and all her fine linen sent to her for compresses as soon as possible. She would go in the morning to the new hospital that had been improvised in Kent & Paine's warehouse and be a nurse for as long as the armies were fighting around Richmond.[501]

She had never done such a thing before, but Roger had sent an order to the committee formed for the relief of the hospitals that his salary as a member of the Confederate Congress be drawn from the treasury and appropriated for care of the wounded.[502] Sara now planned to do her part—to give of herself for their care. She had come to the same conclusion as Kate Cumming in Mobile. "We can not fight," Kate had written in her diary, "so must take care of those who do."[503]

Sara was resolved, as the verse went, to "fold away all [her] bright-tinted dresses, turn the key on [her] jewels today," to "braid back in a serious way [her] tendril-like tresses" and go "to meet the stern needs of the hour."[504]

Every cannon shot from the running battle could be heard in every home in Richmond.[505] The next morning, Sallie Putnam wrote, the rattle of musketry was "like a shower of hail."[506] Ignoring the fearful sounds, Sara made her way to the Kent & Paine's warehouse. It was a large airy building transformed into a hospital immediately after the battle at Seven Pines. When Sara entered it early that morning, she saw cots already occupied on the ground floor, and other cots being readied. An aisle between the rows of narrow beds ran to the rear of the building. Broad stairs led to a second story, where other cots were being laid.

Sara presented herself as a candidate nurse to the matron, who eyed this elegant volunteer dubiously. She had seen Sara's kind before. As Mary Chesnut had written of one family in her diary a year earlier, "Every woman in the house is ready to rush into the Florence Nightingale business." It was a widespread impulse. Mary believed there was "no lack of women's nursing, no lack of women's tears."[507]

A story, probably apocryphal, was going around of one eager would-be Florence Nightingale who approached a wounded soldier in a hospital ward and said, "Can't I do something for you, sir?"

"No thank you, ma'am."

"Is there nothing?"

"No thank you, ma'am."

"Can't I wash your face for you?"

"Well, if you insist, ma'am, all right, but fourteen ladies have washed it already today."[508]

Doctors were said to object to the presence of that other breed of hand-wringing volunteer nurse, the wounded men's wives, believing they invariably killed their patients with kindness.[509]

The matron at Kent & Paine's warehouse could use good help, but she had her doubts about Sara. She hesitated, then said, "The work is very exacting. There are so few of us that our nurses must do anything and everything—make beds, wait upon everybody, and often a dozen at a time."

"I will engage to do all that," Sara promised.

Heading to where she would sign in, she passed the rows of occupied cots and saw a nurse kneeling beside one of them, holding a pan for a surgeon—who was holding over it the red bleeding stump of an amputated arm.

Sara fainted.[510]

ROGER WAS TEN MILES away, in Longstreet's division, and Lee was about to hammer the Federals again. The Confederates were massed on McClellan's right flank and rear. The contours of the terrain were working against Lee. His soldiers had to attack across a network of fields, ravines, and swamps against a strong semicircle of dug-in Union troops. Jackson was still unaccountably late, and Lee's blow was again disjointed. But so was the Union defense. The two sides fought through the day to a standstill, and that evening Fitz-John Porter pulled out of his position, crossed the Chickahominy, and rejoined the rest of McClellan's army.

It was said that Roger was "everywhere where the firing was hottest," something Sara would not want to hear.[511] Her husband wasn't driven by optimism, however. An officer in the Fourteenth Louisiana overheard him say, "I am afraid those devils will get into Richmond in spite of all we can do."[512]

But there was little optimism in "those devils," either. McClellan's great army was in retreat. *New York Tribune* correspondent Charles A. Page described a scene common to all retreats. It was a scene "not . . . to be forgotten," he wrote. "Scores of riderless, terrified horses dashing in every direction; thick-flying bullets singing by, admonishing of danger; every minute a man struck down; wagons and ambulances and cannon blockading the way; wounded men limping and groaning and bleeding amid the throng; officers and civilians denouncing and reasoning and entreating, and being insensibly borne along with the mass; the sublime cannonading; the clouds of battle-smoke, and the sun just disappearing, large and blood-red."[513]

Lee was driving the Union army but paying an exorbitant price in dead, wounded, missing, or captured. The Confederate wounded continued to pour into Richmond. "Every house," Sallie Putnam said, "was a house of mourning or a private hospital." Death was holding "a carnival in our city."[514] In nearby Petersburg the large airy and well-ventilated tobacco factories were also being turned into hospitals. Everywhere, the midsummer heat was stifling.

THE FIRST PERSON Sara saw when a spray of cold water revived her after her fit of "fine-lady faintness," was the hospital matron, standing beside the cot where Sara had been carried and looking down at her. "You see," the matron said, "it is as I thought. You are unfit for this work. One of the nurses will conduct you home."

A night's vigil and a noble resolve, Sara could see, were inadequate preparation for hospital work. So back in her room at the Spotswood, she set about arming herself for a return, steeling herself against the sickening odor of death that mingled with the acids and disinfectants in the hospital—the appalling mixture that she believed had made her faint. She put sal volatile and spirits of camphor in the pockets of her gown and, next morning, returned to the Kent & Paine's warehouse and presented herself again to the matron.

Finally, in the face of Sara's insistence, the matron relented. "I will give you a place near the door," she said, "and you must run out into the air at the first hint of faintness."

Ambulances were streaming in and unloading at the door, and Sara was soon too busy to think of herself. A few drops of camphor on her handkerchief were getting her through the worst of it. As the day wore on, she became more and more absorbed in her work. She didn't faint again.[515]

By Sunday morning, the twenty-ninth, everybody in Richmond was certain the Union army was on the run. The thunder of artillery was growing fainter as the battle drifted farther and farther away down the James. The city knew the siege had been lifted and the threat ended.[516]

But the dead and dying continued to pour into Richmond's hospital wards.

At Kent & Paine's warehouse, Sara was now pulling a regular twelve-hour shift—from seven o'clock in the morning to seven in the evening. By the end of the week, she had been promoted. Now instead of carving fat bacon to complement the corn bread on the hospital's dinner menu, or standing between two cots to shoo flies from bleeding wounds, or fetching water, or putting clean sheets on empty cots, she was assigned regular duty with a single patient. And every day a new harvest of patients appeared at the door.

She was thoroughly reinstated with the surgeons, the matron, and the wounded alike when she appeared one morning accompanied by a man bearing a basket of clean, well-rolled bandages— the harvest from her own linen cupboards and dresser drawers. Items she had written home for had arrived, with the promise of more to come. Her tablecloths, sheets, dimity counterpanes, and chintz furniture covers had been transformed into bandages, in springlike greens and whites, and were applied to mangled arms and legs. Her fine linen underwear and napkins, cut to surgical dimensions by the sewing circle at the Spotswood, were seeing service as compresses.[517]

But despite everything she and every other nurse and doctor and volunteer could do, they couldn't stem the ghastly tide of the wounded who were dying. A gravedigger at the cemetery said, "We could not dig graves fast enough to bury the soldiers."[518] Some women were desperately nursing their own husbands. One was in a streetcar when she heard of the death of her husband. Another glanced out her window and saw a coffin lettered with the name of her husband being carried by.[519] The month of July was a month nobody in Richmond would ever forget. Sallie Putnam later wrote, "We lived in one immense hospital, and breathed the vapors of the charnel house."[520] The war had created a whole new world of "fever wards and dying men."[521]

Sara had said the city had no language but a cry. But the cry had been answered, she was proud to say, by Richmond's women, those "delicate, beautiful women I had so admired when I lived among them. Not once did they spare themselves, or complain, or evince weakness, or give way to despair." Every morning they came to the hospital at the warehouse, bringing any luxuries they could find for the wounded soldiers.[522]

The death of one youthful Confederate soldier in a hospital inspired Marie Ravenel De La Coste, of Savannah, to write words that wept for all the young Southern soldiers who were being carried bleeding and wounded into the fever wards of this still young war. It seemed to Sallie Putnam, living in Richmond's charnel house, that the heart-wrenching "exquisite pathos of the poety" of Marie's words "sent a thrill of ectasy to our hearts, and comfort and sweetness to the bereaved in many far off homes of the South."[523]

Into the ward of the clean, white-wash'd halls
Where the dead slept and the dying lay,
Wounded by bayonets, sabres and balls,
Somebody's darling was borne one day.
Somebody's darling, so young and so brave,
Wearing still on his sweet, yet pale face,
Soon to be hid in the dust of the grave,
The lingering light of his boyhood's grace.
Somebody's darling, somebody's pride.
Who'll tell his mother where her boy died.[524]

There was by now "an abiding ache" in nearly every Southern woman's heart, often wept out "on some dear bosom," or over graves "wet with . . . tears."[525]

Georgiana Gholson Walker would later vividly remember "those terrible . . . battles around Richmond, when I heard the bursting of every shell, the firing & even saw the flash of the cannon, never knowing except day by day that my Husband lived; my timid heart dreading that each bullet took his life."[526]

It was a dread that Sara shared. She confronted the dread every night in the dark loneliness of her room at the Spotswood Hotel. Every night during the running fight that would become known as the Seven Days battles, a courier had come bringing news of Roger. And every night, when she saw the messenger at her door, her heart "would die within me!"

One evening as Sara was resting in her room, exhausted from a hard day at the warehouse, a haggard officer, covered with mud and dust, appeared at her door. He entered, fell across her bed, and cried out, "My men are all dead."[527]

Roger had returned from the Seven Days battles.

He had fought to wildly contradictory reviews from his soldiers that were difficult to reconcile. Lieutenant Colonel Zebulon York, commanding the Fourteenth Louisiana Infantry Regiment under Roger, made note of his "superior ability, sagacity and courage."[528] Major Thomas C. Elder, Roger's commissary officer, wrote his wife, Anna, that the general "greatly distinguished himself." Elder was told that in one fight "he seized the flag of the 14th Alabama regiment in his hands and leading the charge of his brigade rushed up to breastworks and over them to a battery through a fire of the enemy that seemed certain death; yet he escaped unhurt."[529]

Lieutenant Robert H. Miller of Zebulon York's Fourteenth Louisiana, however, wrote home bitterly that more than half of his regiment was destroyed "mainly owing to the miserably and cowardly Generalship of Brig. Gen. R. A. Pryor. . . . He is a *politician-general*, and merits the contempt of all *soldiers*."[530]

But Longstreet's was the final word. That general was more than satisfied with Roger's "gallantry and skill" throughout the seven days.[531]

In the week of vicious fighting, McClellan had failed to take Richmond, despite outnumbering the Confederates two to one. Instead he had to be satisfied with simply saving his army. Lee had both succeeded and failed. He had driven the Union host from the hills of Richmond, saving the city. But he had failed to destroy the enemy, the intended goal of his offensive. And he had paid the cost with twenty thousand casualties, killed, wounded, or missing.

One writer was to write that the fighting had "converted twenty-six miles of swamp and forest into a vast necropolis."[532] Constance Cary mourned those who would never return. "What wrecked hopes it left to tell the tale of the Battle Summer!" she wrote. "Victory was ours, but in how many homes was heard the voice of lamentation to drown the shouts of triumph!"[533]

CHAPTER 12

————•••————

Marching with Lee

"'*The* Great Battle of Richmond,' And what does it tell?"

Ida Dulany, in Uppervillle, Virginia, asked her journal that—then answered her own question. It told "heart-chilling tales of streams of blood and heaps of dead, of shrieks and groans, of mowing men down like heads of wheat, of onslaught and repulse and . . . the battle still undecided."[534]

Nobody, however, knew what it all meant for "this poor, damaged, unhooped Confederacy."[535] Nobody knew what was going to happen next. McClellan lay behind the protective muzzles of his gunboats at Harrison's Landing, driven from the outskirts of Richmond but with an army still huge, lethal, and threatening. Lee knew it might rise up and strike again at any time. A second Federal army had advanced to Culpeper in northern Virginia under Major General John Pope. What did that mean? What was it going to do? Lee must now contend with two Union armies, front and rear.

When elements of Pope's command—the Army of Virginia—began moving out of Culpeper southward, toward Orange Court House and Gordonsville, on August 9, Lee had already posted Stonewall Jackson's corps south of Culpeper and north of the Rapidan, with the idea of striking first. But the Union force under Major General Nathaniel Banks, whom Jackson had embarrassed in his Shenandoah Valley campaign earlier in the spring, delivered the first blow. Banks struck two of Jackson's divisions at Cedar Mountain, and for a time he had them reeling—until a third Confederate division, under the irrepressible A. P. Hill, came up, counterattacked, and drove the Federals back.

It was now clear, if it hadn't been before, that Pope was moving south in a major offensive. Intelligence had also reached Lee that McClellan had been ordered from the James back to Washington to support Pope. The Confederate commander therefore turned his full attention to Pope's Army of Virginia. By August 13 he had turned his back on McClellan and was moving all of his own army from the Peninsula toward Gordonsville. Roger's brigade was marching with it, in James Longstreet's division.

Five days later Pope's army, pressed by Lee's advancing Confederates, pulled back to the north bank of the Rappahannock to await the reinforcements from McClellan, now landing at Aquia Creek, below Washington. On August 25 Lee set Jackson in motion with a flanking movement—one of Jackson's specialties— around Pope, from below the Rappahannock toward Manassas, the vicinity of the first major battle of the war the summer before. The next day Confederate cavalry under Fitzhugh Lee galloped into Manassas Junction and captured the rail point. Skirmishing broke out all along the line to and around Manassas—at Bristoe Station, Bull Run Bridge, Gainesville, Haymarket, Sulphur Springs, and at Manassas Junction itself. By evening Jackson, moving rapidly— another of his specialties—reached Bristoe Station.

Pope didn't know it, but his army had been outflanked. On the morning of Wednesday, August 27, he was confused. Nearly half of the Confederate army was now, somehow, between him and Washington. He abandoned his position on the Rappahannock and sent troops hurrying northward toward Manassas, where Jackson was now destroying facilities and ravaging Union stores.

Jackson, however, was not waiting to be attacked at Manassas. He withdrew on that night of August 27 to a position along the Warrenton Turnpike west of the Old Bull Run battlefield. When Pope arrived at Manassas, he found Jackson gone, and he had no idea where, and his confusion deepened. Reports coming in of Jackson's whereabouts were conflicting and contradictory. Finally, Pope ordered his army to converge on Centreville, where he heard Jackson might be.

Pope found the elusive general on Friday afternoon, August 29, when Jackson fired on one of the Union divisions moving toward Centreville, near Groveton on the Warrenton Turnpike. This was not where Pope had expected to find Jackson. After a fierce fight, Pope made yet another serious miscalculation. Believing that Jackson was retreating, he ordered his forces to concentrate on the rear of that shifty Confederate's division. In the midafternoon, Lee arrived with Longstreet, west of Jackson's position and bypassing it—another development Pope knew nothing of.

The next morning, Saturday, August 30, Pope attacked Jackson, who was not retreating at all, but was dug in along a railroad cut near Groveton. But the Union commander's army, still widely scattered and exhausted from constant marching, struck only piecemeal. Longstreet, with Roger's brigade, came up about noon, and as darkness fell the Confederates were strongly posted along their original line of battle. Pope, still deluded, hit Jackson's corps on the left, as Longstreet, on the right, attacked Union concentrations on Henry House Hill, where Jackson had made his famous stand and won his nickname the year before. As another night fell, Pope's army was beaten, but not routed. Lee had won but had again failed to destroy his enemy, as he had hoped to do.

The next morning, the last day of August, Pope collected his battered command on the heights of Centreville, and began a retreat toward Washington. Lee sent Jackson on another looping flank movement, toward Chantilly on the outskirts of Washington. The next day, September 1, a final severe fight in a heavy rainstorm ended there in the evening, and with it ended the battles that became known as Second Manassas. It had been another Confederate triumph that had cost dearly. Another nine thousand Confederate dead, wounded, and missing heightened the anguish of Southern women. But Federal casualties were even higher, nearly twice Confederate losses— more than sixteen thousand. There were to be as many darkened and sorrowing hearthsides in the North as in the South.[536]

Roger personally darkened two Northern hearthsides himself. Briefly captured, he bolted, seized one of the Yankees' muskets and bayoneted his two captors, killing one and mortally wounding the other. Some called it daring heroism, but because he was a prisoner of war, some called it murder.[537]

AFTER THE SEVEN DAYS battles on the Peninsula, Sara had been remanded by Roger to the mountains near Charlottesville. There she left three of her children—Marie Gordon, Theodorick, and Mary—with her aunt Mary, and took her two youngest boys to a summer resort called Coyners, in the Blue Ridge Mountains, near the railroad. There she could still be along the lines of communication with the army and, she hoped, with Roger, who was somewhere out there marching with Lee.[538]

The hunger for communication and the desperate need to know were agonizing to Confederate women everywhere. And rarely were either speedily satisfied. Susan Caldwell was crying out for all Southern women when she wrote to her husband in Richmond, "Oh! how my heart has yearned but for *one line*."[539] But when that one line—or word from any source—came, they didn't know how much of it to believe. "One hears so many well-authenticated lies nowadays," Susan Middleton wrote her cousin, "the capacity to believe seems slow and deadened."[540] A jaded Mary Chesnut confessed, "I have wept so often for things that have never happened, I will withhold my tears now for a dead certainty."[541]

Elizabeth Wallace, in Virginia, came to believe that "falsehood travels faster than truth."⁵⁴² Lizzie Hardin, in Kentucky, was to write in her dairy, "If we are poor in everything else we are at least rich in rumors." The news, she believed, "is like a Russian bath where you are alternately plunged into hot vapor and thrown into the snow."⁵⁴³ It was "the fickle nature of war," Clara Solomon, in New Orleans, explained, "—one moment victors, the next retreaters."⁵⁴⁴

When the Union armies retreated back into Washington, Lee knew he could not attack them there. So he decided on another bold flanking movement—this time onto Northern soil. He began angling his army toward the crossings of the Potomac near Leesburg, west of Washington. For three days, September 4 to 7, he pushed his soldiers over the crossings as his bands played "Maryland, My Maryland." On September 6, Jackson's soldiers occupied Frederick.

In Washington the discredited Pope was replaced by McClellan, who had been restored to command of the Union armies in the east and charged with reorganizing them to meet this new Confederate threat. Reorganizing as he went, McClellan marched slowly toward Frederick. Knowing nothing at first of the enemy's whereabouts or intentions, he kept his army carefully positioned between where he thought Lee might be and Washington and Baltimore.

The Confederates had pushed on, out of Frederick and westward over the South Mountain passes. By September 15 Jackson, on orders from Lee, had split from the main army, marched back into Virginia, and captured Harpers Ferry. Longstreet had been sent northward toward the Pennsylvania line.

In a stroke of fortune that rarely falls to an army commander, Lee's plans and the disposition of his army fell into McClellan's hands. Three of his soldiers found a copy of the plans for the Confederate campaign wrapped around three cigars in a field outside Frederick. McClellan now knew where Lee was and what he was doing. Temperamentally a slow mover, McClellan quickened his pace. He knew Lee's army was divided in front of him, even if he had no firm fix on its numbers. He pushed up into the South

Mountain passes. Surprised by this usually conservative enemy's sudden vigor, Lee ordered Major General D. H. Hill to slow the Federal force as best he could on South Mountain while he called Longstreet in from up north and Jackson from Harpers Ferry. Lee's widely spread army was in serious jeopardy.

During a ferocious day of fighting, Hill held on precariously at South Mountain as Lee looked for a place to reassemble, turn, and fight. He found it in the little Maryland town of Sharpsburg, in a gently undulating alleyway between a creek in his front, called the Antietam, with the Potomac River and Virginia at his back. By September 15 he was there with Hill and Longstreet, awaiting Jackson, who was marching hell-bent for Sharpsburg with all of his command, save A. P. Hill's division.

McClellan's pursuing army approached cautiously from over the South Mountain passes and set up on the hills across Antietam Creek. After a day of reconnoitering—a precious day lost, just long enough for Lee to recall his scattered army—McClellan had put the right wing of his command across the Antietam on the Confederate left. In the early morning of September 17, he launched the attack from there.

Roger's brigade in Richard H. Anderson's division had been one of several of Longstreet's brigades temporarily detached to join Jackson's corps in its march to Harpers Ferry. The division had set out for Sharpsburg on September 16. It arrived on the morning of the seventeenth and took a position at a sunken road in the center of Lee's line. Under Roger's command again, and not all that happy about it, was the Third Virginia Infantry.

McClellan had intended to strike the Confederates across the entire line, from right to left. But the attack was again uncoordinated and piecemeal and not as he had planned. Rebel forces under Jackson on the Confederate left counterattacked with columns that Lee was shuttling up and down his interior line. By ten o'clock in the morning the Confederates held as the Federal attack on the Confederate left played itself out.

The fight now moved to the center. The thin Rebel force that hunkered down along the sunken road saw a fresh wave of Federal troops massing at its front and marching forward. Roger and his brigade were now about to face the fury of the second phase of the disjointed Union attack.

Roger found himself confronting what looked like Armageddon. To make matters more harrowing, Anderson had been wounded, and Roger, his senior brigadier, was now in command of the entire division—in a very sticky situation. Nothing in his career in law, journalism, and politics had prepared him for this. Desperately pressed, he hurried a courier to Longstreet, requesting artillery reinforcement, with the word "that he would hold his position until the last man was taken or surrender." Longstreet told the courier, "Tell Gen[']l Pryor we did not come here to be taken."[545] He tore the margin from a piece of newspaper and wrote, "I am sending you the guns, dear General. This is a hard fight and we had better all die than lose it."[546] Words of dubious comfort.

This fierce but disjointed Union assault also spent itself, just shy of crushing the thin Confederate line at its center. But this time Roger got only passing and perfunctory praise from Longstreet.[547] He had been in over his head in the bewildering job of commanding a division in a crunch, proving himself a better journalist-politician than he was a general.

The attack on the Confederate right now opened, long after McClellan, more and more frustrated, had intended. The Union Ninth Corps, under Ambrose Burnside, was having trouble crossing the southernmost bridge spanning Antietam Creek. Four hundred Georgia riflemen positioned on the heights above the bridge were making it a crossing into oblivion. When Burnside finally did get across, at great cost, and drove the Georgians from the heights sometime after noon, he halted to regroup his battered force. This would take two hours.

Meanwhile, the last remaining division of Lee's army, under

A. P. Hill, who had been left to mop up at Harpers Ferry, had been called in. It was desperately needed at Sharpsburg. Hill had begun his march at six-thirty that morning, the seventeenth, prodding and whipping his soldiers to top marching speed. As Burnside was completing his regrouping, Hill's division, after seventeen hot miles of hell-bent marching, was crossing the Potomac. Burnside struck Lee's thin defending line about four o'clock in the afternoon and bent it slowly back. When Burnside's troops were at the outskirts of Sharpsburg, nearly between Lee's right flank and across his only line of retreat on the Potomac, A. P. Hill burst on the scene. Just as the tenuous Confederate line was about to give way, he hit Burnside's unsuspecting and unprotected left flank. The momentum of the fighting dramatically reversed. Burnside's corps, surprised and heavily assaulted, was driven back to Antietam Creek. Night soon fell, and when it did, the Confederate army was still—miraculously—holding its position. Lee's army had been snatched from disaster in the face of overpowering numbers.

It had been the single bloodiest day in American military history. Great black columns of smoke had ascended over this killing ground, one Confederate artilleryman observed, and had "hung around the mountains like a pall."[548] Twenty-six thousand men, Union and Confederate, had been killed, wounded, or were missing—more than twelve thousand Union and thirteen thousand Confederate.

All the next day, September 18, Lee waited, ready—despite the weakened condition of his decimated army—to entertain a renewed Union assault. When it didn't come, he left in the night, crossing Boteler's Ford, near Shepherdstown, and falling back into Virginia. Pouring across the Potomac with him were his bloody wounded. In Winchester on September 19, Kate Sperry cried into her diary, "Never saw as many wounded and disabled soldiers in my life—the place is thronged with them—from every regiment—the pavement is very full." The next day she wrote, "They've been coming in all day and are still coming."[549]

Across the South, Confederate women recoiled from the news of the battle. A young widow in Virginia, who was left with only her husband's sword, cried out to a friend, "Oh, Nell, when it's all over, what good will it do? It will just show that one side could fight better than the other, or had more money and men than the other. It won't show that anybody's right. You can't know how it is until it hits you, Nell. I'm proud of him, and proud of his sword; I wouldn't have had him out of it all. I wouldn't have had him a coward. But oh, Nell, I feel that war is wrong! I'm sorry for every Northern woman who has a circle like this around her, and a sword like that hanging on her wall."[550]

Cornelia McDonald, in Winchester, Virginia, wrote in her diary, "To me it seems as if all the flowers of life are withered, and nothing left but the bare, bitter, thorny stems." In this second autumn of the war, when the winds were "whirling away the leaves from the trees," Winchester was in Union hands and even the sunshine looked "cold and sad" to her.[551]

As ROGER WAS surviving the confusion and killing along the bloody sunken road at Antietam, Sara waited at the resort in the Blue Ridge, shut off, knowing very little. She had not been alone with her little boys, however. Indeed, she was in high-powered company. Also at the resort was Confederate General Arnold Elzey, of Jackson's command, who had been wounded in the face at Gaines's Mill on the Peninsula. He had been bandaged up to his eyes and sent to the rear, with a physician, for rest and recovery. With Elzey were his wife and his aide, a captain. The captain's young bride had crossed the Potomac in an open boat to join and marry him there. Dolly Hill, A. P. Hill's wife, was also there, and General and Mrs. Louis Wigfall and their daughter.

The resort's small hotel sat at the head of a little green valley. Stretching behind was a velvet swath of green, a spring and a rivulet in its middle, bounded by a mountain ridge on either side.

Sara's small cottage had windows opening on the mountains, and to her, at night in her bed, the moon and stars as they rose above her seemed so near that she felt she could reach out and pluck them off the hilltop.

The view was more congenial than the company; it was not an entirely happy ensemble. The wives came to Sara to complain about matters of rank and precedence. "I'd like to know *who* this Maryland woman [Mrs. Elzey] is that she gives herself such airs," one complained. "How much longer do you think I'll stand Dolly Morgan [Hill]?" another demanded. "Why, she treats me as though she were the Queen of Sheba." Sara, "with becoming meekness," could only reply, "I'm sure I don't know! I am only a brigadier, you know—the rest of you are major-generals—I am not competent to judge."

But fall was coming on and Sara found the climate "delicious." The valley was "carpeted with moss and tender grass, and thickly gemmed with daisies and purple asters." Before sunrise the morning sky visible between the high hills looked to her to be formed of roses. In the evening, from a hilltop, sky and mountain were "bathed in golden glory."

Sickness soon entered this idyllic scene, however, to deaden her pleasure; Roger Jr. fell desperately ill with typhoid fever, so ill that for many days Sara despaired for his life. Elzey's physician held no hope. Sara wrote the Confederate secretary of war, George Wythe Randolph—a dear friend from her childhood, present at her wedding—desperately imploring him, "Send my husband to me, if but for one hour." He answered, "God knows I long to help and comfort you! but you ask the *impossible*."

Not until all the other guests had departed and Roger had returned with the army from Maryland could she travel with her stricken son. In Charlottesville the little boy suffered a temporary relapse.[552] But his father was alive and well, and Sara knew where *he* was, which was something she could be grateful for.

CHAPTER 13

·•·•·

Alone in the Blackwater

$\mathcal{R}$oger's brigade had always been itself a little confederacy—a grab bag of state allegiances. In it at one time or another were regiments from Virginia, Alabama, Louisiana, Florida, and North Carolina. And it was now being dismantled.

Jefferson Davis wished to reshuffle the army's regiments and brigades. He believed that soldiers would show more loyalty and fight better, with more enthusiasm, under officers from their own states.[553]

By the late fall of 1862 Roger had lost all of his varied brigade and was without a command. Even the Third Virginia had been wrested from him, transferred to Brigadier General James Kemper's brigade, and the men were generally gratified to be rid of Roger. One soldier from the regiment talked of "Old Pryor who we are clear of now."[554] The Second, Fifth, and Eighth Florida, the Fourteenth Alabama, and the Fifth North Carolina had all been stripped away. He was being passed over for brigadiers junior to him. He was without a brigade and at loose ends, a somewhat tainted star in the Confederate military firmament.

Whatever he might have thought of Roger's less than impressive performance in front of the sunken road at Sharpsburg,

Robert E. Lee was outwardly sympathetic. "I regretted, at the time, the breaking up of your former brigade," Lee wrote him on November 25, "but you are aware that the circumstances which produced it were beyond my control. . . . I hope it will not be long before you will be again in the field, that the country may derive the benefit of your zeal and activity."[555]

There was a problem of what to do with this political general of zeal and activity, who appeared unemployed. By Lee's order he was detached from the Army of Northern Virginia, put under the command of Major General Gustavus W. Smith, and ticketed for a departmental command. On November 29 Smith sent him to Major General Samuel G. French for duty around Suffolk. Smith's accompanying letter to French said, "It is intended by the government that he shall have a Virginia brigade as soon as one can be formed for him. In the meanwhile it is General Lee's desire that General Pryor shall serve upon the Blackwater—his own section of the country," and that two regiments of cavalry be put under his command.

Smith's letter went on to say, "General Pryor has already won for himself the reputation of being one of the best, most daring, and energetic officers in the army, highly distinguished in civil life, and one of the most influential men in the state, especially in his own section. He will cooperate with you thoroughly, and I am sure will render good service to the cause and be of great assistance to yourself."[556]

So Roger went from the war's mainstream to a backwater called the Blackwater, a region around Suffolk named for the Blackwater River. Facing him was a large body of Federal troops occupying Suffolk itself. Roger's job was to keep that big enemy off Longstreet's command, which Lee had sent to the region to forage for desperately needed provisions—corn and bacon, in particular, which were in short supply in the Army of Northern Virginia. The main mass of Lee's army was now concentrated around Fredericksburg.

SINCE SHARPSBURG, SARA had gone to Roger wherever she could find him. When Lee's army went into temporary winter quarters at Culpeper, after the battle at Antietam, Sara went there. She found herself in an armed camp. She had not imagined "there were so many soldiers in the world." "You cannot take a step anywhere," another said, "without treading on a soldier!"

Lee probably believed he didn't have enough soldiers and wished he had more, for however many Rebels there were in Virginia, there were even more Federals, "thousands on thousands" of them, Sara believed. They had closed the major rivers and were menacing the railroads. And everything was therefore scarce and expensive. Nobody had much in the way of comforts or luxuries.

In the evenings soldiers came to the house where Sara was staying for at least one available comfort and luxury offered them in their overcrowded world—a snug fireplace in a drawing room in congenial female company. Sara called it "our camp-fire." Around it the soldiers and the women sang that sad and woefully tender and weepy hit love song, wildly popular throughout the Confederacy:

> *It matters little now, Lorena,*
> *The Past is the eternal past,*
> *Our heads will soon lie low, Lorena,*
> *Life's tide is ebbing out so fast;*
> *But there's a future—oh! thank God—*
> *Of life this is so small a part;*
> *'Tis dust to dust beneath the sod,*
> *But* there, *up* there—*'tis* heart *to* heart.[557]

Maggie Howell, Varina Davis's saucy younger sister was noted for her rapier-like wit. One admirer said of her that she was "a nice girl," a "good talker & gentle," with a faultless waist and a very pretty foot.[558] Maggie swore, "There is a girl in large hoops and a calico frock at every piano between this place and the Mississippi, banging on the out-of-tune thing—and looking up into a man's face who wears [the] Confederate uniform." Maggie believed the song "has not had a fair chance," being "squalled so" with "its banged accompaniments—discord itself."[559]

Sara noted that "pretty Nelly," one of the girls around their "campfire," sat at the piano in her hoops and calico frock on these evenings in the Culpeper parlor, banging it out, her blue eyes raised to heaven, with a soldier, Jack Fleming, accompanying her on his guitar, "his dark eyes raised to Nelly."[560]

As Roger turned his own eyes toward Suffolk late in the fall of 1862, Sara focused hers on him, resolved to follow, if possible, to the Blackwater. Roger didn't suspect she would do such a thing—follow him to such a particularly dismal end-of-the-world region. He expected she would find a place among friends and relations in Petersburg and stay there. But by now Sara had no home anywhere. She belonged to the growing legion of Southern refugees. Roger's father's home was home to her when he was in it, but he was no longer in it. He had given up his church in Petersburg and become a chaplain in the army, "where," he said, "I can follow my own church members and comfort them in sickness, if I can do no more."

As soon as Sara learned the whereabouts of Roger's command, she pulled her camp outfit out of storage, packed a trunk or two, and caught the rail cars for the Blackwater. The railroad ended a few miles short of Roger's camp. She and her little boys arrived at the end of the line at twilight and found themselves standing alone on a station platform in the middle of what appeared to be nowhere. Night was coming down and she had no idea where they would sleep. She knew only that she would manage somehow. She always did.

There was a small wooden building nearby that served as a waiting room and post office. The only other building around was a small house in a grove of leafless trees. Sara believed that she had "never before seen such an expanse of gray sky. The face of the earth was dead, bare level, as far as the eye could reach; and much, very much of it lay under water." It was a region of bogs culminating in one great no-man's land called the Dismal Swamp—a "vast desolation" where "cypress, live-oak, the dogwood, and pine struggled for life with the water."[561] Sara could hear no harmonious or civilized sound, no hum of industry or lowing of cattle, only "a mighty concert" of "thousands, nay millions, of frogs."

As the postmaster in this dreary tableau was locking his door and preparing to leave for the day, Sara, liking the look of him, approached and asked, "Can you tell me, sir, where I can get lodging to-night? I am the general's wife—Mrs. Pryor—and to-morrow he will take care of me."

The postmaster surveyed her, her little boys, their trunks, and the box of camping equipment and said, "I can take thee in myself. I am just going home."

"Oh, thank you, thank you," Sara said. "I shall need only the smallest trunk to-night."

"I'm afraid I can hardly make thee comfortable, as I live alone," the postmaster said, "but thee is welcome."

"'Thee'! Oh, joy!" Sara thought. "This is a blessed little Quaker! We'll not part again! Here I rest."

When they entered his door, the postmaster called out for "Charity."

The call was answered by a black girl in a short linsey-woolsey frock, which, whatever its other virtues, failed to hide her ankles and bare feet. Her hair was tied in innumerable little tails, sticking out all over her head like porcupine quills. Sara soon realized she was "the most alert little creature I ever saw, nimble-footed and quick."

"Charity," Sara's host told the girl, "have a good fire made upstairs in the front room at once." Turning again to Sara, he said, "Thee is welcome." And Sara followed the girl up the stairs.

"And so your name is Charity?" Sara asked.

"Charity's meh name an' Charity's meh naycher," Charity informed her.

A young white boy named Dick brought in an armload of

wood, and a fire was soon cheering them. As Sara looked about the room, Charity said, "You needn' be lookin' at de baid. I'll soon sheet it. He's got sto's o' quilts, but I dunno know as he'll s'render 'em."

But he did surrender them, carrying them upstairs himself. They were beautiful quilts, with their bright patchwork, and they made the two beds in the room look warm and inviting.

Charity leaned against the mantel, her bare feet crossed one over the other, and leisurely studied Sara. Sara felt it a wise move to placate her.

"We'll unlock the trunk," Sara said, "and I'll find a pretty ribbon for you."

"I knowed," Charity said, "that you was some punkins soon's I sot eyes on you."

Before Sara was called to a supper of biscuit, fried bacon, and coffee without cream, Charity told her about herself and the kindly postmaster.

"I'se free, I is!" Charity said. "Mo'n dat, he's a Quaker, an' ef you ever seen Quakers, you knows dey don' like no slaves 'roun'. Yas'm. I'se free—an' Dick, he's a po'-white boy. Me'n him does all de wuk cep'n in hawg-killin' time, an' den de fokes come fum de quarters to he'p."

"Are you lonesome?" Sara asked.

"*Dat* I is." Charity confessed. "You see he los' his wife two mont' ago. Dese here quilts is hern. She made 'em."

"I'm so sorry!" Sara said.

Charity had broken down and was sobbing with her head against the mantel.

"Yas'm!" she sobbed. "I cert'nly is lonesum! She jes up an' die, an' de po' little baby daid too."

Sara lay in bed that night, under the bright quilts the postmaster's wife had stitched, and thought of that "dear dead woman." She resolved to be nothing but a comfort to Charity and the Quaker postmaster, and began making plans for their happiness.

With a heart "full of sympathy, full of gratitude, full of hope," she fell asleep and slept "sweetly and long."

A message was sent first thing in the morning from the post office to Roger's camp, which soon brought Roger. It also brought an invitation from the postmaster for Roger to make the postmaster's house his headquarters, which Roger accepted. During the day, he moved in bag and baggage, and a cook was detailed from the camp, for they were to furnish their own table. Their host looked so offended when they also offered to pay rent for their lodgings, that no more was said on the subject.

Finding the thick white china in the house unattractive, Sara consulted with Charity about buying something different. But the only market town nearby was Suffolk, and it was in Union hands.

"He's got painted cups an' saucers, but I dunno's he'll s'render 'em," Charity offered.

"Suppose you ask him!"

"I dun try 'im once," Charity said. "I ax 'im dat time when his mother-in-law cum to see 'im—and he nuvver say nuthin!"

After a few days the postmaster threw a bunch of keys into Sara's lap and said, "Everything in the house and on the plantation belongs to thee."

With Charity as witness, Sara unlocked the old mahogany sideboard and counted out the cups, saucers, and plates—all gilt-edged and decorated with rosebuds.

"Good Gawd!" said Charity. "I *nuvver* though he'd s'render the chany cups!"

"Not one is broken," Sara said. Then, sternly, "If you break one, tell me at once and bring me the pieces, so I can send to Richmond and replace it."

After that they saw but little of their magnanimous host. He virtually lived at the post office, staying late every night to sort the mail and have it ready for early-morning delivery to the camp. He returned home each evening about midnight to eat and sleep. And every night he found a bright fire crackling in the fireplace, a clean-swept hearth, a supper of biscuits, sausage, or broiled ham, and a little pot of coffee prepared by Sara. A table, a lamp, and the latest newspaper were waiting for him beside his armchair.

A few months after Sara left this hospitable house to return to Petersburg, she received a letter from the postmaster. It read: "RESPECTED FRIEND: I have now married. I couldn't stand it. Thy friend, I.P."

From that time on Sara always counseled, "As cure for an incorrigible bachelor, simply...take care of him beautifully for three months and then—leave him!"[562]

THE SECOND CHRISTMAS of the war brought little cheer to the South. "Well, this is Christmas day," Bettie Ancell wrote her brother, from Virginia, "but only in name here, as there are but few, indeed if any, merry hearts, as in days gone by, and if anything, I feel sadder than usual, to think this is or used to be a day of mirth. But, now, no joy or gladness fills my heart." Arabella Pettit, Bettie's sister-in-law, wrote her husband, "It was dull, duller, dullest."[563]

On the last day of 1862, Ella Thomas, in Augusta, wrote of a rising wind that was blowing the old year away. "As its mournful cadence swells around the house," she told her diary, "I can imagine it sighing a requiem for the countless dead who have been ushered into eternity since this year began its course."[564]

When the new year arrived, Kate Cumming, in Chattanooga, nursing Confederate soldiers wounded from the battle raging at Murfreesboro, sighed into her diary, "Another year has commenced, alas! with bloodshed. When will it cease? I ask that question with nothing but echo for my answer."[565]

Coming in with the answering echo, however, was news of a proclamation by President Lincoln, emancipating all slaves in Southern territory occupied by Federal troops in the war. The proclamation, announced following the battle of Antietam and taking force on January 1, was received with mixed emotions in the Confederacy. On official levels it was generally seen as an odious measure "calculated, if not intended, to produce servile insurrection at the South."[566]

Many Confederate women also saw it that way. "Do you think," Arabella Pettit had asked her soldier-husband, at the front, when she first heard of it in November, "that there will be a general massacre of whites before Christmas? I do have the thought."[567]

Roger and Sara, in the Blackwater when they heard, felt the proclamation had very little to do with them. They had never owned slaves. They had servants, but these servants were rented from slaveholders and were paid for their services. Sara didn't believe the proclamation made much difference to the common Southern soldier, either. In her view he "cared little for politics, less for slavery," and had enlisted not to fight for the right to secede or to own slaves, but to resist the invasion of the South by the North—to prevent what he saw as subjugation. He was fighting to drive an invader from his home.[568]

Other Southern women put a different spin from Sara's on the despised proclamation, reacting with more fire and resentment. One of these called it "this new act of tyranny."[569] Kate Stone, the devoutly rebellious Mississippian snarled into her diary, "I wonder what will be the result of this diabolical move. . . . Surely not as bad for us as they intend it to be." She wrote bitter words about its detested author. "I think," she fumed, "there is little chance of a happy hereafter for President Lincoln. A thousand years of repentance would be but brief time to wipe out his sins against the South. How can he ever sleep with the shades of the thousands he has consigned to a bloody death darkening his soul?"[570]

ALL AROUND THE postmaster's house and seemingly sleepless in the new year was the croaking army of frogs. Sara viewed them as a huge choral ensemble, an amphibious orchestra, and believed that nothing like them could be imagined. "They serenaded the moon all night long; a magnificent diapason of mighty voices, high soprano, full baritone, and heavy bass."

A spell of warm humid weather came on toward the end of January. The winter apparently was wanting to be over. Grass was springing up in the swamp, green and lush. The willows were budding. There were no singing birds on the Blackwater yet, the true heralds of spring, but the frogs were obviously "mightily exercised" over the coming season of renewal. Their nightly croaking had taken on a jubilant note.

Roger's job was calling for sleepless vigilance. Brigadier General Raleigh Colston, his immediate commander in the Blackwater district, had written him that *"you must hold the line of the Blackwater to the last extremity."* General French, both Colston's and Roger's superior in overall command in southern Virginia and North Carolina, had counseled Roger that "you must annoy the villains all you can, and make them uncomfortable. Give them no rest. Ambush them at every turn."[571]

Often in the middle of the night Roger summoned John, his manservant, mounted him on a horse, and sent him to call his staff officers to a meeting. From her bed Sara heard them tramping into Roger's bedroom for a council of war. On January 28 Roger confided to her that he intended to make a foray in the direction of the enemy. "He is getting entirely too impudent," Roger told her. "I'm not strong enough to drive him out of the country, but he must keep his place."

The next day he marched away in the direction of that impudent enemy. As he left, the weather suddenly changed; the skies lowered and the horizon became dark and threatening. Sara reported to the hospital tent and put herself at the disposal of the surgeon, an act that had become her accustomed routine when Roger marched away to battle. As she was put to work preparing more bandages, she pressed Charity into service to help pick lint.[572]

Roger's soldiers met the Federals at Deserted House, also

called Kelly's Store, eight miles from Suffolk, on January 30. Roger
later reported that the enemy attacked at four o'clock in the morning with "as furious a cannonade as I have ever witnessed."[573] He
wired Colston in Petersburg: "After three hours' severe fighting,
we repulsed them at all points and held the field." In the end, however, he withdrew, estimating his losses in killed and wounded
did not exceed fifty. In an address to his troops on February 2, he
boasted that the Federals had a five-to-one bulge in numbers, but
were nonetheless repulsed by "your terrible fire."[574] The Confederate Congress was impressed. A resolution was introduced on
February 4 thanking Roger and his command for their "signal gallantry, and cool courage, and patriotic prowess."[575]

Roger's sorties on the Blackwater did not win unmixed praise,
however. Brigadier General Joseph R. Davis, sent to Suffolk to reinforce Roger, had no intention of staying. He asked to return to
North Carolina to serve under French instead. "I cannot see that
this line needs more than a Brigadier's command," he wrote his
uncle Jefferson Davis, "and if it does ought to have a better commander than Gen P———."[576]

It seemed to Sara that Roger and his staff were "forever in the
saddle" during this time, and when he did return, he was usually
too tired to amuse her. During the days he was gone, she busied
herself teaching her little boys, dispensing the food and supplies
Roger's men brought her, and making a study of Charity. The girl
pleased her greatly; she was quick to learn, responsive, and affectionate. And she was Sara's sole female companion. If Charity certainly was lonesome, so was Sara.[577]

Mail was thin on the Blackwater. Few newspapers came, and
even fewer books. But there was the occasional letter. Sara thanked
God in particular for letters from Agnes, her friend in Richmond.

"MY DEARIE," Agnes chided her on January 7. "Have you
no pen, ink, and paper on the Blackwater—the very name of
which suggests ink? I get no news of you at all. How do you amuse
yourself, and have you anything to read?"

Agnes figured not. She was therefore sending Sara a copy of Victor Hugo's latest novel, *Les Misérables*—reprinted by a Charleston firm on the best available paper, which Agnes confessed was "pretty bad." But the novel was wonderful. "You'll go wild over that book," she wrote Sara. "I did—and everybody does." It was a book about hard times, which most Southerners could now relate to personally. Everybody seemed to be reading it, Agnes said—even the army.

Agnes herself was worried about shortages. "Do you realize the fact," she asked Sara, "that we shall soon be without a stitch of clothes? There is not a bonnet for sale in Richmond." Some of the young women were smuggling them in, which Agnes frowned upon. "We have no right at this time," she protested to Sara, "to dress better than our neighbors, and besides, the soldiers need every cent of our money."

Agnes had ripped up her pearl-gray silk bonnet trimmed with lilies of the valley, washed and ironed it, dyed the flowers blue, and thought it now very becoming. She said all the girls intended to plait hats next summer when the wheat ripened. The country girls had made their own bonnets last summer and pressed the crowns over bowls and tin pails.

"Heaven knows," Agnes confided to Sara, "I would costume myself in coffee-bags if that would help" while the country is in such peril, "but having no coffee, where could I get the bags?"

She had read in the newspapers that General French reported the enemy 45,000 strong at Suffolk. This worried Agnes. "How many men has your General?" she asked Sara.

Even as she was writing this letter, Agnes reported, a crowd of blacks was passing through the streets of Richmond, singing as they went. They had been working on the fortifications north of the city and were now going to the south side to work on them there. She noted about the passing blacks what Sara had noted about soldiers: They didn't seem much concerned about Lincoln's emancipation proclamation.

By way of a postscript, Agnes reported she had attended Varina Davis's latest reception. There was a crowd there, all in still "quite passable" evening dress, despite the fashion privations of the day. Agnes had worn her gray silk dress with the eleven flounces that she thought Sara might remember her having worn at Addie Douglas's last reception in Washington. "Doesn't it all seem so long ago," Agnes asked Sara, "—so far away?"

She reminded Sara of the evening the Prince de Joinville of France had escorted her—Agnes—to one of the president's levees. "Now," she wrote, "I attend another President's levee [Davis's] and hear him calmly telling some people that rats, if fat, are as good as squirrels, and that we can never afford mule meat." The day may come, Agnes wrote, when rat meat will be in demand.[578]

In another letter later, Agnes took notice of Roger's sorties against the Federals around Suffolk. She said everybody in Richmond was saying Roger would be promoted to major general. "When he is," Agnes wrote, "I shall attach myself permanently to his staff." The life of "inglorious idleness here is perfectly awful." She told Sara she longed for "a rich experience."

"Give me the *whole* of it—victory, defeat, glory and misfortune, praise and even censure," she wrote, "anything, everything, except stolid, purposeless, hopeless uselessness." The worst effect of inaction, she believed, was felt in Richmond, where "we can manufacture nothing for the soldiers, and only consume in idleness what they need."[579]

Sara welcomed these letters from Agnes, for they brought her "news of the outside world," and she resonated with much that her friend said.[580] But Sara was with Roger at the point of action, not idle, and getting the whole of it, not languishing in hopeless uselessness.

For many women in the South in this new year of the war, the most operative word in "the whole of it" was "misfortune"—and worse. "Death," Susan Caldwell, in Virginia, wrote to her husband, in Richmond, "is knocking at doors all around us." Before the war would end, it would knock twice on her own door. Her husband would lose his mother, and Susan would say, "she was *mine too.*" And Susan's little baby daughter, "our loveliest child," would be swept away by scarlet fever and Susan would know "the deep keen anguish of a Mother's heart," and "find no comfort any where."[581]

Mary Chesnut asked, "Does anybody wonder so many women die? Grief and constant anxiety kill nearly as many women as men die on the battlefield." She told her diary, "I know how it feels to die—I have felt it again and again." She wrote, "It is awfully near—that threat of death—always."[582]

Indeed, death was ever near, ever present, ever busy, and intimately known. "[It] does not seem half so terrible as it did long ago," Kate Stone confessed to her journal in Mississippi. "We have grown used to it. Never a letter but brings news of the death of someone we knew."[583]

A LATE SPRING brought a crisis in Richmond, explained in another letter to Sara from Agnes. On April 4, Agnes wrote, "Something very sad has just happened in Richmond—something that makes me ashamed of all my jeremiads over the loss of the petty comforts and conveniences of life—hats, bonnets, gowns, stationery, books, magazines, dainty food."

A foot of snow had blanketed Richmond in late March. But by April 2 the retreating winter had relaxed its grip and the weather was springlike. Agnes had gone out for a walk to capital square before breakfast, and there, on the west side of the square, she found a crowd of women and boys—several hundred of them—standing quietly together. She sat on a bench nearby, wondering what it meant. One of the women left the others and came to sit down next to her. Agnes noted that she was a pale, emaciated girl, not more than eighteen years old, wearing a sunbonnet and a calico gown.

"I could stand no longer," the girl explained. As Agnes moved down the bench to make room for her, she observed that the girl had delicate features and large eyes, and her hair and dress were clean and neat. But as she raised her hand to remove her sunbonnet and use it for a fan, her loose calico sleeve slipped up and revealed the mere skeleton of an arm. The girl, seeing Agnes's shocked expression, hastily pulled down her sleeve.

With a short laugh, the girl said, "This is all that's left of me!"

She had been a pretty girl—a dressmaker's apprentice, Agnes had judged from the girl's chafed forefinger and the skill evident in the lines of her gown. Agnes asked her about the crowd, "What is it? Is there some celebration?"

"There *is*," the girl said. "We celebrate our right to live. We are starving. As soon as enough of us get together we are going to the bakeries and each of us will take a loaf of bread. That is little enough for the government to give us after it has taken all our men."

The girl turned to Agnes with a wan smile as she rose to rejoin the long line that had now formed and was beginning to move. "Good-bye!" she said, "I'm going to get something to eat!"

"And I devoutly hope you'll get it—and plenty of it," Agnes replied.

Earlier that morning a delegation of the women had called on Governor Letcher, interrupting his breakfast, to appeal for bread. He had promised to meet with them later. But now the crowd had multiplied. It numbered, by Agnes's calculation, more than a thousand. It had continued to swell until it "reached the dignity of a mob," she wrote Sara.

The mob commandeered carts and wagons on its line of march as it swung along Cary and Main Streets, emptying the stores not only of bread but anything else they could seize. Governor Letcher hurried to the scene to reason with the mob, but they ignored him. He ordered the bell in the old guard tower rung, and he sent Mayor Mayo to read Virginia's Riot Act to the mob. But the mayor was also ignored, and the looting continued. Letcher gave the crowd five minutes to disperse and threatened to fire on them if they didn't. The City Battalion came up Main Street, and the mob fell back. But still they didn't disperse. The state's Public Guard soon followed.

President Davis appeared and climbed onto a dray to address the problem. He was somewhat deprived this morning himself. His best horse had been stolen the night before. Some in the crowd hissed. When his reasoning with the mob failed to make headway, he shouted, "You say you are hungry and have no money. Here is all I have; it is not much, but take it." He emptied his pockets and threw the money to the crowd.[584] Two generals, one of them Sara's acquaintance from the Coyners resort in the mountains, Major General Arnold Elzey, now commanding the Department of Richmond, and Brigadier General John H. Winder, the provost marshal, wished to "suppress the women." But Secretary of War James Seddon declined to issue such an order, and the Public Guard soon broke the riot without firing on the crowd.[585]

"While I write," Agnes wrote Sara, "women and children are still standing in the streets, demanding food, and the government is issuing to them rations of rice. This is a frightful state of things." She told Sara in closing, "Your General has been magnificent. He has fed Lee's army all winter—I wish he could feed our starving women and children."[586]

The so-called bread riot outraged Richmond's city councilmen, who only the day before had held municipal elections. They were proud of what they had been doing for the poor and destitute in the city. In December, believing "it is one of the highest duties of every community to see that the necessities of life are provided for its poor," and that the coming winter was going to be particularly severe, they had appropriated twenty thousand dollars for their care. The council called the bread riot "disgraceful" and "uncalled for" and held that it "did not come from those who are really needy, but from base and unworthy women instigated by worthless men who are a disgrace to the City and the community." The council offered a reward of fifty dollars for the conviction of any individual who was engaged in the riot, and a week later it appropriated another twenty thousand dollars for the worthy poor and destitute in the city and for the families of Richmond's soldiers in the field.[587]

The Confederate economy was disintegrating. Relentless inflation had left many Southerners, particularly the poor, no cover from starvation and destitution. Want was everywhere and there seemed to be little the blockaded South could do about it. The bread riot in Richmond was not an isolated incident. Similar protests were breaking out in other cities in the Confederacy. That same April there were hunger protests in Augusta, Milledgeville, and Columbus in Georgia. In March, in Salisbury, North Carolina, women working in government clothing shops couldn't afford food on the wages they were paid, so they marched on the town's stores and offered the merchants "government prices" for flour, bacon, salt, and molasses. When they were refused, they simply took them.

Mary C. Moore, one of the women, wrote Zebulon B. Vance, the governor of the state, "We are all Soldiers Wives or Mothers. . . . How far will eleven dollars [a Confederate soldier's monthly pay] go in a family now when meat is from 75 to $1 00 pr pound, flour $50 pr bll, wood from 4 to 5$ pr load, meal b[ran] 4 an[d] 5 dollars pr bushel, eggs 50 to 60 cts pr dz . . . Molasses $7 00 pr gal?" She wrote, "We are willing and do work early and late to keep off starvation which is now staring us in the face. But the Government only allows us 50 cents a pr for lined pants and 75 cents for coats and there are few of us who can make over a dollar a day and we have upon an average from three to five helpless children to support. . . . Now Sir how we ask you in the name of God are we to live?"[588]

Governor Vance was a magnet for letters such as that. Women all over the state were writing him, with varying degrees of grammatical sophistication, but with a common anguish: "Governor Vance," another wrote, "i set down to rite you afew lins and pray to god that you will oblige me i ame apore woman with a posel of little children and i wil hav to starv or go neked me and my little children if my husban is kep a way from home much longer ... i beg you to let him come tha dont give me but thre dollars a month and fore of us in famely ... i have knit 40 pare of socks fo the solgers and it take all i can earn to get bread ... if you cud hear the crys of my little children i think you wod fell for us i am pore in this world but i trust rich in heven i trust in god ... and hope he will Cos you to have compashion on the pore."[589] Vance did not ignore such pleas. North Carolina would appropriate $2.5 million to relieve families of poor soldiers in the war.[590]

The week before the bread riot in Richmond, Kate Stone, at Brokenburn plantation in Mississippi, had written in her journal what many in the South now believed: "It is a painful present and a dark future."[591] It was difficult to see any other picture.

CHAPTER 14

A Bizarre Resignation

$\mathcal{T}$he time had come when Roger was no longer needed on the Blackwater and was relieved. That meant that Sara was no longer needed there, either. She and the little boys and the camp chest checked out of the postmaster's house in early 1863, left Charity and the chorus of frogs, and hit the road, refugees again.

They were taken in as temporary boarders by a farmer, without the consent of his wife. And there Sara was "of all women made most miserable." The wife of the house had not wanted refugees and their baggage and their woes in her home. So Roger, after a fleeting visit to her from Richmond, where he was now on duty awaiting reassignment, counseled her to push still farther into the Virginia southland to an old watering place called Amelia Springs.[592] Sara was, in the beginning of this third year of the war, "round-wombed," as Shakespeare had put it—pregnant with their sixth child.[593]

Beyond Amelia Springs the war was raging. Between the middle of December 1862 and the middle of the summer 1863, four epic battles were fought, four cataclysms that rocked the country North and South.

IN NOVEMBER OF 1862, after the battle of Antietam, George McClellan had been sacked by Abraham Lincoln for having "the slows."[594] On December 13, his successor in command of the Army of the Potomac, Ambrose Burnside, had sent that army across the Rappahannock at Fredericksburg, through a midmorning fog, to a monumental disaster. Burnside's main assault had been against James Longstreet's corps entrenched on and at the foot of a ridge called Marye's Heights. To the deafening thunder of cannon, soldiers of the Union army slammed into a wall of murderous fire. Until late afternoon they charged toward the ridge, wave after wave, into a slaughter pen. When the hell ended, Burnside's army recoiled back across the river, beaten, bleeding, and decimated— more than twelve thousand dead, wounded, or missing.

Confederate Captain Charles Blackford wrote his wife, Susan, in Lynchburg, "If the world had been searched by Burnside for a location in which his army could be best defeated and where an attack should *not* have been made he should have selected this very spot."[595]

Captain Blackford, in common with most other rebel soldiers, had problems of his own. The Confederate army in victory was also in tatters, and he was no exception. "I am in daily dread my pantaloons will not stand much longer the strain of this cruel war," he wrote his wife. "To be breechless in this weather and in the face of the enemy will not do." Another of his problems was that Fredericksburg was his old hometown. From Marye's Heights he could see the familiar streets of the city and pick out the yard and the house where he had been born and where they had lived and which he still owned. His town now seemed to him a vast mortuary. It was eerie to see it deserted in this way, with corpses of men and horses lying in the streets.[596]

Confederate losses at Fredericksburg were less than half those of the Union army. But they were losses keenly felt. Sallie Putnam, who had endured in Richmond through the Seven Days battles, wrote, "The vacant chairs were multiplied in Southern homes."

She grieved that "every battle added fresh leaves to the mourning chaplet of the South."[597]

In January of 1863 Burnside set out to cross the Rappahannock again, but the attempt was in vain; bogged down in heavy winter rains, it came to be called "the mud march." By the end of January, the Union Army of the Potomac, cold and dispirited, had had enough of marching and fighting. Both the Union and Confederate armies went into winter quarters, hibernating just a river's width across the Rappahannock from one another.

The Union army got yet another new commander, Joe Hooker, and with a rested command restored above and beyond its former strength and numbers and in fighting trim, he pushed across the river in the final three days of the month of April—into yet another disaster.

Lee was faced again with a host twice his size. But ever the daring innovator, with a penchant for slashing flank-attacks, he again defied all rules of warfare, divided his own smaller army in the face of Hooker's larger one, and sent his brash lieutenant and Second Corps commander, Stonewall Jackson, on a lightning march around the Union right. Jackson struck unexpectedly, as usual, in the early evening of May 2, near a crossroads called Chancellorsville, rolling up the Federal flank and driving a bewildered Hooker all the way back to the banks of the Rappahannock. It was another stunning Confederate victory. The battle of Chancellorsville raged for another two days, ending when Hooker backed away and recrossed the river, commander now not of what he had called the "finest army on the planet,"[598] but of yet another Union army stunned by another monumental defeat. In Washington, Lincoln said, "My God! my God! What will the country say! What will the country say!"[599]

What would Southern women say? "Of the mothers in this town," the poet Margaret Junkin Preston wrote from Lexington on May 5, "almost all of them have sons in this battle; not one lays her head on her pillow this night, sure that her sons are not slain . . . oh!

the sickness of soul with which almost every household in this town awaits the tidings to-morrow may bring."[600]

Ambulances rattled into Richmond late into the night. Kate Rowland and her sister Lizzie went out into the wards with lanterns, tin buckets filled with water, sponges to wet wounded brows, and bandages. "Sounds of misery greeted our ears as we entered," Kate told her diary, "some groaning, others crying like children, and some too weak and suffering to do anything but turn a grateful look upon us as we squeezed the cold water from the sponge over their stiffened and bandaged limbs. Our tears fell fast as we moved from bed to bed, such a sight as it was; the men black with dirt and powder, some barefooted, and every form of wound from the maimed hand and broken arm to the bandaged head with perhaps one or both eyes gone and the poor sufferer drawing slow and painful breath with the fatal ball in the chest. Oh, it was fearful. I had no words to say to them, only prayers and tears."[601]

Again the South had to ask if the victory was worth it—more this time than ever. On the night of his stunning flank attack, one of the most spectacularly successful in military history, Jackson was gunned down by mistake by a regiment in his own corps.

At Guinea Station, behind Chancellorsville, Anna Jackson, wife of the wounded general, watched helplessly at his bedside as he died of pneumonia. And after her husband lay in state before the mourning nation in Richmond, she took him home to Lexington, where he had wanted to be put to rest, and laid him in an as-yet-unmarked grave, in a coffin wrapped in a Confederate flag and heaped with flowers.

Sorrow for his passing convulsed the South. Their paladin had fallen, leaving, one mourner wrote, "a name second to none these times have evoked."[602] "We were all plunged into the deepest grief," Sara later wrote. "By every man, woman, and child in the Confederacy this good man and great general was mourned as never man was mourned before"[603]—mourned "like Rachel weeping for her children."[604] Richmond's city councilmen, who went out as a body to meet Jackson's casket at the rail station and follow it to the governor's mansion, where the mourned hero would lie in state, were so "profoundly impressed with the great calamity" that they refrained "from an attempt at eulogy which no language can adequately express."[605]

Margaret Junkin Preston, in Lexington, Jackson's hometown, was devastated. Jackson was her former brother-in-law. She had loved him. "My heart overflows with sorrow," she cried into her journal. "The grief in this community is intense; everybody is in tears. . . . Oh, the havoc death is making! The beautiful sky and the rich, perfumed spring air seemed darkened by oppressive sorrow. Who thinks or speaks of victory? The word is scarcely ever heard. Alas! Alas! When is the end to be?"[606]

When Jackson fell, something seemed to go out of the Confederate will. "The tide of fortune," Sara wrote, "seemed to turn."[607] Kate Featherston Peddy wrote her husband, from Georgia, "I am so sorry, for he was worth ten thousand men to our cause. I fear it will protract the war longer. It looks like we will soon be ruined any way."[608]

The public sorrow only deepened in Richmond as the wounded from the battlefield at Chancellorsville continued to pour in. During the Sunday service in Saint Paul's Episcopal Church, the sexton walked quietly up the aisle and whispered to worshipers whose loved ones had been brought in wounded, dying, or dead. Pale-faced, they rose and followed him up the aisle and out of the church. Mary Chesnut said that it was "a scene calculated to make the stoutest heart quail."[609]

Shaken by the loss of Jackson, whom he called his "right arm,"[610] but riding a high wave of victory after Chancellorsville, Lee once again invaded the North, this time driving across the mountain passes into Pennsylvania. There in the western outskirts of the prosperous little farm town of Gettysburg, at the hub of eleven roads, he collided with the Union Army of the Potomac once again, now under its fourth commander, Major General

George Gordon Meade. For three days, July 1 through 3, Lee fought Meade, was repulsed, and retreated. His strike at the Union jugular had failed again.

Gettysburg was a telling blow to Southern prospects. "Though our men made a charge which will be the theme of the poet, painter and historian of all ages," Captain Charles Blackford wrote his wife, "they could not maintain the enemy's lines much less capture them. The might of numbers will tell." He told her, "the outlook is very far from bright, and this looks much to me as the turning point of the war. As we were the invading party at Gettysburg and made the attack, our failure to carry the enemy's lines amounted to defeat."[611]

Seventeen-year-old Susan Bradford wrote in her diary the last day of the battle, "Another telegram brings more news from Gettysburg—such awful news—death and destruction and perhaps defeat. God help our poor country. Holding my breath I listen and tears come, though I try to be calm. So many of our brave men, who went forward can never come back. Oh, this horrible, horrible WAR!"[612]

The charge and repulse on the third day at Gettysburg, Nellie Gray wrote in her diary, "goes down in history along with Balaklava and Thermoplae. There were more vacant chairs in Virginia, already desolate—there were more broken hearts for which Heaven alone held balm."[613]

Roger Pryor was in Richmond, serving on a court-martial board, when reports of the battle arrived from the front. That evening he called on President and Mrs. Davis and was told that the president was unavailable, but that Mrs. Davis would be pleased to receive him. It was intensely hot in Richmond, as July often was, and Roger felt he mustn't impose a long visit on Mrs. Davis. But she seemed unwilling to be alone, and as he rose to leave, she begged him to stay. After a few moments Davis appeared, "weary, silent, and depressed." Soon the Davis family favorite, Little Joe, barely five years old, entered, in his robe, and kneeled at his father's knee for his evening prayers. The boy repeated a prayer of thankfulness and supplication for God's blessing on the country. Davis laid a hand on the boy's head when he had finished, and said, "Amen."[614]

Denied once again, Lee took his battered army back across the river into Virginia. The losses in the three-day battle, the largest of any in the war, staggered the South. More than twenty thousand Confederate soldiers, a third of Lee's entire force, were killed, wounded, or missing. Even though the Union army had suffered more, over twenty-three thousand casualties, it was small consolation for Lee and the South.

More, even worse, news came on the heels of that from Gettysburg. As the battle was opening on that first day in Pennsylvania, it was apparent in the west that Confederate Vicksburg, under siege for two months by the Union army of Ulysses S. Grant, could not hold out much longer. The city had reached the end of its endurance. Kate Stone, who lived at Brokenburn, the cotton plantation thirty miles northwest of Vicksburg, had been awaking mornings "to the booming of cannon" and going to sleep "to the same music." She found herself too near "'the pomp and circumstance of glorious war' to find it pleasant."[615] She was about to find it more unpleasant still.

At Amelia Springs, there had been little room or little occasion for gaiety for Sara and her fellow refugee women and their children. But on July 4 the proprietor proposed that the ballroom be lit and that a fiddler, a barber in everyday life, play dance tunes to brighten the night. Young feet couldn't resist a waltz or polka beat, and the floor was soon filled with what Sara called "care-forgetting maidens." There were no men there—except the fiddler and the proprietor—giving the stag dance a different, and feminine, twist. A telegram came for the proprietor, and the women stopped dancing to huddle together under the chandelier to hear it read. It told them Vicksburg had fallen—starved into submission. "Surely and swiftly," Sara thought, "the coil was tightening around us. Surely and swiftly would we, too, be starved into submission."[616]

Annie Harper, in Natchez, where the loss of the river was life-threatening, viewed the fall of Vicksburg as "the first notes of the Confederacy's death knell rung with clanging harshness on our ears."[617]

She was right. When Vicksburg capitulated and Port Hudson, downriver, surrendered five days later, the last bastions on the Mississippi fell, and Lincoln said, "The Father of Waters again goes unvexed to the sea."[618] The Confederacy was sliced in half down the big river. The trans-Mississippi West was cut off militarily from the main body. It was a catastrophe transcending even Gettysburg.

Captain Charles Blackford, with Lee's army, felt and deplored the plunge into despair that followed. "Our sky is dark," he wrote Susan, "and the worst feature is that our people seem to be letting down. We have had only our first reverses, yet many people have gone into a fainting fit. The press seems to take infinite delight in publishing everything to increase the depression and chill the enthusiasm of the army. The Richmond 'Enquirer,' I observe, speaks of the present as comparable with the darkest days of the Revolution, and, with apparent glee, quotes the price of gold as an indication of our condition. The language of the 'Enquirer' I regard as treason."[619]

Yet, it had been the gloomiest July of the war. Mary Chesnut was not alone starting her days asking, "What bad news next, I wonder?"[620]

ROGER PRYOR WAS in his own personal funk, in Richmond. He had had about all he could stand of military foot-dragging. Through the winter his discontent had widened to embrace more than just the Federal threat in his front. He believed he had performed well in the Blackwater. But his military record raised mixed reviews. Many agreed with him that he had done well at Suffolk. One of his soldiers wrote home, "A more energetic, vigilant, & ju-

diciously brave officer I have never seen. Since he has been in command, we have been upon the march nearly half the time. I have a
high opinion of his competency & earnestness of patriotism."[621]

Major General French praised Roger for his "successful defense
of that frontier" with his small command.[622] However, the action at
Kelly's farm, near Suffolk, had come to be viewed by some in the
Confederate war department as "a useless battle, with unfortunate
results," and Roger's conduct in command of the Confederate
troops in that engagement was being called into question.[623]

After he had left Suffolk early in the year, several officers in his
command wrote Jefferson Davis, protesting his departure, calling
it a "great injustice," and praising Roger as "one of the ablest generals in the service." They wrote that "placed in command on a
line that has been constantly threatened," he "has conducted the
campaign with such energy, vigor, & skill, as to keep the enemy in
constant terror of attack." They praised him for displaying "so
much gallantry & dash tempered by such prudence & ceaseless
vigilance that the enemy has not only been kept at bay, but have
been driven within their quarters & made to keep a large force for
their protection, which might otherwise have been used for offensive operations at other points on the Confederate lines."[624] Residents in the Blackwater also wrote protesting his departure and
urging his reinstatement, calling his removal "a very serious loss,"
and praising him for giving them protection and saving their property from falling into enemy hands.[625]

But these pleas and petitions brought nothing. By summer
Roger was convinced he was going nowhere in the army. For
months he had been without assignment or brigade, and it was becoming more and more apparent he would never get either, no
matter how hard he lobbied. He had missed Fredericksburg, Chancellorsville, and Gettysburg. The war, which he had done so much
to help detonate, was exploding on without him.

Roger had shown himself utterly courageous and a man of
many talents, but commanding troops in battle apparently wasn't

one of them. He was perhaps better liked by Union soldiers whom he had captured than by many of his own men whom he commanded—hardly a formula for success in one's own army.

Through the winter and spring he had worn out the mails, reminding the secretary of war of his promise of a permanent command. Roger thought he had earned it, after service at Williamsburg, Seven Pines, Mechanicsville, Gaines' Mill, Frayser's Farm, Second Manassas, Sharpsburg, and on the Blackwater. On April 6 he wrote a passionate plea to President Davis himself, complaining that more than a month had passed since he was relieved, with no word of his next assignment. He asked to be returned to active service and not "denied participation in the struggles that are soon to determine the destinies of my country." He argued, "If I know myself, it is not the vanity of command that moves me to this present appeal, but a single and sincere wish to contribute somewhat to the success of our cause."[626]

Friendly fellow officers supported him, urging not only that the army not lose his services, but identifying certain regiments that might easily be assigned him to make up a brigade. Davis was not unsympathetic. He wrote courteous replies, repeating assurances of esteem and telling his secretary of war that Roger "is entitled to a Brigade."[627] But brigades continued to go to officers junior to him. The *Richmond Examiner* and other newspapers began nosing into the matter and picturing Roger as one of a cabal of officers opposing the administration. Roger wrote Davis, assuring him that wasn't true. Davis wrote back gratefully, "The good opinion of one so competent to judge of public affairs, and who has known me so long and closely is a great support in the midst of many and arduous trials."[628]

Finally Roger was finished begging. He had been "dancing attendance in the anterooms for six months, waiting assignment to command," John Jones, the war department clerk, wrote. It appeared to be, as Jones said, "The government don't like aspiring political generals."[629]

On July 15 Roger wrote Davis another letter. "I have considered, calmly and deliberately, what course I should pursue under the circumstances," he told the president, "and my reluctant conclusion is that I have no choice but to resign." This bombshell was immediately followed by another; he was reenlisting as a private. "Perhaps as a Private in the ranks I may be able to render some little service," he said. Count on Sara's husband to do something not only unexpected, but wholly bizarre.[630]

THE FIRST HALF of August brought intemperate heat across the country. At no time day or night did the temperature drop below eighty degrees. Sara had spent long sultry nights in Amelia Springs, nursing her little boys through distressing paroxysms of whooping cough. She was asleep, after a long wakeful night, when she heard Roger's voice, as in a dream. She opened her eyes and saw he was real, seated beside her on the bed.

He urged her to hear him out and bear with patience what he was about to tell her. First, he must leave in an hour to catch the train back to Richmond. Then he told her he had resigned his commission as a brigadier and was enroute to join Fitzhugh Lee's cavalry as a private and a scout.

If this was astonishing news to the world, it was bitter news for Sara. He was slipping away from her again. She implored him, begged him to "stay with me and the children."

"No," he told her. "I had something to do with bringing on this war. I must give myself to Virginia. She needs the help of all her sons. If there are too many brigadier-generals in the service—it may be so—certain it is there are not enough private soldiers."

When his hour was up, he kissed his sleeping boys and hurried to catch the stage to the rail station. After he left, Sara was alone again, as she had been so often in this war, in circumstances now doubly "hard to bear."[631]

CHAPTER 15

———— •◦• ————

War at the Door

*R*oger reported to the Third Virginia Cavalry, Company E—the Nottoway Troop: all friends, hometowners, and admirers—at its campsite on the Rappahannock, on August 25. He fell in at retreat and answered the call of his name, like any private. Then the band of the Second Virginia Cavalry came over that evening, serenaded him—unlike what it would do for just any private—called him out, and he delivered a speech.[632]

Fitzhugh Lee, Roger's new commanding officer, found this self-demotion from general to private somewhat perplexing. Lee was a gifted cavalryman, a nephew of Robert E. Lee, and only twenty-nine years old. He had graduated from West Point, in 1856, where he distinguished himself more for his horsemanship than for his scholarship. He was "overflowing with animal spirits" and was in his element as a brigadier of cavalry, a bachelor, and a "gay cavalier of ladies." He was short, thickset, and drifting toward stoutness. He had a square head and short neck set on broad shoulders, and "a merry eye and a joyous voice of great power," given to singing corn-shucking tunes."[633]

Lee welcomed his new private with a question. On August 26, after Roger had reported for duty, Lee sent him a note: "*Honorable, General, or Mr.*: How shall I address you?" Then, in his usual joyous style, he concluded, "Damn it, there's no difference! Come up to see me. Whilst I regret the causes that induced you to resign your position, I am glad that the country has not lost your active services, and that your choice to serve her has been cast in one of my regiments."[634]

SOON AFTER ROGER LEFT Sara, to report to Fitz Lee, her stay at Amelia Springs ended. It was decided that she should return to Charlotte County, to Aunt Mary, to give birth and wait out the end of the war—as long as it took. Their oldest son, Theodorick, and their two girls, Marie Gordon and Mary, were already there. But marauding parties and guerrillas were everywhere, blocking the way. After repeated failed attempts, she decided to return instead to Petersburg, their old home, and find sanctuary there. She reached Petersburg in the autumn as the leaves were turning.

The autumn weather was dreamlike. In Richmond, twenty miles from Petersburg, Sallie Putnam reveled in "the bracing atmosphere, the delicious, dreamy influence of the beautiful Indian summer." But it could not, she believed, "chase from our doors the dread phantom that lurked on the threshold."

As this third winter of war approached, the capital city itself, Sallie noted, was "growing rusty, dilapidated," and taking on "a war-worn appearance." The Confederate currency was dilapidated and war-worn as well, "frightfully depreciating, (an old story), we were wholly at the mercy of avaricious speculators, (a story quite as old), food was scarce, fuel was scarce"—among so many other things—"and we saw no means of relief in the power of those in authority over us." Richmond, Sallie believed, had "never known such a scarcity of food—such absolute want of the necessaries of life." Fat bacon and Indian peas, sweetened by a dessert of sorghum syrup and cornbread, had become standard fare—a plunging comedown from the elegant menus of antebellum days. The lack of genuine coffee was as irritating as any hardship the South was suffering, and brewing up a halfway satisfactory replacement was taxing human ingenuity. Rye, rice, wheat, potatoes, beans, ground nuts, Chinese sugarcane, chicory, okra seed, sorghum seed, roasted and parched yam, parched corn or parched meal, asparagus—virtually anything that remotely suggested coffee—was resorted to as a substitute. "But after every experiment to make coffee of what was not coffee," Sallie complained, "we were driven to decide that there was nothing coffee but coffee." Articles of clothing that managed to squeeze through the Union blockade were so dear that they were unaffordable. Confederate soldiers on the battlefield fought without shoes, were short of blankets, and subsisted on "the meanest and most scanty fare."[635]

More and more Southern territory was falling into Federal hands and becoming "Yankeedom,"[636] turning the South into a republic of refugees—"fugees," they called themselves,[637] "roughugees," the soldiers called them.[638]

No city in the Confederacy had more of these fugees than Richmond. Since the second year of the war, its "floating population" matched or exceeded its permanent one.[639] But the homelessness was Confederacy-wide. Kate Stone was herself a fugee, forced from Brokenburn plantation in Mississippi after the fall of Vicksburg. She had fled westward over the river into Texas, where "night came on apace wrapped in her sable mantle and unbrightened by a star." She called such as she "storm-tossed wanderers," on "our journey to the unknown."[640]

Tryphena Fox, a Northern transplant to a plantation in Louisiana, wrote her mother in Pittsfield, Massachusetts, on the last day of the battle of Gettysburg, "Oh! Mother! you northern people know nothing of the horrors of war.... Our home is gone— everything there destroyed.... We own nothing now but our clothing & but very little of that." In another letter she wrote, "You have no idea, Mother, how many homeless wanderers this war has caused—wanderers who have been accustomed to every comfort, how deprived of everything & now, know not where to lay their heads." Tryphena in the past year had been stripped not just "of my home & home comforts, of servants, & everything but a little clothing," but "of one of my darlings [a daughter dead of scarlet fever]." But, she sadly wrote, "All of these are nothing when compared with what the next year may take from me."[641]

Susan Blackford wrote from Lynchburg to her husband, in Lee's army, "I must leave to a tenant this delightful home, where I have been so happy and which is endeared to me by a thousand tender associations, and become a homeless wanderer, without even the cheering hope of seeing you. I would not mind it so much if the house was to be shut up, but the thought that strangers are to wander through it, and that the roses are to bloom only for others, makes me very sad."[642]

In Petersburg Sara was very much marching in this army of refugees. She drifted about with her two little boys, seeking a place at a welcoming hearthside. Many of her old friends had left town and had already rented their houses to strangers and other refugees, or left them to the homeless among their own kin. There seemed no room anywhere for Sara, her boys, and their small purse, growing smaller each day. Finally, a brother-in-law offered her a vacant overseer's house on a property he owned. Such quarters bordered on squalid, but the arrangement would only be temporary until one of his town houses became vacant for her.

When Sara drove out to the little house, she found it scarcely more than a hovel. Its kitchen was unplastered, smoke-blackened, and windowless, with loose, gap-toothed planks for a floor, and the bare earth visible beneath. A door opened into a small room with a fireplace, a window, and another door. A short flight of stairs led to an unplastered attic. The house was tenanted by wasps, which had lived there unchallenged for months. So Sara retreated outdoors while a boy on the place made a smudge to drive them away. She borrowed bedding from her relative for the pine bedstead and the low trundle bed underneath. When the trundle bed was drawn out at night, there was no place in the little room to stand, and nothing could be done but to go to bed. For furniture there were a few wooden chairs and a small table. There were no curtains, carpet, or rugs, and no china. There was firewood on a woodpile and a small hoard of meal and rice and a bit of bacon in the overseer's grubby closet. In a nearby cabin lived a woman named Mary and her mate, whom Sara would only know as "Mary's husband," who were in charge of the property. It was an unpromising haven, but it was to be their new winter home, and it was better than nothing.[643] As Kate Cumming had written in her diary, "War is a great leveler, and makes philosophers of us, when nothing else will."[644]

Sara was to find a measure of both solace and philosophy in a new neighbor but old friend, Lucy Laighton. Lucy, a granddaughter of Patrick Henry, soon became a constant comfort to Sara. Sara remembered Lucy as being a brilliant young girl. She and her husband, a Northern man, were "very cultivated, very poor, very kind." Lucy's heart "went out in love and compassion" to Sara, taking it on herself to teach her friend to deal with scarcity. She also helped hold Sara's soul together. Her talk became "a tonic," stimulating Sara to endure with courage.

Lucy taught Sara to float tea on top of a cup of hot water to make it go further than when steeped in the usual way. Every morning she sent Sara a pat of butter the size of a silver dollar, with two or three biscuits and sometimes a bowl of persimmons or stewed dried peaches. Lucy had a cow, and every day she churned its milk into buttermilk for biscuits. It was too precious to drink straight.[645]

A fierce winter tempest lashed Virginia a day or two before Christmas, and Sara's little boys kindled a roaring fire in the cold, unwelcoming kitchen, roasted chestnuts, and set forlorn traps for rabbits and snowbirds. The boys made no complaint about a Christmas as bereft of gifts as their traps were of prey. On Christmas day Sara mended their clothes—there was no material from which to stitch new ones. But she was not "all unhappy." Just having her little boys with her at this bare fireside was consolation for her destitution, and something in her "proudly rebelled against weakness or complaining."

By midnight snow was falling thickly around the little hovel, and Sara suddenly felt very ill. She sent for Mary's husband and begged him to ride to Petersburg three miles away to fetch the doctor. When the doctor arrived she was in desperate pain. "It doesn't matter much for me, Doctor!" she whispered. "But my husband will be grateful if you keep me alive."

When she woke from what seemed to her a wakeless sleep begun "ages ago," the doctor was standing at the foot of her bed, where she had left him. She reached out her hand, and it touched a little warm bundle swaddled beside her. She had delivered a baby girl—a "little stranger."[646] The doctor spoke to her gravely but kindly. "I must leave you now," he said, "and, alas! I cannot come again. There are so many, so many sick. Call all your courage to your aid. Remember the pioneer women, and all they were able to survive."

A woman named Anarchy was in the room with the doctor. She was Mary's friend and had done occasional chores for Sara. The doctor gestured toward Anarchy and said, "This woman is a field-hand, but she is a mother, and she has agreed to help you during the Christmas holidays—her own time. And now, God bless you, and good-by!"

Sara lapsed again into sleep, and when she awoke, "the very Angel of Strength and Peace had descended and abode with me." She resolved to prove to herself that "if I was called to be a great woman, I *could* be a great woman." Staring at her from the bedside were her little boys. They had been taken the night before across the snow to her brother-in-law's house but had awakened at daybreak and "come home to take care" of her.

Eliza Page, Sara's longtime maid, had fallen ill, and Julia, her only remaining servant, had left on Christmas morning, saying she was too lonesome to stay. So Sara hired Anarchy at twenty-five dollars a week for all of her nights. But Anarchy's hands, gnarled by work in the cornfields, were too knotted and rough to touch the baby's delicate skin, so Sara, propped up on pillows, dressed her herself, sometimes fainting from the effort.[647]

Three weeks after the baby was born, Sara was still bedridden. One of her boys, startled by the approach of an apparition he didn't recognize, ran before it into the house shouting, "Oh, mamma, an old gray soldier is coming in!"

The "old gray soldier" entered Sara's bedroom and stood leaning on his saber, staring at her. "Is this the reward my country gives me?" he demanded.

Not until he said those words did Sara recognize Roger. Turning on his heel, he strode out of the house, shouting for John, his manservant.

"John! John!" he shouted. "Take those horses into town and sell them! Do not return until you do so—sell them for anything! Get a cart and bring butter, eggs, and everything you can find for Mrs. Pryor's comfort."

John, who had been with the Pryors a long time, didn't construe so literally this urgent order to sell all the horses. He sold all but Jubal Early, Roger's favorite gray.

Roger had been riding Jubal Early with Fitzhugh Lee's cavalry, tramping through the snow after William Averell's Union cavalry. Roger had suffered through cold and hunger himself, sleeping on the coverless ground, sharing his blanket with John, and using his own horses. He was without furlough and must soon report again for duty. But before he did, he moved Sara and the boys into town into one of their relative's houses that had become vacant in the new year. To shield her somewhat from falling again into so sad and destitute a situation, Roger purchased three hundred dollars in gold—"that universal talisman"[648]—and Sara stitched a girdle to wear about her waist, concealed beneath her gown. The coins were quilted in, each in separate compartments so that with scissors she could extract them one at a time without disturbing what was left.[649]

FROM THE BEGINNING of the war, Petersburg had been shielded from the direct shot, shell, and wreckage raking much of the rest of the South. Petersburg's women had continued tirelessly to listen for the long train whistle and to greet battle-bound soldiers with flowers, fruit, and refreshments, denying themselves every luxury to do it. The tread of marching feet was a familiar beat in the streets, but no enemy footsteps had been heard there, nor had any enemy gun been fired within the city limits. War's angry thunder had been heard afar, from Big Bethel, Seven Pines, and the Seven Days battles around Richmond. But it had been a low growling distant thunder. Petersburg was "a near neighbor" to war, but not of it.[650]

Yet living was hard. The city was virtually cut off now from much of the outside world, and only inadequate supplies were being smuggled in for its crowded host of refugees. Its main highway, the James River, bristled with Federal gunboats enforcing the Union blockade. Markets had long been closed and the stores of supplies exhausted.[651]

Everything was dear—butter cost eight dollars a pound, meat four to five dollars a pound—and that was breathtakingly cheap, Sara would soon learn, compared to prices yet to come. From Agnes's letters Sara supposed Petersburg was suffering more from scarcity than Richmond, where cabinet members were still hosting elaborate dinners and serving wine, as of old. In Petersburg, Sara observed, "We had already entered upon our long season of want." The town had been drained by its women's unselfish gifts to the soldiers—the wounded and those just passing through.[652]

Yet, ironically, never had Petersburg seemed healthier. No garbage was left rotting in the streets. Every scrap of animal or vegetable matter was consumed, the streets swept clean. Flocks of hungry pigeons strutted and cooed after children who were eating bread or crackers and dropping crumbs. Finally, the pigeons themselves vanished, sharing the fate of the bread. People were down to dining on mice and rats, which President Davis had suggested were as tasty as squirrels. But the rats and mice, too, soon disappeared. Caterwauling and emaciated cats staggered about the streets, on the edge of starvation. An ounce of meat a day apiece was a family's ration. Cows, pigs, wheat—anything walking, flying, sitting, or growing that was edible—were either consumed by their owners or stolen from them. Eggs were snatched from nests, and the sitting hens with them.[653]

Making something do for something else had become an art form in the South's world of scarcity. Besides anything and everything interloping as coffee, raspberry, huckleberry, blackberry, and holly leaves were being brewed for tea. Corncob ashes were going for baking soda. Homemade dyes were coloring what cloth Southern women could get their hands on. Indigo plants were making shades of blue, red-oak bark was making red, buds of sweet gum were making purple. Butternut hues were being mixed from barks of certain trees and from walnut hulls. Pokeberry juice was bringing what dark color it could to the everpresent homespun. A rich garnet could be distilled from pine roots, and grays from myrtle bushes. However, "the color most needed in this war-stricken land," Susan Bradford wrote in Florida, "was black, and there is nothing more difficult to dye."[654] Oak-gall juice and sumac were going for ink. Persimmon seeds were making buttons, and thorns were substituting for pins. Cotton seed and ground peas and lard were making kerosene. Wood, cloth, felt, old carpets, and canvas were being turned into shoes. Hats were being fashioned from palmetto straw, rye, wheat, and longleaf pine needles. Medicines, in desperate undersupply, were being concocted from what grew in the fields or by the side of the roads—ironweed for quinine; sassafras, pennnyroyal, and mountain mint for health-restoring teas; willow-bark powder for chills; dried mullein leaves, smoked in a pipe, for asthma; crushed poppy seeds to ease pain.[655]

Roger had left John with Sara and the children. Installed as the little family's chief cook and commissary-general, John was working his culinary magic by virtual sleight-of-hand, from the barest ingredients—no fixings but flour, rice, peas, and dried apples, and such grease or shortening as he could coax from bones he wrangled from the quartermaster, and sorghum molasses. Yet he managed to produce such treats as waffles and pancakes.[656]

Many of the families that had fled Petersburg at the time of McClellan's march on Richmond had since returned. But they had not brought back with them the city's accustomed gaiety—too many of her sons had been slain or were in present danger of being so. And even with these returnees, Petersburg had become virtually a city of old men, women, and children.[657]

Sara's next-door neighbors now were Thomas Branch and a pastor, the Reverend Churchill Gibson. Across the street lived a widow with three daughters. Down the street lived the Bollings, parents of "the superb" Tabb Bolling, the fiancée of Rooney Lee, one of Robert E. Lee's sons. Also in the neighborhood were the William Banisters, with their houseful of beautiful daughters.[658]

"What friends you girls are!" Sara said to these young daughters of her neighbors when she met them walking and talking together.

"We are all going to be old maids together," said one of them, "and so we are getting acquainted with each other."

"Well! it will be no disgrace to be an old maid," said another. "We can always swear our going-to-be-husband was killed in the war."

A sad, wistful look stole over their young faces as each remembered an absent lover.[659]

But wistfulness was fleeting in young hearts. "We'd be crying our eyes out over the accounts of deaths and wounds in some battle," one Alabama beauty confessed, "when suddenly, we'd hear a band—and away we'd fly, wiping our eyes as we went, and laughing and joking the minute we caught sight of brass buttins and the confederate grey. If ever men were 'run after,' southern soldiers were."[660]

Girls with "peach blossom cheeks and May-cherry lips,"[661] had become a serious problem for some of the young boys left behind, too young yet to wear Confederate gray. Kate Stone in Mississippi, wrote of girls who had their "'trot lines' out for all these boys."[662] One of these put-upon teenage boys wrote his bachelor uncle in the army: "I am still flying around with the girls. I tell you they keep me sterred up. I went to a meting . . . at Union and coming home I had to keep company with about a dozen girls and you know that they keep me stirede up. I want you to make haste and kill these old Yankies by Christmas and come home to help me out for I tell you that I have my hands full."[663]

The young girls who visited Sara never complained of the lack of food, but they grieved greatly over their fashionless wardrobes. A fashion essential, the common pin, had become as scarce as food. The girls walked about the city with eyes cast down, mining the ground for strays. Thorns were gathered and dried and substituted for them—anything to keep cloth together and appearances up.

It went to prove, Sara thought, that "the desire for ornament is an instinct of our nature, outliving the grosser affections for the good things of the table." She had often heard that the consciousness of being well dressed "will afford a peace of mind far exceeding anything to be derived from the comforts of religion."[664] She believed it.

ANOTHER SPRING HAD come to the South. But hanging over this one was an unspringlike malaise. Mary Chesnut wrote in her diary, "We are rattling downhill—and nobody to put on the brakes."[665]

A mother in South Carolina whose boy, her only child, had gone to the war, mourned, "With the coming spring instead of peace and joy, when the earth is all beautiful and smiling, we are told to prepare for another fierce attack of our cruel foe and more carnage and blood and slaughter await us. My heart sickens at the thought."[666] The *Richmond Whig* wrote, "Even in times of peace the spring months are months of scarcity. Now they are months of distress."[667]

The war itself was again nearer at hand for Richmond and Petersburg. Distant cannonading now rattled windows in Richmond. Elizabeth Van Lew, a Federal spy and spinster wed to the Union and living a risky undercover life in the Confederate capital, wrote in her "occasional journal," "One cannot imagine the gloom of this place now. Since Monday the atmosphere has been heavy with the smoke of battle. The stores are all closed. We are not to be seen upon the streets. . . . Oh death and carnage so near!" She was awakened May 14 by cannon fire. "We are on the eve of fearful bloodshed," she predicted in her journal.[668]

Storm clouds rolled in over Richmond midmonth, and in the pauses of heavenly lightning and thunder could be heard the distant rumble of earthly artillery. In June, Phoebe Pember, a Confederate nurse, wrote, "For the last three weeks there has been no day or night that the booming of cannon has not been the last sound at night and the first in the morning."[669]

Although the hard hand of war itself had so far spared Petersburg, there was a sense as spring turned toward summer in 1864 that the exemption was about to be revoked. The Federals were stalking the Virginia southside. It was perhaps symbolic that Ben Butler, notorious throughout the South as "Beast Butler," was at City Point, scant miles away, far too close for comfort.

"This brings the War *very* near my home," Georgiana Walker wrote, "only ten miles from Petersburg. . . . Things are assuming a terrible reality, the enemy is very near our Capitol, & truly it is now, with us fighting or death!"[670]

In early May, Ulysses S. Grant, the new general in chief of the Union armies, had crossed the Rappahannock with his multitudes and marched into the Wilderness, a "tangle of honeysuckle and laurel, wild grape and Virginia creeper, impenetrable depths of shadow and fragrance."[671] There he had engaged Lee's Army of Northern Virginia, half the size of his own, in a fire-blasted opening battle of the new spring campaign. Fighting had raged since then between the two armies, in a running battle from the Wilderness to Spotsylvania, Grant trying unsuccessfully—so far—to slip around Lee's right, roll him back, and power his way into Richmond.

The capital was bracing, expecting the worst. "Never," Maria Smith Peek had written her soldier husband-to-be on May 16, "has Richmond been in such a state of excitement as within the last ten days, and never before have we had so great cause for alarm. The Yankees are menacing us on all sides and not a day passes over our heads but that we hear the roar of artillery."[672]

In early June, Grant hit Lee at Cold Harbor, on Richmond's outskirts, with a luckless head-on assault that lost him seven thousand men in lightning time, another deadly, frustrating repulse for Northern arms. But Grant was not retreating, and the days following Cold Harbor were quiet and charged with suspense. Confederate and Federal soldiers wondered what Grant would do next, where he would land the next blow, and how long could Lee hold him at bay.

SARA BELIEVED "no lovelier day ever dawned" than Thursday, June 9, 1864, in Petersburg. The previous few days had been somewhat rainy, but this one was a day that sang to the soul. The magnolia grandiflora, as Southern as she was, was in full flower. Honey locusts, kissed by bees, perfumed the warm summer air, nearly overriding the peachy fragrance of the microphyllous roses. Jasmine garlands drooped gracefully over trellised front porches throughout the city. The morning was so sweet, fragrant, and bright that the women and children of the city were out in the streets, running errands and visiting friends.[673]

ROGER PRYOR IN THE 1850S
Horace Greeley called him the
"eloquent tribune of Virginia,"
widely seen as a firebrand of
secession.   *Library of Congress*

SARA PRYOR IN AN 1855 PORTRAIT
In Washington they called her "the
beautiful *brune*" with soft brown hair
and eyes.   *Virginia Historical Society*

FRANKLIN PIERCE
The young president asked
Roger for advice about his
inaugural address, and
made Sara proud.
Library of Congress

HENRY A. WISE
Running for governor of
Virginia in 1855, he looked like
"a corpse galvanized," but he
was a slayer of Know-Nothings.
Library of Congress

STEPHEN A. DOUGLAS
"The Little Giant,"
senator from Illinois,
was Roger's friend and
Sara's admirer.
Library of Congress

ADELE CUTTS DOUGLAS
Stephen Douglas's wife, she
and Sara became more than
"pasteboard friends."
Library of Congress

ON THE DUELING GROUND
Dueling was a common recourse for settling scores, as indicated in this drawing of the period, when Roger and the code of honor seemed made for each other.   *Library of Virginia*

JAMES BUCHANAN
Sara whispered to him, "Mr. President,
South Carolina has seceded."
Library of Congress

HARPER'S WEEKLY.

JOURNAL OF CIVILIZATION

Vol. V.—No. 227.] NEW YORK, SATURDAY, MAY 4, 1861. [SINGLE COPIES SIX CENTS.
$2 50 PER YEAR IN ADVANCE.

Entered according to Act of Congress, in the Year 1861, by Harper & Brothers, in the Clerk's Office of the District Court for the Southern District of New York.

THE HOUSE-TOPS IN CHARLESTON DURING THE BOMBARDMENT OF SUMTER.

ON THE ROOFTOPS OF CHARLESTON
Charlestonians watched the bombardment of Fort Sumter with
"palpitating hearts and pallid faces." *Library of Virginia*

CONFEDERATE WOMEN HOUNDING THEIR MEN TO WAR
They were "gushing patriotism," spewing fire like lava from Vesuvius.
Museum of the Confederacy

LISTENING FOR THE FIRST GUN
On the tracks to Manassas hearing the dreaded sound of war.
Library of Virginia

CONFEDERATE WOMEN NURSING THE WOUNDED
Every woman was "ready to rush into the Florence Nightingale business."
Library of Virginia

◀ THE JAMES RIVER
Virginia's main thoroughfare, Sara called it "the romantic river of our
country." *Library of Virginia*

RICHMOND BREAD RIOT
One of the marchers in this April, 1863, protest said, "We are celebrating
our right to live." *Library of Virginia*

SOUTHERN REFUGEES
There were tens of thousands of "fugees," as they called themselves, "storm-tossed wanders" on "a journey to the unknown."
Museum of the Confederacy

CONFEDERATE WOMEN IN MOURNING
"What, oh God," they thought, "if I should never see him more!"
Museum of the Confederacy

ROGER AND SARA'S PETERSBURG
The war finally came to its door in June, 1864.
Library of Congress

THE FALL OF RICHMOND
An "immense tongue of fire was devouring the city."
Library of Congress

LINCOLN IN RICHMOND
To Sara's friend he seemed old and tired and ugly, but the blacks cheered
him through the streets. *Library of Virginia*

SARA—THE NEW YORK YEARS
A memorial in *Harper's Weekly*
said, "Bravely, tenderly,
hopefully, she had lived through
great events." *Library of Congress*

ROGER—THE FIRE OF
REBELLION STILLED
"New York received him
gladly, and in time, honored
him greatly," recalled a
memorial tribute.
*Museum of Hampden-Sydney
College*

Just before nine o'clock Anthony Keiley, a thirty-one-year-old lawyer and member of the Virginia General Assembly, a former lieutenant in the army, wounded at Malvern Hill and now exempt from military duty, was sitting in his office reading the morning papers from Richmond, eager for any scrap of news that might tell him of "the situation."

Abruptly, at nine o'clock Petersburg's bells began to peal, interrupting his reading. Keiley reckoned that "all the available bell metal in the corporation broke into chorus with so vigorous a peal and a clangor so resonant, as to suggest to the uninitiated a general conflagration." Usually such an uproar signaled fire. But Keiley also knew, given the times, it could herald the approach of another kind of "devouring element—the Yankees."

He dropped his newspapers and, "in most indecent haste," ran out into the street and confronted the first passerby, demanding to know what all the bell-ringing meant. His excited informant shouted that enemy cavalry, numbering some twenty thousand, were approaching the city down the Jerusalem Plank Road and were within two miles of where the two of them now stood.

Keiley calculated that even discounting the estimate by the usual 75 percent, it was a very uncomfortable prospect. "What forces have we on the Jerusalem Plank Road?" he demanded, "do you know?"

"Not a d———n man except [Col. Fletcher H.] Archer's Battalion," the passerby said, "and not a hundred and fifty of them."

Keiley noted parenthetically that they had not had a revival of religion in the city for some time and that Confederate whiskey would make a nun swear. He also knew that Archer's Battalion was but a militia organization armed for local defense. It consisted of old men crowding sixty and beyond, and young boys under eighteen— a cadre of leftover, uniformed, and ill-armed "non-conscribables" least fit for military service. "Here," Keiley thought, "was what the gentleman of the prize ring would call 'another bloody go.'"

Keiley locked his office door, called by his house to "replenish my commissariat," and set out on the run "prepared (morally speaking) to do battle *a l'outrance,* against all comers of the Yankee persuasion." He confessed to being "somewhat puzzled to know 'wither I should go.'" He was equally vague about what he might do when he got there. But it seemed to him the most useful place to be was "obviously the line of the enemy's approach." And that was with Archer's Battalion, posted about a mile southeast of the cemetery.[674]

As the news heralded by the bells spread across town, its male citizens, either far too old for fighting—or far too young—were dropping everything and running, like Keiley, in the direction of the Jerusalem Plank Road.

The town druggist, old, but not too old, pulled on his battle gear, and charged his partner, older than he, to watch the shop in his absence. "Now," the druggist said, "if you want anything done at home you must talk to somebody else! I am going to the front! I'm just like General Lee. I should be glad if these fellows would go back to their homes and let us alone, but if they won't they must be made to, that's all." His partner, though aged, had a mind of his own and was soon hurrying home to get his musket as well, the drugstore be damned.

William Banister, Sara's neighbor, was the president of the Exchange Bank. He was highly esteemed, even venerable—but frail and half deaf. He was in his office at the bank when the bells began to peal. His wife and two of his daughters, Mollie and Anne, hoped that the old man hadn't heard them. He hadn't. But he did hear soon about what was up. He went home at once, shouldered his musket, and told his loved ones he was headed for the front, wherever that was. They begged him not to go, for he would be unable to hear the orders.

"If I can't hear," he said, "I can fight—I can fire a gun. This is no time for any one to stand back. Every one that can shoulder a musket must fight. The enemy are now right upon us."[675] He marched away, one who saw him go said, "erect as a Mohawk chief . . . full of patriot fire." With his rifle and blanket slung across his shoulders, he seemed "the personification of the Southern cause."[676]

When Keiley arrived at Archer's Battalion, he found "a very stimulating degree of excitement," and preparation blooming as grandly as the magnolia grandiflora.[677] Borrowing the musket of a militiaman on leave and not likely to return, Keiley stepped up to the decaying breastwork. The work was intended to accommodate two pieces of artillery, but Keiley noted that it was "all innocent of ordnance." He saw "nothing in the character of the position to give the assailed any advantage other than that which the breast-work offered in case of a direct attack, the ground being almost a dead level in every direction." Other volunteer defenders, less than a hundred in all and shouldering a bouillabaisse of antique weapons, were stepping up alongside him.[678]

Archer's little force was mostly professional men, whose professions weren't war. It was a motley collection. "No uniforms, battle-flags, or shimmering bayonets invested us with the pomp, pride and circumstance of war," one of them later wrote. "There were wanting even the shrill tootings of the fife and the taps of the drum to excite our martial enthusiasm."[679] They were merchants, professors, teachers, druggists, a dentist, a banker, a town officer, an accountant, a master painter, a tailor, a clerk, a "gentleman," and a laborer. Some were manning breastwork against old age as well as against the Yankees—against assaults of impaired hearing and dimming eyesight. At least one had to carry a pocketknife to cut open his cartridges, no longer having teeth enough to bite them with.[680] Keiley saw it as "perfectly evident that 20,000 cavalry or any respectable minority of the same, would make short work of us."[681]

Joining these ancients and the boys young enough to be their grandsons were inmates from the hospitals and the jail, whom those with a sense of humor called the "patients and penitents." Within sight and earshot, on nearby Bragg's Hill, a band of black musicians had tuned up and was playing "Dixie" and "The Girl I Left behind Me" to try to keep spirits up and fool the approaching enemy into believing reinforcements were coming up. There were those in the Confederate troop who never heard a note of it.[682]

They didn't have long to wait. About eleven thirty, a cloud of dust rising from their front and the thundering of hooves announced the galloping arrival of Union cavalry, sent by Major General Benjamin F. Butler, Grant's commander of the Army of the James, to attempt to get into Richmond from the south, through Petersburg. The next instant, Keiley saw "the glitter of spur and scabbard," revealing a long line of horsemen rapidly deploying under the cover of a wood running parallel to the thin Confederate line and about half a mile from its front. The defending battalion's muskets—mostly old flintlocks from the War of 1812, as aged in some cases as the soldiers holding them—were, in Keiley's estimation, "not worth a tinker's imprecation" at a range greater than a hundred yards. So the Confederates, beyond the range of their musket power, could only "watch the preparations for our capture or slaughter." The Federals sent a small company of troopers to feel out the pitiful little rebel force, as they continued to deploy in a long line double the length of the Confederate rampart. It was obvious to Keiley they intended "to flank us on both sides." The Federals were not only manyfold more in numbers than the Confederates, but they were armed with state-of-the-art repeating rifles, which Keiley believed could fire sixteen times before reloading.

The fight was soon joined, and it raged for nearly two hours until the Federal host had entirely surrounded the "extended and exposed" Confederate front, filed into their rear, and shot the two men nearest Keiley in the back. Union cavalry swarmed over the breastwork, and Keiley found himself a prisoner, yielding "with what grace I could to my fate."[683]

Robert A. Martin, a city councilman also exempt from military service, father of a loving family, and also nearly totally deaf, had rushed to the front with the others. Hearing orders at virtually any decibel level was beyond him. And when the one was given that day to cease firing and the rest of the company had begun to run for its life, he continued to stand fast, load, and shoot. A fleeing comrade pressed his lips to Martin's unhearing ear in passing and shouted, "Stop firing! Stop firing!"

Martin heard that. But obeying it wasn't in his program. "Stop firing!" he shouted in disgust. "Orders? I haven't any orders to stop firing," and he instead kept advancing and pumping out lead. His was the last Rebel shot fired. This ragtag army was ardent, if not high on following orders.[684]

In town, Lossie Hill, Sara's friend and "the daintiest of dainty maidens," was threading her way down the dusty street to spend the morning with old Mrs. Mertens, when she heard a frantic shout, "Get out of the way! Damn the women! Run over them if they won't get out of the way."[685]

These ungallant orders came from generally the most gallant of men, the handsome aristocratic son of a British army officer from northern Ireland, Captain Edward Graham, whose four guns of the Petersburg Artillery were thundering through the streets to the rescue of the slender defense line on the Jerusalem Plank Road. His men, one woman marveled, "leaped from the guns and caissons and with whip and cheers urged on the flying horses as they ran beside them."[686]

Graham's guns were followed by the cavalry of young Brigadier General James Dearing, a former artillerist in Lee's army. The Federal advance was stopped, much to the disgust of Ben Butler, who concluded, correctly, that his best men had been kept at bay in large part by old men and boys, "the cradle and the grave being robbed of about equal proportions."[687] Butler, a lawyer by profession, later questioned Keiley, now his prisoner and also a lawyer, and said he knew the city was virtually empty of soldiers because "if there was a soldier in town, no lawyer would get into the trenches!" Keiley smiled and said, "You speak of Northern lawyers, I presume."[688]

Some graves, sadly, were not robbed in the end. More than half the little force of defenders had been killed, wounded, or captured. Old man Banister, the banker, was carried home dead to his wife and daughters, shot through the head. Patty Hardee's father, another of Sara's friends, was one of the first to report to the Jerusalem Plank Road and one of the first to be borne home dead to his daughter.[689] Nine of Petersburg's citizens had been killed outright and four mortally wounded. Eighteen others had been wounded but lived. Twenty-eight to thirty had been taken prisoner. It was a painfully long casualty list of unbearably familiar names—the banker, the druggist and a tailor, all three dead, each leaving a widow and six orphans; the dentist; the professor of French at the Petersburg Female Academy; a commission merchant's clerk from the town. The professor of music returned with three wounds.[690] "A few gallant Souls were defending the city, with their life's blood," one woman wrote. "One by one, the bodies of the most prominent citizens were brought to their sorrowing friends."[691] Another wrote, "Night closed in, and we sat down face to face with our woe—some to watch the dying, others to keep sad vigil beside their dead."[692] The Reverend William Platt of Saint Paul's Church, conducting funeral services, said, "In the midst of life we are in death."[693]

Three nights later, June 12, Grant quietly, quite in secret, efficiently and rapidly pulled his main army out of its position at Cold Harbor and set it in motion toward the James River. A vanguard, Major General William. F. Smith's Eighteenth Corps, arrived at Petersburg's back door on Wednesday, June 15, with orders to take the city. Residents climbed to the roof of the Iron Front Building, the tallest building in the business district, to watch them come, kicking up dust two or three miles away, leaving in their train in the distance a line of burning farmhouses.[694] It was a force of breathtaking size, such as Petersburg had never seen and could not hope to defend against. It was commanded by Smith, whom Ella Washington—whose unlucky home had stood in his path in Hanover

County—saw as "heavy in the face and figure," with sandy hair and a beard worn pointed on the chin. Her burning, angry, and prejudiced eye saw in him "dull eyes, and a stupid expression." "I can't think," she had spit into her diary, "he is smart or can be much of an officer unless appearances lie greatly."[695]

But Smith was smart enough to be growling at Petersburg's gates to do what Butler had failed to do, and there looked to be no way that the thin Confederate guard commanded by P. G. T. Beauregard, the hero of Sumter and First Manassas, could stop him from powering into the city. However, war mixes inefficiency with efficiency in often unbalanced ratios. Chaos and confusion in the Union host—mixed-up orders, insufficient rations, misleading maps, missed opportunities, maddening delays, numbing fatigue—and another valiant, inspired Confederate stand, far stronger than the old and young men's line of June 9, held it tenuously at bay.

By Friday, June 17, all in Petersburg knew that Grant's entire Union army—one hundred thousand strong—was hovering two miles east of town. All that night thousands of Confederate soldiers and civilians dug a new defense line fronting this gigantic host. Confederate wagons of the Army of Northern Virginia began rolling into the city the next morning, raising suffocating clouds of dust and much anxious speculation.[696]

Some townspeople comforted themselves with the thought that "we are only re-enforcing our defenses." Sara's father-in-law, the Reverend Theodorick Pryor, had arrived unexpectedly. The army corps to which he was attached had made camp near Petersburg.

"I've just met General Lee in the street," he told Sara.

Sara cried in alarm, "Oh, *is* he going to fight here?"

"My dear," the reverend father-in-law said, "you surprise me! The safest place for you is in the rear of General Lee's army, and that happens to be just where you are! The lines are established just here, and filled with Lee's veterans."[697]

So it had come down to what Sara's neighbor, Charles Campbell, the noted Virginia historian and headmaster of the Anderson

Seminary, called "war at the door."[698] The two armies had fought the summer away along the Wilderness–Spotsylvania–Cold Harbor line, only to end it here at Petersburg, which had not known war firsthand before. By the weekend, June 18, Grant concluded that Petersburg could not now be carried by assault. Swiftly he laid siege lines. Lee just as swiftly entrenched.

Hard times enough were behind Sara. Now she was in the middle of the war itself, and even harder times seemed ahead as the fourth summer of fighting began.

CHAPTER 16

———•◦•———

In the Cannon's Mouth

$\mathcal{T}$he Sunday after Ulysses S. Grant laid his siege lines before Petersburg, Reverend John Miller, minister of the Second Presbyterian Church across the street from Sara's house—Theodorick Pryor's old church—rose in his pulpit, bowed his head, and addressed the Higher Power.

"Almighty Father," he prayed, "we are assembled to worship Thee in the presence of our enemies." The amen was delivered by the enemy. With a "serpentlike hiss," a shell burst through the church wall. In an instant the pews emptied.

"And the shell?" Sara inquired.

"It lies upon the [communion] table in the church," the pastor, a former captain of Confederate artillery, said. He had disarmed it and slung it over his shoulder and carried it there, and nobody dared remove it.

It was the first shell to enter Sara's side of town. It wouldn't be the last.[699]

From that moment, Petersburg was shelled at nerve-jangling intervals—endlessly, it seemed. The shelling at first centered on the Old Market area, presumably because the railroad depot was situated there, where soldiers were likely to collect. But the guns soon widened their sweep to the streets of the business section, then to the residential district, until the entire city was filled with "the infernal noise" of "screaming, ricocheting, and bursting... shells."[700] "Zip! zip! crack! bang! the nasty things went everywhere," Nellie Gray exclaimed. Nowhere in the city seemed exempt.[701] Seeing that no part of Petersburg was safe, Lee ordered the hospitals removed beyond the range of the Federal guns.

The shelling thundered on for hours at a time, in "one uninterrupted peal of thunder," lighting the night sky with a "vivid brilliance," and sending up smoke that "rolled in clouds towards the heavens."[702]

As the congregation at Second Presbyterian suspected, the infernal machines had a particular affinity for the houses of the Lord. Steeples made standout targets. For a time this also made churchgoing risky business, inviting premature translation to the hereafter. That was so until Dr. Platt, pastor of Saint Paul's Episcopal Church on Sycamore Street, had had enough. This man of God wrote Major General George Gordon Meade, commander of the Army of the Potomac under Grant, protesting the sacrilege and appealing to him as a Christian soldier to stop waging war against worshipers in the city, who were mostly women and children. At least, he prayed, leave them "the sanctity of the Sabbath, one day's respite of the seven." God had rested on the Sabbath, why not Federal cannon? The plea got through the lines and apparently appealed to Meade's Christianity. From that day, there was no more shelling on Sundays.[703]

There were those in Petersburg who couldn't stand the thunder of the guns any day of the week and so left town. But there were some who couldn't or wouldn't leave, and they dug holes in the ground, five or six feet deep, and covered them with heavy timbers banked with earth. Sara's next-door neighbor, Thomas Branch, piled bags of sand around his house. When the heavy shelling zipped, cracked, and banged, entire families made for these improvised "bomb-proofs."

Another of Sara's neighbors, the historian and seminary head-master Charles Campbell, cleared out the large, dry coal cellar in the seminary. He spread rugs on the floor, furnished this snug refuge with lounges and chairs, and invited Sara, who lived but a block away, to flee there when the shelling became unbearable.

One evening, at the end of a long scorching-hot day, Sara was dead tired and in a deep sleep when the cannons began to speak and the thunder roll. She was oblivious to their shrieking until awak-ened by her maid, Eliza Page. As the windows rattled and banged from the powerful concussion of the shells, Eliza pulled the groggy Sara from her bed and threw blankets around the children. They were fleeing through the street, hurrying to the Campbell cellar, when a shell burst not more than fifty feet in front of them. A geyser of fragments spewed into the air, spraying down debris and hellfire. But not one of them was hurt.

On another day a shell caromed into the front yard and buried itself in the ground. Sara's baby, Lucy, was in her nurse's arms nearby and was fascinated rather than frightened. The first word Lucy ever spoke, Sara believed, was an attempt to imitate the lan-guage of the shells. They made a fluttering sound as they arched through the air and floated down with a frightening hiss to explode or lodge themselves in somebody's yard. Lucy loved it.

"Yonder comes that bird with the broken wing," the servants said.

The shells exploded in midair above them in a puff of smoke "white as an angel's wing," which drifted across the sky and sent particles pattering down like hailstones.[704]

Sara and her little boys, with an ear for its music, soon learned the peculiar deep-base growl of one gun in particular, which seemed barking just for them—their own private death-dealing representative in the Union siege lines. The boys named it Long Tom. For stretches of time—days sometimes—Long Tom rested. But at other times it would grumble, roar, and spit, making up for lost time. Like their baby sister, the boys didn't panic or complain. They seemed to understand that that would be an act of cowardice.[705]

Nor was Sara much afraid of the shells, believing strongly in fate. Two of her neighbors, the Gibsons and Mrs. Meade, shared this conviction, agreeing that courage was, after all, largely a matter of nerves. Many others, unconvinced of fate and predestination but agreeing about the matter of nerves, simply left town. Everything on wheels, from drays to wheelbarrows, was pressed into service by fleeing citizenry.[706]

The long, departing parade passed Sara's door until there was no more of it left to pass. The children watched this migration with fascination. One day, Nannie, the Campbell's little daughter, stood at the gate, watching, with little Lucy in her arms, when a shell plowed into the ground some distance away.

A mounted Confederate officer passing by, reined up and demanded, "Whose children are these?"

"This is Charles Campbell's daughter," Nannie introduced herself, "and this"—indicating the baby—"is General Pryor's child."

The officer said sternly, "Run home with General Pryor's baby, little girl, away from the shells."

As he turned to ride away, he said to her, "My love to your father. I'm coming to see him."

Little Nannie was perplexed. "Who is that man?" she asked a bystander.

"Why, don't you know?" someone said. "That's General Lee!"[707]

In the hellfire of the cannonading, Sara received two messages from the outside world. One was a scolding; one was a plea. Agnes was the scolder. "You dear, obstinate little woman!" she wrote Sara. "What did I tell you? I implored you to get away while you could, and now you are waiting placidly for General Grant to blow you up."[708]

The plea was from her oldest son, Theodorick, lobbying her to let him come from the country to be with her. "If I cannot be of any use," he wrote, "at least I can be *with* you." He followed his letter immediately with himself. And there he was, amid "the wild wail of the storm of misery," small for his age and looking "as fair as a girl" in his linen blouse.[709]

Theodorick came to share not only the wild wail of the shells but the human want the siege had brought with it. No farmer dared venture within the lines, and there was no longer a market in the city. There were also no longer fish in the streams nearby or wild game in the woods. The cannonading had driven them all away, with many of Petersburg's residents.[710]

Virtually half black and half white, Petersburg was peopled by perhaps more free blacks than any other Southern city.[711] And not far from Sara's door, between the hills rising on either side of a sunken road, a community of them had hollowed out space where they sat in the daytime on mats, knitting, and selling small cakes made of sorghum and flour, and little round meat pies, and hymning their antiphonal songs. Sara's family was skirting the edge of hunger, but she was leery of the meat pies. They were made from God knows what—from dead mules, very likely. Sara had seen one lying on the common with a square chunk of flesh cut neatly from its side.

Despite their hunger, Sara and her children never ate rats, mice, or mule meat. Instead, they existed on peas, bread, and sorghum, buying a little milk when they could, mixing it with a drink made from roasted and ground corn picked up by Mr. Campbell's children whenever the army horses were fed.[712]

Sara could empathize with Captain Blackford, of Lee's army, who told his wife, Susan, of his supper of a pone of corn bread and a cup of water, saying, "It is hard to maintain one's patriotism on ashcake and water."[713]

These were the worst of times, and there was a growing infirmness of purpose in many minds in the South, a feeling that continuing the war was no longer worth the sorrow and the price. Sara's friend Agnes felt this in Richmond. "There is a strong feeling among the people I meet," she wrote Sara toward the end of summer, "that the hour has come when we should consider the lives of the few men left to us. Why let the enemy wipe us off the face of the earth? Should this feeling grow, nothing but a great victory can stop it."

Agnes asked, "Don't you remember what Mr. Hunter said to us in Washington? 'You may sooner check with your bare hand the torrent of Niagara than stop this tidal wave of secession.' *I* am for a tidal wave of peace—and I am not alone. Meanwhile we are slowly starving to death."

Agnes saw disheartening signs and contradictions all around her, some of it looking like utter "insanity in our people." President Davis, she wrote Sara, "likes to call attention to the fact that we have no beggars on our streets, as evidence that things are not yet desperate with us. He forgets our bread riot which occurred such a little while ago. That pale, thin woman with the wan smile haunts me."

"Ah!" Agnes wrote, thinking again of the bread riot, "these are the people who suffer the consequence of all that talk about slavery in the territories you and I used to hear in the House and Senate Chamber. Somebody, somewhere, is mightily to blame for all this business, but it isn't you nor I, nor yet the women who did not really deserve to have Governor Letcher send the mayor to read the Riot Act to them. They were only hungry, and so a thousand of them loaded some carts with bread for their children. You are not to suppose I am heartless because I run on in this irrelevant fashion. The truth is, I am so shocked and disturbed I am hysterical. It is all so awful." She signed her letter, "Your Scared-to-death Agnes."[714]

During the long nights the blacks in the sunken road between the hills, within easy earshot of Sara, sang their antiphonal melodies so out of joint and weird to Sara's ear. The droning of their voices rose "above the dull roar of the guns, the keen hiss of the shells as they fell, and the rattle and rumble of the army wagons":

"My brederin do-o-n't be weary,
    De Angel brought de tidin's down.
Do-o-n't be weary
    For we're gwine home!

I want to go to heaven!
    Yas, my Lawd!
I want to see Jesus!
    Yas, my Lawd!

My brederin do-o-n't be weary,
    De angel brought de tidin's down.
Do-o-n't be weary
    For we're gwine home."[715]

Roger rode in and out of this hardscrabble tableau as his duties as a scout for the army permitted. After a time, in 1864, Bushrod Johnson, in the Richmond defenses, asked to borrow Roger for special duty. In early May, Ben Butler had begun to put a move on Richmond and Petersburg from south of the James River. On May 7 Butler's troops struck the Confederates at Drewry's Bluff, seven miles below Richmond, in an action at Port Walthall Junction, but were thrown back. A month later, June 9, Butler had met the old men and boys of Petersburg on the Jerusalem Plank Road.

Roger had distinguished himself at Port Walthall. General D. H. Hill wrote, "The victory at Walthall Junction was greatly due to General Roger A. Pryor. But for him it is probable we might have been surprised and defeated."[716] Bushrod Johnson wrote in his official report, "For the most reliable information I was indebted to Roger A. Pryor, who was active, tireless, and daring in reconnaissances."[717]

The soldiers were also noticing him. At the action at Reams's station on August 24, he "appeared on our battle line a-foot and did some sturdy fighting," a soldier of the Cobb Legion Cavalry wrote. "His presence, coolness and courage amid the roar of artillery and the din of battle, were an inspiration to all as he moved and fought with rank and file."[718]

Following these services around Petersburg, Roger was summoned by Fitzhugh Lee's uncle, Robert E. Lee. Uncle Robert was short on information about Grant's position. He knew that Roger knew Petersburg perhaps better than anybody in his army, having lived in and around the city since boyhood, and having been active in the area throughout the siege.

"Grant knows all about me," Lee told Roger, "and I know too little about Grant. You were a school-boy here, General, and have hunted in the by-paths around Petersburg. Knowing the country better than any of us, you are the best man for this important duty."[719] Lee was still calling Roger "General," too. Once a general, always a general.

Gone from home, at times for as long as a week, Roger would suddenly reappear, often bringing more complications than relief. When things were as bad as they could get, he appeared one afternoon with three guests for tea—and not just any guests. They were the Honorable Pierre Soulé, the Confederate diplomat from Louisiana and former U.S. senator and friend of their Washington days, and Generals D. H. Hill and James Longstreeet. Sara rustled up some bread—she could still buy a little flour with the gold compartmentalized in the money girdle hidden about her waist—and a little tea, which she served in a yellow pitcher without a handle. Mrs. Campbell had sent over a small piece of bacon. Sara served her distinguished guests from her handleless pitcher held with a napkin, the tea sweetened to her guests' individual tastes by a spoonful or two of dark brown sugar.

Pierre Soulé was fastidiously French and "a most attractive conversationalist," who spoke "with singular clearness and force" in either French or English.[720] His manners were Gallic. He said to

Sara, with a gracious bow, "This is a great luxury, Madam, a good cup of tea."[721]

Other times the guests Roger brought home to share the scant board were several social cuts below that distinguished triumvirate. Very early one morning he burst into Sara's room and said, "I am dead for want of sleep." That was nothing new. What he said next, however, was. "I was obliged to take some prisoners," he told her. "They are coming under guard, and you must give them a good breakfast."

As he walked out of the room to find a bed to collapse into, he called back, "Be sure, now! Feed my prisoners, if all the rest of us lose our breakfast."

Five dispirited blue-coated soldiers appeared under guard and lay down under the trees and were soon asleep. What to do? Sara called her little brood together to propose a question. They had only a small pail of meal. Would they be willing to give it to the prisoners? They were, and so five small loaves of bread were baked and the prisoners fed—with sweetened corn-coffee to wash it down.[722]

AUGUST 1864 PASSED for Sara "like a dream of terror." The weather was hot and dry, punctuated by crashing thunder and lurid lightning—nature's cannonading as counterpoint to man's. The "very heavens," Sara said, "seemed in league with the thunderbolts of the enemy." Their section of the city was not under constant siege now. But their "own gun," Long Tom, would bark periodically as if to remind them of his presence and their place. A Confederate battery would answer, and the two would thunder for five or six hours, and Sara and the children would wait out the epic conversation in Campbell's bombproof cellar.[723]

In July Campbell wrote in his diary, "We have the same hot sun, same drought, same dust, same war circumstances, same shellings to-day as on every day."[724] The war was eroding every-body's will and endurance. By late August Sara had seen more than she could stand of bombing and of wounded and dying soldiers. She began to believe she could endure no more.

She learned with a quickening sense of relief that her brother-in-law had moved his family to North Carolina, leaving Cottage Farm, his place three miles from the city, at her disposal. He was leaving it empty but for some furniture and a piano. He would be glad to have her living in it. Sara wrote Bushrod Johnson, the Northern-born Quaker who had somehow become a Confederate general, requesting an army wagon to move them the next morn-ing. All that night she packed and made ready. She had collected a spare sampling of furniture when Roger had moved her into town eight months earlier. She planned to take that with her.

The wagon didn't come when expected, and all day she waited and all the next night—without beds—and all the next day. As she sat looking out the window into the twilight, hoping and watching, a vigorous cannonading commenced. A line of shells rose above her into the darkening sky, etching luminous arcs and breaking into showers of fragments. *Our gun will be next!* Sara thought. *Long Tom will soon speak.* For the first time her strength left her. She began to cry, weeping "over the hopeless doom which seemed to await us." Just then she heard the wheels below her window, and there was her wagon, drawn by four horses, to take her from this hell.[725]

They were delivered, bag and baggage, lares and penates, to Cottage Farm, blessedly beyond the reach of the guns. It wasn't until then that Sara realized how great had been the strain of the past three long months. She literally "went all to pieces," trembling as if with a chill. John, Eliza, and the boys unloaded the wagon in the road before the lawn, and the driver turned his team and started back toward the besieged city. It was nine o'clock at night. There were no lights to show them into the house, nor did they have the strength and will to move their things inside. John said he would stand guard through the night, and they began to spread their blankets on the hard cottage floor.

Within moments, however, half a dozen soldiers came up, led by an officer who cheerfully greeted them as "welcome neighbors." His company was camped nearby, he said, and they had seen her predicament and had come to "set things to rights" and offer her protection. By midnight the soldiers had them moved into the cottage, their beds put up and made, and their boxes all under cover. John's "commissariat" yielded up some biscuits, and there was a well of pure water near the door. They seemed safe at last.[726]

Sara woke the next morning to the cool freshness of a lovely early September morning. Her heart, never long given to darkness, was filled again with light and hope. She saw that a large circle of early fall flowers—chrysanthemums, dahlias, and late-blooming roses—lined the carriage drive to the door. A green lawn ran to the limits of a large yard in the rear of the cottage, and beyond was a garden with a few potatoes to dig, and an apple tree in fruit.

Sara's brother-in-law had left two old family servants at the cottage—Uncle Frank and his wife, Aunt Jinny—as caretakers. To them and to the presence of the company of soldiers, Sara was indebted for the yet unplundered apple tree and potato patch. Aunt Jinny also kept a few fowl. There might now be a morning egg for baby Lucy. Roger's father, chaplain to the army, soon appeared, his corps having camped within riding distance of Cottage Farm. There was a small outbuilding in the yard, into which he moved. But he was often absent for days at a time, ministering to his soldier flock. Roger was also somewhere nearby, but employed day and night, often in peril, scouting for the army his father was praying for.[727]

ONE DAY, SOON AFTER they moved in, young Theo and Roger Jr. ran home thrilling with excitement and bearing grand news. General Robert E. Lee himself had just dismounted at the Turnbulls, a short distance on the road beyond, and set up his headquarters. The Army of Northern Virginia was moving into the neighborhood.

From that moment the whole face of the earth seemed to change. Army wagons began crawling in an unending line along the road past Sara's gate, raising "a fog of dust." All was astir as well in their rear, over a second parallel country road. A short connecting road between the two passed close by the water well near the cottage. It, too, was packed and well traveled. The whir of the well wheel never seemed to Sara to stop, day or night. Major General Cadmus Marcellus Wilcox, an old friend commanding a Confederate division, came to her door asking if he might pitch his headquarters on her back lawn.

The white tents of Wilcox's staff soon reached to her back door. It seemed Sara could not escape war. As another refugee was to say, "What I ran away from I ran into." Sara was literally enwombed within a mighty army, and very likely the most thoroughly protected woman in the South.[728]

Margaret Junkin Preston, the Virginia poet, had an eloquent descriptive verse that fit Sara's new surroundings:

> But thick as white asters in Autumn are found
> The tents all bestrewing the carpeted ground;
> The din of a camp, with its stir and its strife,
> Its motley and strange, multitudinous life.[729]

The pictures and books from their Washington days were pulled from a warehouse in Petersburg and brought to the cottage. Shelves for the books were built in the dining room. Pictures Roger had brought home from his mission to Greece in the fifties were hung on the walls of the two bedrooms and the parlor— "Madonna della Seggiola" over the mantel, Guido's "Aurora" over the piano. She found various delicate carvings in the stored boxes, and her music. There was a baby house and toys for Lucy in another box, and a French trunk with many compartments that held

Sara's collection of evening dresses from happier days. She didn't open it. There would be no need of such finery here in this time and place. She consigned it to the cellar. The house began to look cozy and homelike.[730]

John and the boys laid immediate plans to acquire a cow, chickens, ducks, and pigeons. And it began to happen. Gold from Sara's money belt bought a cow named Rose from a neighboring farmer. John built a shelter for her close to his own quarters, where he could protect her—and her milk in particular—from night callers.

"'Cause," John said, "I knows soldiers! They gits up fo' day and milk yo' cow right under yo' eyelids. Ain't you hear about Gen'al Lee in Pennsylvania? The old Dutch farmers gave him Hail Columbia because his soldiers milked their cows. But Lawd! Gen'al Lee couldn' help it! He could keep 'em from stealin' horses, but the queen of England herself couldn' stop a soldier when he hankers after milk. An' he don't need no pail, neither; he can milk in his canteen an' never spill a drop."[731]

SARA WAS HAPPIER than she had been in a long time. There was a crack in the lowering clouds, a promise of a temporary respite. If the army could avoid a collision with Grant in front of Petersburg for another month or two, both sides would go into winter quarters and everybody could have a blessed rest, so much needed, Sara believed, to fit them for the likely terrors of the coming spring campaign. The Reverend Theodorick Pryor was making clanging predictions, like the jeremiads of a prophet, somewhat darkening the aspect. "We are here for eight years— not a day less," he told Sara.[732]

Sara's next concern was for her little boys and their education. She found schoolbooks for them and became their teacher, as her aunt Mary had been her teacher. Sara knew "a little Latin and less Greek," and she would gravely listen as they recited in the former.

She was admittedly weak in mathematics but hoped they might never discover "the midnight darkness of my mind" on that subject.[733]

The war and its siege was now but a distant murmur, rather than an immediate clanging reality. Two forts in the Confederate line—Forts Gregg and Battery 45—shielded their immediate neighborhood. Occasionally the forts were challenged and there was an answer, but there was no attempt to attack on either side. The most painful reminder of the reality of war was the picket firing at night, often incessant "like the dropping of hail." It was harrowing for Sara, for she knew that men were falling in this endless firing. And there was the constant anxiety for Roger's safety. He was out there in all of that, often in peril, scouting at the edge of the lines, perhaps behind them.[734]

Visitors were dropping by to pay their respects, great men, war names, household names—Generals A. P. Hill and Cadmus Wilcox, Colonel William Pegram, and others. It was a world of men. Indeed, Sara had only two female acquaintances in the midst of all this maleness—the wife and daughter of "old Billy Green," who lived in a farmhouse on a hill a short distance from the cottage. Mrs. Green was kind to Sara and to everybody, and her daughter, Nannie, was a beauty with an amiable nature inherited from her mother. In that setting, and with that nature and her looks, she became an "out-and-out belle," the only young woman in the neighborhood. Tenderly rephrased and improvised lyrics were written to her by many poetic pens in the surrounding army. "Sweet Annie of the Vale" became "Sweet Nannie of the Hill."[735] Many hearts longed to recite these new lyrics tenderly in her ear.

Any winter respite from war for Sara promised to be fleeting. For spring would come again and with it more war—driven more than ever by an undercurrent of impending doom. The stench of defeat was in the air throughout the Confederacy, a sense that it might not be far off.

Unlike Sara, Grace Elmore, in South Carolina, was in a back eddy of the war. But there was horror around her and she felt it. "So much horror . . . and what a terrible uncertainty," she wrote in her diary. "We know not what a day may bring forth, nor at what hour this peaceful town may be spread in ruins, and another instance of barbarous spite added to the long list of outrages committed by the Yankees." Yet her life seemed to flow placidly on. "We hear of battles," she wrote, "we see friend after friend brought home coffined and ready for the churchyard, the mourning garb is no longer uncommon, and the cork leg and one armed men have ceased to attract attention, we have gotten used to it all, war does not interrupt a quiet breakfast nor does it disturb our nights rest."[736]

In Atlanta, however, as in Petersburg, the enemy was at Ella Thomas's door. The end seemed near, and she was bracing for it. "How I do wish this war was over," she wrote in her journal. "I wish to breathe free. I feel pent up, confined—cramped and shall I confess it am reminded of that Italian story of *The Iron Shroud* where daily—daily hourly and momently the room contracts, the victim meanwhile utterly impotent to avert the impending doom."[737] For Minerva McClatchey, in Athens, but a few miles east of Atlanta, the doom had already arrived. It seemed to her "as if all creation was here and all dressed in 'blue.'"

On September 1, Atlanta fell, and Mary Chesnut threw up her hands in resignation. "The end has come," she cried into her diary. "No doubt of the fact. . . . We are going to be wiped off the face of the earth." She felt "as if all were dead within me, forever."[738]

It was a common feeling now in the embattled Confederacy.

CHAPTER 17

—•◦•—

The Riderless Horse

*A*utumn had returned, dressed in red, yellow, and amber, and the lines that had drawn tighter around Petersburg brought Sara at least one much-desired benefit. Roger could usually return to her after reporting each night to Lee. She had ceased feeling so anxious now when he rode away in the mornings on his big gray, Jubal Early. He would generally return in the evenings.

One morning in late November, frost lay on the ground around Cottage Farm. John had squeezed a cupful of milk from Rose—all Rose, on her slender rations, could manage to produce for him. They had boiled it with parched corn, and sweetened it with sorghum molasses. With biscuits well beaten but unmixed with lard or butter, it made a passable breakfast. Sara was seated at the table that morning with her little boys. Dr. Pryor had departed on his daily rounds of mercy, comforting sick and wounded soldiers in the hospitals.

Sara was writing letters this morning—to Agnes, her mother, and her little girls in Charlotte County. She had just finished a long letter to Aunt Mary, telling of their relative content and the prospect of comparative quiet now with the armies soon to settle into winter quarters. She had addressed the letter and was about to seal it, when Cadmus Wilcox entered and took the seat before the fire that he always took when he came to visit her.

"Madam," he began, "is the general at home?"

"No, General," Sara said, "he did not return last night."

"Are you not uneasy?" Wilcox asked.

"Not a bit," Sara said. "He sometimes stops at Mrs. Friend's when he is belated. She's his cousin, you know."

"Of course!" Wilcox said. "All the pretty women in Virginia are cousins to the Virginia officers. Couldn't you naturalize a few unfortunates who were not born in Virginia?" Wilcox was an "unfortunate" born in Tennessee.

Busy sealing and stamping her letters, Sara did not answer Wilcox immediately. When she looked up at him, she was surprised to see his face was pale and his lip quivering.

"You have to know it," he said. "The general will not return. The Yankees caught him this morning."

"Oh impossible!" Sara exclaimed. "Jubal never fails."

"Look out of the window," Wilcox said.

Sara looked, and there stood Roger's riderless horse, Jubal Early. A groom was removing its saddle.

Wilcox hastened to reassure her. "It will be all right," he said. "A little rest for the general, and we will soon exchange him."

Sara's head reeled and her heart sickened. She had never expected this. As she sat shivering beside the fire, she heard the clank of a spur and looked up and saw an officer standing at the door.

"Madam," the officer said, "General Lee sends you his affectionate sympathies."

Through the open window Sara saw Lee on his horse, Traveler, standing by the well. He waited there until his messenger returned and then rode slowly away toward the Petersburg lines.[739]

ROGER THAT MORNING had had a journalist's hankering for a newspaper. He often had it. And when he did he would wave an old newspaper at the Federals across the skirmish lines, and if one of them waved back, he would gingerly approach, meet the man midway between the lines, and exchange a wad of tobacco for the latest Union editions. It was illegal, but many of them did it. Roger had never been one to balk at illegalities. Union generals, in particular, frowned on such interchanges. It let Confederates learn what they were doing. Men who did it were often arrested. They did it anyhow. Tobacco, as everybody knew, had perhaps an even stronger attraction than newsprint.

Roger's attraction, however, was to the newsprint. So he had stood before the Rebel picket line that morning waving a newspaper. He picked a bad day for it. The Federal force in front of him, on the extreme left of the Union line, was from the Ninth Corps. Only days before, one of their number, Captain Henry S. Burrage, of the Thirty-sixth Massachusetts, had done what Roger was doing—had met Confederates between the lines and been taken prisoner for his trouble. The men of the Ninth Corps had considered this a poor reflection on them, and its general applied for and won permission to capture a Confederate officer under similar circumstances in retaliation if the occasion presented itself. Roger appeared across the skirmish line at this inopportune moment, waving a newspaper and seeking an exchange.

Captain Hollis O. Dudley, commanding the Eleventh New Hampshire and two companies of the Thirty-second Maine along the picket line that day, saw him, and mistook him for an officer. Roger saw a newspaper waved in answer, and he slowly advanced, waving his own, to a point nearly midway between the lines. "If you are not cowards," Roger was heard to say, "come out." Roger was not one for diplomatic preliminaries.

Dudley had picked five select men of the Eleventh New Hampshire and numbered them one to five. He ordered Captain Marcus L. M. Hussey of the Thirty-second Maine also to pick five of his best marksmen and coolest men, and numbered them six to ten. All ten were sent forward to the advance post within easy musket range of where Roger stood. This done, Hussey started to step out of the line to meet him. Dudley stopped him. "You cannot leave your post," he said, "I will go." And with ten Union rifles leveled on them, and others at the ready, Dudley approached Roger.

As they met, Roger said, "Where is your newspaper?" and Dudley, instead of delivering newsprint, demanded his surrender. Roger recoiled. "No, by God!" he said. But before the words were out, Dudley grabbed Roger's hand and jammed a six-inch Smith and Wesson six-shooter against his chest. Dudley turned toward his line and hissed at Roger, "A word from you or a particle of resistance and I shall drop you and go to my line." In that position, the two of them moved toward the Federal trenches. Along the Confederate line Rebel soldiers watched, helpless to intervene.

"Treachery, treachery," Roger was heard to say, "this is treachery, by God."

The prisoner was sent up to Ninth Corps headquarters and, from there, to General Grant's headquarters at City Point, then confined on a prison barge moored in the James River. Dudley had reeled in the biggest-name private in the Confederate army. Within an hour the provost marshal of the Ninth Corps, sent by its general, praised Dudley's coup as the greatest achievement yet by an officer of the Ninth Corps. How, the general asked, might he reward him? Dudley modestly said he had only done his duty and that he had but one request—that he be given Roger's revolver, belt, and holster, as a memento of the event.

Since the incident had occurred along his line, Wilcox rode out to study where it had happened. He then asked Lee if he might write General Grant, requesting Roger's release. Grant passed the request on to General Meade, commanding the Army of the Potomac, and Meade emphatically refused, saying he had but recently cashiered Captain Burrage for a like offense and that Roger must suffer the consequences.[740]

The immediate consequence for Roger was an interview with George H. Sharpe, Grant's assistant provost marshal general and the man charged with interrogating captured Confederate prisoners. Roger failed to give him any information he could use, and the interview soon became a social conversation. Roger was shipped the next day to the Old Capitol prison in Washington, where the government kept high-profile Rebel prisoners, smugglers, blockade runners, court-martialed Union officers, seditionists, and miscellaneous other enemies of state. Just across the street from the Capitol, the building had been built in 1815 to temporarily house Congress following the British occupation of Washington in 1814. It later became a boardinghouse, and John C. Calhoun had died there. Now it was a prison. And Roger attracted more than the usual amount of attention as he was escorted there under guard. Many of his former acquaintances in the national capital recognized him.[741]

Inside the prison Roger was searched. Among keepsakes in his pocket was a bottle of brandy that had been slipped into his overcoat by one of those old Washington friends. Everything else was confiscated but the brandy. Returning it to him, the Federal officer said, "Keep it, General! There's an almighty sight of comfort in a bottle of brandy."[742]

LIEUTENANT WILLIAM G. SHEEN, an officer of the Thirty-ninth Massachusetts in the defenses of Washington, had applied to go home on leave. When his leave was approved and as he was preparing to depart, the adjutant general of the district offered to place in his charge a prisoner bound for Fort Warren in Boston Harbor, which would save the young officer the cost of transportation home. Without knowing who it might be, Sheen agreed. Not until he got his orders did he learn who it was. He was impressed. He had known Roger by reputation since boyhood. His prisoner was a famous man.[743]

At the Old Capitol, the prison superintendent handed Roger over to Sheen, advising him to put the prisoner in irons, since he was a dangerous man. Sheen refused, instead requesting Roger's word as a gentleman that he would not attempt to escape while in Sheen's custody. Roger agreed, and the two of them boarded a train at nine thirty the night of December first. At daylight the next morning they pulled into the station in Jersey City, then crossed over into New York on the Courtland Street Ferry.

The hour was early and the two of them stopped for breakfast at the Merchants Hotel. After breakfast, while preparing to leave the hotel for the quartermaster general's department to get orders and transportation, Sheen was surprised to find the rotunda of the hotel packed. For a brief moment Sheen feared his prisoner would be wrested from him. But Roger told him to take his arm, and together they shouldered through the crowd. At the quartermaster general's office, Sheen found his orders changed. He was directed to take Roger to Fort Lafayette in New York Harbor, rather than to Fort Warren.

Sheen and Roger caught the ferry to Fort Lafayette, the Union government's bastille for political prisoners. Sheen turned Roger over to the prison commandant, Colonel Martin Burke, an officer from the Old Army, who gave the young captain a receipt in return. Roger spoke kindly to Sheen as they shook hands to part, extracting a promise from him that if it were his fate to be wounded or a prisoner at Richmond during the war, he should make himself known to Sara, who would respond to any appeal from him. Sheen never had to exercise the option.[744]

The first public confirmation of Roger's capture reached Sara, in Petersburg, in a dispatch from the Union army to the *New York Herald* on November 30. Later, a mysterious personal note reached her through the *New York News*, saying, "Your husband is in Fort Lafayette, where a friend and relative is permitted to visit him." It was signed, "Mary Rhodes."[745]

With Roger gone from her, perhaps forever, Sara faced the approaching winter much as Sallie Putnam in Richmond was facing it—"with shuddering apprehensions."[746] By Christmas she could agree with Grace Brown Elmore, in South Carolina, who wrote in her diary, "Christmas eve! And where is our joy, what festival have we?"[747]

The prospect was not merry.

CHAPTER 18

---•◦•---

The Tightening Noose

*O*n Christmas the year before, Sara had given her little family a new baby sister. This year she intended to give them a Christmas dinner.

John had devised a way of mixing sorghum molasses with a little flour and walnuts baked in a "raised" crust to make a Christmas pie. He baked several of those, and Sara, with money from her golden girdle, bought a piece of corned beef for fifty dollars and boiled it with peas.

As they were about to seat themselves at their festive table, they saw a ragged and forlorn company of soldiers from Lee's army pass the door, back from a raid begun the week before. Snow was falling and the soldiers, with weary dispirited faces and little Christmas cheer, plodded past toward nothing in particular.

Sara stared at them for a moment, then said to her sons, "Boys, are you willing to send the dish of beef and peas out to them?"

The boys agreed, only if they might be the ones to carry it out to the soldiers. They wanted to do that more than they wanted to eat it themselves. Besides, the taste would last longer. They were full of it for days afterwards.[748]

Sara's situation was the grimmest it had ever been—how to maintain her children and herself for the first time in the war unsupported and alone. Roger was a prisoner in Yankeedom. She had lost his rations. Her only food supply now was from her father-in-law's ration as an army chaplain. She had part of a barrel of flour sent from a relative in a county now completely cut off from them, but that was all. She had sent Roger's horse, Jubal Early, to the country to be stabled with a farmer, since she had no means of feeding him.

A number of their old Washington servants had followed Sara to Cottage Farm, but she could no longer support them. John and Eliza, the two closest to her and Roger, elected to stay on without pay. Aunt Jinny and Uncle Frank, the old couple left on the property by Sara's brother-in-law also stayed. And a one-armed boy named Alick, reared in Reverend Pryor's family, had appeared and attached himself to the family as the chaplain's servant.

Soon after, John came to her with what Sara described as "a heart-broken countenance and a drooping attitude of deep dejection." The agent of the estate to which he belonged as a slave was in the city and had advised him to tell Sara that for their safety all its slaves were to be sent to the Louisiana plantation. The whites who had hired them for the year were to be reimbursed.

"How do you feel about it, John?" Sara asked him.

"It will kill me," he said. "I'll soon die on that plantation."

His years of affectionate, faithful service, his hardship for their sakes, crowded into Sara's memory and tugged at her heart. She went immediately to plead his case with the agent. There she learned she could save John from being sent away only by buying him. Without hesitation she unbuckled her money girdle and counted what gold was left—$106. She offered all of it to the agent, a noted slave trader, and although it fell far short of the asking price, he wrote her a receipt for a bill of sale. A dollar in gold in those inflated times was worth $100 in currency, making the price Sara had paid to buy John's freedom $10,600. Sara later told John she never regretted it.

Overjoyed, he exulted that he now belonged to her.

"You are a free man, John," Sara protested. "I will make out your papers and I can very easily arrange for you to pass the lines."

"I know that," John said. "Marse Roger has often told me I was a free man. I never will leave you till I die. Papers indeed! Papers nothing! I belong to you—that's where I belong."[749]

Now John was foraging everywhere, returning home with peas and dried apples and an occasional half-dozen eggs or small bag of corn, which he pounded on a wooden block to make hominy. Sara never inquired deeply into where he acquired such things. Once a week the government permitted her to purchase a small ration of rice and the head of a bullock—horns and all—from the commissary. It was just heads and horns—every other part had been enlisted in the army. What food remained to buy was no longer in Sara's price range. In the inflated currency of the time, flour cost fifteen hundred dollars a barrel, bacon and butter twenty dollars a pound each, beef fifteen dollars a pound, a chicken or a pair of shad fifty dollars. Before the war that same pair of shad had cost ten to fifteen cents.

With the new winter the temperature plunged and the food supply tightened still more. Rose could yield but her one scant cup of milk on her own slim diet—the bit of hay spared her daily from what the officers in the yard fed their horses. But Sara never thought of converting Rose to beef; she was part of the family. The bitter cold found them without wood enough to burn to keep away the chill. So Sara began cutting down trees in the yard, and Wilcox brought her a load of rails from a fence that had been unaccountably spared by the soldiers.

Sara's children, like the soldiers in Lee's army, were perpetually shoeless. Sara made slippers of carpet lined with flannel for the baby. And when a large bronze morocco pocketbook fell into her hands, she translated it into boots for the little one. Out prowling in the fields, Alick found a couple of leather bags from which an army cobbler fashioned shoes for each of Sara's boys. Sara's own most urgent sartorial need was steel that women used for corset stays. That problem was also answered by Lee's army. One of the officers on Wilcox's staff had a pair made for her by the government gunsmith. She believed it the best pair she ever owned.[750]

The family had grown attached to the men in the army camped around them. The officers from Wilcox's staff took an interest in the boys' educations and the books on Sara's shelves, which she circulated to them. In return they brought her candles. Wilcox himself, with his West Point education, became Theodorick's visiting professor of calculus.[751]

The great men of the army began dropping by. Lee often passed the door on his way to the lines and paused to inquire of their welfare. Wilcox, A. P. Hill, and Colonel William Pegram visited her when they could. Sara had known Dolly Hill at Coyners in the Blue Ridge Mountains, and Dolly's husband, the "preux chevalier" (the brave knight) of the army, rode into Sara's yard "with easy grace."[752] Hill was what one of his friends described as a "men's man." He had a high brow, a large nose and mouth, and a full dark beard. He was a renowned fighter, but his uniform bore little ornamentation, hardly more than the insignia of his rank on his collar, and he often wore only an unadorned red woolen shirt in battle.[753]

Like Sara's small company, the army was also hungry—on a far larger scale. A soldier occasionally brought his slim ration—a small square of beef—for Sara to cook for him, or a few grains of coffee to trade with John for a few biscuits—when there was flour with which to bake. Sara sternly forbade taking anything from the soldiers. Instead she had John augment the coffee, in the soldier's presence, with toasted corn, then grind it, and serve it to him with the biscuits. Later Sara would hear a soft footfall in the hall, and the next morning she would find a soldier's ration of precious coffee left for her, and her heart would ache.[754]

Stationery, ink, and candles, items ever abundant and taken for granted in happier days, were as scarce now as everything else. Recycling was a way of life. Confederate women were turning envelopes inside out and reusing them. Sara tore the blank pages from some of the books for stationery, and she manufactured ink from the galls of oak trees—the abnormal growth on leaves and twigs caused by insect larvae. Candles were particularly scarce and most missed of all, for Sara often stayed up late into the night to sew and patch by their dim solitary light. Often all she had were "Confederate candles" that she and Eliza made from long wicks dipped in yellow wax and wound around a bottle.[755]

Wilcox, who was often in the saddle late into the night, said to her, "Your candle is the last light I see at night—the first in the morning." She told him, "I should never sleep."[756]

Sara tried to hide her needs from the soldiers, for she didn't want to deny them what was theirs, and she knew they would give more than they could if they knew her plight. But they found her out anyhow. And at night as she sat sewing beside a "dim, glow-worm light" fast burning down, she would hear a footfall in the hall and find a brown paper parcel on the piano, near the door, full of a soldier's ration of candles.[757]

Sara was now broke, the pockets of her golden girdle empty, and she didn't know where the next dollar to buy the next scrap of food was to come from. She must find some way to earn money. But where could she go, what could she do? There seemed no answer anywhere, no opening for her, for she could not leave the children.

One night, wakeful in her bed, she remembered the unopened trunk from her Washington days, which John and Alick had carried to the cellar when they first arrived at Cottage Farm. Early the next morning she sent them down and they brought it up. With Eliza, Aunt Jinny, and the children gathered around, Sara opened it. It was packed with her old Washington finery.

There was one truth Sara knew about women. Every one of them, in war or peace, had a "natural desire for beautiful raiment." She had it herself. She was grateful to be somewhat restrained from that universal longing, however, in such a time of want.[758] In these straitened times, they were making do with whatever material came to hand. As it was heard said of "a great get-up" at a wedding reception:

> *"Let me whisper: this dress, that I now wear for thee,*
> *Was a curtain of old, in Philadelphee!"*[759]

Sara began dragging everything from the trunk, and with it the accompanying memories. There were half a dozen or more white muslin gowns, flounced and trimmed with Valenciennes lace—many yards of it. There were three evening gowns—a rich bayadere silk gown fully trimmed with guipure lace, a green silk gown with gold embroidery, and a blue-and-silver brocade. There was a paper box holding the shaded roses she had worn to Lady Napier's ball, at which she and Addie Douglas had dressed alike in gowns of tulle. There was another box with the garniture of green leaves and golden grapes that went with the green silk gown. There was yet another box with blue and silver feathers for the brocade. There was an opera cloak trimmed in fur, a long purple velvet cloak, a purple velvet "coalscuttle" bonnet trimmed with white roses, and a point lace handkerchief. There was not only Valenciennes and guipure lace, but Brussels lace, and at the bottom of the trunk there was a package of sky blue zephyr, awakening in Sara the recollection of a passion she had once cherished for knitting shawls and "mariposas" from that soft and airy favorite fabric.

Also in the trunk, wrapped in the velvet cloak, Sara found the two books President Pierce had given her at the end of his presidency. Their weight had pressed the imprint of the cloak's cords and tassels into the fabric, ruining it, sacrificing it to protect everything else.[760]

But what Sara really found in that trunk full of finery and memories was salvation. She was convinced, more than ever, that the consciousness of being well dressed brought more peace of mind even than religion.[761]

She began ripping and sewing, and burning in earnest those

glowworm candles that Wilcox saw flickering at her window long into the night. She stripped the lace from the evening gowns and transformed them into the collars and undersleeves then in vogue. John found an extinct dry-goods store in town with a cache of clean paper boxes. Her first shipment of lace collars sold out at Price's store in Richmond, and Price wrote her that all of her work would find buyers. There were ladies in Richmond, as Agnes had suggested in her letters, who could still afford them, and the Confederate court was still in business, offering a showcase for fashion, such as it was.

After she had converted all of the laces into collars, cuffs, and sleeves, and had sold her silk gowns, her opera cloak, and point lace handkerchiefs, Sara began trimming the edges of the artificial flowers and separating the long wreaths and garlands into clusters for bonnets and corsage bouquets. When she had stripped the muslin gowns of their trimming, she had to decide what to do with the gowns themselves. The muslin flounces, minus their lace, had raw edges no self-respecting belle, even a Confederate in hard times and homespun, would have worn. So she edged them with a spiral line of blue zephyr. She then embroidered a dainty vine of forget-me-nots on bodices and sleeves. She found the result "simply ravishing," flounces any Confederate beauty would be proud to wear.[762]

Some of this was more than Aunt Jinny could stand. "Honey," she said to Sara, "don't you think, in these times of trouble, you might do better than tempt them po' young lambs in Richmond to worship the golden calf and bow down to mammon? We prays not to be led into temptation, and you sho'ly is leadin' 'em into vanity."

"Maybe so, Aunt Jinny," Sara said, "but I must sell all I can. We have to be clothed, you know, war or no war."

"Yes, my chile, that's so," said Aunt Jinny, "but we're told to consider the lilies. Gawd Almighty tells us we must clothe ourselves in the garment of righteousness, and He—"

Eliza, who loved everything about Sara's project, interrupted.

"You always 'pear to be mighty intimate with God A'mighty," she hissed at Aunt Jinny. "Now you just go 'long home an' leave my mistis to her work. How would *you* look with nothin' on but a garment of righteousness?"[763]

When the largess from the Washington trunk was exhausted, Sara attacked Roger's wardrobe. He didn't need it now as much as she did. She cut up his dress coat and designed a lady's glove with gauntlets made of watered silk lining. From the interlining of gray flannel she fashioned gray gloves that brought in yet more money. From the thirteen small fragments of flannel left over, she stitched a pair of drawers for little Willy, her youngest boy.[764]

With her new earnings the first thing she purchased was a barrel of flour, for thirteen hundred dollars. With it John baked hot biscuits three times a day.[765]

Hunger, cold, and poverty were not the sum of Sara's problems. Petersburg was enduring the longest military siege any American city had ever experienced. It was a Sevastopol. The *London Times* was calling it "the graveyard of the Confederacy."[766]

The time and the place were made ever more dark and cheerless by the news from the army, news so grim and unpromising it was difficult for her to keep up a cheerful front for the children's sake. Wilcox's division was being eaten away by desertions, some fifty every twenty-four hours. Wilcox wondered how long he could hold it together. By January in this fourth year of the war, Sara perceived that the soldiers were seeing the cause was lost. They could read its doom in the starvation and suffering around them, in the faces of their officers, in the news drifting in from other fronts, from the siege itself. Their wives and children were suffering worse than they, and many of the men were stealing away in the night to go home. They were deserting, not to the enemy, but to a higher obligation. Nonetheless, some were being found, returned, and executed.[767]

There were nights now when the incessant picket firing, the famine, the military executions for desertion, and the thought of

Roger sick in a Federal bastille in New York Harbor were more than Sara could endure—even for the children's sake. On one of those nights she sighed deeply and audibly, and Theodorick, who slept nearby, asked, "Why can you not sleep, dear mother?"[768]

Theodorick had been a comfort to her throughout this ordeal. He had always been, from infancy, a child of great outer and inner beauty. Sara called him her "goodly child." He was unusually gentle and retiring, yet extraordinarily quick and precocious, and of a highly inquisitive disposition. He and his older sister, Marie Gordon, his companion through his earliest boyhood, had learned to read at an early age. When not yet eleven years old he had trembled in bed remembering the witches he had just read of in Shakespeare's *Macbeth*, convinced their own house was haunted. He had been only five when the Crimean War attracted his scholarly attention. And when Roger ran for the U.S. Congress, Theodorick followed the campaign, mastered the issues, and exulted at the polls on election day with every vote cast for his father. As he approached his teenage years, he was growing into a bookish, brilliant, and scholarly young man.[769]

For their sakes Sara had tried to send Theodorick and Roger Jr., her two eldest sons, presently twelve and ten, to the country to stay with relatives where there was less want and more comfort and safety. But they soon returned unsummoned, footsore and dust covered. They had run away to be with her.

Now here in this night of wakeful unhappiness, Sara turned to Theodorick and said, "Suppose you repeat something for me." He at once began, pulling from his memory his conception of comfort from one of Sara's favorite poems:[770]

> *Tell me not in mournful numbers,*
> *Life is but an empty dream!—*
> *For the soul is dead that slumbers,*
> *And things are not what they seem . . .*

Not enjoyment, and not sorrow,
Is our destined end or way;
But to act, that each tomorrow
Finds us farther than today . . .

Lives of great men all remind us
We can make our lives sublime,
And, departing, leave behind us
Footprints on the sands of time . . .

Footprints, that perhaps another,
Sailing o'er life's solemn main,
A forlorn and shipwrecked brother,
Seeing, shall take heart again . . .

Let us then be up and doing,
With a heart for any fate;
Still achieving, still pursuing,
Learn to labor and to wait.[771]

The laboring and the waiting were wearing thin throughout the South, and not just for Sara in Petersburg. As 1864 was ending—another wrenching year—Grace Elmore wrote in her diary, in South Carolina, "Today the last of 64, a gloomy dark day, the end of a gloomier year. Each year as it closed has found us bereft of a portion of our inheritance, and further from our independence. This year God help us we are almost at the end of the log."[772] Kate Sperry wrote in her diary, in Winchester, Virginia, "Farewell old 1864 . . . you have treated our brave soldiers in the most tragic way."[773] Sarah Morgan, in Louisiana, greeted the year with simple dread. "What new changes will it bring?" she asked her diary. "Which of us will it take?"[774]

Union Major General William T. Sherman had just hacked a path of devastation through the Deep South from Atlanta to Savannah. Many in the way of his going in Georgia had lived what Mary

Jones Mallard called "a horrible night mare, too terrible to be true." Soldiers, defying Sherman's strictures against pillaging homes and private property, repeatedly ransacked Montevideo, Mary's plantation home in Liberty County. "Everyone that comes," she wrote, "has some plea for insult or robbery. Was there ever any civilized land given up for such a length of time to lawless pillage and brutal inhumainities [*sic*]?" Her widowed mother, Mary Sharpe Jones, suffering at her daughter's side, cried, "Where will all the perfidy, insult & injury to the helpless, the Fatherless & the widow end." Staring at the desolation of her once stately home, the mother wrote, "All our pleasant things are laid low.... Our homes & all we possess on earth have been given up to lawless pillage.... I scarcely know how we have stood up under it."[775] Eliza Andrews, who also lived in Sherman's track, hissed into her journal, "I can't believe that when Christ said 'Love your enemies,' he meant Yankees."[776]

Grace Elmore called the march to the sea "the Sherman horror," and she knew it would soon be turning toward her in the Carolinas. "But now where shall we find safety," she demanded of her diary, "where can we lay our weary heads and sickened hearts ... Now it has come, 'tis a trial of fire. There is not a spot to which we can flee & find safety. And oh the terrible wrath that is to be expended on us. We are Carolinians that is our crime, what will be our doom?"[777] "Fire and sword for us here," Mary Chesnut wrote in Columbia.[778]

In February the doom was moving slowly northward, day by day, sowing consternation and panicked flight in its path, and leaving blackened ruin in its wake. Sherman's guns were now distinctly audible in Columbia, moving nearer and nearer, toward the city, up the Orangeburg road. "If he moves slowly," Columbia's Joseph LeConte thought, "it is only to pillage more thoroughly."[779] "Sherman has come," young Malvena Warning wrote in her diary in Columbia on February 15. "He is knocking at the gate. Oh, God! Turn him back! Fight on our side, and turn Sherman back!"[780]

But there was no God or foe in his path to turn Sherman back. Grace Elmore wrote in her diary, "T'is at last here, no longer a mith but a fearful reality. Tomorrow the Yankee takes possession of Columbia."[781]

Sherman's coming was like the coming of the Four Horsemen of the Apocalypse. "Thousands of Yankees coming in," a distraught woman in Liberty Hill wrote as Sherman's multitudes swept though Columbia and rolled northward toward her. "One command follows another in quick succession; all robbing and plundering . . . burning and destroying everything on the face of the land!" The skies about her were "lit by burning fires" and she was sleepless with suspense, "expecting every hour to have the torch set to the house we were in."[782]

The dreadful coming carried with it a sleepless foreboding for everybody and everything. "The cats and goats," Margaret Crawford Adams marveled, "seemed to feel it in the air that something was approaching, for they had disappeared, and did not reappear for days."[783] Waves of Yankees—Kate Cumming, in Georgia, had called them "these fiends in human shape"[784]—invaded the LeConte home in Columbia for nearly two weeks, ransacking the house anew, entering every room, and taking whatever they pleased.[785] As Federal soldiers pillaged her home and threatened to burn it over her head, Pauline DeCaradeuc cringed in a corner through another long night, frantic and terrified, unable to close her eyes. She had not undressed or gone to bed for six nights. "My God!" she wrote in her diary after they left and her house still stood. "I suffered agony, I trembled *unceasingly* till morning."[786]

By the end of February, Sherman had passed through and out of South Carolina, leaving fire and ruin in his wake. Grace Elmore wrote in her diary, "The horror has been and gone. Has devastated and passed over us."[787] Nobody in Columbia was more devastated, more bitter, more aghast—or more passionate—than seventeen-year-old Emma LeConte, Joseph's daughter. "My God!" she wrote in her diary. "What a scene! . . . Imagine night turned into noonday, only with a blazing, scorching glare that was horrible—a copper colored sky across which swept columns of black, rolling smoke, glittering with sparks and flying embers. . . . Everywhere the palpitating blaze walling the streets with solid masses of flames as far as the eye could reach, filling the air with its horrible roar. On every side the crackling and devouring fire, while every instant came the crashing of timbers and the thunder of falling buildings. A quivering molten ocean seemed to fill the air and sky. . . . Oh, that long twelve hours! Never surely again will I live through such a night of horrors. . . . It would be impossible to describe or even to conceive the pandemonium and horror." She believed that "a heavy curse has fallen on this town—from a beautiful bustling city it is turned into a desert."[788]

Sherman's fiery track of desolation and ruin had left in shambles every room where Anna Thomas was staying. All the silver not hidden had been stolen. "This morning," she wrote, "we used seashells for spoons." It was for her a literal nightmare, the next night more miserable than the last.[789]

Sherman was now moving through North Carolina, and Kate Edmonston, in Halifax County near the Virginia line, was nerving herself for what she saw coming. "God grant us strength to endure what he has in store for us," she confided to her journal.[790]

Carolinians, North and South, did endure, but they awoke from the nightmare after it had passed "to realize we were destitute," and to conclude that the Confederacy "seemed suddenly to have changed, a glory had passed from it, and, without acknowledging it, we felt the end was near."[791]

Not all of the horror was Sherman-induced. This new, more doom-driven malaise was gripping the South from Richmond to the Gulf, and women were finding it harder and harder not to be overcome by it. Parthenia Antoinette Hague wrote, "The newspapers brought news of defeat after defeat; day by day they told us of the inexorable advance of the Federal troops; day by day the conviction strengthened with us that, struggle as we would, we were on the los-ing side, and ours was to go down to history as 'the lost cause.' Our soldiers were living on parched corn, as they had been for a year; they were going into battle ragged and barefoot and half-starved— in vain." Parthenia set out on the road from Alabama to Georgia as soon as the railroads could be repaired and the bridges rebuilt, to see after her father, whose house had been in Sherman's path to the sea. Along the road she saw "the ruins of grim-visaged war," and grew more rebellious and bitter. "Oh thou great God of Israel!" she cried, "why hast thou permitted this dire calamity to befall us? Why is it that our homes are so despoiled?"[792]

The kinder past, "with its many hallowed associations," seemed to many in the Confederacy ever more distant, ever more precious, ever more lost. One soldier wrote:

> *Ah!* those *days were very bright—Billy*
> *And* now *they seem to me—*
> *Like some fair enchanted isle*
> *As seen in a desert sea.*[793]

Vanished memories, sighed nineteen-year-old Lucy Buck, in Front Royal, Virginia, they "come back to us 'as sad as earth, as sweet as heaven.'"[794]

But for all the anguish, all of the mourning over an irrecoverable past, a "hectic gaiety and excitement" had seized Dixie in its darkest hour.[795] In part it seemed a letting go in the face of hopelessness. Mary Chesnut had called it "days of unmixed pleasure, snatched from the wrath to come."[796]

"Oh what a falling off is there!" one woman wrote the *Montgomery Daily Advertiser*, "a change and such a change, has come over the spirit of their dream. The Aid Societies have died away; they are a name and nothing more. The self-sacrifice has vanished; wives and maidens now labor only to exempt husbands and lovers from the perils of service. . . . Never were parties more numerous. . . . Never were the theatres and places of public amusement so resorted to."[797]

If "privation, hunger, cold, sickness, wounds, death" were "the daily menu in a daily entertainment," as one Virginian put it,[798] there was also a compulsion to dance the horror away, to glide "swiftly on glancing feet"[799]—to ease the stress, the deprivation and the sense of doom. It was as if Southerners believed they must seize the moment wherever and whenever it could be found, and fill it with as much joy as they could muster, for tomorrow they might be dead—as often they were. Entertainments, balls, amateur theatricals, and musical evenings abounded—many of them to raise money out of patriotism or charity. Even as Sherman rolled into South Carolina, there was singing in parlors, and going to bed, as Joseph LeConte and his friends did, "with our hearts still full of music—the music of kind feelings and happy hearts."[800]

Young people in Dixie, like young people everywhere, could hardly keep from trying to "snatch a fearful joy" wherever they could find it.[801] Elizabeth Randolph Preston's group of young folks, in Lexington, Virginia, threw a party in the Christmas season that winter. She had been only twelve years old four Christmases before when she had heard the word *secession* for the first time in her life. She quickly learned to consider Lincoln a "monster," and to sing "Dixie" and "The Bonnie Blue Flag." Now she was sixteen and it seemed to her "as if war had always been, and would always be, and my unquenchable hope reached out for whatever was to be had of *joie de vivre*."[802]

Most women throughout the South had to take their joie de vivre in unfashionable unbleached homespun, as coarse as slave dresses, instead of in billowy cottons, silks, and linens. In higher social circles, however, fancy dinner parties were still being staged. Theater was booming as never before—farces, melodramas, magic acts, and blackface minstrel shows.[803]

Even in circles where the fare was as spartan as the dress, there was a perverse contentment. "We sipped our Confederate tea," Sallie Putnam wrote, in Richmond, "swallowed quickly our Confederate coffee (frequently without sugar), dined on fat bacon and

Indian peas, and took our dessert of sorghum-syrup and corn bread, with as much cheerfulness and apparent relish as we formerly discussed the rich viands on the well-filled boards of the old Virginia housewives."[804]

The revelry played to mixed emotions. "I did not think two months ago," Kate Stone had written in her journal in the middle of the summer in 1864, "I would ever dance or care to talk nonsense again. But one grows callous to suffering and death. We can live only in the present, only from day to day. We cannot bear to think of the past and so dread the future." The refugees, of which she was now one, reminded her "of the description of the life . . . the nobility of France lived during the days of the French Revolution—thrusting all the cares and tragedies of life aside and drinking deep of life's joys while it lasted."[805]

Richmond was "full of people, and suffering, and crime," one visitor wrote, but the beau monde and its fashionable ladies "dress and walk the streets as if there was no war."[806] It was said that the city "laughed while it cried, and sang while it endured, and suffered and bled."[807] Nellie Gray, who was there, never remembered having more fun in her life, even when "sometimes we were hungry, and while the country, up to our doors, bristled with bayonets, and the air we breathed shook with the thunder of guns." She marveled that there were "hunger and nakedness and death and pestilence and fire and sword everywhere, and we, fugitives from shot and shell, knew it well." But, she said, they put on their bonnets of homemade straw trimmed with chicken feathers and "laughed and sang and played on the piano—and never believed in actual defeat and subjugation."[808]

There were those, however, in whom all laughing and singing and playing and dancing had died—or was at least in remission. Nobody frowned deeper on such mindless frivolity than Augusta Jane Evans, the tall, brown-haired, Yankee-hating novelist and arch-Rebel whose relentlessly unsmiling wartime work *Macaria, or Altars of Sacrifice* had been published in Richmond in 1864. Her novel was a paean to sacrifice and to strong, independent, self-denying womanhood—both in common currency in the wartime South—and was dedicated to the Confederate army. So was its author. To her that army was a holy instrument, and the war a sacred cause. Her most striking physical feature was her polychromatic eyes—one blue, the other brown. But she saw good and evil in clear black and white. She was a stone-willed foe of sin and folly in any form and was wholly intolerant of the idea of taking this war with anything but grim-faced seriousness. "Can mirth and reckless revelry hold high carnival in social circles," she demanded, "while every passing breeze chants the requiem of dying heroes, and is burdened with the lamentations of stricken wives and wailing orphans? Are Southern women so completely oblivious of the claims of patriotism and humanity, that in this season of direst extremity, they thread the airy mazes of the dance, while the matchless champions of freedom are shivering in bloody trenches, or lying stark on frozen fields of glory? . . . 'Shame! shame upon your degeneracy! You dance over our bleaching and unburied bones!'"[809]

Sara Pryor was not dancing. At Cottage Farm she had invitations from friends in town to join in, but she accepted none. She had "no heart for gayety" and not a moment's time to spare from her sewing. "It is passing strange—," she thought, "this disposition to revel in times of danger and suffering." But like Kate Stone, she knew it was not without precedent. Florence, she remembered, was never so gay as during the plague.[810] Even the frowning Jane Evans had to admit that "a sorrow's crown of sorrow is remembering happier things."[811]

Petersburg had its "starvation parties," marked for their lack of refreshments, which were impossible to come by. It had foodless balls, where "the soldier met and danced with the lady of his love at night, and on the morrow danced the dance of death in the deadly trench out on the line."[812]

There was yet another counterpoint to war and its desolation—a rash of weddings. Richmond was famous for its large number of beautiful and single women. And as the *Richmond News Leader* would one day observe, looking back, "Girls looked no less lovely [or available] because they dressed in calico instead of silk. They danced as gracefully at 'starvation parties' as ever they had at great levees."[813]

Phoebe Pember believed that every girl in Richmond was engaged or about to be.[814] Sallie Putnam agreed, noting that "while the god of war thundered from the ramparts, not less busy was the artful boy-god.... Cupid's victories," she said, were many, and there was an epidemic of weddings during this very hard winter. Often "death, remorseless, cruel Death, claimed the warrior bridegroom, and the snowy robe of the bride ... [was] exchanged for the weeds of the widow, the sable robe of the heart's deepest affliction."[815] But the bondings went on.

IN THIS BIZARRE TIME of terrible want coupled to desperate partying, Robert E. Lee sent Sara Pryor a note. "My dear Mrs. Pryor," the note read. "General Lee has been honored by a visit from the Hon. Thomas Connolly [Conolly], Irish M. P. [Member of Parliament] from Donegal. He ventures to request you will have the kindness to give Mr. Connolly a room in your cottage, if this can be done without inconvenience to yourself."

Sara could spare him a room, certainly, but just as surely, she could not feed him. The messenger bringing the note hastily reassured her. He had been instructed by the general to tell her that Conolly would dine with Lee. Nobody was quite sure why this scion of one of the leading families of the Victorian Irish gentry and Tory backbencher was in the stricken South at all. He had arrived on the North Carolina coast on the *Owl*, one of the last vessels to slip through the Union blockade, and had been visiting in Richmond and Petersburg.

Conolly turned out to be an ardent Confederate partisan and

"a fine-looking Irish gentleman," Sara thought, with "an irresistibly humorous, cheery fund of talk"—a charmer too engaging to dislike, a most agreeable guest. Sara put him in John's care and John soon became devoted to his service. The robust MP often dropped in during their biscuit toasting, and he assured them they were better fed than the commanding general.

"You should have seen 'Uncle Robert's' dinner to-day, Madam!" He exclaimed in his Irish brogue. "He had two biscuits, and he gave me one." Another time he said, "We had a glorious dinner to-day! Somebody sent 'Uncle Robert' a box of sardines." Lee was scarcely forgotten. Farm wives regularly sent him pails of buttermilk, and all of it—and every vegetable he was given—he sent to the hospital for the scurvy-ridden soldier-patients.

Conolly believed Sara to be "one of the nicest Ladies I ever saw." He called Cottage Farm, "a smiling farm house,"[816] and soon became fascinated with the Pryor boys and their Latin studies. "I am going home," he vowed, "and tell English women what I have seen here: two boys reading Caesar while the shells are thundering, and their mother looking on without fear." Sara demurred. "I am too busy keeping the wolf from my door," she told him, "to concern myself with the thunderbolts."[817]

He very likely intended to tell the Englishwomen that as well.

CHAPTER 19

————— ·•·•· —————

The Northern Bastille

$\mathscr{S}$ara was desperate to have Roger free and returned to her. He had written her a letter from Fort Lafayette five days before Christmas that turned like a knife in her heart.

"My philosophy begins to fail somewhat," he wrote. "In vain I seek some argument of consolation. I see no chance of release. The conditions of my imprisonment cut me off from every resource of happiness."[818]

From the day in late November when Wilcox had told her Roger was captured and she had seen his riderless horse, little hope lived in her heart that he might be rapidly exchanged as Wilcox had optimistically predicted. At the end of January, when Roger had been gone for two months, Wilcox came to her door again, with news of some hope. Lincoln had agreed to meet in Hampton Roads with three authorized Confederate commissioners to discuss possible peace terms and an end to the war.

Wilcox told her that the three Confederate negotiators—Vice President Alexander Stephens, Senator R. M. T. Hunter, and former justice of the U.S. Supreme Court and now the assistant Confederate secretary of war, John A. Campbell—had just arrived in Petersburg enroute to meet with Lincoln.

"I thought you might come out and listen to the cheering," Wilcox suggested. "It is echoed by the enemy. There seems to be no doubt of the feeling on both sides."

Wilcox loaned her an ambulance and Sara drove out to the front where the commissioners were to cross the lines. The Confederate troops at Fort Gregg and Battery 45, not far from the rear of her garden, had come out and were cheering. There seemed to be a momentary truce, cheer answering cheer all along the line. Sara's ambulance drew up to the side of the road and stopped, and presently an open carriage carrying the mayor and the three commissioners pulled up before crossing over.

With a wildly beating heart, Sara left her ambulance and hurried to their carriage. There Hunter, a longtime friend, greeted her kindly and introduced her to his two fellow commissioners. Sara felt a good deal about Hunter as Louis Wigfall felt about him—but for different reasons. Wigfall had said early in the life of the Confederacy, "I don't know what we Southern men would do without Hunter; he is the only one among us who knows anything about finance." Sara didn't know much about finance, either, but she believed this old friend might help free Roger.

Trembling with emotion, she said, "My errand is to you, dear Mr. Hunter. You are going to see President Lincoln or his representative. I entreat you, I implore you, to remember your friend General Pryor. He is breaking his heart in prison. Beg his release from Mr. Lincoln."

"I will—we will," they promised her, and Sara was heartened.

The carriage drove on, and as it crossed the line, a final cheer went up from the hundreds of soldiers, Confederate and Union, who were looking on with hope in their own hearts. In an instant, however, after the carriage had passed, the lines fell back as they were. The two sides were enemies again. Sara turned her ambulance and hastened out of the range of fire.[819]

———

FORT LAFAYETTE, WHERE Sara's thoughts turned daily, jutted up from a two-and-a-half-acre rock island in the Verrazano Narrows at the mouth of New York Harbor. It was built there, opposite Fort Hamilton between Brooklyn and Staten Island, in 1822 as one of three sentinels guarding the main entrance to the harbor. The fort was octangular, with its angles pointing out to the sea, the bay, and the two shores, and armed, as one observer put it, with "two tiers of grinning cannon."[820] Its walls were eight feet thick and twenty-five to thirty feet high, and it had two stories of casemates, ten to each story. It was a compact entity with a hollow center open to the air 120 feet square and bordered by a pavement about 25 feet wide.

Since there was no particular need in this war for its "grinning cannon," the fort, named for the Marquis de Lafayette, the French hero of the American war for independence, was turned into a prison in July 1861. Since it specialized in housing political offenders, it was widely considered "the American Bastille." Among its first eighteen inmates, also the first prisoners of state ever jailed in this country, were four suspect Baltimore police commissioners, four Rebel-minded accomplices caught giving aid to the enemy, an errant government official, two spies, and a Broadway bully.[821]

In its day in this war Fort Lafayette had housed a who's who of otherwise respectable society. There had been governors of states, foreign ministers, members of congress, virtually the entire Maryland state legislature (to head off passage of an act of secession), a mayor, police commissioners, army and navy officers, doctors civil and military, lawyers, merchants, farmers, mechanics, inventors (generally considered a particularly dangerous class), newspaper editors, spies, pirates—and, of course, Confederates.[822]

A captured Confederate blockade runner bound for Lafayette said it loomed up before him "in all its dreariness."[823] Another inmate who served time there, Francis K. Howard, one of the Maryland legislators incarcerated early in the war, wrote of it, "A gloomier looking place ... both within and without, it would be hard to find in the whole State of New York, or, indeed, any-where."[824] "Heaven!" grumbled another arrested Maryland official, "my County Jail is a palace to such a place." Said yet another captive official from the Old Line State, "Is it possible that freemen are to be huddled together in such an infernal hole?"[825]

The prisoners were housed in two main gun batteries and in four casemates on the lower tier. Open entrances had been bricked over to make them escape-proof. The two batteries, paved with brick, were twenty-four by sixty feet, but diminished in living space by five large thirty-two-pounder cannon jutting into the room eight feet apart, with beds wedged in among them. The four casemates were fourteen-by-twenty-four-foot rooms with low-vaulted ceilings only eight feet high at their apex. They were lit by three small loopholes in the outer and inner walls, letting in "perpetual twilight" and ventilation from the sea. They were dungeons by their nature—dank and damp. Some forty Confederate captives, mostly officers, were housed there in late 1864 and early 1865. Prominent among them was Roger Pryor, the private called a general.[826]

Roger was held in casemate number two with about twelve other prisoners; he slept on a straw mat on the floor. The daily menu was conducive to weight loss—a small piece of meat and a thin slice of bread for breakfast; another slender piece of meat, a cup of rice or bean soup, and a thin slice of bread for dinner; and for supper, another small slice of bread. The inmates cooked this spartan fare on a small coal-burning grate, fetching the coal themselves from the cellar, and glad of it for the exercise. When Roger left the prison, he would be replaced in the casemate by a haughty young officer who refused to fetch his own quota of coal. "And so," said Colonel Burke, the prison commandant, "you are too great a man, are you, to fetch your coal? I had General Pryor here. He brought up his coal! I think, sir, you'll bring up yours!"[827]

Colonel Burke was the kind of man who would definitely fetch. He had served with Winfield Scott in the Mexican War, and

Scott said of him that he was "famous for his unquestioning obedience to orders. He was with me in Mexico, and if I had told him at any time to take one of my aides-de-camp and shoot him before breakfast, the aide's execution would have been duly reported."[828] His inmates at Fort Lafayette, not fearing to be shot before breakfast, enjoyed taunting him. With coal for a pencil, they drew caricatures of him on the casemate walls, a fresh picture every morning: "Burke as a baby," "Burke in his first pants," "Burke in love," and so on.[829]

Burke had a particular aversion to improvised saws, "the old knife with the gapped edge," occasionally fashioned by inmates to answer for a refined saw, with which to violate prison bars. There was small hope these gap-edged creations could successfully saw through anything more challenging than the daily beef ration. But Colonel Burke regularly mounted a reconnaissance to find bars that had been sawed at, and when he found one, he made a major fuss and launched a search.[830]

One of Roger's cell mates in casemate number two was Captain J. D. Allison, a Confederate officer operating out of Canada and suspected in connection with a plot to burn New York City. Allison had been one of John Hunt Morgan's Confederate raiders, and the Northern press called him "The Notorious Jack Allison, one of Morgan's men, a Guerrilla & Ridge Runner." He had been released in November 1864 but was rearrested eleven days later and returned to Fort Lafayette, where his friends and fellow inmates crowded around to congratulate him on having, so far, escaped hanging. He and Roger were given to gambling at cards. But Allison was something of a cardsharp. After a particularly heavy snowfall in early February, Roger had lost his bedding to him, in a game of euchre. In another game he lost his shirt, cravat, collars, and a mince pie he was expecting from an outside friend. Before the month was out, the two of them had "some sharp words" and agreed to have nothing more to say to one another.[831] The card games and Roger's losses tailed off.

A cell mate more notorious even than Jack Allison was also in casemate number two, with an aura of doom about him. John Y. Beall, an officer of the Confederate navy, was another of those Canada-based Rebel agents bent on subversion in the North, implicated, like Allison, in the conspiracy to burn New York City. He was also charged with scuttling, burning, robbing, and hijacking vessels, with an eye to freeing Confederate prisoners in Northern prisons. Considered a major menace in the North, he had been arrested mid-December, in civilian dress, attempting to throw a passenger train from the track near Buffalo, New York. He had been tried as a spy, guerrilla, outlaw, and would-be murderer and sentenced to hang. Like Roger, Beall was an aristocrat with deep Virginia roots, a graduate of the University of Virginia law school, and equally fiery and impetuous.[832] He was not yet thirty years old and was thought by the ladies to be "young and very good-looking."[833] As a Confederate soldier fighting with Stonewall Jackson early in the war, he had taken a bullet in the breast that had broken three ribs and entered his right lung. He had gone to Pine Hill, north of Tallahassee, Florida, to convalesce under the care of Dr. Edward Bradford, and after several months of quiet there was again service ready. However, because of his wound, he was no longer considered fit for active fighting, so he entered the secret service in Lee's army.[834]

In Canada he had led bands of guerrillas on the Great Lakes in attacks against Yankee shipping. He had asked that Roger be allowed to act as his attorney, but the war department, having an aversion to convicts lawyering for convicts, wouldn't hear of it. After his trial and sentence he was sent back to the casemate at Fort Lafayette to await his fate. The South had reacted with threats of reprisal. Hang Beall, and the Confederate authorities vowed that they would string up a number of prominent Northerners in their custody. Lincoln's secretary of war, Edwin Stanton, a hard case, had countered with a threat to hang Beall's hoped-for lawyer,

Roger Pryor, which he was inclined to do, anyhow. This sword of Damocles hanging commonly over their heads, among other things, made Roger and Beall sympathetic cell mates. Beall told Roger he had no hand whatsoever in the attempt to burn hotels in New York, nor had he transgressed the laws of war in his attempt to derail railway trains. His regard for Roger was such that he entrusted him with his diary before leaving the prison to be hanged.[835]

On February 13 Colonel Burke came to the casemate and called for Beall. "I have bad news for you Captain," the colonel said, "but I know you are a brave man and can stand it." All the other inmates were moved to a battery, "a great cold barn" of a place, leaving Beall in the casemate alone under heavy guard. At nine o'clock that evening, the prisoners learned he was to be hanged on the eighteenth. "Oh: God what a lamentable death," Jack Allison wrote in his own prison diary, "and for one from home & friends, a prisoner in the hands of his bitter, bitter enemies."[836]

At nine o'clock in the morning, February 16, a tug tied up at the prison to take Beall to Governors Island for his execution. His former cell mates in the battery watched as he walked from the casemate into the yard. He saw them and saluted, spoke pleasantly to those nearest him, and walked out with a steady step to the tug.[837]

Though not condemned to die—yet—Roger found the winter of imprisonment was nonetheless going hard, seriously undercutting not just his spirit but his physical well-being. By February he was slipping in both health and spirits. He wrote Sara, "I am as contented as is compatible with my condition. My mind is ill at ease from my solicitude for my family and my country. Every disaster pierces my soul like an arrow. . . . How I envy my old comrades their hardships and privations. I have little hope of an early exchange, and you may be assured my mistrust is not without reason. *Except some special instance be employed to procure my release, my detention here will be indefinite.* I cannot be more explicit. While this is my conviction, I wish it distinctly understood that I would not have my government compromise any scruple for the sake of my liberation. I am prepared for any contingency—am fortified against any reverse of fortune."[838]

Sara was no more sanguine than he. The peace commissioners, whom she had petitioned on his behalf, had returned diplomatically empty-handed and unable to bring Sara an encouraging word. Hunter wrote her that they had remembered Roger as promised, "but his release would not be considered."[839]

Unknown to Roger or Sara, however, other eyes were watching, primarily Washington McLean, a noted "pen-driver,"[840] editor of the *Cincinnati Enquirer*, who had met Roger when he was in the U.S. Congress. Also watching was John W. Forney, another Northern editor and Roger's onetime colleague on the *Washington Union* in the early 1850s. They saw that Roger was being held as hostage for the safety of the Union officer Captain Henry S. Burrage, whom the Confederate government had threatened to hang. With Roger's life in precarious balance, they decided to act.

They first approached Grant, who refused to intercede. McLean then went to see the secretary of war. Stanton received him in the library of his home, where McLean found him with his little daughter in his arms.

"This is a charming fireside picture, Mr. Secretary," McLean said. "I warrant that little lady cares nothing for war or the Secretary of War! She has her father, and that fills all her ambition."

"You never said a truer word, did he, pet?" said Stanton, pressing her curly head to his bosom.

"Well, then," McLean said, risking it all on one throw of the dice, "you will understand my errand. There are curly heads down there in old Virginia, weeping out their bright eyes for a father loved just as this pretty baby loves you."

"Yes, yes! Probably so," Stanton conceded.

"Now," said McLean, "there's Pryor—"

Before he could finish the thought, Stanton pushed the child from his knee and thundered, "He shall be hanged! Damn him!"[841]

McLean's toss of the dice had come up snake eyes.

So he ratcheted the effort up one more notch. Armed with the support and a letter of introduction from his fellow editor Horace Greeley, of the *New York Tribune,* who knew and had leverage with Lincoln, McLean went to see the president himself. Greeley had written, "Roger A. Pryor, now a prisoner of war in Fort Lafayette, was captured under circumstances which seem to give him special claims to exchange. My friend Mr. W[ashington] McLean of Cincinnati is authorized to offer any reasonable exchange for Mr. Pryor, and I hope it may be effected." Joshua Speed, Lincoln's attorney general, had written Lincoln on February 15, "Mr. McLean of Cincinnati is very anxious to get Roger Pryor ... now at Fort Lafayette exchanged. He says that he would stake his fortune on Pryors complying with any promise he would make or for the fulfilment of the terms upon which he accepts a parole."[842]

Lincoln knew of Roger. He had read some of his editorials in antebellum days. He also had heard of Roger's uniformly generous treatment of Union prisoners who at various times had fallen into his custody earlier in the war, particularly of his capture at Second Manassas of an entire camp of Federal wounded, surgeons, and ambulance corps, and his kindness and prompt parole of them. He also knew that Roger had fed the party of Union prisoners at Petersburg at the expense of Sara's impoverished larder. "The man who can do such a kindness to an enemy," Lincoln said, "cannot be cruel and revengeful." The president listened attentively to McLean's plea, and after listening, issued an order to Colonel Burke to deliver Roger into the Cincinnati editor's custody. With Lincoln's order in his hand, McLean entrained for Fort Lafayette.[843]

There his order from Lincoln won Roger's immediate release. The New York papers on February 19 reported that the general turned private had been paroled to report to John W. Forney.[844] McLean and Roger entrained immediately for Forney's home in Washington.

When news of Roger's release reached Stanton, the secretary—a man with an adamant mind of his own—issued orders to seize him wherever he could be found, with the intent of seeing him hanged. When Forney learned this, he sent his secretary, John Russell Young, to the various Washington newspapers to give each a brief account of how Roger had passed through Washington that evening and, under parole, had passed into Rebel lines. It wasn't true, but this was war. Roger hunkered in at Forney's house for two more days to see if the diversion would work. It did. Stanton, believing his quarry had escaped, disgustedly abandoned the hunt.[845]

Forney had also written Lincoln on February 18, as McLean was in New York freeing Roger, saying, "I do not think that the release of Roger A. Prior [sic], according to your generous card given to Washington McLean yesterday, would be followed by any but the very best consequences. He has Mr. Greeley's letter to you asking for his deliverance. A fair and honorable exchange is offered by his friends. I am full of sorrow that Mr. Stanton should object to the fulfilment of your promise in his behalf, and I now write this note in the hope that you will permit your own wishes to be carried out."[846]

The day Washington McLean was rescuing Roger from the Northern bastille, word reached the casemate that Lincoln had granted John Beall a temporary reprieve. The newspapers and Beall's former cell mates speculated that it was to permit his mother to see him one more time. Nobody knew how long the reprieve would last.[847] There was still slim hope he might not be hanged. Not only was Roger intensely interested in trying to intercede on Beall's behalf, but by now so were McLean and Forney. McLean suggested that a personal appeal to the president on Beall's behalf by his cell mate Roger Pryor might prevent the execution. McLean telegraphed Lincoln, requesting an interview. The president agreed.

The next evening, February 23, Roger, McLean, and Forney called at the White House. The visit had two aims—to get Roger paroled or exchanged and Beall saved from the noose. Lincoln received them cordially, and Roger at once made his pitch for Beall's salvation. It was a last-ditch effort; the clock was ticking. The president listened. He seemed interested in all that Roger was saying. But after a prolonged discussion, Lincoln took a telegram from his desk from General John Dix, commanding the Department of the East, headquartered in New York. The telegram assured Lincoln that Beall's execution was necessary for the security of Northern cities. It was apparent that Beall's reprieve was but temporary and that the president had no intention of stopping the execution.[848]

Indeed, Lincoln had something else on his mind. He turned the conversation to his recent Hampton Roads conference with the three Confederate emissaries who had crossed the lines behind Cottage Farm. Lincoln was disappointed with its results. He told Roger that had the Confederates agreed to reestablish the Union and abolish slavery, Lincoln's two main goals, the South might have been compensated for the loss of its slaves and protected by a universal amnesty. But Davis had made Southern independence a condition sine qua non of any negotiations, which Lincoln could not accede to. Lincoln told Roger that it was obvious the Southern armies would soon be crushed and that Davis would be responsible for every drop of blood shed in the further prosecution of the war. Lincoln dwelt so long and so ardently on the subject that Roger inferred he still hoped the people of the South would override Davis and renew negotiations for peace. The president could not believe Davis's senseless obstinacy represented the true sentiments of the South. It was also obvious to Roger, as the three callers departed, that Lincoln desired him to sound out the leading men of the South on the subject when he returned home.[849]

Returning home was now in Roger's immediate future. The next day, February 24, Lincoln wired Ulysses S. Grant at City Point, asking him to let Roger pass through the lines. Grant, who had earlier opposed letting the notorious prisoner go, wired back: "Send Pryor on here and we will exchange him. He can do us no harm now." That same day, Lincoln wrote out a pass: "Allow the bearer, Roger A. Pryor, to pass to Gen. Grant, and report to him for exchange."[850]

And that same day, John Y. Beall was executed on Governors Island. As he marched soldierlike to the gallows, stepping in slow time to his own death-dirge, he exclaimed, "How beautiful the sun is! I look upon it for the last time!"[851]

CHAPTER 20

Death Knell

General Robert E. Lee had been a point of light in darkest Petersburg, just as he had been the South's beacon since the Seven Days battles when he had driven George McClellan's multitudes from the gates of Richmond. He was the champion of the Confederacy, the embodiment of its hopes, the one reassuring presence in "those abominable trenches" of Petersburg.[852] It was his sword, as one hopeful Georgia wife wrote, "to which the Southern people looked for liberty and independence."[853]

He often rode alone behind the Petersburg trenches on his horse, Traveler, without courier or staff, always "of mien so dignified that no man could presume on familiarity, and yet so gracious that a child might approach him."[854] He was far more even than that. Thomas Conolly, the visiting Irish M.P., described him as "the idol of his soldiers & the Hope of His Country" and "also the handsomest man in all that constitutes the real dignity of man that I ever saw."[855] Another visiting Englishman, Colonel Arthur J. L. Fremantle, believed him "almost without exception, the handsomest man of his age I ever saw."[856]

An admiring cousin had written of him years before that he looked "more like a great man than any one I have ever seen."[857] He was described wearing "a well-worn long gray jacket, a high

black felt hat, and blue trousers tucked into his Wellington boots."
He carried no arms—looking like a man of peace. The only marks
that betrayed his military rank were the three stars on his collar.
Fremantle reported, "Throughout the South, all agree in pronounc-
ing him to be as near perfection as a man can be," with apparently
"none of the small vices, such as smoking, drinking, chewing, or
swearing, and his bitterest enemy never accused him of any of the
greater ones." His only faults appeared to stem from his "excessive
amiability."[858] "No fault to be found if you hunted for one," Mary
Chesnut said. "He looks so cold and quiet and grand."[859]

He as often rode out to consult with his lieutenants as he sent
for them to come to him. The sight of him on the roadside, in the
trenches, or at Sara's well "was as common as that of any subor-
dinate in the army. When he approached and or disappeared, it
was with no blare of trumpets or clank of equipments. Mounted
upon his historic warhorse, 'Traveler' he ambled quietly about,
keeping his eye upon everything pertaining to the care and defense of his army."[860]

Cottage Farm lay on the road between Lee's headquarters and
Fort Gregg, the fortification that held Grant at bay on that part of
the line. Lee almost daily passed on his way there or to Battery 45.
Regularly, on Sundays, he rode by on his way to a little wooden
chapel, nearer to his quarters than Saint Paul's Church in Petersburg, where most of the army's high command worshiped. He wore
his faded gray overcoat and slouch hat, bending his head against the
sleet on stormy winter mornings. Sara had often seen him.[861]

As was her wont, early one morning she sat sewing in her little
parlor, when an orderly entered and said, "General Lee wishes to
make his respects to Mrs. Pryor."

Lee followed immediately. With the courtesy and kindness that
always marked his manner—and with anticipation this time lighting his eye—he asked after her welfare. He took the baby, Lucy, in
his arms and asked, "How long, Madam, was General Pryor with
me before he had a furlough?"

"He never had one, I think," Sara answered.

"Well, did I not take good care of him until we camped here so close to you?"

"Certainly," Sara said, puzzled by the drift of these preliminaries from this great man.

"I sent him home to you, I remember," Lee continued, "for a day or two, and you let the Yankees catch him. Now he is coming back to be with you again on parole until he is exchanged. You must take better care of him in future."

Sara gasped, too much overcome by her emotions to stammer out more than a few words of gratitude.

After a moment, Lee added teasingly, "What are you going to say when I tell the General that in all this winter you have never once been to see me?"

"Oh, General Lee," Sara answered, "I had too much mercy to join in your buttermilk persecution."

"Persecution!" he exclaimed. "Such things keep us alive! Last night, when I reached my headquarters, I found a card on my table with a hyacinth pinned to it, and these words: 'for General Lee, with a kiss!'" Lee tapped his breast and said, "Now, I have here my hyacinth and my card—*and I mean to find my kiss!*"

He looked down at Lucy and was amused by her earnest stare as she gazed up into his face. "They have a wonderful liking for soldiers," Lee said, speaking of children generally.

Sara was struck by the general's "singular calmness." It was a calmness she had often heard of. Sara didn't know it that morning, but under the outward calm, Lee was perhaps the most troubled man in the Confederacy. He knew the apparent hopelessness of the Southern cause. He knew he had but a ragged, undermanned army of not more than 33,000, spread over forty miles of trenches—little better than a skirmish line. He knew that Grant, facing this thread-thin defensive line, had a host exceeding 160,000 troops. He knew that with these numbers it was out of the question for him to mount any kind of successful offensive thrust.[862] He knew the end was near. After exchanging a few more words and leaving a message for Roger to come see him on his return, he rose, walked to the window, and looked out over the fields.

Sara was moved to say, "You only, General, can tell me if it is worth my while to put the ploughshare into those fields."

"Plant your seeds, Madam," Lee replied, adding sadly after a moment, "the doing it will be some reward." Sara realized then that the hope of the Confederacy had himself very little hope left.[863] Throughout the South, as its beacon was dimming, there was but a common anguish. Kate Cumming wrote in her diary in Georgia, "Not one ray of light gleams from any quarter. It seems like hoping against hope."[864]

ROGER RETURNED TO SARA, pale and thin. Her houseguest, Tom Conolly, and the officers encamped in her yard, called on him, joyful of his release, keenly anxious to hear his story. Sara's friends in Washington had wished to send gifts home for her with him, but Roger had declined them, accepting only two cans of pineapple. Conolly sent out for the "boys in the yard"—the officers—and helped Sara divide the fruit into helpings so all would have a taste. Conolly himself passed the tray around with the pineapple divided up on all the saucers and butter plates they could find in the house. "Oh, lads!" he cried. "It is just the *best* thing you ever tasted!"[865]

Roger had yet an obligation to fulfill—to the enemy's leader. So, soon after he returned, he went to Richmond. There he talked to Hunter and others and told them of his interview with Lincoln. All the prominent men he talked to, with one voice, told him nothing could be done about Davis, and the South could only await "the imminent and certain catastrophe."[866] It would come soon enough.

April 2, a Sunday morning following All Fools' Day, the weather was surpassingly beautiful, the sky was cloudless, the sunlight was brilliant. To one Union officer it seemed "that a more perfect day could not have dawned on earth since the creation."[867]

"The April woods," one of Lee's staff officers wrote, "were budding... the odors of spring were in the air, the green fields and the broad prospect of woods and hills formed an inspiriting contrast to the close earthworks behind which [the Rebel army] had so long lain."[868]

The first swallow had returned to North Carolina, as it always had, as precise and dependable as clockwork. Kate Edmonston saw it and "the sight of him made me heartsick with hope deferred. I have so often hailed him as the harbinger of Peace & been disappointed."[869]

That Sunday morning Roger and Sara were up early. A farmer friend had sent a load of peas, potatoes, dried fruit, hominy, and a little bacon as a welcome home for Roger. They had heard that the hospitals in Petersburg were scurvy-ridden, and they had boiled some of the hominy, prepared the dried fruit, and bagged the potatoes to send to the sick.

The cannonading all the night before had been ferocious— more thundering than normal. It shook the earth and rattled the windows and kept Roger awake. Over breakfast he said to Sara, "How soundly you can sleep! The cannonading was awful last night. It shook the house."

"Oh, that is only Fort Gregg," she said. "Those guns fire incessantly. I don't consider them. You've been shut up in a casemate so long you've forgotten the smell of powder."

After breakfast Sara had gone to the kitchen to fill pails with food for the sick and the wounded in the hospitals, and to send John and Alick on their morning errands. Roger walked out to the fortification beyond the garden. A new, low earthwork had been thrown up in the night near the house, and Roger stood on it to look out toward the trench line. In a moment he sent a message calling urgently for Sara. When she arrived, he held out his hand and drew her up beside him.

The scene before them was alive with movement. Black laborers were passing, wheeling barrows filled with the spades they had been using. Below, on the plain, ambulances were collecting at intervals, stopping and going. A thin gray defense line stretched across under the guns of the nearest earthwork. Fort Gregg and Battery 45 were snarling, answered by Union guns all along the line. As Roger and Sara watched, the woods opposite leaped into life. Out from it flushed an entire division of bluecoats, with muskets glinting and banners whipping.

"My God!" Roger exclaimed. "What a line! They are going to fight here right away. Run home and get the children in the cellar." He would soon follow.

When Sara reached the Confederate encampment in the yard behind the house, she found everything in confusion. Tents were being struck and loaded into wagons. One of the officers rode up to her and urged her to leave immediately, and Sara reminded him that he had once promised not ever to allow her to be surprised.

"We are ourselves surprised," he said; "believe me, your life is not safe here a moment." Tapping his breast, he said, "I bear despatches proving what I say."

There was no time to consult Roger. Sara ran into the house and gathered up the children. She ordered the servants to remain. If things grew hot, they had the cellar. Perhaps their presence would save their own goods and hers should the day go against the Confederates. In any event, she believed they would be safe. Uncle Frank departed immediately for the shelter, needing no coaxing.

"I have only one order," Sara told the others, "hide the General's flag." As she left, bareheaded—she couldn't find her bonnet in the confusion—she heard Uncle Frank call from the portholes of the cellar, "For Gawd's sake, Jinny, bring me a gode of water."[870]

The morning was close and warm as she and the children set out, fleeing "before the bullets" across fields plowed by shot and shell. Sara felt the want of her bonnet.[871] Presently, ahead on the road came a carriage driving rapidly from town. In it was Mr. Laighton, her former Petersburg neighbor, who had just safely settled his wife and little girls and was now coming for Sara. He proposed that as they were at the moment out of musket range, she rest along the road under the shade of a tree while he went on to the farm to see if he could save something—what did she suggest? Sara asked that he bring a change of clothing for the children and her medicine chest.

When Laighton returned, he said that he had seen Roger, and that all the cooked provisions where being handed out to Confederate soldiers and more was being prepared. He told Sara he had promised Roger he would care for her until he could follow. John had put the silver service into the buggy and Eliza had packed a trunk, for which Laighton was to return—the French trunk, in which Eliza had put a change of clothing.

They were all soon in Laighton's buggy on their way to town. Laighton asked, "Where shall I take you?"

Sara hadn't the faintest idea. She thought she would trust to chance and hope for an invitation from someone to stay somewhere. But in town they found the streets teeming with refugees as homeless as Sara and her children and as uncertain of shelter. Few of Sara's friends were left in Petersburg. Most of them had fled when the siege was laid.

As they drove slowly through the streets looking for some sign of lodgings, they met a man Sara recognized as Roger's tailor. He told them a house had been left vacant by one of his customers, who had authorized him to rent it. "I now rent it to General Pryor," he said, and led them to it, a residence in Sara's old neighborhood on Washington Street. A man that the tailor addressed as Robert answered the bell, and the tailor told him that Sara and the children had become his master's tenants and that Robert and his mother, now in the house, would not be required to leave.

"Take good care of this lady," the tailor ordered. "I will see that your wages are paid and that you are suitably rewarded." Laighton left the silver service on the front porch, and there, in front of her new temporary lodgings, Sara sat down and waited.[872]

About noon, John found her. He was carrying Sara's champagne glasses and a basket of biscuits. Sara sent him back to the farm with strict orders to care for Roger's regimental flag. John told her he had hidden it in the cellar under some fence rails. No, he had no news of the battle, except that "Marse Roger is giving away everything on the earth. All the presents from the farmer will go in a little while."[873]

The next "envoy" from Cottage Farm was Alick, leading Rose, the cow, by a rope. Go back? No, *ma'am*, he told Sara, not if he knew his name was Alick. As he walked off to take Rose a pail of water, he said, "You'n me, Rose, is the only folks I see anywhar 'bout here with any sense."[874]

Neighbors soon discovered Sara, and to her joy she found that Mrs. Gibson, Mrs. Meade, and Mr. Bishop—one of her father-in-law's church elders—all old friends and neighbors, were still in their houses, very near her new temporary home. Her father-in-law, she later learned, was with the hospital corps, which had been sent to the rear. Lee had ordered the hospitals moved early in the day, and three thousand sick and wounded men had been evacuated. Sara saw this as a striking indication of Lee's estimate of the probabilities of the day.[875]

In the evening Sara's boys came in with war news. Sara had left the farm about ten o'clock in the morning. By one o'clock in the afternoon, Lee was holding the Confederate battle line through her garden.[876] Sara remembered, with a pang of anguish, the important family papers she had locked in the trunk in her room at the farm—all of Roger's letters; the correspondence from his time in Greece, in the East, and in Egypt; the letters from statesmen and authors in the years before the war. She sent Theodorick and Campbell Pryor, Roger's twelve-year-old half brother, back to the farm to break open the trunk, set fire to the contents, and not leave until they were consumed—to keep them from falling into enemy hands and made sport of. In time the boys returned, having burned the letters but bearing between them a huge bundle—a bedsheet full of papers. "Father's sermons," Campbell explained.[877]

The day had gone against Lee's army. Grant had at last broken through. The city was to be surrendered on the heels of Lee's evacuation at midnight.

Roger came in from the farm that evening ahead of the re-treating Confederate army. He was in such an excited state and so physically exhausted that Sara feared when the army passed he might try to go with it. At bedtime she found three upper rooms prepared for them. She put the boys in one, first slipping the large silver tray between two mattresses and hiding six pieces of the service in a hamper in the corner, under soiled towels and pinafores. A smaller room she had reserved for Roger. Now she locked him in it, slipped the key into her pocket, and took her seat at the window to listen to the sounds of the night.[878]

The doorbell rang. Startled, Sara opened the door and found Petersburg's mayor, W. W. Townes, standing there. He had come to ask if Roger, soon to be virtually the only Confederate soldier left in town and a former leading citizen, would go out with the flag of truce to surrender the city.

Sara was aghast. "Oh, he cannot—he cannot," she exclaimed. "How can you ask him to surrender his old home? Besides, he is worn out, and is now sleeping heavily."[879]

Back at her window after the mayor left, Sara saw General Lee pass with his staff. Soon there was a shattering explosion, another, then another. The city's bridges were being blown up and the to-bacco warehouses torched.

Still at her window at dawn, Sara saw the first Federal pickets enter the city, silently, watchfully. Sara ran to wake her boys. "Get up, boys!" she ordered. "Dress quickly. Now remember, you must be very self-controlled and quiet, and no harm will come to you."

Almost immediately the door to her room was thrown open and Robert entered with three armed Federal soldiers.

"What do you want?" Sara demanded.

"To search the house," they answered.

"You will find nothing worth your while," she said, "There is my shawl! I have just run in from the lines. Here are my children."

"We don't want your clothes," said one, "we want your prisoner."

Roger, who had not undressed, knocked at his locked door.

When Sara unlocked the door, he came out, fastening his collar, saying "Here I am." Before Sara could think or protest, they had marched him out of the house, and she was left alone with Robert, who was trembling with fear and excitement.

Sara turned on him, outraged by his betrayal of them, "Leave this house!" she screamed.

"What for?" he said, turning sullen.

"Because you are no friend of mine. This is now my house. You are not to set foot in it again."

Sara had brought with her from the farm a black servant, Lizzie, who had been hired by Eliza "to amuse the baby." Lizzie had carried Lucy to the basement kitchen when the trouble started. Now Sara heard a loud stomping and singing in the basement, and from the top of the stairs she called out to Lizzie, who ran up, frightened, with the baby in her arms. A soldier glared up at them from the bottom of the stairs.

"What are you doing here?" Sara demanded.

"Getting breakfast," he replied.

"You'll get none here," she told him.

The soldier started up the steps with his bayonet set. Sara stepped back and bolted the door.

Out in the street, a young Union officer was passing on horseback. Sara ran out and cried to him, "Is it your pleasure we should be murdered in our houses?" she demanded. "My kitchen is full of soldiers."

"Where, where?" the officer said, as he dismounted and ran into the house.

Sara led him to the bolted door and unbolted it. She then had "the satisfaction of watching him lay about the soldiers with the flat of his sword." When finished with them, the officer ordered them out and stationed a guard at the house.[880]

Out the window, the approach of another Federal army corps brought Sara yet more agony. She saw, borne in triumph at the head of the marching command, Roger's regimental banner, which she had tried so hard to keep from Union hands. As they passed her window the soldiers sang:

> *John Brown's body is a-mouldering in the ground,*
> *   As we go marching on!*
> *Oh, glory hallelujah,*
> *   As we go marching on!*

Down the line of march the song was caught up by the soldiers following:

> *Hang Jeff Davis on a sour apple tree,*
> *   As we go marching on.*
> *Oh, glory hallelujah,*
> *   As we go marching on!*

Sara thanked God Roger was not there to see it. But Alick saw it. "Ole Frank's at de bottom of dis business," he told Sara. Indeed Sara didn't doubt that Uncle Frank had purchased favor with the invading Union troops by revealing the banner's hiding place in the cellar.[881]

Roger soon returned, having been released after he had presented Lincoln's card that read "parole until exchanged." Together he and Sara sat all the rest of that day in the front parlor of the house and watched as Union soldiers marched past in pursuit of Lee's army. There seemed to be but one slim thread of a hope now for the Confederate cause—that Lee could unite with Joseph E. Johnston's army to the south and hide out in the Virginia mountains until he could rest and recruit his command back up to strength.[882]

IN RICHMOND, TOO, on that Sunday morning, a radiant sun pierced the soft haze that hung over the city. The steeple bells had called their congregations to worship. Their peal, the editor of the *Richmond Examiner* later remembered, "rose into the cloudless sky, and floated on the blue tide of the beautiful day."[883] The usual congregation filled Saint Paul's, with President Davis, "grave and tall and grey . . . straight, quiet, and attentive," seated in his customary pew, number sixty-three, on the aisle in the middle of the congregation. It was the Sunday of Holy Communion, and the celebration of the Lord's Last Supper. The sun slanted through the open windows, "very golden, very quiet." The Reverend Charles Minnigerode, the pastor at Saint Paul's, was reading the antecommunion service and the congregation was on its knees. The sexton, William Irving, a large man in a blue suit, brass buttons, and ruffled shirt, appeared in the center aisle and made his way to Davis's pew. He handed the president what appeared to be a telegram, and Davis rose instantly, put on his overcoat, and walked quietly out of the church "with a quiet grace and dignity."[884] Sara's friend Agnes noted that "his face [was] set, so we could read nothing."[885]

As Dr. Minnigerode read another of his "stirring and fervid" communion sermons, the sexton entered repeatedly to call out from the congregation first one, then another, of the men connected with the government and the military, who also quickly rose and left the church. An uneasy rustle rippled through the congregation, and with it, a growing sense of dread. The sexton now approached the chancel railing and whispered to the assistant pastor. Dr. Minnigerode quickly closed his sermon and went briefly to the vestry. When he returned, the congregation was streaming from the church, knowing something ominous had happened, without being told.[886]

Agnes hurried home to the Spotswood, where she lodged, and sent a note to the proprietor, asking for news. He answered her that Petersburg was being evacuated by Lee's army. It was by no means certain they could hold Richmond. He asked Agnes to keep it quiet and not fuel excitement or panic in the hotel. Agnes sat and tried to read in the quiet of her little parlor, but was literally in "a fever of anxiety." She soon gave that up and descended to the main hotel foyer. Nobody was there but two or three children with their nurses. She walked out into the street and met a Richmond city judge, William H. Lyons. He confessed that there was no point in further evading the truth. The lines were broken at Petersburg, and both it and Richmond would be surrendered late that night; he was going with the mayor and a committee of citizens with a flag of truce to surrender the city. He told her that locomotives were already fired to carry away the archives and bank officials. Davis and his cabinet would probably leave at the same time.

"And you, Judge?" Agnes asked.

"I shall stand my ground. I have a sick family, and we must take our chances together."

"Then seriously—really and truly—Richmond is to be given up, after all, to the enemy?"

"Nothing less! And we are going to have a rough time, I imagine."

Agnes would not be satisfied until she had seen Judge John A. Campbell, the Supreme Court justice of her Washington days and the Confederate assistant secretary of war, a man "of high character and position"[887] whom "we so much relied on for good, calm sense."[888] Campbell was elderly and bald, bowed and pale, seasoned by years of public service, "with a look on his face full of all disappointment and sadness, yet of great dignity."[889] Agnes found him with his hands full of papers, which he waved deprecatingly as she entered.

"Just a minute, Judge!" Agnes exclaimed. "I am alone at the Spotswood and—"

"Stay, there, my dear lady!" he said. "You will be perfectly safe. I advise all families to remain in their own houses. Keep quiet." He told her he was glad to know that the colonel, Agnes's husband, was safe. "He may be with you soon now," he assured her.

Agnes returned with that advice to the Spotswood, to reassure and comfort the proprietor, who immediately issued a notice to his other guests. Agnes then went out to pass the news to the families she knew best in the city.[890]

By late afternoon the "rough time" Judge Lyons had predicted arrived. Panic swept the capital. Everybody now knew Lee's lines had been broken at Petersburg. The news had hit "like a bombshell in a peaceful camp and dismay reigned supreme."[891] Captain Charles Blackford wrote his wife that night that "the streets were full of scared people . . . all in great distress, all powerless to prevent or accomplish anything."[892] Wagons rolled furiously through the streets to the various government departments, loading up archives and records and carrying them to the depot of the Richmond and Danville Railroad. All the cars of the rail line were pressed into service to evacuate government officials and the Confederate records.[893]

Thousands of citizens prepared to leave with the government. Transportation was in short supply and drawing exorbitant prices. "Vehicles with two horses, one horse, or even no horse at all," a reporter wrote, "suddenly rose to a premium value that was astounding." All over the city, the reporter said, it was the same— "wagons, trunks, band-boxes and their owners, a mass of hurrying fugitives filling the streets," mixing with porters carrying huge loads and wagons piled with baggage, all swarming toward avenues of escape.[894] Banks throughout the city threw open their doors to depositors and were getting their own bullion ready to ship out of town.

Half a dozen city councilmen met around a rude table in a dingy corner room on an upper floor of the capitol building[895] and ordered all liquor and spirits—"distilled damnation," some called it[896]—confiscated and poured into the gutters, for fear drunkenness would further compound the chaos. The vapors impregnated the air, and men, women, and boys rushed out with buckets, pails, pitchers, hats, and boots to catch what they could of the golden streams of brandy, whiskey, and rum.[897] It apparently seemed to many that no emergency, however serious, warranted wasting good liquor. Some of the alcohol burst into flames and the gutters became "a Niagara" of running fire.[898]

Night fell warm and still. A soft wind, "touched with the perfumes of earliest flowers and the first buds of spring," moved softly from the west.[899] But little sleep came with it. In the streets mob rule had taken over. Under the cover of night, crowds surged from store to store, unhinging doors and smashing windows, robbing some stores, torching others. In the alarm and terror, guards at the state penitentiary fled and inmates set fire to the workshops and escaped, stealing clothing wherever they could find it and casting off their prison garb. Many of them joined the surging mobs, roaming and plundering the helpless city, Sallie Putnam said, "like fierce, ferocious beasts." She wrote, "No human tongue, no pen, however gifted, can give an adequate description of the events of that awful night."[900]

There was scarcely less confusion and excitement in homes throughout the city. Fear had penetrated every household. Women collected and hid their valuables and cherished correspondence. "All through that long night," Mary Fontaine wrote, "we worked & wept, & bade farewells, never thinking of sleep."[901] Sallie Putnam wrote, "Fathers, husbands, brothers and friends clasped their loved ones to their bosoms in convulsive and agonized embraces, and bade an adieu, oh, how heart-rending!—perhaps, thought many of them, forever."[902]

Around midnight a train on the Danville line carried away the officers of the Confederate government. More trains full of fleeing people left throughout the night. The roads out of Richmond and the canal were the only avenues of escape left. The roads became jammed and the canals filled with boats thronged with refugees— all seeking safety in directions, Charles Blackford believed, "in which safety was not to be found."[903] John H. Reagan, the Confederacy's postmaster general, leaving with the government, believed that "the pen of man cannot be dipped in ink black enough to draw the darkness of that night which fell over Richmond."[904]

Mary Fontaine heard in the distance the shouts of soldiers and the mob as it ransacked stores. Under her window wagons rumbled and drums beat, all in a clashing, confused medley of sound.[905] At the first gray streak of dawn, explosions rocked the city with a roar "like that of a hundred cannon at one time."[906] Foundations shook, and windows more than two miles distant were shattered. Beds in the Union hospital at City Point heaved as in an earthquake. The Confederate boats in the James and the bridges across the river were being detonated. The earth, one witness wrote, "seemed fairly to writhe as if in agony, the house rocked like a ship at sea, while stupendous thunders roared around."[907] Emma Mordecai heard "the incessant roar of one explosion after another, or of many together . . . multiplied by the repeated reverberations from hill to hill, in terrible grandeur."[908]

For Sallie Putnam the scene that morning was unforgettable. Richmond's four main tobacco warehouses had been torched, and the fires raged, racing through the city "with fearful rapidity." The roaring, hissing, and crackling of the flames rose above the confusion and clamor of the plundering in the streets. From the city's lower side, near the river, dense black clouds of smoke rose "as a pall of crape to hide the ravages of the devouring flames," which were now leaping from building to building. As the racing fires reached the arsenal, more earsplitting explosions rocked the city. "All the horrors of the final conflagration, when the earth shall be wrapped in flames and melt with fervent heat were," it seemed to Sallie, "prefigured in our capital."[909] Agnes called it "a morning of horror, of terror!"[910]

Alfred Paul, the French consul, stood on one of Richmond's seven hills and stared in horror at the "immense tongue of flame" devouring the city.[911] The entire business district was on fire. Richmond seemed "one sea of flame."[912] Elizabeth Van Lew, the Yankee spy living in her mansion on Church Hill, however, looked on the holocaust, "the burning bridges, the roaring flames" adding such "a wild grandeur to the scene," as just retribution. "Square after square of stores," she wrote in her journal, "dwelling houses and factories, warehouses, banks, hotels, bridges, all wrapped in fire, filled the sky with clouds of smoke as incense from the land for its deliverance. What a moment! Avenging wrath appeased in flames!" It was no wonder, she marveled, that "the walls of our houses were swaying; the heart of our city a flaming altar, as this mighty work was done."[913]

Mary Fontaine closed the shutters at her windows in the night, to block out the sights and sounds of Armageddon. Everything within became "still as death, while immense fires stretched their arms on high all around me. I shuddered at the dreadful silence. Richmond burning & no alarm. It was terrible. I cannot describe my feelings as I stood at a window overlooking the city in that dim dawn." She saw the sun rise, "a great, red ball veiled in a mist."[914]

From the street the cry, "Yankees!" reached her window. Majors A. H. Stevens and E. E. Graves of the Fourth Massachusetts Cavalry, with forty horsemen, had just taken the city's surrender note. Mayor Mayo, who had said he would sooner die than surrender his city, had just surrendered it. The Yankee cavalrymen now rode steadily into Richmond toward the capitol through the smoke-laden air. Mary didn't move—"I could not—but watched the blue horseman ride to City Hall, enter with his sword knocking the ground at every step, & throw the great doors open, & take possession of our beautiful city; watched two blue figures on the Capitol . . . saw them unfurl a . . . flag, & then I sank on my knees, & the bitter, bitter tears came in a torrent."[915] Through the roaring, hissing, crackling flames, through the explosions and shouting, rose the strains of "The Star Spangled Banner." "For us," Sallie Putnam lamented, "it was a requiem for buried hopes."[916]

Then came the Union army. A lady of Richmond watched as it came: "Stretching from the Exchange Hotel to the slopes of

Church Hill, down the hill, through the valley, up the ascent to the hotel, was the array, with its unbroken line of blue, fringed with bright bayonets." As the phalanx, marching to the beat of regimental bands, turned at the Exchange Hotel into the upper street, each regiment burst into wild cheering. "Through throngs of sullen spectators; along the line of fire; in the midst of the horrours of a conflagration, increased by the explosion of shells left by the retreating army; through curtains of smoke; through the vast aerial auditorium convulsed with the commotion of frightful sounds, moved the garish procession of the grand army, with brave music, and bright banners and wild cheers."[917]

No city in Christendom, a Northern reporter entering with the Union army wrote, had "stood longer, more frequent, and more persistent sieges." The Union had been "shivering our thunderbolts against it for more than four years." The city, he wrote, "is the Rebellion; it is all that we have directly striven for; quitting it, the Confederate leaders have quitted their sheet-anchor, their rooftree, their abiding hope."[918]

Nellie Gray saw the invading army and thought sadly of the popular song, "Richmond Is a Hard Road to Travel." The Yankees had always found it so, but here they finally were.[919] And Richmond, that center of "refinement, elegance, and hospitality of the olden days," was now "the grave of dead heroes and the grave of dead hopes."[920]

By one o'clock in the afternoon on April 3, the confusion was at its peak. A south wind had sprung up, threatening to carry the surging flames to the northwestern side of the city. Federal troops were now fighting the fires. To Sallie Putnam all of the "horrors of Pandemonium" seemed screaming over Richmond. It was sundown before "the awful reverberations" of exploding shells stopped. And in the evening a deathlike quiet settled over the city. The hot, fierce fire had finally burned itself out. But it had razed the business district and gutted the heart of the city. All through another night an uncertain Richmond kept "a fearful vigil," listening "with beating heart and quickened ears" for the faintest sound that might portend other and more terrible horrors.[921]

IN PETERSBURG ON April 3, Roger and Sara continued to watch the Union legions march past their door. It soon became known the Pryors were there, and they began receiving visits from old Washington friends who had followed the Union troops into the city. Congressman Elihu B. Washburne called and so did Senator Henry Wilson.

Lincoln himself, having stood by on the vessel *River Queen* at City Point, had taken a special train that morning for Petersburg, to meet with Grant. The two met at Thomas Wallace's comfortable brick house on South Market Street. Settling in high-backed wooden chairs on the front porch, where Lincoln could dangle his long legs over the side and Grant could smoke his cigar, they talked for an hour and a half. In the course of the day Lincoln inquired after Roger, who had excused himself from meeting him on the grounds that he was still a paroled prisoner, that Lee was still in the field, and that he could therefore hold no conference with the commander-in-chief of the opposing army.[922]

The next morning, Lincoln entered Richmond, thirty-six hours after Jefferson Davis had left the city. The day was unseasonably warm, the air thick with dust and heavy with smoke from the still-smoldering fires. About nine o'clock he arrived at the landing at Rocketts, Richmond's dockside, on Admiral David D. Porter's flagship, the *Malvern*, a captured Confederate blockade runner. The president set out immediately for uptown—on foot, dressed in a long black overcoat, high silk hat, and black suit, walking rapidly and towering above the crowd, flanked on his right by Admiral Porter and on his left by his little son, Tad.[923] Porter had hurriedly sent to the commander of the occupying army for a military guard to escort the fast-striding president. Lincoln had been recognized and was now surrounded by mobs of jubilant blacks.[924]

As he passed on his way to the Confederate White House on Clay Street, the headquarters of Major General Godfrey Weitzel, commanding the new occupation, Agnes saw him clearly. To her he seemed tired and old—"and I must say, with due respect to the President of the United States, I thought him the ugliest man I had ever seen."[925] Lincoln sat wearily in Davis's chair and asked for a glass of water. He later met with Agnes's friend John Campbell, the only high-level Confederate official left in Richmond.

On April 5 Agnes wrote Sara a letter she was not sure she would ever receive. "I am obliged to acknowledge," she wrote, "that there is really no hope now. . . . Everybody says so. My heart is too full for words. General Johnson says we may comfort ourselves by the fact that war may decide a *policy*, but never a *principle*. I imagine our *principle* is all that remains to us of hope or comfort." But without hope, Agnes was grateful for life. "Your General lives. My colonel lives," she wrote. "What words can express our gratitude? What is the loss of home and goods compared with the loss of our own flesh and blood? Alas! Alas! for those who have lost all!"[926]

Four days later, April 9, all hope ended. Cornered at Appomattox Court House by Grant's relentlessly pursuing army, Lee surrendered. "Agony piled upon agony," mourned Emma Mordecai in Richmond.[927] Seventeen days later, April 26, Joseph E. Johnston, whom many hoped Lee might unite with in order to fight on, surrendered to General William T. Sherman, in North Carolina. As the idiom of the times had it, the Confederacy had "gone up the spout."[928] All of the South had become Yankeedom. "God help us!" Judith McGuire cried when Lee surrendered, "We must take refuge in unbelief." When Johnston surrendered, she wrote, "My native land, good-night," and closed her diary.[929]

It was suddenly over—all the suffering, Sara thought, and the bloodshed and the death—and "all for nothing!"[930] "Can it be true?" a disbelieving Pauline DeCaradeuc cried into her diary. "Is the Confederacy subjugated? Have the chivalry of the South given their lives in vain?"[931] For many women in the South, the sentiment was the same. Lizzie Hardin wrote in her diary in Kentucky, "It seemed as though the sun had gone out at noonday."[932] "Was it to this end we had fought and starved and gone naked and cold?" Nellie Gray cried as Petersburg and Richmond fell, "To this end that the wives and children of many a dear and gallant friend were husbandless and fatherless? to this end that our homes were in ruins, our State devastated? to this end that Lee and his footsore veterans were seeking the covert of the mountains?" When Lee surrendered, she wrote, simply, "Hope was dead at last."[933]

Rebecca Thompson Bayless felt the hard hand of defeat in the parlor of her plantation in Tuscumbia, Alabama. "Unless you have experienced it," she later wrote, "one cannot know the horror, the unspeakable horror of the feeling of having the negroes run in the house and say: 'The Yankees are Coming!' That and the sound of cavalrymen wailing, the rowels of their spurs dragging on the floor, the clanking of their sabers will follow me like a nightmare to the end of my days."[934]

Abram Joseph Ryan, a Roman Catholic priest-poet, wrote:

> *Furl that Banner for 'tis weary,*
> *'Round its staff 'tis drooping dreary,*
> *Furl it, fold it, let it rest:*
> *For there's not a sword to save it,*
> *And there's not a hand to wave it,*
> *And its foes now scorn and brave it,*
> *Furl it, fold it, let it rest.*[935]

Nannie Thomas, one of the tearful Virginians who had watched the Union army march into Richmond through smoke and fire on that Monday morning, April 3, wrote, "This war has been comparatively a skeleton fighting against a giant." Like many in the South, she marveled that the giant with all of its mighty resources hadn't buried the skeleton long before this.[936]

CHAPTER 21

---·•·•·•---

Shattered Lives

*I*t was spring again, but the South and its survivors were in a cold winter of defeat and despair. A Confederate officer saw "sad & withered hearts . . . throughout this broad land," people moving mournfully about "with stealthy steps," accosting one another "with mournful looks." Nothing remained but "abject submission." The conqueror held the South "by bayonets & sabers. . . . The citizens consider all lost & the fact is the country is."[937]

Another, in Mississippi, wrote, "Our fields every where lie untilled. Naked chimneys, and charred ruins all over the land mark the spots where happy homes, the seats of refinement and elegance, once stood. Their former inhabitants wander in poverty and exile, wherever chance or charity affords them shelter or food. Childless old age, widows, and helpless orphans beggared and hopeless, are every where." And an editor in Georgia later wrote, "Those who strew flowers over the graves of departed heroes will feel that the quiet dreamers in the dust are far happier than those who still walk the rugged paths of a distracted world. . . . For them the wreath of wild flowers, for us the crown of thorns."[938]

Eliza Andrews, in Georgia, saw "a new pathos" to the demoralization "in a crutch or an empty sleeve, now that we know it was all for nothing." She told her journal that after supper they had all retired to the parlor for some music. "We tried to sing some of our old rebel songs," she said, "but the words stuck in our throats. Nobody could sing, and then Clara Harris played 'Dixie,' but it sounded like a dirge." The soft Southern nights now had a hard edge. She felt "a settled gloom, deep and heavy" hanging over everything. "We spent a miserable evening," she wrote, "in the beautiful moonlight that we knew was shining on the ruin of our country."[939]

"The country," Clarissa Adger Bowen wrote in her journal in northwestern South Carolina, "is in a wretched state." It seemed to her that the only law now was "the old one that 'he should take who has the power and they should keep who can.'"[940]

"So we . . . have *peace*," Laura Nisbet Boykin wrote in her diary in Georgia. "But what a melancholy peace!"[941] "I used to dream about peace, to pray for it," Emma LeConte confided to her diary, "but this is worse than war. What is such peace to us?"[942]

"*Conquered, submission, subjugation.*" Those were bitter words breaking Kate Stone's heart. "Yet," she told her diary, "I feel we are doomed to know them in all their bitterness." The degradation seemed more than she could bear. "How can we bend our necks to the tyrant's yoke?" she demanded. "Our glorious struggle of the last four years, our hardships, our sacrifices, and worst of all, the torrents of noble blood that have been shed for our loved Country—all, all in vain. The best and bravest of the South sacrificed—and all for nothing. Yes, worse than nothing. Only to rivet more firmly the chains that bind us."[943]

Not every Southern heart despaired so deeply as Kate's. Some saw, if dimly, silver lining in the dark cloud. Laetitia Lewis's home on the western rim of the Shenandoah Valley had been plundered by the invading Union army. She had lost all. "I have not in the whole house," she cried, "*one single* thing that was ever given to me as a token of affection or remembrance. . . . The Gold of Ophir could not give me back my little simple treasures." But still she took comfort through her "sense of utter bereavement" that "Life's blessings are still intact with me. The enemy could not carry away God's sunshine, & the sweet airs; so with me they could not carry away the affection and remembrances of my heart that have made the sunshine of life to me."[944]

For the notorious firebrand Roger Pryor, the fire had died, the sunshine had dimmed. He was resigned. "We have been fairly whipped," he said. "For myself, I yield that the cause is hopeless.... I will go back to the plough and my duty as a loyal citizen."[945]

APRIL 16 WAS A QUIET Sabbath in Richmond, and the church bells were ringing worshipers to vesper services. But throughout the city, groups of people were pausing, arrested by unbelievable news from the North: "The President is killed!" Many on their way to church returned home, or to the homes of friends, to see if this staggering news was really true. Many disbelieved, some thought it a "sabbath day rumor." They had endured many such Sunday rumors in the past four years.[946]

The news of Lincoln's assassination reached Roger and Sara in Petersburg on April 17. They—all of Petersburg, Sara believed— were "unspeakably shocked." That Lincoln had fallen "by the hand of an assassin ... by a Confederate and avowedly in the interest of the Confederate cause" distressed the Pryors. They feared the entire South would be blamed for it—as if its cross was not already heavy beyond bearing.[947] After the news reached Petersburg the people of the town, in a mass meeting organized by Roger and two others, adopted resolutions framed by him deploring Lincoln's death as a major blow to the restoration of peace, denouncing the assassination, regretting it more than any military defeat the South had suffered, and expressing "indignation and sympathy."[948]

Sara believed the resolutions mirrored "the earnest and universal sentiment of Virginia." She questioned if in any quarter of the country, "the virtues of Abraham Lincoln—as exhibited in his spirit of forgiveness and forbearance—are more revered than in the very section which was the battle-ground of the fight for independence of his rule."[949] Roger and Sara could give personal witness to the slain president's forgiveness and forbearance, and it swayed their reaction.

Others in the South, however, put a much more bitter and unforgiving spin to the assassination. Kate Stone, made homeless by the war, wrote in her journal, "It is a terrible tragedy, but what is war but one long tragedy?" And "what torrents of blood Lincoln has caused to flow." She could not be sorry for his fate; she believed he had reaped his just reward.[950]

Alarming reports had sifted in to Roger and Sara from outlying southside counties of marauding parties plundering private homes and preying on defenseless women, with no government now to protect them. Roger went to Nottoway County to see what was happening with his sisters. He had not heard from his father since the Union troops had broken through at Cottage Farm.

Left alone in Petersburg with the children, Sara watched as a group of Confederate prisoners were marched past under guard on the streets. Petersburg had been made a holding center for Rebel prisoners of war who had not been paroled. They were being crowded into the surviving tobacco warehouses in the city, down by the river, the same buildings that had held Union prisoners during the war.

The Confederates passing her in the street were a forlorn body of ragged, hatless, barefoot men. The women of Petersburg stood at their doors with their hearts aching, but they smiled, trying to cheer the men as they passed, as they had done so many times before for passing soldiers. One of the Confederates suddenly darted from the ranks, approached Sara, embraced her, and slipped a watch into her hand. As he continued on, she looked inside the watch and found his name. She was shocked to realize he was a valued friend, a young colonel whom she hadn't recognized in his ragged barefoot condition.

Sara's boys, her volunteer intelligence unit, learned where the prisoners were being confined and that at Federal headquarters citizens were being issued permits to take some of them home. But an adult had to sign for them and it had to be done in person. So Sara went, with her boys, who were also her volunteer escort, to see Major General George L. Hartsuff, now in command of the occupation forces in Petersburg. She found Hartsuff at "Centre Hill," the home of the wealthy Petersburg tobacconist, Robert B. Bolling, which Hartsuff had turned into his headquarters. General Hartsuff was of the Union Army of the James, a West Pointer who had fought in all the major battles in the east during the war. He enjoyed the reputation of a rigid disciplinarian.

Sara made her plea directly to him and was asked how many prisoners she wanted. She thought she could accommodate eight, but could only name one, the young colonel who had slipped his watch into her hand. Hartsuff, a man with a concrete exterior but a sympathetic interior, said she could select her prisoners, and said, "Would to God I could release them all."

Sara found the makeshift prison a stifling oven, and its odors nearly unendurable. She didn't see how any human being could live in it. She was helped by the guards to choose her men, and then presented herself with them and her order from Hartsuff. Her name and theirs were entered into an army register, with an order to report daily until the command moved on. Back home with her prisoners Sara took the precious silver tray, which she had hidden and protected through four years of war, to the Northern sutler and pawned it for two hundred dollars. With that she bought shoes, handkerchiefs, and hats for them all, and kept them with her for a week or more until they were administered the oath of allegiance and liberated—as Hartsuff had wished.[951]

EARLY ONE MORNING after they had gone, Sara was called from her room by Alick. Four gentlemen were downstairs demanding to see her. Going down, she found four Federal officers. As soon as she appeared, one of them asked gruffly, "How many rooms are in this house?"

"I think there are eight or ten," Sara answered.

"General Sheridan wants the house for his adjutant's office."

Sara was aware that General Philip Sheridan, the Union cavalry commander, had arrived in Petersburg the day before and had commandeered the elegant Hamilton mansion and one of its outbuildings, on the next street over. Sheridan had been ordered to headquarter in Petersburg, to block any advance north by Joseph E. Johnston's Confederate army, which had not yet surrendered and now hovered around Durham, North Carolina.

Sara answered her four visitors coldly, "I cannot oblige General Sheridan. My house is small. I need it for my own family."

One of the officers crossed the room and stood before her. "Madam," he said, "you seem to be unaware that when General Sheridan sees a house that suits him, he knows how to make the terms for it."

"Ah, well," Sara replied, "I had forgotten that fact for the moment. Do I understand my family must go in the street? How much time can you give me to remove them?"

The officers withdrew into the hall and conferred. Soon one of them, a Captain Lee, returned and courteously informed her that they had concluded after all not to annoy her. He told her they were aware they were addressing Mrs. General Pryor and were happy to spare her an inconvenience.

Sheridan, however, wasn't. The next morning Sara was awakened by a commotion in the parlor. She threw on her gown, thrust her feet into her carpet slippers, and peered over the banister. Captain Lee was standing at the foot of the stair, writing a note on top of the newel post.

When he looked up and saw her, he said, "I was writing to you, Madam. General Sheridan has ordered us to take your house. It is a military necessity. I pray you will try to be patient, and I will do all I can to save you annoyance."

"How soon must I leave?" Sara asked.

"Not at all! We can allow you two rooms—the one you already occupy and the one below it."[952]

Sara turned the second room into a dining room and sitting parlor, and moved beds from a rear room to her own room for the rest of the family. Still she was very nearly crowded out, if not by people, then by books. Roger had boxed their library for safekeeping, with the help of Union soldiers—because, they said, they considered him "a friend."[953] Roger's benevolence was remembered. John had piled the boxes into a corner of her reception room.

It was intensely hot for April in Petersburg, too sweltering to sit inside with closed doors. So Sara locked the doors to her bedroom during the day, and the family lived in the yard unless the rain drove them to cover. The noise in the house was as incessant and pervasive as the heat. The rest of the house-cum-adjutant's office was a center of ceaseless turmoil—tramping in and out and loud talking—night and day. There was, indeed, virtually no night. The gas burned constantly. Sara had no idea to what purpose her seized rooms were put; she only knew they were rarely silent. She came to believe that all the business of a great army was being transacted there.

Sentries were stationed so close about her doors that she could not enter the yard or garden without passing them. And that was a demeaning ordeal. As she passed one of them on her way outside to give the baby air, he said, "We've caught Jeff Davis."

When she returned, her eyes downcast to avoid him if possible, he stepped close to her and hissed, "He shall be *hanged*."

Sara had had enough. Leaving the baby with the little boys, she walked to the veranda of the Hamilton mansion and asked for General Sheridan. She was ushered into a room where a number of officers were sitting around a table, and announced herself.

"I am Mrs. Pryor," she began, "whose house you have taken for an adjutant's office. Sentinels have been placed around my house who insult me when I cross the threshold."

One of the officers, whom Sara recognized as Sheridan, rose and said, "What can we do for you, Madam? What do you demand?"

"That the sentry around my house be removed to the street enclosure."

He invited her to sit, but she said she would prefer to stand. Sheridan took some paper and began writing out an order. Standing there, Sara was suddenly aware of her want of fashion. "What I must have looked like to those officers," she later mused. Her gown was of chocolate-hued percale, with a white spot on it. Enormous hoops were then in fashion, but she had none, having long since abandoned them for the sake of the hard-strapped Confederacy. She fancied she resembled "the wooden Mrs. Noah" on the ark in the deluge, checking the animals two by two into the ark.

She took Sheridan's order, bowed her thanks, and walked home through a line of soldiers, but with larger liberty for her and her children clutched in her hand.[954]

The hard times were daily getting harder in what Sara called "my captivity." She now had no dining room and very little to eat except the biscuits her neighbor Mr. Bishop brought in and a daily tray sent over by Mrs. Meade, who had Northern men paying rent to board in her house and could therefore afford to patronize the Northern sutler. But men must smoke, and the proprietor of the cigar shop the Pryors had patronized regularly in better times hired Sara's boys and Campbell as a "walking agency" to sell cigars to officers and soldiers. They were making the only income the family now had and were getting reacquainted with U.S. pennies, nickels, and dimes.[955]

Sara's only cheer seemed to be visits from friends. Often Captain Lee, not necessarily a friend, came in complaining about Southern women. He was being snubbed by the Petersburg beauties. He had picked up a dropped veil for one of them, and she had turned her head away when she reached to take it—as if the veil might not be tainted but the giver was. He was a Northern man, that was true, Lee complained, but he also considered himself a gentleman.

The most gentlemanly thing he did, in Sara's view, was the day he came in and told her they had marching orders. They were leaving. "We go to-night!" he told her. "I know you are pleased! We have given you so much trouble!"

"Not more, I suppose," Sara said, "than was necessary!"

"Well, I must say," Lee said, "you have been very patient." He then told her that General Sheridan was in the office and wished "to make his respects to you."

Sheridan entered and thanked her for the manner in which she had endured the inconvenience. It seemed to Sara that for some reason the general wished her not to think ill of him and the way he had treated them, so he began explaining the Northern philosophy of war.

"It was the very best thing to do," he said. "The only way to stamp out this rebellion was to handle it without gloves."

This wasn't the most endearing and winning thing he could have said, and if he expected either agreement or argument from Sara, he got neither. Instead he got stony silence. After an embarrassing pause, he began berating the Confederate government for its own bad management.

"Ladies," Sheridan told her, "should be better cared for." He said he had "unearthed, within forty miles of this place, enough provisions to keep you in perfect comfort." That was news to Sara.

The general looked down and saw the baby's brown eyes fixed steadfastly on his face. As General Lee had said, children have a wonderful liking for soldiers. Lucy apparently did, and whether the uniform was gray or blue did not seem to matter to her.

"I think I must borrow this little lady," Sheridan said. "It is not often General Sheridan has anything in his arms as sweet as this."

He turned and left the room with the baby in his arms—Lucy gladly going with him. When she was presently returned, she held in her little arms a parcel with figs, bananas, cakes, and nuts. Little Lucy and all her charms had become the family's best provider.

That evening the adjutant's office was closed. They had shouldered into her house and her life and stayed for ten days. And when they went, they left the place "polluted with dirt" and Sara with a whopping unpaid gas bill. But she had her house back.[956]

Roger returned shortly after and reported again to the Federal authorities. He would not be paroled until Joseph E. Johnston surrendered to William T. Sherman in North Carolina, in late April. But he was allowed to go to Richmond to seek work of some kind to support his family. And he went.[957]

When the Union troops passed on, leaving only Hartsuff's guard, the small tobacco business of her little boys went into abrupt decline. They were now so destitute, Sara was faced with letting the servants, all who were left, go. She told Eliza Page, "I can no longer maintain you or give you wages." Eliza offered to stay on "for the good you have already done us." But Sara wouldn't allow it, and Eliza left to return to her husband.[958]

The hardest to let go was John. Sara simply couldn't keep him. And it was difficult to explain that to him

"I will never leave you," he protested.

"You *must*, John!" she said. "You must go home to your father in Norfolk. He will advise you."

"The old man is in the oyster business," John said. "What do I care about oysters? All I care for is Marse Roger and these boys."

"You really must go to your father, John," Sara insisted. "How much money have you?"

He had five dollars. Sara also had five, which she gave him.

"Now don't let me see you again," she said. "Write to me from Norfolk."

John sadly protested. But next morning he was gone, the only slave Sara had ever "owned."[959]

Next she turned to her most urgent need—how to feed her family. Her only recourse seemed to be to draw rations from the invading army, which had to be done in person. With her little guard—her sons "understood they were to escort me everywhere"—she set out for Federal headquarters. It was another stunning spring day in Petersburg. Sara thought she had never seen a lovelier one. "How," she marveled, "could nature spread her canopy of blossoming magnolia and locust as if nothing had happened? How could the vine over the doorway of my old home load itself with snowy roses, how could the birds sing, how could the sun shine as if such things as these could ever again gladden our broken hearts?"[960]

At the desk, a young officer asked, "Have you taken the oath of allegiance, Madam?"

"No, Sir," she said, although she was prepared to do so.

The officer studied her seriously for a moment and said, as he wrote out the order, "Neither will I require it of you, Madam!"

Buoyed by that pleasant encounter, Sara sent Alick, with the order, to the commissary. He soon returned wearing a woebegone face. He had drawn a fish that was so rancid he couldn't bear to bring it into her presence. And the meal he had been issued was crawling with caterpillars.

Sara foresaw another direct encounter with General Hartsuff. She immediately wrote him a letter.

"Is the commanding general," she wrote, "aware of the nature of the ration issued this day to the destitute women of Petersburg?"

She sent it and Alick, with the bag of caterpillar-infested meal, to Hartsuff. The boy returned later with no response. But in a few minutes a tall orderly appeared at her door, touched his cap, and handed her a note from Hartsuff. "Major-General Hartsuff is sorry he cannot make *right* all that seems so wrong," the note read. "He sends the enclosed. Some day General Pryor will repay." Hartsuff had attached, on an official letterhead, an authorization to the quartermaster and commissary to furnish Sara with all she might demand or require and to charge it to his private account.

This was generous, but it would not do. Sara answered that she was not insensible to his offer, but he "*ought to have known*" that the ration allowed the destitute women of Petersburg must be enough also for her. She needed no special consideration.

As she sat alone in the house contemplating another sale of a piece of the silver service, there was a jangle of harness outside the front door. From a handsome carriage in the street emerged an elegant lady, who bustled in with a lace-edged handkerchief to her eyes and announced that she was Mrs. Hartsuff. The ever fashion-conscious Sara noted that she was superbly gowned in violet silk and lace. She was wearing a small *fanchon* bonnet (a small kerchief-type headpiece with lace trimming cascading about the ears) fixed atop an enormous cushion of hair. It was the first fashionable chignon that Sara had seen, an arrangement called a "waterfall," a coil of hair worn at the back part of the head and down the nape of the neck—an exaggeration of the superabundant distended "bun" Englishwomen had worn a few years before.

"Oh, my dear lady," Mrs. Hartsuff began, "we are in such distress at headquarters! George is in despair! You won't let him help you! Whatever is he to do?"

"I really am grateful to the General," Sara assured her, "but you see there is no reason he should do more for me than for others."

"Oh," Mrs. Hartsuff disagreed, "but there *is* reason. You have suffered more than the rest. You have been driven from your home! Your house has been sacked. George knows all about you. I have brought a basket for you—tea, coffee, sugar, crackers."

"I cannot accept it," Sara protested. "I am so sorry."

"But what are you going to do? Are you going to starve?"

"Very likely," Sara said, "but somehow I shall not very much mind."

"Oh, this is too utterly, utterly dreadful," Mrs. Hartsuff exclaimed as she left the house.

The next day the ration for Petersburg's women was changed. Fresh beef, canned vegetables, bread, and coffee were issued all around. And Mrs. Hartsuff took to calling daily on Sara.

"Not that George has gotten over it," she said. "His feelings are constantly hurt here."[961]

Neither General or Mrs. Hartsuff knew it, but Sara was about to hurt his feelings yet again.

CHAPTER 22

———◆—◆—◆———

Into the Arms of the Enemy

$\mathcal{I}$t had been six weeks since the lines at Petersburg had been broken, and the refugees who were driven away by Union siege guns were returning. Among them, and wanting their house back, came the owners of Sara's temporary haven. They were refugees no more, but Sara was about to become one again.

Her eyes turned in the only direction that offered sanctuary—Cottage Farm. But she had been told that on no account would she be safe back there without a guard. That, then, called for another meeting with Hartsuff. So with her little-boy escort, she went up to the stately Bollings mansion, past the two handsome marble greyhounds that guarded its entrance, and asked to see the general.

She waited on the long veranda in the rear of the mansion with its lofty pillars and stared in appreciation at the sweeping grounds beyond, planted in evergreens and dominated by a magnificent magnolia grandiflora, then in springtime bloom. The grounds were graced by white marble statues and marble benches. A rustic staircase led down to a conservatory. The mansion stood on an elevation that sloped sharply to the street below, and Sara knew that a legend-haunted subterranean passage below led from the mansion to the street and to a shrub and vine-shielded entrance. The beauty and serenity of it all contrasted sharply with the chaos in their lives.

As she waited for Hartsuff to receive her, the young officer waiting with her praised the beauty of the veranda and the grounds beyond. "I should like to fight it out on this line all summer," he said, playing on what General Grant had said about the "bloody line from the Wilderness to Spotsylvania."

Sara remembered the Bollings, who had been driven from all this, and said wickedly, "That would be most unfortunate for you. This place is very sickly in summer—deadly, in fact. Typhoid fever is fatal in this section." She was in fine sarcastic form, ready to face Hartsuff.

As she entered, the general neither looked up nor greeted her, but continued writing at a table. Sara waited a moment, then threw herself against his wall of concentration. "General," she began, "I have come to ask if I may have a guard. I am about to return to my home—Cottage Farm."

Still no answer. Only the rapid scratching of pen on paper. "General Hartsuff," Sara said after a moment, "are you still angry with me because I did not feel I could accept your kind offer? I couldn't take it! I couldn't trust myself with it! I should have given a ball and ruined you."

Hartsuff laughed and threw down his pen. "It is impossible for you to go to Cottage Farm," he said. "There are fifty or more negroes on the place. You cannot live there."

"I must!" Sara protested, "it is my only shelter."

Hartsuff was a discerning man, and he knew there was not much point in arguing with this headstrong young woman. "Well, then," he said, resigning himself to it, "I'll allow you a guard, and Mrs. Hartsuff had better take you out herself, that is, if you can condescend to accept as much."

Sara was not aware that Mrs. Hartsuff, of the cascading hairdo, had entered the room and was standing behind her, listening—until she heard her speak. "And I think, George," Mrs. Hartsuff said, "you ought to give Mrs. Pryor a horse and cart in place of her own that were stolen."

"All right, all right," said Hartsuff, who was now clearly outnumbered and overmatched. "Madam, you will find the guard at your door when you arrive. You go this evening? All right—good morning."

Late in the afternoon Mrs. Hartsuff appeared at her door with an ambulance and four horses.[962]

At Cottage Farm the two women found desolation. The earth was ploughed and trampled, the grass and flowers uprooted. Carcasses of six dead cows lay in the yard, filling the evening air with the nauseating odor of decaying flesh. When they opened the front door, swarms of flies flew out.

"If this were I," said Mrs. Hartsuff, gathering her skirts as closely about her as her hoops would allow, "I should fall across this threshold and die."

"I shall not fall," Sara said proudly. "I shall stand in my lot."

Inside was unspeakable filth, in every corner of the house. Pieces of pork fat lay on the floor. Molasses oozed from the library shelves, where spilled bottles lay uncorked. Filthy opened tin cans were scattered about. Nothing of use, not even a tin dipper to drink from the well, was left in the house, only a bottomless chair and a bedstead rigged together with bayonets. Picture frames were stacked against the wall, all of them absent their pictures. A portrait of an old lady, with a saber slash across her face, clung to one wall.

"Now, what in the world are you going to do?" asked Mrs. Hartsuff.

"The best I can," Sara said.

Aunt Jinny had now discovered their presence. With a curtsy to Mrs. Hartsuff, she took Sara's baby in her arms.

"This is a hard home-coming for you, my po' lamb!" she said to Sara. "But never mind! Jinny has got plenty of clean bedclothes and things." Then, to Mrs. Hartsuff, she said, "Yes, marm, I can take care of 'em!"

There was the matter of the fifty or more blacks camping out on the farm. They had moved in after the Yankees had swept through. In the eyes of the two women, they were menacing. Now free, what would they do? How would they act? Were they intending to take over the farm? In bondage there was always the latent threat, dreaded by Southern whites, that their black slaves would turn on them in rebellion. There were now no restraints, nothing shielding the women from retribution and violence. Hartsuff had sent a guard with Sara, but still she worried: "Suppose they should overpower the guard and murder us all?"

Sara asked Jinny about them.

"The colored people?" Aunt Jinny said. "Oh, the colored people will give no trouble. They are very peaceable."

Jinny swept a room for Sara and her children and spread quilts on the floor. Later in the evening, an ambulance sent by Mrs. Hartsuff drove up with a tin box of bread-and-butter sandwiches, some tea, an army cot, and army bedding. The guard Hartsuff had sent, a great, tall fellow, reported to Sara for orders. She directed him to watch through the night at the roadside of the house, and she would sit up and keep watch in the opposite direction.

The children fell asleep on the floor, and as the night wore on, Sara grew "extremely anxious about the negroes" and what Jinny had told her of the sacking of the house. Jinny thought there were not more than fifty blacks. They filled every outbuilding except the kitchen. Everything was quiet at the moment, but Sara was unable to sleep.

Deep into the night she was startled by a shrill scream coming from the kitchen building. A door opened suddenly and slammed shut, and a voice cried out, "Thank Gawd! Thank Gawd A'mighty." Then all was still again. Was this a signal? the overwrought Sara wondered. She held her breath, listened, then softly rose, closed the shutters and fastened them, and crept to the door and bolted it from the inside. The guard apparently had not heard it. Probably asleep on the porch, Sara thought. The children were also asleep, oblivious to the terror.

More awake than ever, Sara resumed her watch at the window,

pressing her eyes against openings in the slats. A pale half moon hung low in the night sky. At a little distance Sara could see by its light the newly dug soldier's grave Alick had discovered and reported to her earlier. A heavy eroding rain had fallen in the early hours of the night, and a stiff arm and hand now protruded eerily from the shallow grave, seeming to appeal upward to heaven. Tomorrow, Sara thought, she would cover over the supplicating arm, be it clad in blue or in gray, and mark the spot.[963]

As the sun rose Aunt Jinny emerged from the kitchen, and Sara opened the shutters to greet her. The old servant brought in a cup of coffee and was distressed to learn that Sara hadn't slept all night. She asked if Sara had heard anything, and Sara told of the scream from the kitchen. It had been "Sis' Winny," Aunt Jinny explained. She got happy in the middle of the night "an Gawd knows what she would have done, if Frank hadn't ketched hold of her and pulled her back in the kitchen! Frank 'an me is pretty nigh outdone an' discouraged 'bout Sis' Winny. She prays constant all day; but Gawd A'mighty don't count on bein' bothered all night. Ain' he 'ranged for us all to sleep, an' let Him have a little peace? Sis' Winny must keep her happiness to herself, when folks is trying to git some res'."[964]

Hartsuff's guard came to Sara's window as uneasy as she had been. He told her the blacks refused to leave, that he might have to threaten them with his pistols.

"Oh," Sara protested, "you wouldn't shoot, would you?" Greatly distressed, she asked that the blacks be called to the back door so she could speak with them. She soon found herself facing some seventy-five blacks—men, women, and children. Sara told them she was "sorry to see so many of them without homes," and one of them who struck Sara as "an intelligent looking man" interrupted her.

"We are not without homes," he said. "I planted and worked on this place for years before the war. It is right I should have some choice in the land the government promises us, and I have come here because I shall ask for the land I have worked."

Sara told him he must be mistaken, that the farm belonged to her brother-in-law, not her. She explained that she was there "through his kindness, and I am perfectly willing that you should remain through mine until you find other shelter, provided you consider my husband master here, give no trouble, and help me clean up this place." She told them that all who were not willing to do that must leave, that they "must distinctly understand that this is private property which will be protected by the government."

"That's so!" seconded the guard.

An old gray-haired man stepped forward and said he was Abram, who had "toted young Marse Roger on my back to school many a time," and that he and his family would stay. "Come, now!" he said to the others. "You all hear what the Yankee gentleman say! Git to work now on them dead cows—hurry up!"

Sara sent Abram to the quartermaster to borrow a team to haul away the carcasses and other filth. Aunt Jinny produced chairs and a table, and by nightfall the place was comparatively clean and livable.[965]

To Sara's joy and relief, Roger soon returned from Richmond. But there had been no prospect there for employment. He had been a lawyer, editor, diplomat, politician, and soldier. All of these callings now seemed closed to him because of the Federal government's hard line toward those who had been leaders in the rebellion, in the Confederate government, and in its armies.

"There seemed to be," Sara mourned, "no room for a rebel in all the world." Roger had nothing left but "a ragged uniform, his sword, a wife, and [six] children—his health, his occupation, his place in the world, gone; his friends and comrades slain in battle; his southern home impoverished and desolate. He had no profession, no rights as a citizen, no ability to hold office."[966]

Moreover the charge of treason was hanging over his head.

Immediately after Lee's surrender at Appomattox, the U.S. Circuit Court held a session in Norfolk and indicted Lee, Confederate Secretary of War John Breckinridge, Roger, and others. Roger could feel no sense of personal security. A cloud hung over them all. Deprived of every source of livelihood, they somehow had to pick up what shattered pieces of their lives they could and begin anew.[967]

As he would later describe it, Virginia was "the Niaobe of nations [a queen in a classic story], veiled and weeping the loss of her sons, her property confiscated and her homes in ashes."[968]

Indeed, all of the South lay in ruin. The Confederacy was gone, never to be recalled. Southern fields, once so fertile and giving, were desolated. Many of its towns and cities were now charred, smoking vestiges. Slavery, the South's basic labor system for decades, was forever dead. And once-proud Dixie was under Yankee rule.

Lizzie Hardin mourned in her diary in Kentucky: "I wish I had the power to describe the state of this country. The Constitution so much waste paper, the civil law a dead letter, slavery in such a condition that neither masters nor Negroes know whether it exists or not, lawlessness of every shade, from the lawlessness of the government at Washington to that of the Negro who steals his master's chickens, and in the midst of it all, between the Southerners and Union people a hatred, bitter, unrelenting, and that promises to be eternal."[969]

Kate Stone returning to Brokenburn in the train of the Confederate surrender, wrote in her journal, "But never, never, never more echoes back to our hearts like a funeral knell at every thought of the happy past. We must bear our losses as best we can. Nothing is left but to endure."[970] Young Malvena Waring, from South Carolina, wrote in her diary, "Changed are we, and changed our home, in everything but loving hearts."[971]

Agnes was also thinking of how changed things were. She wrote Sara in May that she was "aggrieved and indignant at the sermons people are preaching to us," saying the war had been a blessing. She was impatient with "this attempt to extort good for ourselves out of the overwhelming disaster which brought such ruin to others; to congratulate ourselves for what is purchased with their blood. Surely, if for no other reason, for the sake of the blood that has been spilt, we should not hasten to acquiesce in the present state of things. If I catch my Colonel piously affirming too much resignation, too prompt a forgetfulness of the past, I'll—well, he knows what I am capable of saying!"

Agnes then told Sara, "We cannot remain here. We are literally stripped to the 'primitive' state my reverend brother thinks so good for us. We are woefully in need of 'silk, cotton, and something they call capital,' and we'll never get it here. And so my Colonel and I are going to New York. He has secured a place in some publishing house or other. I only wish it were a dry-goods store."

Agnes wrote, "Of course our social life is all over. I have taken my resolution. There are fine ladies in New York whom I used to entertain in Washington. Just so far as they approach me, will I approach them! A card for a card, a visit for a visit. But I imagine I shall not be recognized. I am content. There will be plenty to read in that publishing house. I shall not repine. All the setting, the *entourage*, of a lady is taken from me, but the lady herself has herself pretty well in hand."[972]

At Cottage Farm Roger and Sara still had their loving hearts, but they were also finding it impossible to take up their life again as it once was. The cords that bound them to the past were severed, frayed loose ends now, beyond hope of retying. In the weeks that followed the end of the war they suffered for want of some way to occupy themselves. Sara had no war chores anymore—no garments to mend or make, no household to manage. They sat and stared sadly out on the grim landscape dotted by chimneys without houses, "standing stark sentinel over blackened heaps where our neighbors had made happy homes." They had no heart for reading. As the various Federal brigades moved away from the neighborhood, a few plain articles of furniture taken from the house were returned—a few tables and chairs, but nothing handsome or of value. An itemized list Sara furnished brought only that little bit of furniture—no books, pictures, bric-a-brac, or other furnishings. And the sultry, down days of summer had set in bringing with them endless hours of "listless endurance, followed by troubled sleep."[973]

Tourists began passing by out in front of the cottage, where, Sara recalled, General Lee had ridden daily to the lines at Petersburg. The curious stood at the site of Lee's headquarters. They plucked a few blades of grass from the deep depression, called the Crater, left by the Federal explosion in the summer of 1864, and visited the abatis, lunettes, and fortifications where the Union army had broken through on April 2. Sometimes a passing tourist asked to call on Sara and Roger, claiming some common acquaintance. It was an intrusion Roger resented. Their sympathetic attitude offended him. The Pryor's friends in town were in too much poverty and sorrow themselves to visit. "A deadly silence and apathy had succeeded the storm," Sara said. It would be a long time before Petersburg showed signs of waking from its nightmare—not until the coming of the cool invigorating weather of autumn. The blood-soaked soil and the lingering stench of the dead animals would taint the atmosphere itself until the fall frost came to drive it out.[974]

Malaria struck the family and hung on for weeks. One after another the children fell sick with the fever and lay painfully on pallets on the floor. Then Sara came down with it, violently ill. Their only nurse was Roger, and soon after they recovered, he came down with it himself, wracked by ague and fever. When he, too, recovered, he continued to sit listlessly and "in hopeless despair," gazing out on the desolate moonscape around them.[975]

General and Mrs. Hartsuff came to visit. When the Pryors were down with the fever, they sent in messages from outside the gate. After they had recovered, Hartsuff came himself, and then in the early fall sent his commissary general, Captain Gregory, to see Sara. The captain, speaking for Hartsuff, reasoned seriously with her.

Roger, he said, must go away. Punishment and retribution were a constant threat there, in Virginia. He argued that Roger would die if he stayed. Hartsuff had approached Roger with the same argument, but Roger had refused vehemently to leave his family.

"Where, oh, where could he go?" Sara pleaded with the captain. "He does think sometimes of New Orleans."

"Madam," said the captain, "there is a future before your husband. New York is the place for him."

New York was becoming a haven for former Confederates. Many in Roger's position were going there, to friendly receptions and renewed opportunities. The city was filled with sympathetic Democrats who related to their former Southern friends and associates.[976]

But Sara was uncertain about Roger. "He will never, never consent to go there," Sara said.

"Well, then," the captain said, "we must use a little diplomacy. Send him by sea to shake off his chills. Mark my words—as soon as he registers in New York, friends will gather around him. Only *send* him—and speedily."

Young Theodorick had overheard this conversation, and when the captain left, he implored Sara to do what Hartsuff urged.[977]

Sara perhaps remembered the letter Agnes had written her from Richmond in early May about their moving to New York. Without consulting Roger, she hitched the horse Hartsuff had given her to the little cart, and she and Theodorick drove into town. She took her watch, which she had once before tried unsuccessfully to sell, and looked for a banker who would take it as collateral on a loan. After several failures, she found one. She added to the watch a cherished antique cameo ring set in diamonds that Roger had given her before their wedding and which had never left her finger. Leaving these two precious items in hock for three hundred dollars, she bought some quinine for Roger's fever, ordered a suit of clothes to replace his threadbare Confederate gray, and went home to argue with him.

It was not an easy sell, but she finally persuaded him to accept the idea of a short sea voyage to New York "to break the chills that shook him so relentlessly every third day." He agreed to go for a week. That was really all that Sara had in mind. Her idea was that he would go to New York briefly, get his footing, and return. "Nothing was further from my thought or wishes," she later wrote, "than a permanent residence in New York."[978]

Whatever she thought, Sara was sending her husband "into the arms of the enemy."[979]

When the week was up, instead of Roger's return, Sara got a letter. "What will you think," he wrote, "when I tell you that several gentlemen suggest to me to settle here? Dare I 'then to beard the lion in his den——the Douglas in his hall!'" He said he had "half a mind to try it. 'The world is all before us where to chose.'"

General Hartsuff was looking like a prophet.

Close on that letter came another: "I'm not yet determined when to return. I was to leave this morning, but Mr. Ben Wood of the [*New York Daily*] *News* has requested me to remain a day or two that he might have a talk with me. What this means, I am not sure. I conjecture he will propose some connection with his paper. By the last of the week you may expect me with you."

The last of the week—it was now early October 1865—found him still in New York. He had accepted a proposition from Wood, "for the present," to write for his intensely pro-Southern *Daily News*, which would earn him twenty-five dollars a week. The only hitch in this arrangement was that Roger was still refused a pardon, and charges were still pending against him in Washington. The government mustn't know he would be writing for the *News*. He would have to write anonymously or under an assumed name.

"I am going to work like a beaver," Roger promised Sara, "and with no other purpose now than to earn a living for my dear wife and children."

He had taken a room at 47 West Twelfth Street and had asked

Sara to send him his winter clothes. Worried for the children, he advised her that they must try, "whatever is left undone, to send the boys to school."

After a week or two Roger had become discouraged by the high cost of living in New York and was wavering again. "Sometimes I sink in despair," he wrote Sara in one of his letters, "but then I rally and press on. Don't you think heaven will prosper me for *your* sake? The obstacles to success of 'a rebel' in this city are almost insurmountable."

He wrote her that "I feel I cannot bear a long separation from my dear family—my darling little ones. And yet how can I maintain them here? Is it not a cruel fortune which tears us asunder when our delight in each other is about the only source of happiness left us in this world? I shall lose, in this hopeless grind, all the elastic energy of my mind. I cannot live without you!"

But by early December 1865 Roger was still in New York, and still the victim of sporadic ague and fever—"the worst I ever suffered"—and still living without her. But he was also no longer wavering. "For I *have* entered the fight!" he wrote. "The die is cast—and here I mean to remain, 'sink or swim, survive or perish.'"

He explained to her how it had all come about. Sitting one evening with Ben Wood in the *Daily News* office, the editor had said to him, "General, why don't you practice law? You would make ten thousand dollars a year."

"For the best of all possible reasons," Roger argued, "I am not a lawyer."

The idea of his making so great a sum in a profession long since abandoned was too preposterous for Roger to give it serious thought. But Wood pressed the matter. Roger hadn't said anything of it at the time to Sara because, for a time, he had not decided whether to act on Wood's urgings. But then a lawyer in New York had offered him desk space in his office and the use of his library. Roger had been borrowing books and studying law ever since.

Now he was writing Sara that he had resolved to apply for admission to the bar, had done so, and had been admitted. He was a lawyer again.[980]

Just after Christmas 1865, he wrote her that his prospects had brightened somewhat. He had been retained, provisionally, as counsel for the National Express Company, from which he might make a little something. "Dearest Sara," he closed this post-Christmas letter, "let us endure these trials with all possible fortitude. If only you can keep happy, I can bear my portion of the burden."[981]

IN THE LONG LONELY winter without Roger, Sara struggled "to sustain my hopes," and "for his sake" not allow her heart to break. One morning in early February, old Abram, who had become a help and comfort to her, approached with furrowed brow.

"What we all goin' to do now for wood, Mistis?" he asked.

"What you have done all along, I suppose," Sara said.

"No'm," the old man said. "Dat's onpossible. We done burn up Fort Gregg an' Battery 45. Der ain' no mo' fortifications on de place as I knows of."

"Fortifications!" Sara exclaimed. "Why Abram! You surely haven't been burning the fortifications?"

"Hit's des like I tell you, Mistis. De las' stick's on yo' wood-pile now."

"Well, Abram," said Sara sadly, "if we have destroyed our fortifications—burned our bridges—the time has come to change our base. We will move into town."[982]

Roger and the fortifications were not all that were gone from Cottage Farm. Rose, their little cow, had died. The turnips and potatoes Abram had planted and harvested were all gone. The two pigs he had reared had "fulfilled their destiny," and the government rations had ceased. And now Abram wished in his old age to leave, also, to return to his old home and to his old master from a plantation to the south, who longed to welcome him.

Without food or fuel and without Abram, Sara and the children could no longer live in the country. The fields around them were still a wasteland, with no fences to protect crops or keep cattle, and Abram saw no hope for cultivation—nothing to "work on." She would indeed have to change her base.

The afternoon before they left to move back into town, early in the new year 1866, the weather was again "so deliciously balmy" that Sara walked over the garden and grounds one more time, thinking of "the great drama" that had been enacted there. Spring had come early again to Virginia's southside counties, "to touch all scars with her gentle finger-tips." Already the grass was greening on Cottage Farm, and on the branches of the trees around the well where General Lee had so often stopped, leaves had appeared. Sara noted that "over all the battle-torn ground, over the grave of the young soldier who had lain so long under my window, over the track ploughed by shot and shell," the newborn season had spread "a delicate bloom like a smile on the lips of the dead."

Sara spent much of that last night on the farm at the window from which she had watched the night of her first homecoming. Cottage Farm had been "polluted, sacked, desecrated," yet she admitted she was "leaving it with regret. Many a hard battle with illness, with want, with despair had been fought within those walls." It all seemed to Sara now "like a long, dark night in which neither sun nor moon nor stars had appeared; during which we had simply endured, watching ourselves the while, jealous lest the natural rebound of youthful hope and spirit should surprise us, and dishonour those who had suffered and bled and died for our sakes."

In March Roger sent money to send the children, now all together with her in town, to school. To help him mend their fortunes and to keep her "old friend the wolf" from the door, she persuaded seven of her neighbors to send their children to her for piano lessons.[983]

In New York Roger was finding the law an uneven calling. He had rented a little dollar-a-day office in New York City—a bare room with a carpetless floor, plain uncovered table, and three chairs—one for himself, and two for possible clients. There, he wrote Sara, he had hung his "modest shingle soliciting the patronage of the public." He began attending court regularly to listen to leading New York lawyers but found no clients to sit in his two chairs and no opportunity to practice himself.

The New York papers had found him and were calling him "the Rebel Pryor." "The great difficulty in my way," he believed, "is the lingering prejudice against 'rebels.'" But he intended to tough it out; he said it may be "my last cast—and I am resolved to succeed or perish in the attempt."

In February, as Sara was moving from Cottage Farm back into the city, he wrote her that he had made a reckoning of his earnings since he had come to New York. Admitted to the bar about the first of December and "practicing" now for about two and a half months, he had earned $356 and been retained by the Express Company. Most of his earnings had gone to pay past debts. He had some little money yet owing him, and some doubtful claims, and the other court lawyers were treating him "with marked courtesy." In a hurried postscript to this letter, he wrote, "a client interrupts me! Don't be depressed, Sallie! A gleam of light gilds our horizon, which has been dark, God knows, long enough. Next summer we must have our *home,* and won't it be a happy home? God grant it."

In his next letter, however, he was again depressed. There had been a fading of his "gleam of light." He thought he had two good cases, but the would-be clients decided not to proceed. "Oh how weary I am of this life!" he wrote.[984]

As the year progressed without much relief, he began writing again for the *Daily News* to bring in money. "The law is so slow—so uncertain," he wrote Sara, "that I almost despair." The children, he wrote—"I trust they all care a little for me! Poor papa, so lonely and sad without his home! Kiss them all for me. I love them more than all the world."

Soon after, the gleam was rekindled. He had tried and won a case that brought him a thousand dollars, and he was soon employed in other cases. Moreover, he was now enjoying good health. The ague and fevers were gone. But by the winter 1866–67, in the up and down fortunes of the law, the Express Company had gone under, bankrupt and insolvent, denying him an expected three-thousand-dollar fee. This forced another maddening and indefinite delay of a reunion with Sara and the children. So "Work, work, work," he wrote, "is my destiny; your welfare the goal that beckons me on. I contemplate nothing else—I desire nothing else."[985]

While the close of 1866 brought no new hope, it did bring Roger—for a Christmas visit. They all, Sara and the children, begged him to abandon the plan to live in New York. They were all against it, having small hope of ever being able to exist in that city, with its high rents and high cost of living. Not wishing to grieve Sara, Roger did not oppose them, but neither did he stay. He wrote her from New York on January 23, sending her two hundred dollars, which he was "sorely pressed" to raise, to redeem the silver tray she had hocked at war's end to buy shoes for the prisoners. With it he wrote, "I love you all more and more every day of my life, and I would sacrifice everything to be with you." But, he said, it must be in New York. "Next spring you *must* join me. Do let us make the experiment."

By March he was still struggling, still pressed for money, but still with not the least idea of abandoning the experiment. He wrote Sara that his practice was growing slowly but surely, and he believed it was based on a trust of his own competence. "Thank God," he wrote, "what I have accomplished, though small, has been achieved by my own unaided exertions, and without the least obligation to a human being. I have no patron. I have never solicited business. My only arts are, work and devotion to study . . . and when the victory is achieved I shall feel inexpressible gratification in saying, with Coriolanus, '*Alone* I did it.'"

"And now one more word," he wrote. "You must come to me. I cannot live without you. Is not poverty better than such an existence? May we not live here humbly, but in one another's presence? I do not see that it is possible for me to get employment in Virginia. Let us abate something of our pride and ambition, and be content to live poorly and obscurely. We can at least be sustained by our mutual love and admiration. What care we for the world?"

Whatever hope that stirred in Sara was dulled by a slow spring for Roger that followed those brave words. He was suffering acutely now from neuralgic headaches and no new legal cases were coming in. "I cannot account for it!" he grieved. "Everything looks so much less promising—but really now I *must* remain here. I have no money to get away! Never have I been so sick at heart. I often fear I can bear no more."

He was now writing Sara every day, his mood swinging wildly with each letter, ashamed of his last one, but in no less despair. "If a breeze does not come soon," he wrote, "I shall be at a standstill. What then? My family is dependent exclusively upon my scant earnings. If they fail, I see no hope in another quarter. This is the apprehension that kills the soul within me. The catastrophic haunts me like a spectre, and clouds my spirit with a perpetual gloom."

The breeze he sought did come—in April 1867. Eight cases had come in with the new season, one of them promising to bring him two thousand dollars if he won it; otherwise nothing. He won it, and in July the time had also finally come—after two long years—for Sara and the children to join him in New York.[986]

Within two weeks she wound up all of her small affairs in Petersburg, kissed her tearful little band of music scholars good-bye, and sent Marie Gordon and little Mary to Charlotte County to be with Aunt Mary for the rest of the summer while she moved. She persuaded her laundress, Hannah, to accompany them to New York, and booked passage for her and the other children.[987]

One more time Sara found herself on the James River. On a hot July morning, she sailed from City Point to the Atlantic and northward on the *Saratoga,* one of two steamboats of a line running biweekly from Richmond to that "great unknown world" that was New York City. Her baggage was one trunk holding her own garments, the children's clothes, the silver service, and a few damaged books saved from Cottage Farm—"the melancholy wreckage" of what had been a home "enriched with . . . treasures."

Sara was *"tired*—tired unto death," and her heart "heavier than my boxes," as the *Saratoga* pushed off into the river from City Point—Grant's teeming port of entry to the siege of Petersburg, now quiet and deserted.

"Truly," Sara thought, evoking verse of Robert Burns:

> *All backward as I cast my e'e*
> *Seems dark and drear;*
> *And forward though I canna' see*
> *I doubt and fear.*[988]

Turning one last time from battle-ripped Petersburg, watching one more time the great mansions along the river slide past and then from view, she, too, now went, following Roger, into the arms of the enemy.

EPILOGUE

---•◦•---

The Sweetheart of My Life

*S*ara and the children found Roger waiting for them on the dock in New York City, and Sara thought him very thin and wan and "sadly in need of us." They crossed, in the ferry, to Brooklyn and there caught the "horse cars," and rode through what seemed to Sara endless miles of lit streets to the little house Roger had rented for them.[989]

There they began what Marie Gordon would later call "these Brooklyn years."[990] It was an unsubstantial little house, "narrow as a ladder and filled with unattractive furniture," on the edge of what appeared to Sara as nowhere. It was a house without a furnace or a stove—nothing but open grates to keep away the chill, in a sparsely settled neighborhood, in a row of look-alike houses amid a sprinkling of vacant lots. It fronted on "an uninteresting sidewalk of a hot, dreary street." All seemed to Sara "so desolate, so hopeless, for us in this great unknown world. We knew ourselves not only strangers but aliens, outcasts." Her "sickening sense of loneliness" was accented by the "far-off hum of the city, and the mournful fog-horns and whistles of the river." Hannah, the laundress who had been talked into coming with them, called it "dis Gawd-forsaken place." She soon left, to return to Virginia, despite

Sara's urgent pleas to stay, and Sara filled her place with an Irish-woman named Anne.[991]

This wasn't Sara's first exposure to New York. She had visited this biggest of American cities when she was fifteen and Aunt Mary "suddenly discovered that the child was a woman. She must see the world." They had come to New York in the autumn of that year and had stopped at the Astor House, on Broadway, where her seat at the dining-room table was near that of ex-president John Quincy Adams. Sara's room overlooked the park opposite the Astor House, where scarlet flamingos stood around a fountain on toothpick legs. Sara had walked in Bowling Green Park, then New York's fashionable promenade, taken tea on Bleeker Street, and bought a set of turquoise jewelry, a jeweled comb, and a white topaz broach at Tiffany's. They had visited Niagara Falls, where the heavy thunder of the waters and the immensity of their power had filled her with terror. The best part of the trip for Sara had been returning home to Charlottesville.[992] She knew how Hannah felt.

Early in the spring after Hannah left, they moved to Brooklyn Heights, to a house on Willow Street near the ferry and much nearer Roger's office on Liberty Street in New York City. Brooklyn was a huge overgrown village, a separate entity from the big city across the river, and the third largest city of the North.[993]

There, for the next ten years, they waged a war of survival, often in the near clutches of poverty, always working, it seemed to Sara, "to the utmost limit of human endurance." She later wrote, "Our 'destiny was work, work, work'—and patiently we fulfilled it." With her own hands she made every garment their children wore, even their winter coats, sewing, stitching, and hemming deep into the night. It smacked of war's hard times all over again, of the long candle-lit nights at Cottage Farm.[994] As Roger was to say, quoting an aphorism, "The immortal garland is not to be run for without dust and heat."[995]

But there was no war now, and there were the trappings of a normal life, and a gradual climbing out of the pit. Their daughters were growing into beautiful young women, after their mother, magnets for girlfriends and for handsome young men alike. They moved to a house on Thirty-third Street in Manhattan, in a city that seemed to Sara "the most undesirable in the country for a new beginner in any enterprise."[996]

She described their new neighborhood in a letter to Agnes. On one side was the rear of a big hotel, its kitchens fronting on the house. Sara said she would as soon hear shrieking shells as its clanging of pots and pans. Behind them was a sash-and-blind factory kicking up "dust and noise unspeakable." On the other side a neighbor had planted a garden, erected an awning, and there held card and wine parties that Sara called "revels." The patch of blue sky they looked out on seemed narrow compared to the broad open skies of Virginia. The stifling heat of the New York summer, she wrote Agnes, "cannot be imagined." But Sara worked beauty into their lives, with climbing nasturtium and morning-glory vines in window boxes. And the little house became "the theater of many pleasant events." There, in its parlor, their daughter Lucy was married.[997]

Roger was a changed man in both his profession and in what he professed. From the ardent secessionist passionately badgering South Carolina to fire the first shot at Fort Sumter and catapult Virginia into the war within an hour by the Shrewsbury clock, he became an equally ardent and eloquent Unionist. In a letter to the *Richmond Whig* in October 1867, he answered criticisms of him in Virginia that he was a turncoat. "When I renewed my oath of allegiance to the Union," he wrote, "I did so in good faith and without reservation; and as I understand that oath, it not only restrains me from acts of positive hostility to the government, but pledges me to do my utmost for its welfare and stability. Hence, while I am more immediately concerned to see the South restored to its former prosperity, I am anxious that the whole country, and all classes, may be reunited on the basis of common interest and fraternal regard." This objective, it appeared to him, "can only be attained by conceding to all classes the unrestricted rights guaranteed them by the laws and by obliterating as speedily and as entirely as possible the distinctions which have separated the North and the South into hostile sections."

Roger now regarded civil war as the "sum and consummation of all human woe." Another such catastrophe, he believed, must be averted at whatever cost in energy and ability. In private discourse with his friends in the South, Roger seized "every appropriate . . . opportunity" to plead for "moderation and magnanimity." He advised his fellow Southerners to "accept the situation" and adjust to the changed state of things, to "recognize and respect the rights of the colored race," to "cultivate relations of confidence and good-will toward people of the North," to shun "profitless agitations of political debate"—the practice of which he was a proven master—and to turn their energies to more useful work.

In part Roger was seeking redemption. He was hoping "in some measure, and in a quiet way, to repair the evil I contributed to bring upon the South." Passion, he wrote the *Whig*, "precipitated us into secession; reason must conduct us back into the path of peace and prosperity." He knew his views courted personal animosity among his old friends in the South, but "at whatever risk of personal obloquy and at whatever sacrifice of personal interest" he was "resolved to employ all the energy and intellect I may command in the incessant endeavor to promote peace and good-will among the people of the lately belligerent states."[998] He was to back this resolve time and again in speech and action through the rest of his life.

Sara summed up what it had all come down to in the end: "This was war," she wrote, "war that spares not the graybeard, childhood, aged women, holy nuns—nobody! . . . I humbly pray, He has forgiven, as we have forgiven, and I trust been ourselves for-given. No southerner, however, can wholly forget."[999]

Roger's new Unionism made him some strange bedfellows. Perhaps the most belief-defying of these was his friendship, per-sonal and professional, with Ben Butler, the notorious Union general, called "Beast" in the South, who had thundered at Peters-burg's gates and insulted the women of New Orleans—the man Kate Stone, in Mississippi, suspected had been reincarnated with "the soul of Nero."[1000]

Butler retained Roger to defend his son-in-law, the former Union General Adelbert Ames, the reconstruction governor of Mississippi, against impeachment charges. Conviction seemed cer-tain, but Roger got the impeachment charges dropped, permitting Ames to resign with his reputation intact.[1001]

No less surprising was Roger's acquaintance with Horace Greeley, the self-confessed ink-slinging editor of the *New York Tribune* and would-be politician-president.[1002] When Greeley was nominated by the Democratic Party in 1872 to run against Grant, who was bidding for a second term in the White House, Greeley asked Roger to campaign for him throughout Virginia and the South.[1003] Roger declined. The thought of such a bizarre teaming was surreal. Roger's friend the journalist John Russell Young wrote him that the spectacle of "the Harry Hotspur of the Southern Rev-olution—the one orator who had clamored so impatiently for the Shrewsbury clock to strike," now championing Horace Greeley defied imagination. "Can the irony of events have a deeper illus-tration?" Young marveled. "*Miserare!* How the world is tumbling! What can we expect next? Jefferson Davis and Frederick Douglass [the renowned black abolitionist-orator] running on the presiden-tial ticket, in favor of Chinese suffrage!"[1004]

Theoretically, such an alliance as Greeley-Pryor in Democratic politics was not impossible. Roger often said he was "born a Pres-byterian and a Democrat" and that he had never faltered in either belief. He became active in party councils again in the years following the war. In 1876 he was a delegate to the Democratic National Convention that nominated Samuel J. Tilden.[1005]

In 1877 Roger was invited by leading Brooklynites to deliver an address on Decoration Day, at the Academy of Music. He went as far as it was possible for a onetime fire-eater to go in recanting his past. In the coda to the speech, he said, "From the vantage ground of a larger observation, with a more calm and considerable meditation on the causes and conditions of national prosperity, I, for one, cannot resist the conclusion that, after all, Providence wisely ordered the event [the Civil War], and that it is well for the South itself that it was disappointed in its endeavor to establish a separate government. Plain it is that, if once established, such a government could not have long endured. It was founded on principles that must have proved its downfall."

The speech signaled Roger's ultimate amalgamation into the Northern and national culture. The firebrand orator for secession had become the firebrand orator for reconciliation. The *New York Evening Express* said that the speech "wins golden opinions," that it was "brave, patriotic, and statesman-like." Pryor, it editorialized, is "one of the few men who have a to-morrow." The *Wilmington (North Carolina) Star* called it " 'logic on fire.' "

A prominent preacher of the time, Richard S. Storrs, wrote, "I do not see how you could possibly have treated the theme . . . more delicately or more grandly—with a finer touch, or a more complete mastery of all its proper relations and suggestions." Sara saw the speech as "a fitting close to the first twelve years of our life of trial and probation."[1006] Three years later, in 1880, the Congress itself ended the probation officially, passing a law removing Roger's "political disabilities." Fifteen years after the war ended, he was finally forgiven.[1007]

The Pryors were now seasoned New Yorkers and prominent fixtures in the city's social circles. The *Brooklyn Eagle* described Roger as a "striking figure" in his Northern adopted city, "tall, almost gaunt, with long hair and typical features of a North American

Indian...always impressive."[1008] He was now a leading New York lawyer "truly enamored of [the law and] her austere and rugged beauties."[1009]

He was on the team of attorneys for the plaintiff in 1875 when Theodore Tilton, a brilliant journalist-orator-reformer, charged the eminent preacher Henry Ward Beecher with committing adultery with his wife, Elizabeth, debauching her, and ruining Tilton's life. It was a sensational case, called at the time "the most celebrated jury trial in America for the past half century...one of the most remarkable in the history of jurisprudence." It scandalized the nation for months and employed the most high-powered New York lawyers. Roger, described by an observer as "a man of large erudition and of a marvelously alert mind," was entrusted with the delicate and obscure questions of law in the case on the plaintiff's side.[1010] His reply to William M. Evarts, of the Beecher defense team, was his highlight moment. His closely reasoned argument was "the greatest surprise of the day," wrote one reporter. His execution was "prodigious...a *tour de force*.... A volcanic torrent of speech...lightning-like." He "drives onward," the reporter wrote, "like a Jehu rushing into battle. He has no moderate passages." Yet the diction, "with all its headlong speed, is perfect in precision and force, and no less in elegance."[1011]

More than one observer was impressed. "Among all the lawyers who represented the plaintiff," one analyst later wrote, "there was none, in my estimation, who in discussion of the relevancy of testimony reached greater heights than those reached by Mr. Pryor. He was a dramatic figure, with his long black hair and high cheek bones, and seemed almost the counterpart of an Indian Chief on the warpath.... Where there was a question that required learning or the apt quotation of the legal principle from the reported case, the chapter and page were on the tip of his tongue."[1012] Another writer said of him that he was still "this duelist in field and forum"[1013]—a calumny Roger would deny. Asked about his duels in later years he said, "They were indiscretions of my youth. Let's not talk about them."[1014]

The titillating case ended, after all that, with the jury unable to reach a verdict, an outcome vindicating the defendant. Roger came to believe that was the proper result. "Whenever I go to the Borough of Brooklyn and see the statue of Beecher standing under the windows of the court room where we sought to drag his name in the mire," he later told a friend, "I say to myself, 'How gloriously history has vindicated him and condemned us!' "[1015]

Roger was a major player in many landmark cases of the day. He was the first lawyer to win a suit against the Elevated Railroad Company for damages to adjoining property. He was a leading appeals counsel in the defense of the anarchists in the sensational Haymarket bombing in Chicago in 1886 that killed one and wounded several. Arguing their innocence before the U.S. Supreme Court, Roger looked almost the anarchist himself with his angular form, his "massive, granite-like jaw, coal-black eyes and long, black hair."[1016] He believed the accused innocent of anything but their opinions. "If there was a [bomb] plot in existence," he told reporters, "do you suppose they would have had their wives and children there?"[1017] He was the lead attorney in a suit to break up the sugar trust in New York. This last case, which he won, was the first litigation in any court of any state to break up combinations in restraint of trade. Other states soon followed New York's—and Roger's—lead, dooming the forming of trusts as a way to legally consolidate an industry.[1018]

In 1890 his gifts as a lawyer elevated him to the bench—as a judge of the Court of Common Pleas of New York, the oldest judicial tribunal in the state, twice as old as the nation.[1019] Four years later when that court was merged into the state supreme court, he sat on that bench for another five years. Who would have thought it of this fiery Southern secessionist of unhappier times?

There was still a large residue of the South in Roger Pryor, mellowed by the passing years. One writer has said of him that he was "a gentle, gracious, kindly gentleman of the old school—kind in the home, kind on the bench."[1020] His favorite passage in Shakespeare was from *Measure for Measure:*

> *No ceremony that to great ones 'longs,*
> *Not the king's crown, nor the deputed sword,*
> *The marshal's truncheon, nor the judge's robe,*
> *Become them with one half so good a grace*
> *As mercy does.*[1021]

Roger's forte as a lawyer had been divorce and corporation law. As a divorce lawyer he was generally found defending the woman in the case, his Southern chivalry never dimming. He took these pro-feminist leanings with him to the bench. The *New York World* wrote, "The Justice here has furnished a whiff of the old chivalry of the South before the war...in his treatment of litigants." The *World* reported that he "one day startled the courtroom by declaring he would not believe the confession of a co-respondent backed by the statements of a private detective against the unsupported denial of a woman."[1022]

As a jurist he was thought to have a clear and searching mind, together with his unusual chivalry toward litigants.[1023] A fellow jurist said of him, "Mr. Pryor's arguments, if they do not always convince, always enlighten the mind and conscience of the court." He was said to have "an iron energy, with all the instincts and ambition of the student and the scholar."[1024] Sara said, proudly, that he brought to the bench "the habits of self-denial and unremitting study he had practiced for twenty years."[1025]

And Sara brought to New York her unique and winning grace. One writer said of her that she was "adorably Southern and ever exquisitely feminine."[1026] "Handsome, entertaining, literary," another writer has since described her.[1027]

She became a writer herself—she called it "a babbler of Reminiscences." She dipped "my pen in my heart" and wrote of "the memories which happen to linger in the brain of the old like bits of drift-wood floating round and round in the eddies of a back-water." She said she had "lived in the last two-thirds of the splendid nineteenth century, and [had] known some of the men and women who made that century notable."[1028] Her two books of memoirs, *Reminiscences of Peace and War* and *My Day,* were published in the early 1900s. In these her friend LaSalle Corbell Pickett said that Sara gave "to the reading world beautiful pictures of the lights and shadows that had fallen over her life."[1029]

Her first "timid venture" into writing since her love story for the *Saturday Evening Post* years before, was an occasional article or essay for *Cosmopolitan Magazine,* the *Delineator*—a popular fashion magazine—and other periodicals.[1030] In 1899, after Roger retired from the bench, Sara began writing in earnest. Her first book, about the mother of George Washington and her times, appeared four years later and was praised by a reviewer as "a very entertaining and attractive book," a "sane and correct view . . . a fair picture of the mother of the greatest American."[1031] It was followed by a history of Jamestown, Virginia, and the two books of memoirs. Sara once told John Russell Young that "darning stockings had a debilitating effect upon literary aspirations," but she continued darning and writing, anyhow.[1032]

One admirer wrote of her that "suffering has not made her bitter, nor misfortune crippled a beautiful nature." Marie Gordon would later write of her mother that she "ever placed above even the golden word, the Golden Deed."[1033] She became one of the founders of the Home for Friendless Women and Children in New York, the impresario of a concert that earned four hundred dollars for the cause. She was gracious of manner, of distinguished appearance, and a gifted raconteur[1034]—and therefore a gifted fundraiser. She raised three thousand dollars for the monument to Mary Washington, George's mother. When the yellow-fever epidemic stalked Florida in 1888, she organized society benefits that raised seven thousand dollars for relief. And when the Galveston flood drowned thousands in Texas in 1900, she raised fifty-one thousand dollars for the relief of its children who had been made homeless orphans. She said, "The greatest work I ever did was for Jacksonville and Galveston—for fever and for flood."[1035]

As they had always—in antebellum Virginia and Washington and in the war-ravaged Confederacy—Roger and Sara continued to move in the highest social circles, even in New York. To the last they were "in touch with the prominent shapers of events."[1036]

Many of Brooklyn's most noted citizens were their neighbors in Brooklyn Heights. Among their many friends were former Union generals—Ulysses S. Grant, Winfield Scott Hancock, James Fry, Henry Slocum, Fitz-John Porter, Daniel Butterfield, and George McClellan. William T. Sherman and his daughter Rachel were visitors at their house on Thirty-third Street, and Sara said, when first introduced to him, "Oh, General Sherman! *Never* did I think I should find myself in the same boat with *you!*" "Now see here!" Sherman answered. "I'm not as black as I am painted."[1037]

In October 1890 John Russell Young threw a dinner in Roger's honor, at the Astor House, after Roger was elevated to the bench—"a quiet, private gathering." Among the celebrated guests were Sherman, Grover Cleveland, Dan Sickles, Henry George, Mark Twain, Thomas Nast, and Murat Halstead—among the most famous in their callings in the country. Alexander McClure, another national luminary who was present, said, "Such an assemblage was impossible prior to the rebellion, and there has been none such since, and it is not likely that any man at this table will ever look upon its like again." It was an improbable collection of forty movers and shakers, saying improbable things. Sherman laid a reconciling hand on Roger's shoulder and said, "We would have done all this for him long ago, but he had to be such a rebel!"[1038]

Among Sara's close friends were the wives of two of the most famous men in the country—Winfield Scott Hancock and Ulysses S. Grant. Sara spent much time with Mrs. Hancock, and Roger consulted with the former Union general on political matters and spoke for him when Hancock headed the Democratic ticket in the presidential election campaign of 1880.[1039]

Two days after Hancock's defeat in the presidential race, Sara was lunching with Julia Grant at the Fifth Avenue Hotel, and Julia invited her to a reception at her home for General Philip Sheridan. The recollection of her confrontations with Sheridan in the days following the fall of Petersburg came coursing back through Sara's memory.

"Of course you'll not go," Roger said. "How can you meet General Sheridan?"

"Why not?" Sara said. "If he can stand it, I can."

Sara went, and took Lucy. It was a long jump from the last time they had met in Sara's house-cum-adjutant headquarters in Petersburg to the drawing room of the wife of Sheridan's old commander. When the general saw her, he was at first too astonished to speak.

"Do you remember me, General Sheridan?" Sara asked.

In a moment both of his hands grasped hers. "Indeed, indeed I do, dear lady—and I am grateful to Mrs. Grant for giving me this opportunity to tell you that no man in this country more cordially rejoices at General Pryor's success than I do."

He remembered Lucy, too, the little baby he had held in his arms in the house in Petersburg, who had stared so steadfastly into his eyes and to whom he had given the figs, bananas, cakes, and nuts, and who was now taller than he.[1040]

Of all of Roger's and Sara's seven bright children—the seventh, Fanny, had arrived in 1868—Theodorick was the brightest. Marie Gordon, the sister and playmate of his younger years, later wrote that in him they had "entertained an angel unawares." Sara, to whom he had recited Longfellow's "A Psalm of Life" in that lowest of nights in Petersburg, said he was "no ordinary boy." A mathematics professor, after the war, called him "a mathematical genius." And Theodorick was just as proficient in everything else—Latin, Greek, English literature, history—a born student.

His mind was "well stored," his memory "prodigious," his analytical powers "remarkable."[1041] Tom Conolly, the visiting member of Parliament from Donegal in their Cottage Farm days, had thought him "one of the finest boys I ever saw . . . very forward in Mathematics & Geometry."[1042]

He had matriculated at Princeton and graduated, in 1870, with first honors and the school's coveted mathematical fellowship, which sent him for a year of study to Cambridge in England. His bent had been toward a career in theology—the ancestral call of the ministry was in him. But he went instead into the study of law to become his father's partner, splitting his time between the Columbia Law School and Roger's law office. He was brilliant in that calling, too.

The autumn of 1871 was a dying time. Summer was putting on its final show of color, the flowers were fading and leaves were falling. It was a time of the year that saddened, and it was affecting Theodorick, making him melancholy.

On a Saturday evening that October, he was at home, asking his mother to play for him on the piano. She played for him for two hours, selections she knew he loved best. The next evening, a little after nine o'clock, after attending church with a friend and after reading for a few moments, he went out into the hall, put on his coat and hat, told Sara he felt warm and would take a walk to cool off, and left the house.

They never saw him alive again. On Monday morning his body was found floating in the East River. His coat, watch, and purse were missing, but there were no marks of violence on him. Nobody ever knew what had happened. He was buried at Princeton—"in this classic ground," his eulogist called it. He was only twenty years old.[1043]

It was a tragedy far worse than war for Roger and Sara. And before they died, they would see yet another of their boys go before them—William, also luminously brilliant. He became one of the country's most noted obstetricians and gynecologists, who,

Sara wrote, was "most richly endowed, physically and mentally, and . . . gave to suffering humanity all that God had given him."[1044] He died on August 26, 1904, from what physicians called "a complication of diseases."[1045]

The other five children lived on, their stories happier than Theodorick's or William's. Roger Jr. became a lawyer. Marie Gordon, their oldest, married Henry Rice and returned to Virginia to live on a large tobacco plantation. The other girls also married, their weddings witnessed by many of the rich and famous— among them John D. Rockefeller, Frederick D. Grant, Daniel Butterfield, P. G. T. Beauregard.[1046]

Roger resigned from the bench in 1899, when he reached seventy, the age limit for judges in New York, and returned to his law practice. In 1912 he was appointed an official referee by the appellate division of the New York supreme court. When he and Sara celebrated their sixtieth wedding anniversary, in 1908, more than a thousand people came to New York to celebrate with them.[1047]

Sara returned to Petersburg on visits during their New York years. She drove out to the battlefields around the city and saw that nature had erased the scars. Daisies now whitened the fields where the Federal soldiers had encamped, and covered the graves by the wayside. Nature, Sara thought, "had not forgotten these lonely unmarked graves, nor will she ever forget, until time shall be no more."[1048]

It seemed that sad retrospection would be a part of the American psyche for as long as they all lived. Charlotte Bostwick of Brooklyn had written after war's end, "So many changes; so many breakings-up; so many farewells to the departing to the distant lands and to the 'better land.' Oh, what a world of mutation! How laden is the air with sighs from the sorrowful."[1049]

Sara knew what those sighs signified—that "the old life will not come back and the old friends are gone."[1050] It seemed so long ago, that day at the wedding reception in Washington when she had told President Buchanan that South Carolina had seceded. She now knew that that breathtaking act of defiance had launched the cataclysmic events that were to "change all our lives, give them poverty for riches, mutilation and wounds for strength and health, obscurity and degradation for honor and distinction, exile and loneliness for inherited homes and friends, pain and death for happiness and life."[1051]

She perhaps remembered Ben Shepard, whom beautiful Helen had urged to fields of glory so many years ago on the rail platform in Petersburg. He had died in battle, carrying his love for her and the banner of that lost cause, the banner, Sara thought, that had "led the armies of the South through fire and blood to victory, to defeat, in times of starvation, cold, and friendlessness . . . the banner of a thousand histories," now furled forever.[1052] And the Helens of the South were too many to number, for as the popular song had it, "But many a sweetheart mourns the loss / Of a Southern Soldier Boy."[1053]

Sara perhaps remembered the wounded Confederate soldier whom she and Fanny Poindexter had rescued from the roadside before the Seven Days battles, and whom they never went to see again at the hospital. Two years later Sara had been approached at a railway station by a handsome young officer who said he had "never forgotten, would never forget" her. He was that young soldier, recovered, still alive, and now Lieutenant Ernstorff.[1054]

Neither would she ever forget. But many, Sara knew, wanted to forget. As one survivor, who had sent her husband to war, would later write, "That time is a blank horror in my life. I remember only tears."[1055]

In writing and thinking about the war years, Sara often wondered what would have happened to them had Roger fired that first shot at Fort Sumter when the young artillery officer on Johnson Island offered him the lanyard. Even had his life been spared, she believed, he certainly would not have become an eminent New York lawyer and jurist.[1056]

On the morning of February 15, 1912, Sara died of chronic pernicious anemia, four days short of her eighty-second birthday, and was buried in Princeton beside her two boys. It was said of her that she was "as harmonious as music, as gentle as a summer's breeze, as steadfast as a star," that "there was no place in her heart where fear or meanness or envy lurked. Bravely, tenderly, hopefully she lived through great events."[1057] For the gritty survivor who had "seen so many setting suns," hers had finally set.[1058] What she had wished years before, in God's name, for a young newly married couple, had come to pass for her and Roger: They had grown old together.[1059]

Four years before she died, on her sixtieth wedding anniversary, she had written a poem, called "My Day." The last verse said what she thought about all this:

> *I have lost my rose, forgotten my song,*
> * But the true heart that loved me is mine alway;*
> *The stars are alight—the way not long—*
> * I had my day!*[1060]

WHEN SHE DIED Roger mourned and said, "I have lost the sweetheart of my life."[1061]

SEVEN YEARS AFTER her death, at ten o'clock in the evening, March 14, 1919, Roger, age ninety, died of pneumonia in their home on West Sixty-ninth Street. When he died, he was the last survivor of the firing on Fort Sumter, the last surviving prominent antebellum editor, the last antebellum member of the U.S. Congress, the last member of the Confederate Congress, one of the last general officers of the Confederate army, and among the last of its privates.[1062] The *New York Herald* wrote that "in no other country save our own could such a career as that of Roger A. Pryor be possible."[1063]

One tribute to him said that he died "full of years and honor.... He was for a very considerable part of his long life, a striking and commanding figure. His appearance was picturesque, his charm of manner great. He seemed born to distinction. . . . New York received him gladly, and in time, honored him greatly." The tribute said, "His career is closed, but it will be long before his memory is forgotten."[1064]

His body was carried to Princeton and buried beside the sweetheart of his life—his rightful place, for he had also been the sweetheart of hers. In life and in death these two rebel hearts had been meant for each other.

A Word of Thanks

Writing a book is an excellent way to attract help, which is a good thing, for no book of history can possibly be written without it. Not only is that help deeply appreciated, but those who give it must be vigorously thanked.

My thanks, as always for any book I write, begins with my wife, Kathleen Lively, who showed no undue suspicion when I disappeared for days into the nineteenth century, and no jealousy when I fell in love with Sara Pryor.

Neither would this book be nearly as good—and I like to presume it is good—without the skilled harassment of my editor at Harcourt, Walter Bode. He irritated me no end at times, but practically everything he suggested made this a better book. Fortunately I had the wisdom to listen to him. David Hough, Harcourt's managing editor, who took the baton from Walter for the wrap-up phase, has a done a careful, professional job and has my thanks as well. And without my agent and dear friend, Mike Hamilburg, and his always helpful associate Joanie Kern, the book would never have gotten into Walter's and David's capable hands in the first place.

I am greatly indebted to three outstanding historians and friends who at various junctures in the pursuit of this work lent an invaluable hand: Grady McWhiney, the distinguished professor of history emeritus from Texas Christian University, a leading Civil War scholar for better than half a century, who gave of his strong friendship throughout; Lynda L. Crist, who as editor of the papers of Jefferson Davis continues to make enormous contributions to Civil War scholarship and is always ready with special expertise and help; and Robert K. Krick, the world's leading expert on the Confederate Army of Northern Virginia, who guided me to some sources I would never have found without him.

My needs were also well and congenially served by John M. Coski, historian for the Museum of the Confederacy in Richmond, and by Chris Calkins at the Petersburg battlefield, who pointed me to the sites of the various residences of Roger and Sara Pryor in that beleaguered city.

Genealogical help came to my side on several occasions from Joan Martin, an expert genealogist, who also happens to be the mother of my son-in-law, Scott Martin. Like his mother, my son-in-law was a great help at several junctures during the process when I couldn't figure out my computer. John Gatewood Pryor, a descendent of the Pryor line from Atlanta, also sent me materials about Roger and Sara that were very helpful.

Help came in bunches from any number of librarians, who, next to spouses, are truly indispensable ingredients in researching any book of history. I must thank particularly Trudi Ensey, who, as the interlibrary loan librarian at the Arlington, Texas, Central Library, pulled in from every corner of the country books that I could not have gotten otherwise. She, and therefore I, relied heavily in this task on two librarians at the Fort Worth Public Library, Mary Sikes and Dale Rogers. Susan McDonald, senior archivist at the Robert W. Woodruff Library at Emory University, also offered a hand along the way. I am indebted immeasurably to the libraries of the three great universities in my part of the country: University of Texas at Arlington, Southern Methodist University in Dallas, and Texas Christian University in Fort Worth. And I spent many profitable hours in the rich collections of the Library of Virginia and the

Virginia Historical Society in Richmond, and the Earl Gregg Swem Library at William and Mary College, in Williamsburg.

I also owe thanks to four special people at Hampden-Sydney College, Roger Pryor's alma mater. Elna Ann Mayo, in the college library; Mary C. Herdegen, curator of the Esther Thomas Atkinson Museum; college chaplain William E. Thompson; and professor of classics and Hampden-Sydney historian John Luster Brinkley were all particularly helpful.

Among those who also helped me gather material at critical times was another relative, Kenneth Crumbly, of Williamsburg, Virginia. I also had help in Williamsburg from newspaper columnist–historian Will Molineux. V. Elaine Thompson, in Lynda Crist's office, and Jane "Budge" Weidman, in Washington, helped me pull materials from the National Archives. And George Stone, an expert swordsman, helped me get a grip on the world of dueling, which Roger had such kinship with.

Finally, what could I have done without Sara Pryor? Because she wrote so enchantingly and so thoroughly about her life with Roger and their lives together in the Civil War, this book now lives. If she were here I would give her a huge hug.

Endnotes

In the notes that follow, only the author's last name, the short title of the work, and the page numbers are cited. The full bibliographical information for every work can be found alphabetically listed in the bibliography, beginning on page 395.

1. This is a phrase from Schurz, *The Reminiscences of Carl Schurz*, 2:164.
2. The account of how Buchanan learned of South Carolina's secession is from Sara Pryor's two books of memoirs, *My Day*, 153–55, and *Reminiscences of Peace and War*, 110–12.
3. Pryor, *My Day*, 1.
4. Rice, "Sara Agnes Pryor," 4277.
5. De Leon, *Belles, Beaux, and Brains of the 60's*, 157.
6. Turner, "Some Early Nottoway County History," 270.
7. Turner, *Old Homes and Families in Nottoway*, 1–2, 12.
8. Epes, "Roger Atkinson Pryor," 11.
9. Suplée, *The Life of Theodorick Bland Pryor*, 7–8.
10. Both quotes are from ibid., 9.
11. *Dictionary of American Biography*, s.v. "Bland, Richard."
12. Campbell, *The Bland Papers*, xx.
13. A detailed biographical sketch of this Revolutionary War Theodorick, from which this description is taken, is in Campbell, *The Bland Papers*, xiii–xxxi. Also see *Dictionary of American Biography*, s.v. "Bland, Theodorick"; and Abbott, *Official Report of the Trial of Henry Ward Beecher*, xxii.

14. For the Pryor line, see Watson, "Notes on Southside Virginia," 173; and Suplée, *The Life of Theodorick Bland Pryor*, 19–20.

15. Suplée, *The Life of Theodorick Bland Pryor*, 20.

16. Claiborne, *Seventy-five Years in Old Virginia*, 84.

17. Epes, "Roger Atkinson Pryor," 11.

18. Watson, "Notes on Southside Virginia," 175. There is good background on Roger's father on pp. 173–76. Also see Epes, "Roger Atkinson Pryor," 10–11.

19. Theodorick's character is pictured by a daughter-in-law, Anne Campbell Pryor, in "Recollections Concerning Dr. Theodorick Bland Pryor," 1–6.

20. Epes, "Roger Atkinson Pryor," 11.

21. Ibid., 10.

22. Ibid., 11; Suplée, *The Life of Theodorick Bland Pryor*, 78.

23. For a delightful history of Hampden-Sydney College, see Brinkley, *On This Hill*, particularly pp. 195 n, 203, 205, 208, 208 n, and 227 for material used here.

24. My description of Roger is framed largely from Epes, "Roger Atkinson Pryor," 10; and Watson, "Notes on Southside Virginia," 177.

25. The Charlottesville setting is lyrically described in Suplée, *The Life of Theodorick Bland Pryor*, 28–29, 42–43. I have borrowed from it wholesale, for both quoted and paraphrased passages. See also Pryor, *My Day*, 43.

26. Pryor, *My Day*, 43.

27. Eggleston, *A Rebel's Recollections*, 47.

28. Pryor, *My Day*, 24.

29. Avary, *A Virginia Girl in the Civil War*, 109.

30. Pryor, *My Day*, 5–6.

31. Pryor, *Reminiscences of Peace and War*, 34.

32. Suplée, *The Life of Theodorick Bland Pryor*, 21–23. See also Thompson, "First in War, Foremost in Peace," 9.

33. Taylor, *Virginia Baptist Ministers*, 3rd series, 397–401.

34. The journey is described by Sara in *My Day*, 7–9. Her feelings next morning and after are from pp. 9 and 39.

35. Sara's aunt Mary is described in ibid., 37, 75; and in Rice, "Sara Agnes Pryor," 4273.

36. Pryor, *My Day*, 10–12.

37. Ibid., 10, 11, 18.

38. Ibid., 38, 40.

39. Sara remembers this first encounter in her life with a great man in ibid., 34–35.

40. The move to Charlottesville and Sara's adventures in learning are also recounted in *My Day*, 43–53. For an augmenting account of her early steeping in literature and the arts and her musical education, see Rice, "Sara Agnes Pryor," 4273.

41. Pryor, *My Day*, 75–76.

42. Rice, "Sara Agnes Pryor," 4274.

43. Pryor, *My Day*, 56.

44. Ibid., 64–65.

45. Ibid., 57; Rice, "Sara Agnes Pryor," 4274.

46. Pryor, *My Day*, 75.

47. Ibid., 79–81.

48. Roger's visit and Sara's reactions are from ibid., 65–68.

49. Ibid., 68, 70.

50. Eaton, *The Waning of the Old South Civilization*, 28.

51. Roger's graduation and matriculation to the University of Virginia is briefly addressed in Holzman, *Adapt or Perish*, 12–13; Epes, "Roger Atkinson Pryor," 11–12; and Thompson, "First in War, Foremost in Peace," 8. For profiles of Schele, McGuffey, and Minor see *Dictionary of American Biography*, s.v. "Schele de Vere, Maximilian," "McGuffey, William Holmes," and "Minor, John Barbee." Courtenay is profiled in *Appletons' Cyclopaedia of American Biography*, s.v. "Courtenay, Edward Henry."

52. Pryor, *My Day*, 70, 75.

53. Ibid., 78.

54. Ibid., 83.

55. *New York Times*, 6 November 1898.

56. Epes, "Roger Atkinson Pryor," 12; *New York Tribune*, 15 March 1919.

57. Pryor, *My Day*, 83.

58. Ibid., 84.

59. *New York Evening Post*, 15 March 1919.

60. Pryor, *My Day*, 169.

61. Wyatt, *Preliminary Checklist for Petersburg*, 253; Claiborne, *Seventy-five Years in Old Virginia*, 91–92.

62. Lebsock, *The Free Women of Petersburg*, 2.

63. Ibid., 12.

64. Additional detail about Petersburg in this paragraph is from Scott and Wyatt, *Petersburg's Story*, 3; Claiborne, *Seventy-five Years in Old Virginia*, 40, 43–44.

65. Henderson, *The Unredeemed City*, iii.

66. Claiborne, *Seventy-five Years in Old Virginia*, 63, 67, 91.

67. Pryor, *My Day*, 84.

68. Claiborne, *Seventy-five Years in Old Virginia*, 91.

69. Ibid., 92.

70. Pryor, *My Day*, 392, 451–52.

71. Pryor, "The Bar and Forensic Oratory," 111.

72. Pryor, *My Day*, 104.

73. Benjamin Perley Poore, a Washington journalist, describes Kossuth in *Perley's Reminiscences*, 1:404–5.

74. Pryor, *My Day*, 85–88.

75. Ibid., 84–85.

76. Claiborne, *Seventy-five Years in Old Virginia*, 92.

77. Thompson, "First in War, Foremost in Peace," 9.

78. Pryor, *My Day*, 100.

79. Pryor, *Reminiscences of Peace and War*, 4.

80. Pryor, *My Day*, 138.

81. "Washington City," 8; Pryor, *My Day*, 139.

82. Pryor, *Reminiscences of Peace and War*, 9.

83. Ibid., 14; Pryor, *My Day*, 139.

84. The description of the conditions and mood at Pierce's inaugural borrow heavily from Pryor, *Reminiscences of Peace and War*, 15–19.

85. Forney, *Anecdotes of Public Men*, 1:12, 2:418.

86. Poore, *Perley's Reminiscences*, 1:420–21.

87. Pryor, *My Day*, 91.

88. Pryor, *Reminiscences of Peace and War*, 29.

89. Ibid., 29–30.

90. Ibid., 30; *Dictionary of American Biography*, s.v. "Irving, Washington."

91. Pickett, *Across My Path*, 139–40.

92. Ibid., 141–42.

93. Much of the flavor and description of Washington social life and fashion are distilled here from Clay-Clopton, *A Belle of the Fifties*, 27, 86–88, 90, 95, 118.

94. Pickett, *Across My Path*, 137.

95. Clay-Clopton, *A Belle of the Fifties*, 44, 47.

96. Pryor, *Reminiscences of Peace and War*, 34–35.

97. Holzman, *Adapt or Perish*, 16.

98. Abbott, *Official Report of the Trial of Henry Ward Beecher*, xxii.

99. Pryor, *My Day*, 106–7; Nichols, *Franklin Pierce*, 279.

100. Forney, *Anecdotes of Public Men*, 1:57.

101. This brief sketch of Thomas Ritchie owes much to Forney, *Anecdotes of Public Men*, 1:107–8; Cappon, *Virginia Newspapers*, 171; Hudson, *Journalism in the United States*, 268–70; *Dictionary of American Biography*, s.v. "Ritchie, Thomas."

102. Clay-Clopton, *A Belle of the Fifties*, 26.

103. Pryor, *My Day*, 108–9.

104. For detail on Roger's mission to Greece, see Wriston, *Executive Agents in American Foreign Relations*, 660–63.

105. Pryor, *Reminiscences of Peace and War*, 40; and *My Day*, 110–11.

106. Clay-Clopton, *A Belle of the Fifties*, 60.

107. Pryor, *My Day*, 109–10.

108. Anspach, *The Sons of the Sires*, 9–10.

109. "Secret Societies—The Know-Nothings," 94, 97.

110. Zacharias, "The Know-Nothing Party and the Oratory of Nativism," 219.

111. Gay, "The Campaign of 1855 in Virginia and the Fall of the Know-Nothing Party," 319–20.

112. Wise, *The Life of Henry A. Wise*, 67–68, 173–74.

113. Forney, *Anecdotes of Public Men*, 1:135.

114. *Gainesville (Alabama) Independent*, 14 July 1855, and *Lexington Kentucky Statesman*, 22 May 1855, quoted in Zacharias, "The Know-Nothing Party and the Oratory of Nativism," 230.

115. *Dictionary of American Biography*, s.v. "Wise, Henry Alexander"; Eaton, "Henry A. Wise and the Virginia Fire Eaters of 1856," 497.

116. Quoted in Gay, "The Campaign of 1855 in Virginia and the Fall of the Know-Nothing Party," 329.

117. Hambleton, *A Biographical Sketch of Henry A. Wise*, 353; Rice, "The Know-Nothing Party in Virginia," 68.

118. Wise, "The Fire-Eaters," 8.

119. Overdyke, *The Know-Nothing Party in the South*, 94. Overdyke's book offers a good history of Know-Nothingism south of the Mason-Dixon line. Rice's two-part article, "The Know-Nothing Party in Virginia," and Gay's, "The Campaign of 1855 in Virginia and the Fall of the Know-Nothing Party," are brief accounts of the Know-Nothings, their political rise, and the campaign in Virginia in 1855. A good general brief account of the party's rise and fall everywhere is in Billington, *The Protestant Crusade*, 380–436.

120. Pryor, *My Day*, 125–26.

121. Wise, *The Life of Henry A. Wise*, 203.

122. Overdyke, *The Know-Nothing Party in the South*, 155.

123. Pryor, *My Day*, 126.

124. I am indebted for this brief summary of the situation in the country to Craven, *The Growth of Southern Nationalism*, 2–4, 34.
125. *Frank Leslie's Illustrated Newspaper*, 25 April 1857.
126. Nichols, *The Disruption of American Democracy*, 113.
127. Johannsen, *Stephen A. Douglas*, 705–6.
128. The reporter, Murat Halstead, describes Yancey in Halstead, *Three Against Lincoln*, 8, 52. Also see Alfriend, "Social Life in Richmond during the War," 232.
129. Yancey's oratorical gifts are described in Craven, *The Coming of the Civil War*, 276–77; Dillard, "William Loundes Yancey," 155; Halstead, *Three Against Lincoln*, 55; Morrissette, "Social Life in the First Confederate Capital," 13; and Alfriend, "Social Life in Richmond during the War," 232.
130. Wender, *Southern Commercial Conventions*, 170.
131. Ibid., 213–14.
132. DuBose, *The Life and Times of William Loundes Yancey*, 368, 375.
133. Ibid., 359.
134. Van Deusen, *The Ante-Bellum Southern Commercial Conventions*, 64–65; Wender, *Southern Commercial Conventions*, 214.
135. Wender, *Southern Commercial Conventions*, 214.
136. Peterson, "Speaking in the Southern Commercial Conventions," 212; Heidler, *Pulling the Temple Down*, 123; Van Deusen, *The Ante-Bellum Southern Commercial Conventions*, 65.
137. Wender, *Southern Commercial Conventions*, 217. Also see Shanks, *The Secession Movement in Virginia*, 83–84.
138. Wish, *George Fitzhugh*, 244–45.
139. Wender, *Southern Commercial Conventions*, 220.
140. *New York Weekly Tribune*, 20 August 1859, quoted in Wish, *George Fitzhugh*, 235.
141. Pryor, *My Day*, 126.
142. Braden, *Oratory in the Old South*, 3, 6, 17–18.

143. Pryor, *My Day*, 126–27, 129–30.

144. These three descriptions of Roger's rhetorical powers are quoted by Sara in ibid., 129–30.

145. Ibid., 130, 127.

146. Brandy-peaches are discussed in ibid., 128, 136.

147. Pryor, *Reminiscences of Peace and War*, 42.

148. Ibid., 71.

149. The fashion note on Buchanan's Washington is from Clay-Clopton, *A Belle of the Fifties*, 89–90.

150. *New York Herald*, 7 February 1904.

151. Pryor, *Reminiscences of Peace and War*, 81; Clay-Clopton, *A Belle of the Fifties*, 86.

152. Pryor, *Reminiscences of Peace and War*, 84–85.

153. Clay-Clopton, *A Belle of the Fifties*, 86.

154. Pryor, *Reminiscences of Peace and War*, 82, 90.

155. Clay-Clopton, *A Belle of the Fifties*, 128.

156. Their champagne-christened reunion is described by Sara in *Reminiscences of Peace and War*, 67–68.

157. McLean, "When the States Seceded," 283.

158. Pryor, *Reminiscences of Peace and War*, 68.

159. The description of Adele Douglas is framed from Milton, *Eve of Conflict*, 255–57; Clay-Clopton, *A Belle of the Fifties*, 36, 106; and Pryor, *Reminiscences of Peace and War*, 68.

160. Clay-Clopton, *A Belle of the Fifties*, 138; Pryor, *Reminiscences of Peace and War*, 98.

161. Conkling, *The Life and Letters of Roscoe Conkling*, 94; Pryor, *Reminiscences of Peace and War*, 98.

162. McLean, "When the States Seceded," 282.

163. Pryor, *Reminiscences of Peace and War*, 99.

164. Clay-Clopton, *A Belle of the Fifties*, 58.

165. McLean, "When the States Seceded," 282.

166. Young, *Men and Memories*, 434.

167. Pryor, *Reminiscences of Peace and War*, 94.

168. Craven, *The Growth of Southern Nationalism*, 317.

169. Potter, *The Impending Crisis*, 389.

170. Pryor, *Reminiscences of Peace and War*, 93, 95.

171. Rhodes, *History of the United States*, 2:409.

172. Young, *Men and Memories*, 433.

173. *Watertown (Wisconsin) Democrat*, 19 April 1860.

174. *Congressional Globe*, 36th Cong., 1st sess., 493.

175. Roger's maiden speech on the floor is in ibid., 48–50.

176. Sherman, *Recollections of Forty Years*, 1:177.

177. *Congressional Globe*, 36th Cong., 1st sess., 281–86. This exchange with Republicans on the floor was reprinted by the Democrats as a pamphlet entitled *The Principles and Policy of the Black Republican Party* and widely circulated.

178. *Congressional Globe*, 36th Cong., 1st sess., 493.

179. Sherman, *Recollections of Forty Years*, 1:177.

180. Young, *Men and Memories*, 435.

181. *Congressional Globe*, 36th Cong., 1st sess., 655. For a brief biographical sketch of Pennington see *American National Biography*, s.v. "Pennington, William."

182. The speaker impasse and its resolution are ably described in Nichols, *The Disruption of American Democracy*, 270–76.

183. Adams, *An Autobiography*, 43–44.

184. Cox, *Three Decades of Federal Legislation*, 27, 74.

185. Adams, *An Autobiography*, 44–45. Fifty years later, in 1911, when biases had faded and tempers had long since cooled, Adams met Roger again face-to-face in New York. It was at a reception of the New York Genealogical Society, and Adams had agreed to read a paper for the occasion. Roger, now a distinguished New York lawyer and former jurist, had come expressly to hear him speak. He was sitting on one of the front benches, and Adams recognized him the moment he entered the room, and at once approached him and introduced himself. Roger, Adams recounts, was plainly gratified, and "so was I at seeing him there. On both

sides, all the old feeling was gone. In the quieter rays of a setting sun, I like to think it was so!" (See Adams, *An Autobiography*, 45–46, for this reminiscence.)

186. Thompson, "First in War, Foremost in Peace," 12.

187. Pryor, *Reminiscences of Peace and War*, 97–98.

188. Watson, "Notes on Southside Virginia," 176.

189. Pryor, *My Day*, 6.

190. Watson, "Notes on Southside Virginia," 176.

191. Roger's duel with Finney is recounted in Patterson, *The Code Duello*, 50.

192. *Congressional Globe*, 36th Cong., 1st sess., 540.

193. *New York Herald*, 19 January 1860.

194. Sabine, *Notes on Duels and Duelling*, 39.

195. Adams, *The Great Secession Winter of 1860–61*, 15.

196. For a discussion of the essence of dueling and its role in Southern society, see Stowe, *Intimacy and Power in the Old South*, 5–10, 47. The euphemisms for poor whites are from Williams, *Dueling in the Old South*, 76.

197. Wise, "The Fire-Eaters," 9.

198. For this very brief discussion of the customs, purpose, practice, and rationale for dueling, I am indebted to Bruce, *Violence and Culture in the Antebellum South*, 29–31, 40–41; Truman, *Duelling in America*, 17–18; and Williams, *Dueling in the Old South*, 12, 27, 76–77.

199. Hallum, *The Diary of an Old Lawyer*, 27.

200. Williams lists the professions most prone to dueling in *Dueling in the Old South*, 11–12, 34.

201. Murry, *The Code of Honor*, 9.

202. Williams, *Dueling in the Old South*, 9.

203. Conkling, *The Life and Letters of Roscoe Conkling*, 98.

204. Schurz, *The Reminiscences of Carl Schurz*, 2:165.

205. Poore, *Perley's Reminiscences*, 2:50–51.

206. Cox, *Three Decades of Federal Legislation*, 75.

207. This description of Barksdale is by Murat Halstead in *Three Against Lincoln*, 15.

208. Crawford is quoted in Nevins, *The Emergence of Lincoln*, 2:124. For a brief description of him see *Dictionary of American Biography*, s.v. "Crawford, Martin Jenkins."

209. The full, verbatim account of this confrontation, from start to finish, is in the *Congressional Globe*, 36th Cong., 1st sess., appendix, 202–7. The quoted passages, beginning with Lovejoy's opening words to Martin's epithet, are all from it, unless otherwise cited.

210. *New York Times*, 10 and 14 April 1860.

211. *Congressional Globe*, 36th Cong., 1st sess., 1667–68.

212. Riley, "The Pryor-Potter Affair," 31.

213. Craven, *The Coming of the Civil War*, 424–25.

214. The pseudonyms for the bowie knife are from Forney, *Anecdotes of Public Men*, 2:302; and *New York Times*, 20 April 1860.

215. Rhodes, *History of the United States*, 2:395; *New York Times*, 16 April 1860; *Chicago Tribune*, 24 December 1882. "Tom-cat terms" is from Wise, "The Fire-Eaters," 8.

216. Miller, *Thaddeus Stevens*, 21.

217. Hesseltine, "The Pryor-Potter Duel," 408. See Hesseltine, 400–9, and Riley, "The Pryor-Potter Affair," 29–40, for two accounts of the brouhaha.

218. Riley, "The Pryor-Potter Affair," 33.

219. Hazelton, "The Chicago Convention of 1860 and the Man It Nominated," 269; *New York Times*, 15 May 1919.

220. Nichols, *The Disruption of American Democracy*, 287.

221. *Congressional Globe*, 36th Cong., 1st sess., 3303.

222. Pryor, *Reminiscences of Peace and War*, 104.

223. Keitt, "Sue Sparks Keitt to a Northern Friend," 83.

224. Edmondston, "*Journal of a Secesh Lady*," 10.

225. Phillips, "The Correspondence of Robert Toombs, Alexander H. Stephens, and Howell Cobb," 450.

226. Epes, "Roger Atkinson Pryor," 13.

227. Hardin, *The Private War of Lizzie Hardin*, 1.

228. McLean, "When the States Seceded," 282.

229. Hardin, *The Private War of Lizzie Hardin*, 5.

230. These conclusions are nicely summarized in Harris, *A Review of the Political Conflict in America*, 189–91.

231. "Augusta J. Evans on Secession," 65.

232. This sardonic view of the capital is from "Washington City," 1–2, 8.

233. Evans, *Macaria*, 228.

234. McLean, "When the States Seceded," 282.

235. Pryor, "My Day," 146—also the source for "little *mot*" in the next paragraph.

236. Evans, *Macaria*, 241.

237. *American National Biography*, s.v. "Buchanan, James"; Chesnut, *Mary Chesnut's Civil War*, 417; Clay-Clopton, *A Belle of the Fifties*, 90.

238. Wise, *The End of an Era*, 73.

239. Much of this description of Buchanan is taken from *American National Biography*, s.v. "Buchanan, James."

240. Pryor, *Reminiscences of Peace and War*, 101.

241. Ibid., 47.

242. Edmondston, *"Journal of a Secesh Lady,"* 24.

243. Saxon, *A Southern Woman's War-Time Reminiscences*, 15.

244. Phillips, "The Correspondence of Robert Toombs, Alexander H. Stephens, and Howell Cobb," 517.

245. From an editorial in the *Chicago Press & Tribune*, 19 January 1860, quoted in Baringer, *Lincoln's Rise to Power*, 134.

246. U.S. War Department, *The War of the Rebellion: A Compilation of the Official Records of the Union and Confederate Armies*, ser. 1, vol. 51, pt. 2: 3–4. Henceforth this 70-volume 128-part official record, will be cited as *O.R.*

247. *Congressional Globe*, 36th Cong., 2nd sess., 220, 346.

248. Roger's speech is printed in full in ibid., 601–3. It was reprinted as *Independence of the South: Speech by Roger A. Pryor, of Virginia,* Washington, D.C.: Henry Polkinhorn, 1861.

249. Blackford, "The Great John B. Minor and His Cousin Mary Face the War," 442, 445.

250. Clay-Clopton, *A Belle of the Fifties,* 151.

251. De Leon, *Four Years in Rebel Capitals,* 21.

252. Pryor, *My Day,* 155.

253. De Leon, *Belles, Beaux, and Brains of the 60's,* 42.

254. This description of Washington on Inauguration Day is drawn from De Leon, *Four Years in Rebel Capitals,* 19–20.

255. Pryor, *My Day,* 155.

256. De Leon, *Four Years in Rebel Capitals,* 19.

257. Ibid., 20.

258. *O.R.,* ser. 1, vol. 1: 263.

259. Harper, *Annie Harper's Journal,* 8.

260. Eggleston, *A Rebel's Recollections,* 58, 62; Harrison, "Virginia Scenes in '61," 161.

261. Eaton, "Henry A. Wise and the Virginia Fire Eaters of 1856," 495, 509.

262. *Congressional Globe,* 36th Cong., 2nd sess., 882.

263. Ibid., 1191.

264. "The Change of Secession Sentiment in Virginia in 1861," 83, 86.

265. Lee, "Secession Is Nothing but Revolution," 5–6.

266. Stephenson, *The Day of the Confederacy,* 13.

267. Halstead, *Three Against Lincoln,* 41.

268. The quotes are from Wait, "Reminiscences of Fort Sumter," 186, 187.

269. I owe a debt to Wise, *The End of an Era,* 330, for this description of Beauregard. For background on his origins and military career, see Roman, *The Military Operations of General Beauregard,* 1:2–8.

270. For the account of South Carolina's decade-long project to arm itself, see Halsey, "South Carolina Began Preparing for War in 1851," 8–13.

271. *O.R.*, ser. 1, vol. 1: 284.

272. The phrase "cuckoo song" is from Dillard, "William Loundes Yancey," 157.

273. *O.R.*, ser. 1, vol. 1: 297.

274. Greeley is quoted in the *Bulletin of Hampden-Sidney College* 14 (April 1919), 27.

275. Russell, *My Diary North and South*, 111.

276. For excerpts from Roger's speech I have used slightly varying texts from the *Charleston Mercury* and the *Charleston Daily Courier*, 11 April 1861. Accounts of the speech are also in Crawford, *The Genesis of the Civil War*, 305; Pryor, *My Day*, 158–59; and Largent, "Virginia Takes the Road to Secession," 141–42. It was widely reported in newspapers in both the North and South the following day.

277. A brief biographical sketch of Chesnut is in *American National Biography*, s.v. "Chesnut, James, Jr." Also for information about him see Mary's biographical sketch in the same source, s.v "Chesnut, Mary Boykin Miller."

278. Chisolm is sketched in *American National Biography*, s.v. "Chisolm, Alexander Robert." Also see Chisolm, "Notes on the Surrender of Fort Sumter," 82.

279. For an account of this first Confederate visit to Sumter I have used Crawford, *The Genesis of the Civil War*, 422–24. Crawford was the surgeon of the Union garrison at Sumter. He accompanied Anderson to the boat to see the Confederates off. Also see Lee, "The First Step in the War," 75; and *O.R.*, ser. 1, vol. 1: 59.

280. This second boat trip to Sumter, with Roger aboard, is from Lee, "The First Step in the War," 75–76; *O.R.*, ser. 1, vol. 1: 60. Roger's reason for remaining in the boat and not going into the fort is suggested by Chisolm, "Notes on the Surrender of Fort

Sumter," 82. Wigfall's comment on Chesnut's rendezvous in the other world is from Chesnut, *Mary Chesnut's Civil War*, 55.

281. Lee, "The First Step in the War," 76.

282. "Who Fired the First Gun at Sumter?" 502.

283. I use Crawford, *The Genesis of the Civil War*, 426, for my weather report. But descriptions of anything back in time can have a Rashomon aspect; another observer had the morning dark and cloudy, not a star in the sky, and a heavy mist covering earth and sea. See Fletcher, *Within Fort Sumter*, 41.

284. Ruffin, *The Diary of Edmund Ruffin* 1:588.

285. Thompson, "Eye Witness to Fort Sumter," 276.

286. Lee, "The First Step in the War," 77.

287. Chesnut, *Mary Chesnut's Civil War*, 41, 44–46.

288. Holmes, *The Diary of Miss Emma Holmes*, 25.

289. *The Battle of Fort Sumter and First Victory of the Southern Troops*, 4.

290. Holmes, *The Diary of Miss Emma Holmes*, 25–26.

291. *The Battle of Fort Sumter and First Victory of the Southern Troops*, 5, 6.

292. The wailing and sobbing image of the wind is borrowed from Evans, *Macaria*, 60.

293. Taliaferro, "Memoir of Mrs. Harriotte Lee Taliaferro," 417.

294. *The Battle of Fort Sumter and First Victory of the Southern Troops*, 7; Crawford, *The Genesis of the Civil War*, 435, 437.

295. Doubleday, *Reminiscences of Forts Sumter and Moultrie*, 158.

296. Edmondston, "*Journal of a Secesh Lady*," 48. The line, quoted by Edmonston, is from Samuel Taylor Coleridge's, *The Rime of the Ancient Mariner*, part 2, stanza 8, lines 117–18.

297. Chesnut, *Mary Chesnut's Civil War*, 44, 12.

298. For Wigfall's bizarre visit I have combined three different sources, all differing somewhat in detail: Chester, "Inside Sumter in '61," 72–73; Fletcher, *Within Fort Sumter*, 56–59; and O.R., ser. 1, vol. 1: 32.

299. This second visit of the day to Sumter is sketched from *O.R.*, ser. 1, vol. 1: 23–24, 64–65; and Lee, "The First Step in the War," 78–79.

300. Crawford, *The Genesis of the Civil War*, 442 n; Doubleday, *Reminiscences of Forts Sumter and Moultrie*, 169–70.

301. Crawford, *The Genesis of the Civil War*, 442.

302. *O.R.*, ser. 1, vol. 1: 64–65.

303. This poetic description of the harbor on the day of evacuation is taken from Stephenson, *The Day of the Confederacy*, 22–23.

304. Jones, *A Rebel War Clerk's Diary*, 1.

305. Chesnut, *Mary Chesnut's Civil War*, 51.

306. Boney, *John Letcher of Virginia*, 103.

307. Largent, "Virginia Takes the Road to Secession," 143–44.

308. *O.R.*, ser. 1, vol. 51, pt. 2: 11; Largent, "Virginia Takes the Road to Secession," 144.

309. I am indebted for this description to Jones and Rogers, "Montgomery as the Confederate Capital," 2–4; and Russell, *Pictures of Southern Life*, 16.

310. De Leon, *Four Years in Rebel Capitals*, 28; incidental information from Jones and Rogers, "Montgomery as the Confederate Capital," 4.

311. Russell, *Pictures of Southern Life*, 75.

312. Russell, *My Diary North and South*, 165, 167.

313. De Leon, *Four Years in Rebel Capitals*, 23.

314. Russell, *My Diary North and South*, 168.

315. Herd, "Lawrence M. Keitt's Letters from the Provisional Congress of the Confederacy," 22.

316. Curry, *Civil History of the Government of the Confederate States*, 46.

317. Jones and Rogers, "Montgomery as the Confederate Capital," 10, 12.

318. For this breakdown of the provisional congress, I am indebted to Fitts, "The Confederate Convention," 83–84. Also

see Lee, *The Confederate Constitutions*, 155–58, which has slightly different figures.

319. Goode, "The Confederate Congress," 97–98.

320. De Leon, *Four Years in Rebel Capitals*, 30.

321. Kirwan, *The Confederacy*, 38.

322. Herd, "Lawrence Keitt's Letters from the Provisional Congress of the Confederacy," 21.

323. De Leon, *Four Years in Rebel Capitals*, 26.

324. Kirwan, *The Confederacy*, 42.

325. Yearns, *The Confederate Congress*, 12.

326. Phillips, "The Correspondence of Robert Toombs, Alexander H. Stephens, and Howell Cobb," 537.

327. Curry, *Civil History of the Government of the Confederate States*, 52.

328. Davis, *Jefferson Davis: A Memoir by His Wife*, 2:18–19.

329. Curry, *Civil History of the Government of the Confederate States*, 56–57.

330. "Sigma" of the *Charleston Courier* reported Davis's arrival, in Jones and Rogers, "Montgomery as the Confederate Capital," 29–30. Also see 30 n.

331. "When the Band First Played 'Dixie,'" 234; Glass and Singer, *Singing Soldiers*, 8. For detail on the origins of the tune, its debut at Davis's inaugural, and its transfiguration into the Confederacy's unofficial anthem, see Abel, *Singing the New Nation*, 30–34.

332. Davis's inaugural was reported in the *Montgomery Advertiser*, reprinted in Jones and Rogers, "Montgomery as the Confederate Capital," 31–34. Also see 33 n–34 n. For the crowd size and the snippet from the opening prayer, see Manly, "The Diary of Dr. Basil Manly," 148.

333. Davis, *Jefferson Davis: A Memoir by His Wife*, 2:32–33.

334. De Leon, *Four Years in Rebel Capitals*, 37, 39.

335. "Sigma" describes the flag-raising in Jones and Rogers, "Montgomery as the Confederate Capital," 44–45. The flag is described on 45 n.

336. "Beautiful Reception," 129–30.

337. Jones, *A Rebel War Clerk's Diary*, 14–15.

338. Davis, *"A Government of Our Own,"* 324.

339. Thomas R. R. Cobb to his wife, 7 February 1861, in Cobb, "Extracts of Letters to His Wife," 281.

340. Jones and Rogers, "Montgomery as the Confederate Capital," 76.

341. Ruffin, *The Diary of Edmund Ruffin*, 2:5, 9–10.

342. De Leon, *Four Years in Rebel Capitals*, 76.

343. Wright, *A Southern Girl in '61*, 55.

344. Henderson, *Petersburg in the Civil War*, 27.

345. Putnam, *Richmond during the War*, 38.

346. These early preparations are described in Manarin, *Richmond at War*, the edited minutes of the Richmond city council during the war, 2.

347. Collier et al., *White House of the Confederacy*, 7, 13, 15.

348. Putnam, *Richmond during the War*, 33–34; Manarin, *Richmond at War*, 2.

349. Putnam, *Richmond during the War*, 41.

350. Davis, *Jefferson Davis: A Memoir by His Wife*, 2:86.

351. Manarin, *Richmond at War*, 2–3.

352. De Leon, *Four Years in Rebel Capitals*, 86, 93, 96; McCrady, *Formation, Organization, Discipline, and Characteristics of the Army of Northern Virginia*, 12, 14.

353. Jones and Rogers, "Montgomery as the Confederate Capital," 54, 78.

354. Chesnut, *Mary Chesnut's Civil War*, 130.

355. Rhett, "The Confederate Government at Montgomery," 108.

356. Morrissette, "Social Life in the First Confederate Capital," 7.

357. Goode, "The Confederate Congress," 103.

358. Eggleston, *A Rebel's Recollections*, 68.

359. Bird, *The Granite Farm Letters*, 3.

360. Wallace, *3rd Virginia Infantry*, 9–10.

361. Pryor, *My Day*, 163.

362. Putnam, *Richmond during the War*, 18.

363. *Richmond Examiner*, 15 April 1861.

364. The scene in Richmond is remembered by Sara in *Reminiscences of Peace and War*, 121–24. Hunter's quote is on p. 124.

365. Putnam, *Richmond during the War*, 20.

366. Pryor, *Reminiscences of Peace and War*, 122–23.

367. Curry, *Civil History of the Government of the Confederate States*, 44.

368. Keitt, "Sue Sparks Keitt to a Northern Friend," 86.

369. Cumming, *Kate*, 38.

370. De Leon, *Belles, Beaux, and Brains of the 60's*, 213.

371. Ibid., 63.

372. Pryor, *Reminiscences of Peace and War*, 131–32. The quote is from Avary, *A Virginia Girl in the Civil War*, 28.

373. Pryor, *Reminiscences of Peace and War*, 132–33.

374. Maury, Diary, entries for 26 June and 3 July 1861.

375. Avary, *A Virginia Girl in the Civil War*, 3.

376. Cumming, *Kate*, 64.

377. Preston, *Beechenbrook*, 20.

378. Chesnut, *Mary Chesnut's Civil War*, 167.

379. Morrissette, "Social Life in the First Confederate Capital," 11.

380. Blackford, *Letters from Lee's Army*, 59, 94.

381. Putnam, *Richmond during the War*, 39.

382. McLean, "A Northern Woman in the Confederacy," 451.

383. Cumming, *Gleanings from Southland*, 36–37.

384. McDonald, *A Diary with Reminiscences of the War and Refugee Life in the Shenandoah Valley*, 17, 20.

385. Pryor, *Reminiscences of Peace and War*, 129.

386. Jones, *A Rebel War Clerk's Diary*, 14.

387. Pryor, *Reminiscences of Peace and War*, 129–30.

388. Letter from MANY LADIES to the *Charleston (South Carolina) Daily Courier*, 15 August 1861, quoted in Faust, "Altars of Sacrifice," 1209.

389. Chesnut, *Mary Chesnut's Civil War*, 411.

390. Scott and Wyatt, *Petersburg's Story*, 170.

391. These good-byes are described by Sara in *Reminiscences of Peace and War*, 134–35. Also see Claiborne, *Seventy-five Years in Old Virginia*, 191–92, 195.

392. Scott and Wyatt, *Petersburg's Story*, 170.

393. Pryor, *Reminiscences of Peace and War*, 134–35.

394. Magill, *Women, or Chronicles of the Late War*, 7.

395. Pearson, "A Middle-Class Border-State Family during the Civil War," 320.

396. Thomas, *The Secret Eye*, 185, 189–90, 193.

397. Magill, *Women, or Chronicles of the Late War*, 6.

398. Bird, *The Granite Farm Letters*, 50.

399. Harper, *Annie Harper's Journal*, 17.

400. Avary, *A Virginia Girl in the Civil War*, 11, 31. Nellie Gray was not her real name, but one she used in her memoirs.

401. Pryor, *Reminiscences of Peace and War*, 135.

402. Gray, "Life in Confederate Arkansas," 61.

403. Pryor, *Reminiscences of Peace and War*, 135.

404. Chesnut, *Mary Chesnut's Civil War*, 79, 69.

405. Le Grand, *The Journal of Julia Le Grand*, 52.

406. Cuttino, *Saddle Bag and Spinning Wheel*, 14, 81.

407. Bell, *Men and Things*, 179.

408. *Selma (Alabama) Sentinel*, 1 October 1863, quoted in Jackson, *The Story of Selma*, 200.

409. Gay, *Life in Dixie during the War*, 201.

410. Sara's account of getting from Petersburg to the James is from, *Reminiscences of Peace and War*, 136.

411. Harrison, "A Virginia Girl in the First Year of the War," 613.

412. Clay-Clopton, *A Belle of the Fifties*, 175.

413. Harrison, "A Virginia Girl in the First Year of the War," 613.

414. Sara's introspection is from *Reminiscences of Peace and War*, 141–42.

415. Ibid., 143.

416. Ibid., 143–45.

417. This account of Roger's trouble with the Marion Rifles is from Wallace, *3rd Virginia Infantry*, 11.

418. Harrison, "Virginia Scenes in '61," 161–62.

419. Chesnut, *Mary Chesnut's Civil War*, 76.

420. McGuire, *Diary of a Southern Refugee*, 40.

421. McDonald, *A Diary with Reminiscences of the War and Refugee Life in the Shenandoah Valley*, 28, 51.

422. Sperry, "Kate Sperry's Diary," 44.

423. Sara describes Dr. Rice's plantation and his ear to the ground in *Reminiscences of Peace and War*, 146–48, 158–59.

424. Pryor, *Reminiscences of Peace and War*, 160.

425. Jones, *A Rebel War Clerk's Diary*, 34.

426. Cobb, to his wife, 24 July 1861, in "Extracts from Letters to His Wife," 289.

427. A phrase quoted in Cumming, *Kate*, 75.

428. Erwin, *Like Some Green Laurel*, 116–17.

429. Pryor, *Reminiscences of Peace and War*, 160.

430. McDonald, *A Diary with Reminiscences of the War and Refugee Life in the Shenandoah Valley*, 29.

431. Chesnut, *Mary Chesnut's Civil War*, 312, 346.

432. McLean, "A Northern Woman in the Confederacy," 443–44.

433. *Richmond Daily Whig*, 22 July 1861, quoted in Thomas, *The Confederate State of Richmond*, 54.

434. Beers, *Memories*, 25.

435. Chesnut, *Mary Chesnut's Civil War*, 107.

436. Magill, *Women, or Chronicles of the Late War*, 129, 366.

437. Manarin, *Richmond at War*, 65 n, 83.

438. McLean, "A Northern Woman in the Confederacy," 444.

439. Manarin, *Richmond at War*, 210.

440. Sara's introspection is in *Reminiscences of Peace and War*, 160.

441. Her resolve, preparations to leave, and her trip to and arrival in Smithfield are described in ibid., 161–62, 165; and in *My Day*, 163–64.

442. Roger Pryor to the Confederate War Department, 9 August 1861, National Archives.

443. Pryor, *Reminiscences of Peace and War*, 162.

444. Ruffin, *The Diary of Edmund Ruffin*, 2:157.

445. Warner and Yearns, *Biographical Register of the Confederate Congress*, 197.

446. Pollard, "The Confederate Congress," 749–50.

447. De Leon, *Four Years in Rebel Capitals*, 163, 164.

448. Pryor, *Reminiscences of Peace and War*, 84.

449. Goode, "The Confederate Congress," 106.

450. "Proceedings of First Confederate Congress—First Session," 103.

451. Frobel, *The Civil War Diary of Anne S. Frobel*, 82.

452. Manarin, *Richmond at War*, 194 n.

453. Bird, *The Granite Farm Letters*, 83.

454. Cook, *The Siege of Richmond*, 104.

455. The account of Sara's change of base from Smithfield to Richmond is from *Reminiscences of Peace and War*, 164–66.

456. Roger's falling out with the Portsmouth Grays is described in Wallace, *3rd Virginia Infantry*, 22–23; and in Hanrahan, "The Portsmouth Grays," 89–92.

457. Chesnut, *Mary Chesnut's Civil War*, 327.

458. Pryor, *Reminiscences of Peace and War*, 166–67.

459. Wallace, *3rd Virginia Infantry*, 19.

460. Davis, *The Papers of Jefferson Davis*, 8:150.

461. LeConte, *When the World Ended*, 83.

462. Molineux, "The Battle of Williamsburg," 30.

463. Ibid., 32.

464. Ibid.

465. *O.R.*, ser. 1, vol. 11, pt. 1: 567.

466. Thomas C. Elder to his wife, Anna Fitzhugh Elder, 15 May 1862, Elder Papers.

467. *O.R.*, ser. 1, vol. 11, pt. 1: 589.

468. Quoted passages are from Townsend, *Rustics in Rebellion*, 100–101.

469. *O.R.*, ser. 1, vol. 11, pt. 1: 941.

470. McClellan, *McClellan's Own Story*, 338; Davis, *History of the 104th Pennsylvania Regiment*, 110.

471. De Leon, *Four Years in Rebel Capitals*, 85.

472. Harrison, "A Virginia Girl in the First Year of the War," 610.

473. Bird, *The Granite Farm Letters*, 71.

474. Harrison, "A Virginia Girl in the First Year of the War," 610–11.

475. De Leon, *Four Years in Rebel Capitals*, 200.

476. Harrison, *Recollections Grave and Gay*, 82.

477. Avary, *A Virginia Girl in the Civil War*, 40–41.

478. Putnam, *Richmond during the War*, 133.

479. Harrison, "A Virginia Girl in the First Year of the War," 611; Chesnut, *Mary Chesnut's Civil War*, 311.

480. Harrison, *Recollections Grave and Gay*, 83.

481. Bacot, *A Confederate Nurse*, 123, 125, 128.

482. Harrison, *Recollections Grave and Gay*, 84.

483. Harrison, "A Virginia Girl in the First Year of the War," 613.

484. Walthall, *Hidden Things Brought to Light*, 33.

485. Harrison, "A Virginia Girl in the First Year of the War," 613.

486. Description and quotes from Pryor, *Reminiscences of Peace and War*, 170–71.

487. Ibid., 172.

488. Ibid., 174.

489. Sara describes their parting from their husbands in ibid., 174–76.

490. Putnam, *Richmond during the War*, 133.

491. Ibid., 145.

492. The wounded soldier incident is from Pryor, *Reminiscences of Peace and War*, 176–77.

493. Putnam, *Richmond during the War*, 146; Pryor, *Reminiscences of Peace and War*, 178.

494. This fear is vividly expressed by Ida Dulany in Andrews, *Scraps of Paper*, 17.

495. This image of the guns is borrowed from Jones, *A Rebel War Clerk's Diary*, 85.

496. Sara's evening of waiting, watching, and remembering at the window is from *Reminiscences of Peace and War*, 178–80.

497. Sara's memory has the chronology wrong here. Scott was actually killed four days later, on June 30, at Frayser's Farm.

498. Pryor, *Reminiscences of Peace and War*, 180–81.

499. Cumming, *A Northern Daughter and a Southern Wife*, 50.

500. Putnam, *Richmond during the War*, 146.

501. Pryor, *Reminiscences of Peace and War*, 180.

502. Hopley, *Life in the South*, 2:43.

503. Cumming, *Kate*, 39.

504. From the *Charleston (S.C.) Courier*, quoted in full in Cumming, *Kate*, 162, 163 n.

505. Alfriend, "Social Life in Richmond during the War," 229.

506. Putnam, *Richmond during the War*, 146.

507. Chesnut, *Mary Chesnut's Civil War*, 85, 217.

508. *Richmond News Leader*, Bicentennial Issue, 8 September 1937, 75. Also see Pryor, *Reminiscences of Peace and War*, 186.

509. Cumming, *Kate*, 93.

510. Sara's introduction to the hospital in Kent & Paine's warehouse is described in *Reminiscences of Peace and War*, 181–82.

511. Hurst, *History of the Fourteenth Regiment Alabama Volunteers*, 12.

512. Leech, "The Battle of Frazier's Farm," 161.

513. Page, *Letters of a War Correspondent*, 8.

514. Putnam, *Richmond during the War*, 151.

515. Pryor, *Reminiscences of Peace and War,* 182–83.

516. Putnam, *Richmond during the War,* 147.

517. Pryor, *Reminiscences of Peace and War,* 184–85, 187–88.

518. Putnam, *Richmond during the War,* 151–52 n.

519. Edmondston, *"Journal of a Secesh Lady,"* 213.

520. Putnam, *Richmond during the War,* 154.

521. Pember, *A Southern Woman's Story,* 169–70.

522. Pryor, *My Day,* 169; *Reminiscences of Peace and War,* 185.

523. Putnam, *Richmond during the War,* 153.

524. The lyrics are reproduced from Glass, *Singing Soldiers,* 228–29. John Hill Hewitt wrote the music.

525. The quoted phrases are, in order, from Dawson, *Our Women in the War,* 11; Bird, *The Granite Farm Letters,* 296; and Barr, *The Civil War Diary of Henrietta Fitzhugh Barr,* 6.

526. Walker, *The Private Journal of Georgiana Gholson Walker,* 78.

527. Pryor, *Reminiscences of Peace and War,* 184–85, 191–92.

528. *Supplement to the Official Records,* ser. 2, p. 448.

529. Thomas C. Elder to Anna Fitzhugh Elder, 8 July 1862, Elder Papers.

530. Robert H. Miller to his father, Joseph E. Miller, 23 July 1862, in Miller, "Letters of Lieutenant Robert H. Miller to His Family," 87.

531. *O. R.,* ser. 1, vol. 2, pt. 2: 759.

532. Evans, *Macaria,* 397.

533. Harrison, "A Virginia Girl in the First Year of the War," 614.

534. Andrews, *Scraps of Paper,* 40.

535. Chesnut, *Mary Chesnut's Civil War,* 358.

536. I am much indebted to E. B. Long's *The Civil War Day by Day,* 249–59, for this summary of Second Manassas. For the best full treatment of the campaign see John Hennessey's *Return to Bull Run.*

537. McCabe, *The Grayjackets,* 191–93; Thomas C. Elder to Anna Fitzhugh Elder, 1 September 1862, Elder Papers; Johnson, *The Papers of Andrew Johnson,* 9:99–100.

538. Pryor, *My Day*, 176–77.

539. Welton, *"My Heart Is So Rebellious"*, 220.

540. Leland, "Middleton Correspondence," 35.

541. Chesnut, *Mary Chesnut's Civil War*, 500.

542. Wallace, *Glencoe Diary*, 91.

543. Hardin, *The Private War of Lizzie Hardin*, 235, 239.

544. Solomon, *The Civil War Diary of Clara Solomon*, 324.

545. McWillie Notebooks, Mississippi Department of Archives and History.

546. Pryor, *Reminiscences of Peace and War*, 194.

547. *O.R.*, ser 1, vol. 12, pt. 2: 567; and ser 1, vol. 19, pt. 1: 842.

548. Quoted from a letter in Frobel, *The Civil War Diary of Anne S. Frobel*, 192.

549. Sperry, "Kate Sperry's Diary," 56.

550. Avary, *A Virginia Girl in the Civil War*, 68.

551. McDonald, *A Diary with Reminiscences of the War and Refugee Life in the Shenandoah Valley*, 97, 99.

552. This account of Sara at Coyners in the Blue Ridge is taken from Pryor, *My Day*, 177–79.

553. Davis, *The Papers of Jefferson Davis*, 7:358–60.

554. Quoted in Wallace, *3rd Virginia Infantry*, 32.

555. *O.R.*, ser. 1, vol. 21: 1032.

556. Pryor, *Reminiscences of Peace and War*, 211. For Lee's desire to assign Roger to the Blackwater see *O.R.*, ser. 1, vol. 21: 1036–37.

557. Sara describes Culpeper and her stay there in *Reminiscences of Peace and War*, 195–96. The snatches of quoted comments and the stanza of the song "Lorena" are from those two pages.

558. Conolly, *An Irishman in Dixie*, 48.

559. Chesnut, *Mary Chesnut's Civil War*, 451.

560. Pryor, *Reminiscences of Peace and War*, 197.

561. This terse description of the Dismal Swamp is from Russell, *My Diary North and South*, 88–9.

562. The account of Sara's decision to follow Roger, her journey and arrival in Suffolk, and their stay in the postmaster's house, with all the attendant quotes, is taken from *Reminiscences of Peace and War*, 213–18. In all cases when conversation is reported in dialect, as here and elsewhere, it is precisely as Sara wrote it in her memoirs.

563. Turner, *Civil War Letters of Arabella Speairs and William Beverley Pettit*, 1:82, 84.

564. Thomas, *The Secret Eye*, 214.

565. Cumming, *Kate*, 84.

566. Goode, "The Confederate Congress," 107.

567. Turner, *Civil War Letters of Arabella Speairs and William Beverley Pettit*, 1:68.

568. Bartlett, *"My Dear Brother"*, 68.

569. Barr, *The Civil War Diary of Mrs. Henrietta Fitzhugh Barr*, 18.

570. Stone, *Brokenburn*, 145–46.

571. Pryor, *My Day*, 179–80.

572. Except as noted, the account from the croaking frogs to Roger's departure to fight the Federals in front of Suffolk is from Pryor, *Reminiscences of Peace and War*, 220, 230–31.

573. *O. R.*, ser. 1, vol. 18: 143.

574. Roger's wire to Colston and his words to his troops are in Pryor, *Reminiscences of Peace and War*, 233. His wire to Colston is also in *Supplement to the Official Records*, ser. 2, p. 398.

575. "Proceedings of the First Confederate Congress—Third Session," 56.

576. Davis, *The Papers of Jefferson Davis*, 9:74.

577. Pryor, *Reminiscences of Peace and War*, 218–19.

578. Agnes's letter with postscript is reproduced in full in ibid., 226–28.

579. This letter is reprinted in ibid., 235–36.

580. Ibid., 226.

581. Welton, *My Heart Is So Rebellious*, 173, 203, 238, 238 n, 240, 248.

582. Chesnut, *Mary Chesnut's Civil War*, 371, 377, 528.

583. Stone, *Brokenburn*, 258.

584. Davis, *Jefferson Davis: A Memoir by His Wife*, 2:375.

585. Jones, *A Rebel War Clerk's Diary*, 184.

586. Agnes's account of the meeting with the girl on the bench and the bread riot are in her letter to Sara reprinted in *Reminiscences of Peace and War*, 237–39.

587. Manarin, *Richmond at War*, 247–48, 311–13, 317.

588. Ramsdell, *Behind the Lines in the Southern Confederacy*, 48–49.

589. Wiley, *The Plain People of the Confederacy*, 45. Wiley quotes from many of these letters in this excellent little book about the common people of the South during the war.

590. Ramsdell, *Behind the Lines in the Southern Confederacy*, 62, 65.

591. Stone, *Brokenburn*, 185.

592. Pryor, *My Day*, 187.

593. *King Lear* 1.1.14.

594. Smith, *The Francis Preston Blair Family in Politics*, 2:145.

595. Blackford, *Letters from Lee's Army*, 145–46.

596. Ibid., 141, 146, 149.

597. Putnam, *Richmond during the War*, 201–2, 198–99.

598. McClure, *Colonel Alexander K. McClure's Recollections of Half a Century*, 347.

599. Brooks, *Washington in Lincoln's Time*, 61.

600. Allan, *The Life and Letters of Margaret Junkin Preston*, 163.

601. Quoted in Jones, *Ladies of Richmond*, 166–67.

602. Kean, *Inside the Confederate Government*, 60.

603. Pryor, *Reminiscences of Peace and War*, 243.

604. Magill, *Women, or Chronicles of the Late War*, 324.

605. Manarin, *Richmond at War*, 323–24.

606. Allan, *The Life and Letters of Margaret Junkin Preston*, 165.

607. Pryor, *Reminiscences of Peace and War*, 243.

608. Cuttino, *Saddle Bag and Spinning Wheel*, 168.

609. Chesnut, *Mary Chesnut's Civil War*, 477.

610. Dabney, *Life and Campaigns of Lieut.-Gen. Thomas J. Jackson*, 716.

611. Blackford, *Letters from Lee's Army*, 188–89.

612. Eppes, *Through Some Eventful Years*, 203.

613. Avary, *A Virginia Girl in the Civil War*, 260.

614. Pryor, *Reminiscences of Peace and War*, 249–50.

615. Stone, *Brokenburn*, 181.

616. Pryor, *My Day*, 187–88.

617. Harper, *Annie Harper's Journal*, 18.

618. Lincoln, *Collected Works*, 6:409.

619. Blackford, *Letters from Lee's Army*, 197.

620. Chesnut, *Mary Chesnut's Civil War*, 494.

621. Samuel Harper Pulliam to Eliza M. Jackson, 19 January 1863, Pulliam Letter.

622. *O. R.*, ser. 1, vol. 18: 145.

623. This is explained in Barham, "War Record of T. G. Barham," 9.

624. Davis, *The Papers of Jefferson Davis*, 9:85; letter to Jefferson Davis, 28 February 1863, National Archives.

625. Letter to the Confederate war department, 21 March 1863, National Archives.

626. Roger Pryor to Jefferson Davis, 6 April 1863, National Archives; Pryor, *Reminiscences of Peace and War*, 240.

627. Davis, *The Papers of Jefferson Davis*, 8:459.

628. Pryor, *Reminiscences of Peace and War*, 240–41; Pryor, *My Day*, 190–91. Davis's grateful answer to Roger is reprinted in Rowland, *Jefferson Davis, Constitutionalist*, 5:449.

629. Jones, *A Rebel War Clerk's Diary*, 261.

630. Roger Pryor to Jefferson Davis, 15 July 1863, National Archives. Davis was reluctant to accept Roger's resignation. He hoped for a less drastic solution. See Davis, *The Papers of Jefferson Davis*, 9:282.

631. Pryor, *My Day*, 189, 192; *Reminiscences of Peace and War*, 241–42.

632. *Richmond Sentinel*, 31 August 1863.

633. This spirited description of Fitzhugh Lee comes from a contemporary, John S. Wise, in *The End of an Era*, 334–36. For his fondness for corn-shucking songs see Chesnut, *Mary Chesnut's Civil War*, 590.

634. Pryor, *My Day*, 192–93.

635. Sallie's observations are in Putnam, *Richmond during the War*, 79–80, 262–63, 303, 315. For substitutes for coffee, also see Porcher, *Resources of the Southern Fields and Forests*, xii, 435.

636. The phrase, "Yankeedom" is borrowed from Welton, *"My Heart Is So Rebellious,"* 86.

637. Harrison, "A Virginia Girl in the First Year of the War," 609.

638. Blackford, *Letters from Lee's Army*, 155.

639. Putnam, *Richmond during the War*, 320.

640. Stone, *Brokenburn*, 247, 190, 188.

641. Fox, *A Northern Woman in the Plantation South*, 135–36.

642. Blackford, *Letters from Lee's Army*, 218.

643. Sara's coming to Petersburg and to the overseer's house is described in *Reminiscences of Peace and War*, 251–53.

644. Cumming, *Kate*, 98.

645. Sara's description of her friendship with Lucy Laighton is from *Reminiscences of Peace and War*, 253–54, and *My Day*, 195–96.

646. In the nineteenth century the birth of a baby was nearly always announced as the arrival of "the little stranger." Pregnancy was then, in the minds of the women going through it, viewed as "being sick." See Ethel Simpson's introduction in Huckaby and Simpson, *Tulip Evermore*, 4, 10.

647. This Christmastime coming of their sixth child, a daughter, Lucy Atkinson, is described by Sara in *Reminiscences of Peace and War*, 254–56, and in *My Day*, 195–97.

648. Clay-Clopton, *A Belle of the Fifties*, 178.

649. The account of Roger's return is from Pryor, *Reminiscences of Peace and War*, 256–57.

650. A phrase borrowed from Scott and Wyatt, *Petersburg's Story*, 171.

651. This summary of Petersburg in the war owes much to Sara's reflections in *Reminiscences of Peace and War*, 257, 252–53.

652. Ibid., 261.

653. This picture of Petersburg, healthy despite the want, and picked clean, is distilled from ibid., 267.

654. Dannett and Jones, *Our Women of the Sixties*, 33.

655. The rundown of substitutes is distilled from ibid., 33–35; Wiley, *The Plain People of the Confederacy*, 9, 51–52; Eno, "Activities of the Women of Arkansas during the War between the States," 7–8; and Andrews, *The Women of the South in War Times*, 21–22, 26.

656. Pryor, *Reminiscences of Peace and War*, 261.

657. Ibid., 258–59, 270.

658. Sara introduces these new neighbors in ibid., 258.

659. Ibid., 259.

660. Morrissette, "Social Life in the First Confederate Capital," 15.

661. Halstead, *Three Against Lincoln*, 116.

662. Stone, *Brokenburn*, 271.

663. Wiley, *The Plain People of the Confederacy*, 60.

664. Millinery and fashion notes courtesy Sara, in *Reminiscences of Peace and War*, 264–66.

665. Chesnut, *Mary Chesnut's Civil War*, 550.

666. Quoted in Wright, *A Southern Girl in '61*, 164.

667. *Richmond Whig*, 15 April 1864, quoted in Kirwan, *The Confederacy*, 155.

668. Van Lew, *A Yankee Spy in Richmond*, 25, 93–94.

669. Pember, *A Southern Woman's Story*, 192.

670. Walker, *The Private Journal of Georgiana Gholson Walker*, 93.

671. Andrews, *Scraps of Paper*, 152.

672. Blackiston, *Refugees in Richmond*, 32.

673. Pryor, *Reminiscences of Peace and War*, 274.

674. Keiley, *Prisoner of War*, 6–7. For slight variations in Keiley's account, see Claiborne, *Seventy-five Years in Old Virginia*, 217–19, and McCabe, *The Grayjackets*, 212–20.

675. Sara tells of the druggist and the banker going to war in *Reminiscences of Peace and War*, 274–76. Also see Archer, "The Defense of Petersburg on the 9th of June, 1864," 148 n; and Robertson, *The Battle of Old Men and Young Boys*, 37–38.

676. Glenn, "Brave Defence of the Cockade City," 8.

677. McCabe, *The Grayjackets*, 214.

678. Keiley, *Prisoner of War*, 8–9; McCabe, *The Grayjackets*, 215.

679. Glenn, "Brave Defence of the Cockade City," 2.

680. This rundown of professions of the men and some of their infirmities is from Robertson, *The Battle of Old Men and Young Boys*, 59.

681. Keiley, *Prisoner of War*, 9.

682. Scott and Wyatt, *Petersburg's Story*, 178; Pryor, "Incidents in the Life of a Civil War Child," 1–2.

683. The quotes, the situation, and the action on the exposed, thinly defended Petersburg front are from Keiley, *Prisoner of War*, 9–11, with an assist from Glenn, "Brave Defence of the Cockade City," 2.

684. Pryor, *Reminiscences of Peace and War*, 276; Archer, "The Defense of Petersburg on the 9th of June, 1864," 141.

685. Pryor, *Reminiscences of Peace and War*, 274.

686. Archer, "The Defense of Petersburg on the 9th of June, 1864," 134.

687. Pryor, *Reminiscences of Peace and War*, 277.

688. Keiley, *Prisoner of War*, 22.

689. Pryor, *Reminiscences of Peace and War*, 275–76.

690. Archer, "The Defense of Petersburg on the 9th of June, 1864," 121–22; Henderson, *Petersburg in the Civil War*, 110–11; and Harrison, "Petersburg's Ninth of June," 12. The casualty figures vary. I've used Archer's.

691. Walker, *The Private Journal of Georgiana Gholson Walker*, 106.

692. Robertson, *The Battle of Old Men and Young Boys*, 83.

693. Henderson, *Petersburg in the Civil War*, 111.

694. Ibid., 112.

695. Washington, "An Army of Devils," 21–22.

696. Henderson, *Petersburg in the Civil War*, 114–15.

697. Pryor, *Reminiscences of Peace and War*, 278.

698. Henderson, *Petersburg in the Civil War*, introduction.

699. Pryor, *Reminiscences of Peace and War*, 278–79; "Second Presbyterian Church of Petersburg," 3.

700. Pryor, *Reminiscences of Peace and War*, 279–80.

701. Avary, *A Virginia Girl in the Civil War*, 304.

702. Suplée, *The Life of Theodorick Bland Pryor*, 56.

703. Claiborne, *Seventy-five Years in Old Virginia*, 76–77.

704. I have leaned strongly on Sara's account of the digging of "bomb-proofs," and their life under fire, in *Reminiscences of Peace and War*, 280–82, and *My Day*, 201–2.

705. Pryor, *My Day*, 201.

706. Pryor, *Reminiscences of Peace and War*, 282–83; *My Day*, 200.

707. Pryor, *My Day*, 200–1.

708. Pryor, *Reminiscences of Peace and War*, 292.

709. Suplée, *The Life of Theodorick Bland Pryor*, 49, 55.

710. Pryor, *My Day*, 207–8.

711. Henderson, *The Unredeemed City*, ii.

712. The blacks selling their meat pies and Sara's fare are from *My Day*, 203–4, and *Reminiscences of Peace and War*, 283.

713. Blackford, *Letters from Lee's Army*, 272.

714. *Reminiscences of Peace and War*, 293–94.

715. Pryor, *My Day*, 203.

716. Ibid., 206.

717. O.R., ser. 1, vol. 36, pt. 2: 240.

718. Howard, *Sketch of Cobb Legion Cavalry*, 12.

719. Pryor, *My Day*, 206–7.

720. Gorgas, *The Civil War Diary of General Josiah Gorgas*, 72–73.

721. Pryor, *Reminiscences of Peace and War*, 284.

722. Ibid., 288–89.

723. Ibid., 292.

724. Campbell, "Diary of the War," entry of 5 July 1864.

725. Pryor, *Reminiscences of Peace and War*, 296–97; *My Day*, 210.

726. Pryor, *Reminiscences of Peace and War*, 297–98.

727. Ibid., 298–300.

728. Sara describes being surrounded by Lee's army in ibid., 300, and in *My Day*, 211. The refugee quote is from Blackford, *Letters from Lee's Army*, 280.

729. Preston, *Beechenbrook*, 52.

730. Pryor, *Reminiscences of Peace and War*, 301; *My Day*, 211–12.

731. Pryor, *My Day*, 212; *Reminiscences of Peace and War*, 298–99. John's little speech on milk-stealing soldiers is an amalgam of two versions by Sara, which differ slightly. Again, the dialect is as Sara wrote it in her memoirs.

732. Pryor, *Reminiscences of Peace and War*, 301–2.

733. Ibid., 302.

734. Ibid.; Pryor, *My Day*, 213.

735. Pryor, *Reminiscences of Peace and War*, 300, 304.

736. Elmore, *A Heritage of Woe*, 71.

737. Thomas, *The Secret Eye*, 235.

738. Chesnut, *Mary Chesnut's Civil War*, 645, 648.

739. Pryor, *Reminiscences of Peace and War*, 306–7; *My Day*, 216–17.

740. Wilcox's request and Meade's refusal are in *O. R.*, ser. 1, vol 42, pt. 3: 739, 753.

741. This account of Roger's capture is shaped from various statements, news reports, and eyewitness accounts compiled in 1889 by Roger Pryor Jr. and published under the title, *The Capture of Gen. Roger A. Pryor*. See specifically pp. 1–6, 8–11. Roger Jr. compiled the work to refute an account in a North

Carolina newspaper that Roger had not been captured, but had deserted from the Confederate army. Also see the account in Houston, *The Thirty-second Maine Regiment of Infantry Volunteers*, 413–17.

742. Pryor, *My Day*, 222.

743. Roger's captors were as puzzled about how to view this famous enemy as the Confederates were—whether to treat him as a private or a general. Therefore, they also assigned a brigadier general, Henry W. Wessells, as an escort. But Wessells proved far more elusive than the prisoner. After Sheen and Roger had taken their seats on the train in Washington, Wessels appeared for the first time, made himself known, and asked to be introduced to the prisoner. At Jersey City he disappeared entirely, turning up only one more time—when Sheen turned Roger over to the prison commandant at Fort Lafayette.

744. Sheen described his trip with Roger in a letter forty-three years later, 10 July 1908, to Sara's brother, W. L. Rice, the mayor of Bristol, Virginia. It is reprinted in Pryor, *My Day*, 218–20. Orders for the transfer are on p. 221. I have also used information from p. 222. Roger's arrival was also reported in the *New York Evening Post*, 30 November 1864.

745. Pryor, *My Day*, 217–18.

746. Putnam, *Richmond during the War*, 321.

747. Elmore, *A Heritage of Woe*, 82.

748. Pryor, *Reminiscences of Peace and War*, 319.

749. Ibid., 310–11, 329.

750. This rundown of Sara's plight, her want, and some of the solutions are distilled from ibid., 310–11, 316–17, 320, 329, 332; and from *My Day*, 224–26, 229–30, 237–238.

751. Pryor, *Reminiscences of Peace and War*, 319–20; Suplée, *The Life of Theodorick Bland Pryor*, 59.

752. Claiborne, *Seventy-five Years in Old Virginia*, 246.

753. Pryor, *Reminiscences of Peace and War*, 320; Wise, *The End of an Era*, 331.

754. Pryor, *Reminiscences of Peace and War*, 316.

755. Suplée, *The Life of Theodorick Bland Pryor*, 59–60; Pryor, *My Day*, 229. For turning envelopes see Leland, "Middleton Correspondence," 100.

756. Pryor, *My Day*, 229.

757. Ibid.

758. Ibid., 101.

759. De Leon, *Belles, Beaux, and Brains of the 60's*, 396.

760. Sara thus describes the contents of the trunk in *Reminiscences of Peace and War*, 312–13; and in *My Day*, 227.

761. Pryor, *Reminiscences of Peace and War*, 266.

762. All this ripping and cutting and sewing is recounted in ibid., 313–16; and in *My Day*, 227–28.

763. Pryor, *Reminiscences of Peace and War*, 315.

764. Pryor, *My Day*, 230.

765. Pryor, *Reminiscences of Peace and War*, 316.

766. Scott and Wyatt, *Petersburg's Story*, 167.

767. Pryor, *Reminiscences of Peace and War*, 320–22.

768. Ibid., 323.

769. Suplée, *The Life of Theodorick Bland Pryor*, 27, 30–31.

770. Pryor, *Reminiscences of Peace and War*, 323–24.

771. Excerpted from "A Psalm of Life," by Henry Wadsworth Longfellow, in Cook, *One Hundred and One Famous Poems*, 123.

772. Elmore, *A Heritage of Woe*, 87.

773. Sperry, "Kate Sperry's Diary," 73.

774. Dawson, *The Civil War Diary of Sarah Morgan*, 604.

775. Jones and Mallard, *Yankees A'Coming*, 45, 62, 68, 72–73.

776. Andrews, *The War-Time Journal of a Georgia Girl*, 149.

777. Elmore, *A Heritage of Woe*, 82, 87.

778. Chesnut, *Mary Chesnut's Civil War*, 671.

779. LeConte, *'Ware Sherman*, 78, 81–83.

780. From "A Confederate Girl's Diary," in Taylor et al., *South Carolina Women in the Confederacy*, 1:275.

781. Elmore, *A Heritage of Woe*, 98.

782. Mrs. C. P. Poppenheim, "Personal Experiences with Sherman's Army at Liberty Hill," in Taylor et al., *South Carolina Women in the Confederacy,* 1:259–61.

783. Margaret Crawford Adams, "Tales of a Grandmother," in ibid., 1:223.

784. Cumming, *Kate,* 209.

785. LeConte, *'Ware Sherman,* 30.

786. Heyward, *A Confederate Lady Comes of Age,* 68–69.

787. Elmore, *A Heritage of Woe,* 99.

788. LeConte, *When the World Ended,* 45–46, 48, 58–60.

789. Thomas, "The Diary of Anna Hasell Thomas," 137–38.

790. Edmonston, *"Journal of a Secesh Lady,"* 687.

791. Margaret Crawford Adams, "Tales of a Grandmother," in Taylor et al., *South Carolina Women in the Confederacy,* 1:224–25.

792. Hague, *A Blockaded Family,* 142–43, 170–71.

793. Huckaby and Simpson, *Tulip Evermore,* 50.

794. Buck, *Sad Earth, Sweet Heaven,* 11.

795. The quoted phrase is from Eaton, *The Waning of the Old South Civilization,* 82.

796. Chesnut, *Mary Chesnut's Civil War,* 433.

797. Letter to the *Montgomery Daily Advertiser,* 15 June 1864, quoted in Faust, "Altars of Sacrifice," 1220.

798. Claiborne, *Seventy-five Years in Old Virginia,* 250.

799. Morrissette, "Social Life in the First Confederate Capital," 25.

800. LeConte, *'Ware Sherman,* 80.

801. Chesnut, *Mary Chesnut's Civil War,* 574.

802. Allan, *A March Past,* 110–11, 173.

803. An excellent description of this phenomenon is in Eaton, *The Waning of the Old South Civilization,* 82–87. I have borrowed from it liberally for this paragraph.

804. Putnam, *Richmond during the War,* 315.

805. Stone, *Brokenburn,* 292–93.

806. Bird, *The Granite Farm Letters,* 234–35.

807. Tucker, "The Fall of Richmond," 154.

808. Avary, *A Virginia Girl in the Civil War*, 356–57, 359.

809. Quoted in Kunkle, "'It Is What It Does to the Souls,'" 57–58. The description of Augusta Jane Evans that precedes the quote is synthesized from De Leon, *Belles, Beaux, and Brains of the 60's*, 393, and from Fidler, *Augusta Evans Wilson*, 82–83, 86, 150, 157–158.

810. Pryor, *Reminiscences of Peace and War*, 326.

811. Evans, *Macaria*, 78.

812. Claiborne, *Seventy-five Years in Old Virginia*, 244.

813. *Richmond News Leader*, Bicentennial Issue, 8 September 1937, p. 78.

814. Pember, *A Southern Woman's Story*, 187.

815. Putnam, *Richmond during the War*, 342–43.

816. Conolly, *An Irishman in Dixie*, 57, 51.

817. Conolly and his stay at Cottage Farm are described by Sara in *Reminiscences of Peace and War*, 330–31. For supporting detail see Conolly's diary, *An Irishman in Dixie*, 3, 130–31.

818. Pryor, *My Day*, 223.

819. Sara's account of her appeal to the three commissioners is in *Reminiscences of Peace and War*, 327–29. Wigfall's view of Hunter is from Wright, *A Southern Girl in '61*, p. 30.

820. *Home Talk*, 21 August 1939.

821. Ibid.

822. This rundown of Fort Lafayette's clientele is from Sangston, *Bastiles of the North*, 27.

823. Clark, *Histories of the Several Regiments and Battalions from North Carolina*, 5:444.

824. Howard, *Fourteen Months in American Bastiles*, 18.

825. Brewer, *Prison Life!*, 7.

826. The description of Fort Lafayette is distilled from Lonnie Speer's *Portals to Hell*, a study of military prisons in the Civil War, 35–36; Howard, *Fourteen Months in American Bastiles*, 18–19; Sangston, *Bastiles of the North*, 23, 26–27; *Home Talk*, 2 August 1939; *New York Times*, 3 February 1960; *Brooklyn Daily Eagle*, 15 August 1861; *Harper's Weekly*, 7 September 1861; and Roger

Pryor to Mrs. Ranny Scott, 18 March 1865, Scott Family
Correspondence. The old fort, its stone weathered by time, was
leveled, and its island obliterated in the early 1960s to make way
for the Verrazano Narrows Bridge spanning the harbor from
Brooklyn to Staten Island.

827. Pryor, *My Day*, 222–23; Allison, Diary, 3, 5.

828. Thompson, *Photographic History of the Civil War*, 7:56.

829. Pryor, *My Day*, 223.

830. "*Fort-La-Fayette Life*," 33–34; Allison, Diary, 5.

831. Allison, Diary, 3, 6, 7, 8.

832. Much of this detail on Beall is from Headley, *Confederate
Operations in Canada and New York*, 241–43, 358–59. Also see
Baker, *Memoirs of Service with John Yates Beall*, 4.

833. Susan Bradford, of Pine Hill, in Florida, daughter of the
doctor to whom Beall was sent to recuperate from his war
wounds, so described him. See Eppes, *Through Some Eventful
Years*, 201.

834. The detail on Beall's wounding and recuperation is from
ibid., xxiv; and Headley, *Confederate Operations in Canada and
New York*, 242–43.

835. Baker, *Memoirs of Service with John Yates Beall*, 63; notes of
a conversation with Roger Pryor by Isaac Markens in New York
City, 14 May 1904, in Markens Papers.

836. Allison, Diary, 7–8.

837. Ibid., 8.

838. Pryor, *Reminiscences of Peace and War*, 309–10.

839. Ibid., 329.

840. The term for journalists is from De Leon, *Belles, Beaux,
and Brains of the 60's*, 172.

841. Pryor, *Reminiscences of Peace and War*, 339–40.

842. The notes to Lincoln from Greeley and Speed are in Lincoln
Collected Works, 8:314 n.

843. Pryor, *Reminiscences of Peace and War*, 340; Lamon,
Recollections of Abraham Lincoln, 225.

844. Allison, Diary, 8.

845. Pryor, *My Day*, 249–50.

846. Lincoln, *Collected Works*, 8:314 n, 315 n.

847. Allison, Diary, 8.

848. Conversation with Pryor by Isaac Markens in New York City, 14 May 1904, Markens Papers. Also see Markens, *President Lincoln and the Case of John Yates Beall*, 8: and Pryor, *Reminiscences of Peace and War*, 341.

849. Pryor, *Reminiscences of Peace and War*, 341–42.

850. Lincoln, *Collected Works*, 8:314, 314 n, 317; *O. R.*, ser. 2, vol. 8: 191. For the Lincoln-Grant exchange concerning Roger's pardon, see *O. R.*, ser. 1, vol. 46, pt. 2: 668.

851. Beall, *Memoir of John Yates Beall*, 82–83; undated news clipping in Brady Papers.

852. Huckaby and Simpson, *Tulip Evermore*, 51.

853. Boykin, *Shinplasters and Homespun*, 33.

854. Claiborne, *Seventy-five Years in Old Virginia*, 246.

855. Conolly, *An Irishman in Dixie*, 52.

856. Fremantle, *Three Months in the Southern States*, 248.

857. Marietta Fauntleroy Turner Powell, quoted in Andrews, *Scraps of Paper*, 199.

858. Fremantle, *Three Months in the Southern States*, 248–49.

859. Chesnut, *Mary Chesnut's Civil War*, 116.

860. Wise, *The End of an Era*, 343.

861. Pryor, *Reminiscences of Peace and War*, 334–35; *My Day*, 234–35.

862. I've borrowed some of these figures of the relative strength of the two armies from Pollard, *The Lost Cause*, 679–80.

863. Sara's encounter with Lee very closely follows her account of it in *Reminiscences of Peace and War*, 335–37.

864. Cumming, *Kate*, 266.

865. Pryor, *Reminiscences of Peace and War*, 339.

866. Pryor, *My Day*, 252.

867. Bruce, "The Capture and Occupation of Richmond," 125.

868. Long, *Memoirs of Robert E. Lee*, 411.

869. Edmondston, *"Journal of a Secesh Lady,"* 686–87.

870. This chain of events is described by Sara in *Reminiscences of Peace and War*, 343–45; and *My Day*, 252–54.

871. Sara was to recall April 2, 1865, as the day "when I fled before the bullets." See *My Day*, 110. The fields plowed by shot and shell are noted in Suplée, *The Life of Theodorick Bland Pryor*, 67.

872. Sara's flight into Petersburg is distilled from her account in *Reminiscences of Peace and War*, 346–47; and *My Day*, 254–55.

873. Pryor, *Reminiscences of Peace and War*, 347.

874. Ibid., 347–48.

875. Ibid., 348.

876. Suplée, *The Life of Theodorick Bland Pryor*, 67; Pryor, *My Day*, 256.

877. Pryor, *Reminiscences of Peace and War*, 349.

878. Ibid., 349–50.

879. Ibid., 350.

880. This description of the Federal invasion of her house closely follows Sara's account in ibid., 350–52.

881. Pryor, *My Day*, 256–57; *Reminiscences of Peace and War*, 352.

882. Pryor, *My Day*, 252–53.

883. Pollard, *The Lost Cause*, 693.

884. The scene in St. Paul's and Davis's call by the sexton are beautifully described in Weddell, *St. Paul's Church*, 1:241–46. Also see Tucker, "The Fall of Richmond," 155–56.

885. Pryor, *Reminiscences of Peace and War*, 354.

886. Tucker, "The Fall of Richmond," 155–56; Weddell, *St. Paul's Church*, 1:243–44.

887. Kean, *Inside the Confederate Government*, 97.

888. Pryor, *Reminiscences of Peace and War*, 355.

889. Page, *Letters of a War Correspondent*, 329.

890. Agnes's activity is from her letter to Sara reprinted in *Reminiscences of Peace and War*, 354–55. Agnes says it was James Lyons, a Richmond lawyer, she met outside the hotel. But it must

have been William Lyons, the Richmond judge who was in Mayor Mayo's surrender party.

891. Sulivane, "The Fall of Richmond: The Evacuation," 725.

892. Blackford, *Letters from Lee's Army*, 292.

893. Putnam, *Richmond during the War*, 363.

894. The confused scene is pictured by Charles Page in *Letters of a War Correspondent*, 332.

895. The council's meeting place is described in Pollard, *The Lost Cause*, 694.

896. Quoted in Wiley, *The Plain People of the Confederacy*, 26.

897. Putnam, *Richmond during the War*, 363–64; Pryor, *Reminiscences of Peace and War*, 356.

898. The image of a Niagara of whiskey is borrowed from Page, *Letters of a War Correspondent*, 333.

899. Bruce, "The Capture and Occupation of Richmond," 127.

900. Putnam, *Richmond during the War*, 364.

901. Jones, *Ladies of Richmond*, 294.

902. Putnam, *Richmond during the War*, 364.

903. Blackford, *Letters from Lee's Army*, 292.

904. Reagan, *Memoirs with Special Reference to Secession and the Civil War*, 198.

905. Jones, *Ladies of Richmond*, 294.

906. Putnam, *Richmond during the War*, 365.

907. Leyburn, "The Fall of Richmond," 94.

908. Mordecai, Diary, 118.

909. Putnam, *Richmond during the War*, 365–66.

910. Pryor, *Reminiscences of Peace and War*, 356.

911. Spencer, "A French View of the Fall of Richmond," 182.

912. Leyburn, "The Fall of Richmond," 94.

913. Van Lew, *A Yankee Spy in Richmond*, 105–6.

914. Jones, *Ladies of Richmond*, 294.

915. Ibid.

916. Putnam, *Richmond during the War*, 367.

917. Pollard, *The Lost Cause*, 696–97.

918. Townsend, *Rustics in Rebellion*, 262.

919. Avary, *A Virginia Girl in the Civil War*, 69.

920. Magill, *Women, or Chronicles of the Late War*, 292–93.

921. Putnam, *Richmond during the War*, 368–69.

922. Pryor, *Reminiscences of Peace and War*, 353; Henderson, *Petersburg in the Civil War*, 137; Pfanz, *Abraham Lincoln at City Point*, 55–56. Porter, *Campaigning with Grant*, 449–52.

923. This image of Lincoln walking is sifted from a description in Page, *Letters of a War Correspondent*, 335.

924. Porter, *Incidents and Anecdotes of the Civil War*, 302.

925. Pryor, *Reminiscences of Peace and War*, 357.

926. Ibid., 354, 357.

927. Mordecai, Diary, 134.

928. Hardin, *The Private War of Lizzie Hardin*, 223.

929. McGuire, *Diary of a Southern Refugee*, 352, 360.

930. Pryor, *Reminiscences of Peace and War*, 371.

931. Heyward, *A Confederate Lady Comes of Age*, 74.

932. Hardin, *The Private War of Lizzie Hardin*, 232.

933. Avary, *A Virginia Girl in the Civil War*, 364, 373.

934. Sterkx, *Partners in Rebellion*, 168.

935. From "The Confederate Flag," in Andrews, *Scraps of Paper*, 228.

936. Nannie Thomas to Tom Conolly, 27 April 1865, in Conolly, *An Irishman in Dixie*, 117.

937. Tompkins, "The Occupation of Richmond," 195–98.

938. Quotes from R. S. Holt to Joseph Holt, 11 April 1865, and the *Augusta Weekly Constitutionalist*, 29 April 1868, are from Coulter, *The South during Reconstruction*, 16.

939. Andrews, *The War-Time Journal of a Georgia Girl*, 155, 169, 254, 223.

940. Bowen, *The Diary of Clarissa Adger Bowen*, 74.

941. Boykin, *Shinplasters and Homespun*, 33.

942. LeConte, *When the World Ended*, 90.

943. Stone, *Brokenburn*, 339–40.

944. Mordecai, Diary, 109–10, 108.

945. *New York Times,* 21 May 1865.

946. Putnam, *Richmond during the War,* 380.

947. Pryor, *My Day,* 258.

948. Henderson, *Petersburg in the Civil War,* 145; *Harper's Weekly,* 29 April 1865.

949. Pryor, *My Day,* 258.

950. Stone, *Brokenburn,* 333.

951. The account of Sara and the Confederate prisoners is distilled from *Reminiscences of Peace and War,* 361–63.

952. Sara describes Sheridan's takeover of her house in ibid., 363–65.

953. Gavin, *Campaigning with the Roundheads,* 637; Wilkinson, *Mother, May You Never See the Sights I Have Seen,* 346.

954. Pryor, *Reminiscences of Peace and War,* 365–67.

955. Ibid., 367–68.

956. This section, embracing visits from Captain Lee and General Sheridan, closely follows Sara's account in ibid., 368–69. Also see *My Day,* 259–60.

957. Pryor, *Reminiscences of Peace and War,* 370; Pryor, *My Day,* 261.

958. Pryor, *Reminiscences of Peace and War,* 373.

959. Sara letting John go can be found in ibid., 373–74.

960. These musings are from ibid., 376.

961. Sara's bid for food and her confrontations with General and Mrs. Hartsuff are from ibid., 376–80.

962. Sara's visit to the Bolling house and her interview with Hartsuff are also from *Reminiscences of Peace and War,* 380–82.

963. Her arrival at Cottage Farm and her long night vigil are described in ibid., 383–86.

964. Ibid., 386–87.

965. Sara's conversation with the guard and her meeting with the black refugees are from ibid., 387–88.

966. Pryor, *My Day,* 272, 453–54.

967. Pryor, *Reminiscences of Peace and War*, 372.

968. Pryor, "Virginia's Part in American History," 962.

969. Hardin, *The Private War of Lizzie Hardin*, 279–80.

970. Stone, *Brokenburn*, 364.

971. Malvina Waring, "A Confederate Girl's Diary," in Taylor et al., *South Carolina Women in the Confederacy*, 1:287.

972. From a letter to Sara reprinted in Pryor, *Reminiscences of Peace and War*, 374–76.

973. Pryor, *Reminiscences of Peace and War*, 390–91, 396–97; *My Day*, 273, 277.

974. Pryor, *Reminiscences of Peace and War*, 391–92, 394.

975. Ibid., 397–98.

976. For an excellent account of the Confederate migration to the North after the war, see Sutherland, *The Confederate Carpetbaggers*.

977. Hartsuff's urgings for Roger to go to New York are from Pryor, *My Day*, 278–79; and *Reminiscences of Peace and War*, 398.

978. Pryor, *Reminiscences of Peace and War*, 398–99; *My Day*, 279–80.

979. *New York Times*, 16 February 1912.

980. Roger's early days in New York, his anguish, indecision, and final resolve are from Pryor, *My Day*, 280–83, and *Reminiscences of Peace and War*, 399.

981. Pryor, *My Day*, 284.

982. Pryor, *Reminiscences of Peace and War*, 400; *My Day*, 289.

983. Sara's decision to move from Cottage Farm and her introspection are distilled from *My Day*, 288–91. Also see *Reminiscences of Peace and War*, 400.

984. Roger's letters, from which I have drawn this short section, are in *My Day*, 283–86. See p. 297 for what the New York papers were calling him.

985. Ibid., 292, 294–95.

986. This chronicle of Roger's highs and lows follows closely Sara's account in ibid., 298–303.

987. Ibid., 303.

988. Ibid., 303–6, 332.

989. Ibid., 310.

990. Rice, "Sara Agnes Pryor," 4275.

991. Pryor, *My Day*, 310–12, 314–15, 317, 321, 332.

992. Ibid., 68–69, 320.

993. For a look at wartime Brooklyn, see Livingston, *President Lincoln's Third Largest City*.

994. Pryor, *My Day*, 339–40.

995. Pryor, "The Bar and Forensic Oratory," 96.

996. Sara Pryor to Walter Allen Watson, 18 June 1896, Watson Papers.

997. Pryor, *My Day*, 395–97, 415.

998. This new Roger Pryor and his views are taken from his letter to the *Richmond Whig*, 5 October 1867, reprinted in *My Day*, 326–29. A typescript copy of the letter is in the Miscellaneous Manuscripts Collection, Manuscript Division, Library of Congress.

999. Pryor *My Day*, 403.

1000. Stone, *Brokenburn*, 126.

1001. Holzman, *Stormy Ben Butler*, 181.

1002. Trietsch, *The Printer and the Prince*, 248.

1003. Pryor, *My Day*, 350.

1004. John Russell Young to Roger Pryor, 16 September 1872, quoted in ibid., 352.

1005. Pryor, *My Day*, 448.

1006. Roger's words and the reaction to them are from ibid., 367–71.

1007. *Congressional Record*, 46 Cong., 2nd sess., vol. 10: 1493, 1906, 2479.

1008. *Brooklyn Eagle*, 15 March 1919.

1009. Pryor, "The Bar and Forensic Oratory," 96–97.

1010. Donovan, *Modern Jury Trials and Advocates*, 412–13.

1011. From the *Dayton (Ohio) Herald and Empire*, quoted in Pryor, *My Day*, 357–58.

1012. Auerbach, *The Bar of Other Days*, 194.

1013. Epes, "Roger Atkinson Pryor," 17.

1014. *New York Sun*, 15 March 1919.

1015. Auerbach, *The Bar of Other Days*, 199.

1016. David, *The History of the Haymarket Affair*, 380.

1017. Calmer, *Labor Agitator*, 114–15.

1018. Roger's role in New York's legal attack on the sugar trust is fully described in Eichner, *The Emergence of Oligopoly*, 132–51.

1019. Brooks, *History of the Court of Common Pleas of the City and County of New York*, 9.

1020. Epes, "Roger Atkinson Pryor," 17.

1021. *New York Times*, 19 April 1914. The passage from *Measure for Measure* is in act 2, scene 2, lines 64–67.

1022. *New York World*, 24 December 1898.

1023. *Dictionary of American Biography*, s.v. "Pryor, Roger Atkinson."

1024. Stiles, *Civil, Political, and Ecclesiastical History*, 1247.

1025. Pryor, *My Day*, 450–51.

1026. Quoted in Rice, "Sara Agnes Pryor," 4277.

1027. Reniers, *Springs of Virginia*, 252.

1028. Pryor, *My Day*. The phrase, dipping "my pen in my heart" is in a letter from Sara to a Mr. and Mrs. Bacon, 24 July 1896, Gregory Family Papers.

1029. Pickett, *Across My Path*, 142.

1030. Pryor, *My Day*, 409.

1031. *Virginia Magazine of History and Biography*, 11 January 1904, 343–44.

1032. Quoted from a letter by Young, reprinted in Pryor, *My Day*, 351.

1033. Rice, "Sara Agnes Pryor," 4277.

1034. James et al., *Notable American Women*, 3:104.

1035. Rice, "Sara Agnes Pryor," 4275, 4277.

1036. Ibid., 4277.

1037. Pryor, *My Day*, 392–93, 400–1.

1038. Young, *Men and Memories*, 326–28; Pryor, *My Day*, 449–50.

1039. Pryor, *My Day*, 371–72.

1040. The encounter with Sheridan is from ibid., 374, 376–77.

1041. This description of Theodorick is from Suplée, *The Life of Theodorick Bland Pryor*, 34, 72–75, 94.

1042. Conolly, *An Irishman in Dixie*, 72.

1043. Theodorick's career path and the chain of events leading to his death and his burial in Princeton are in Suplée, *The Life of Theodorick Bland Pryor*, 173–75, 178–79, 184–87, 189–191. Suplée's biography is a loving account of the boy's short life.

1044. Pryor, *My Day*, 347–48.

1045. *New York Times*, 26 August 1904.

1046. The wedding announcements for Lucy and Fanny, with guest lists, are in the *New York Herald*, 26 February 1886; and the *New York Times*, 1 April 1897.

1047. *New York Times*, 15 March 1919.

1048. Pryor, *Reminiscences of Peace and War*, 401.

1049. Charlotte Bostwick to Katharine H. Cumming, in Cumming, *A Northern Daughter and a Southern Wife*, 95.

1050. Pickett, *Across My Path*, 139.

1051. Pryor, *Reminiscences of Peace and War*, 112.

1052. Ibid., 371.

1053. Lyrics to "The Southern Soldier Boy" are in Glass and Singer, *Singing Soldiers*, 254.

1054. Pryor, *Reminiscences of Peace and War*, 178.

1055. Morrissette, "Social Life in the First Confederate Capital," 10.

1056. Pryor, *Reminiscences of Peace and War*, 121.

1057. Willcox, "A Light is Out!" 6.

1058. Pryor, *My Day*, 407.

1059. Sara Pryor to Mr. and Mrs. Bacon, 24 July 1896, Gregory Family Papers.

1060. Pryor, *My Day*, vii.

1061. *New York Law Journal*, 18 March 1919.

1062. *New York Times*, 15 March 1919; *Bulletin of Hampden-Sydney College*, 14 April 1919, p. 29.

1063. *New York Herald*, 16 March 1919.

1064. "In Memoriam," in United Confederate Veteran Collection, New York Camp, Museum of the Confederacy.

Bibliography

Abbott, Austin, ed., *Official Report of the Trial of Henry Ward Beecher, with Notes and References.* New York: George W. Smith & Company, 1875.

Abbott, Martin, "Southern Reaction to Lincoln's Assassination." *Abraham Lincoln Quarterly* 7 (September 1952): 111–27.

Abel, E. Lawrence. *Singing the New Nation: How Music Shaped the Confederacy, 1861–1865.* Mechanicsburg, Pa.: Stackpole Books, 2000.

Adams, Charles Francis Jr. *Charles Francis Adams, 1835–1915: An Autobiography.* 1916. Reprint. Westport, Conn.: Greenwood Press, 1973.

Adams, Henry. *The Great Secession Winter of 1860–61 and Other Essays.* Edited by George Hochfield. New York: Sagamore Press, 1958.

Alexander, E. Porter. Papers. Southern Historical Collection, University of North Carolina, Chapel Hill, N.C.

Alfriend, Edward M. "Social Life in Richmond during the War." *Cosmopolitan* 12 (1892): 229–33.

Allan, Elizabeth Preston. *The Life and Letters of Margaret Junkin Preston.* Boston: Houghton, Mifflin & Company, 1903.

————. *A March Past: Reminiscences of Elizabeth Randolph Preston Allan.* Edited by Janet Allan Bryan. Richmond: Dietz Press, 1938.

Allison, J. D. Diary. Typescript. Filson Club Historical Society Library, Louisville, Ky.

American National Biography. Edited by John A. Garraty and Mark C. Carnes. Published under the auspices of the American Council of Learned Societies. New York: Oxford University Press. 1999.

Andrews, Eliza Frances. *The War-Time Journal of a Georgia Girl, 1864–1865.* Edited by Spence Birdwell King Jr. 1908. Reprint. Macon, Ga.: Ardivan Press, 1960.

Andrews, Marietta Minnigerode. *Scraps of Paper.* New York: E. P. Dutton & Co., 1929.

Andrews, Matthew Page, comp. *The Women of the South in War Times.* Baltimore: Norman, Remington Co., 1920.

Anspach, Frederick R. *The Sons of the Sires: A History of the Rise, Progress, and Destiny of the American Party.* Philadelphia: Lippincott, Grambo & Co., 1855.

Appletons' Cyclopaedia of American Biography. Edited by James Grant Wilson and John Fiske. New York: D. Appleton & Company, 1888.

Archer, Fletcher H. "The Defense of Petersburg on the 9th of June, 1864." In *War Talks of Confederate Veterans.* Edited by George S. Bernard. Petersburg, Va.: Fenn & Owen, 1892.

Auchampaugh, Philip Gerald. *James Buchanan and His Cabinet on the Eve of Secession.* Privately Printed, 1926.

Auerbach, Joseph S. *The Bar of Other Days.* New York: Harper & Brothers, 1940.

"Augusta J. Evans on Secession." *Alabama Historical Quarterly* 3 (Spring 1941): 65–67.

Avary, Myrta Lockett. *Dixie after the War: An Exposition of Social Conditions Existing in the South, during the Twelve Years Suc-*

ceeding the Fall of Richmond. New York: Doubleday, Page & Company, 1906.

———. *A Virginia Girl in the Civil War, 1861–1865: Being a Record of the Actual Experiences of the Wife of a Confederate Officer*. New York: D. Appleton & Company, 1903.

Bacot, Ada W. *A Confederate Nurse: The Diary of Ada W. Bacot, 1860–1863*. Edited by Jean V. Berlin. Columbia: University of South Carolina Press, 1994.

Baker, William Washington. *Memoirs of Service with John Yates Beall, C. S. N.* Edited by Douglas Southall Freeman. Richmond, Va.: Richmond Press, 1910.

Barham, Theophilus G. "War Record of T. G. Barham." Typescript. Files of the Petersburg National Battlefield, Petersburg, Va.

Baringer, William. *Lincoln's Rise to Power*. Boston: Little, Brown & Company, 1937.

Barnes, John S. "With Lincoln from Washington to Richmond in 1865." *Appleton's Magazine* 9 (May 1907): 515–24; (June 1907): 742–51.

Barr, Henrietta Fitzhugh. *The Civil War Diary of Mrs. Henrietta Fitzhugh Barr (Barre), 1862–1863, Ravenswood, VA (West Virginia)*. Edited by Sallie Kiger Winn. Marietta, Ohio: Marietta College, 1963.

Bartlett, Catherine Thom, ed. *"My Dear Brother": A Confederate Chronicle*. Richmond, Va.: Dietz Press, 1952.

The Battle of Fort Sumter and First Victory of the Southern Troops. Charleston, S.C.: Steam Power Presses of Evans & Cogswell, 1861.

Beall, John Yates. *Memoir of John Yates Beall: His Life; Trial; Correspondence; Diary*. Montreal: John Lovell, 1865.

"Beautiful Reception at First White House of the Confederacy." *Alabama Historical Quarterly* 18 (Spring 1956): 126–30.

Beers, Fannie A. *Memories: A Record of Personal Experience and*

Adventure during Four Years of War. Philadelphia: J. B. Lippincott Company, 1888.

Bell, Hiram P. *Men and Things: Being Reminiscent, Biographical, and Historical.* Atlanta: Foote & Davies Company, 1907.

Bill, Alfred Hoyt. *The Beleaguered City: Richmond, 1861–1865.* 1946. Reprint. Westport, Conn.: Greenwood Press, 1980.

Billington, Ray Allen. *The Protestant Crusade, 1800–1860: A Study of the Origins of American Nativism.* 1938. Reprint. Gloucester Mass.: Peter Smith, 1963.

Biographical Directory of the American Congress, 1774–1996. Alexandria, Va.: CQ Staff Directories, 1997.

Bird, Edgeworth, and Sallie Bird. *The Granite Farm Letters: The Civil War Correspondence of Edgeworth & Sallie Bird.* Edited by John Rozier. Athens: University of Georgia Press, 1988.

Blackford, L. Minor. "The Great John B. Minor and his Cousin Mary Face the War: Correspondence between the Professor of Law and the Lynchburg Blackfords, 1860–1864." *Virginia Magazine of History and Biography* 61 (October 1953): 439–49.

Blackford, Susan Leigh, comp. *Letters from Lee's Army, or Memoirs of Life in and out of the Army in Virginia during the War between the States.* New York: Charles Scribner's Sons, 1947.

Blackiston, Henry C., ed. *Refugees in Richmond: Civil War Letters of a Virginia Family.* Princeton, N.J.: Princeton University Press, 1989.

Boatner, Mark W., III. *The Civil War Dictionary.* New York: David McKay Company, 1959.

Boney, F. N. *John Letcher of Virginia: The Story of Virginia's Civil War Governor.* Tuscaloosa: University of Alabama Press, 1966.

Book Review of *The Mother of Washington and Her Times,* by Sara Agnes Pryor. *Virginia Magazine of History and Biography* 11 (January 1904): 343–44.

Bowen, Clarissa Adger. *The Diary of Clarissa Adger Bowen, Ashtabula Plantation, 1865.* Compiled by Mary Stevenson.

Pendleton, S.C.: Foundation Historic Preservation in Pendleton Area, 1973.

Boykin, Laura Nisbet. *Shinplasters and Homespun: The Diary of Laura Nisbet Boykin*. Edited by Mary Wright Stock. Rockville, Md.: Printex, 1975.

Braden, Waldo W., ed. *Oratory in the Old South, 1828–1860*. Baton Rouge: Louisiana State University Press, 1970.

Brady, James Topham. Papers. Virginia Historical Society Library, Richmond, Va.

Breckinridge. Lucy Gilmer. *Lucy Breckinridge of Grove Hill: The Journal of a Virginia Girl, 1862–1864*. Edited by Mary D. Robertson. Kent, Ohio: Kent State University Press, 1979.

Brevard, Keziah Goodwyn Hopkins. *A Plantation Mistress on the Eve of the Civil War: The Diary of Keziah Goodwyn Hopkins Brevard, 1860–1861*. Edited by John Hammond Moore. Columbia: University of South Carolina Press, 1993.

Brewer, John M. *Prison Life!* Baltimore: S. S. Mills, 1862.

Brinkley, John Luster. *On This Hill: A Narrative History of Hampden-Sydney College, 1774–1994*. Hampden-Sydney, Va.: Hampden-Sydney, 1994.

Brooklyn Daily Eagle.

Brooks, James Wilton. *History of the Court of Common Pleas of the City and County of New York*. New York: Published by subscription, 1896.

Brooks, Noah. *Washington in Lincoln's Time*. Edited by Herbert Mitgang. New York: Rinehart & Company, 1958.

Brown, Louis A., ed. "The Correspondence of David Olando McRaven and Amanda Nantz McRaven, 1864–1865." *North Carolina Historical Review* 26 (January 1949): 41–98.

Bruce, Dickson D., Jr. *Violence and Culture in the Antebellum South*. Austin: University of Texas Press, 1979.

Bruce, George A. "The Capture and Occupation of Richmond." In *Papers of the Military Historical Society of Massachusetts*.

Vol. 14. 1918. Reprint. Wilmington, N.C.: Broadfoot Publishing Company, 1990.

Buck, Lucy Rebecca. *Sad Earth, Sweet Heaven: The Diary of Lucy Rebecca Buck during the War between the States.* Edited by William P. Buck. 2nd edition. Birmingham, Ala.: Buck Publishing Company, 1973.

Bulletin of Hampden-Sydney College.

Calmer, Alan. *Labor Agitator: The Story of Albert R. Parsons.* New York: International Publishers, 1937.

Campbell, Charles. "Diary of the War." Papers. Earl Gregg Swem Library, College of William and Mary, Williamsburg, Va.

————, ed. *The Bland Papers: Being a Selection from the Manuscripts of Colonel Theodorick Bland, Jr.* 2 vols in 1. Petersburg, Va.: Edmund & Julian Ruffin, 1840.

Campbell, Edward D. C., Jr., and Kym S. Rice, eds. *A Woman's War: Southern Women, Civil War, and the Confederate Legacy.* Richmond and Charlottesville: The Museum of the Confederacy and the University Press of Virginia, 1996.

Campbell, John A. "A View of the Confederacy from the Inside," *Century Magazine* 38 (October 1889): 950–54.

Cappon, Lester J. *Virginia Newspapers, 1832–1935: A Bibliography with Historical Introduction and Notes.* New York: D. Appleton-Century Company, 1936.

Channing, Steven A., and the Editors of Time-Life Books. *The Civil War: The Southern Home Front.* Alexandria, Va.: Time-Life Books, 1984.

Charleston Daily Courier.

Charleston Mercury.

Chesnut, Mary. *Mary Chesnut's Civil War.* Edited by C. Vann Woodward. New Haven, Conn.: Yale University Press, 1981.

Chesson, Michael B. "Harlots or Heroines? A New Look at the Richmond Bread Riot." *Virginia Magazine of History and Biography* 92 (April 1984): 131–75.

Chicago Tribune.

Chisolm, A. R. "Notes on the Surrender of Fort Sumter." In *Battles and Leaders of the Civil War.* Vol. 1. Edited by Robert Underwood Johnson and Clarence Clough Buel. 1887. Reprint. Secaucus, N.J.: Castle, n.d.

Claiborne, John Herbert. *Seventy-five Years in Old Virginia.* New York: Neale Publishing Company, 1904.

Clark, Walter, ed. *Histories of the Several Regiments and Battalions from North Carolina in the Great War, 1861–1865.* Vol. 5. 1901. Reprint. Wilmington, N.C.: Broadfoot Publishing Company, 1991.

Clay-Clopton, Virginia. *A Belle of the Fifties.* New York: Doubleday, Page & Company, 1904.

Cobb, Thomas R. R. "Extracts from Letters to His Wife, February 3, 1861–December 10, 1862." *Southern Historical Society Papers* 28 (1900): 280–301.

Coffin, Charles Carleton. *Four Years of Fighting.* Boston: Ticknor & Fields, 1866.

Cole, Arthur C. "Lincoln's Election an Immediate Menace to Slavery in the States?" *American Historical Review* 26 (July 1931): 740–67.

Collier, Malinda W., John M. Coski, Richard C. Cote, Tucker H. Hill, and Guy R. Swanson. *White House of the Confederacy: An Illustrated History.* Richmond, Va.: Cadmus Marketing, 1993.

The Confederate General. 6 vols. Edited by William C. Davis and Julie Hoffman. Harrisburg, Pa.: National Historical Society, 1991.

Congressional Globe. 46 vols. Washington, D.C., 1834–73.

Congressional Record. 1880. Washington, D.C.

Conkling, Alfred R. *The Life and Letters of Roscoe Conkling, Orator, Statesman, Advocate.* New York: Charles L. Webster & Company, 1889.

Conolly, Thomas. *An Irishman in Dixie: Thomas Conolly's Diary of the Fall of the Confederacy.* Edited by Nelson D. Lankford. Columbia: University of South Carolina Press, 1988.

Cook, Joel. *The Siege of Richmond: A Narrative of Military Operations of Major-General George B. McClellan during the Months of May and June 1862.* Philadelphia: George W. Childs, 1862.

Cook, Roy J., comp. *One Hundred and One Famous Poems with a Prose Supplement.* Revised edition. Chicago: Cable Company, 1929.

Corson, William Clark. *My Dear Jennie.* Edited by Blake W. Corson. Richmond, Va.: Dietz Press, 1982.

Coulter, E. Merton. *The Confederate States of America, 1861–1865.* Vol. 7 of *A History of the South.* Edited by Wendell Holmes Stephenson and E. Merton Coulter. Baton Rouge: Louisiana State University Press and the Littlefield Fund for Southern History of the University of Texas, 1950.

———. *The South during Reconstruction, 1865–1877.* Vol. 8 of *A History of the South.* Edited by Wendell Holmes Stephenson and E. Merton Coulter. Baton Rouge: Louisiana State University Press and the Littlefield Fund for Southern History of the University of Texas, 1947.

Cox, Samuel S. *Three Decades of Federal Legislation, 1855 to 1885.* 1885. Reprint. Freeport, N.Y.: Books for Libraries Press, 1970.

Crandall, Andrew Wallace. *The Early History of the Republican Party, 1854–1856.* Gloucester, Mass.: Peter Smith, 1960.

Craven, Avery O. *The Coming of the Civil War.* New York: Charles Scribner's Sons, 1942.

———. *Edmund Ruffin, Southerner: A Study in Secession.* New York: D. Appleton & Company, 1932.

———. *The Growth of Southern Nationalism, 1848–1861.* Vol. 6 of *A History of the South.* Edited by Wendell Holmes Stephenson and E. Merton Coulter. Baton Rouge: Louisiana State University Press and the Littlefield Fund for Southern History of the University of Texas, 1953.

Crawford, Samuel Wylie. *The Genesis of the Civil War: The Story of Sumter, 1860–1861.* New York: Charles L. Webster & Company, 1887.

Crenshaw, Ollinger. "The Speakership Contest of 1859–1860." *Mississippi Valley Historical Review* 29 (December 1942): 323–38.

Crossley, Martha Jane. "A Patriotic Confederate Woman's War Diary, 1862–1863." Edited by H. E. Sterkx. *Alabama Historical Quarterly* 20 (Winter 1958): 611–17.

Cumming, Kate. *Gleanings from Southland: Sketches of Life and Manners of the People of the South before, during, and after the War of Secession*. Birmingham, Ala.: Roberts & Son, 1895.

———. *Kate: The Journal of a Confederate Nurse*. Edited by Richard Barksdale Harwell. Baton Rouge: Louisiana State University Press, 1987.

Cumming, Katherine H. *A Northern Daughter and a Southern Wife: The Civil War Reminiscences and Letters of Katherine H. Cumming, 1860–1865*. Edited by W. Kirk Wood. Augusta, Ga.: Richmond County Historical Society, 1976.

Curry, J. L. M. *Civil History of the Government of the Confederate States with Some Personal Reminiscences*. Richmond, Va.: B. F. Johnson Publishing Company, 1900.

Cuttino, George Peddy, ed. *Saddle Bag and Spinning Wheel: Being the Civil War Letters of George W. Peddy, M.D., Surgeon, 56th Georgia Volunteer Regiment, C. S. A., and His Wife Kate Featherston Peddy*. Macon, Ga.: Mercer University Press, 1981.

Dabney, R. L. *Life and Campaigns of Lieut.-Gen. Thomas J. Jackson, (Stonewall Jackson)*. 1865. Reprint. Harrisonburg, Va.: Sprinkle Publications, 1983.

Dannett, Sylvia G. L., and Katherine M. Jones. *Our Women of the Sixties*. Washington, D.C.: U.S. Civil War Centennial Commission, 1963.

David, Henry. *The History of the Haymarket Affair: A Study in the American Social-Revolutionary and Labor Movements*. 2nd edition. New York: Russell & Russell, 1958.

Davis, Jefferson. *The Papers of Jefferson Davis*. Edited by Haskell M. Monroe, James T. McIntosh, Lynda Lasswell Crist, Mary

Seaton Dix, and Kenneth H. Williams. Vols. 7–10. Baton Rouge: Louisiana State University Press, 1992–1999.

————. *The Rise and Fall of the Confederate Government*. 2 vols. New York: D. Appleton & Company, 1912.

Davis, Varina Howell. *Jefferson Davis, Ex-President of the Confederate States of America: A Memoir by His Wife*. 2 vols. 1890. Reprint. Freeport, N.Y.: Books for Libraries Press, 1971.

Davis, William C. *"A Government of Our Own": The Making of the Confederacy*. New York: Free Press, 1994.

Davis, William Watts Hart. *History of the 104th Pennsylvania Regiment, from August 22nd, 1861, to September 30th, 1864*. Philadelphia: James B. Rodgers, Printer, 1866.

Dawson, Francis W. *Our Women in the War: An Address . . . Delivered at the Fifth Annual Re-union of the Association of the Maryland Line*. Charleston, S.C.: Walker, Evans & Cogswell Company, 1887.

Dawson, Sarah Morgan. *The Civil War Diary of Sarah Morgan*. Edited by Charles East. Athens: University of Georgia Press, 1991.

De Leon, T. C. *Belles, Beaux, and Brains of the 60's*. New York: G. W. Dillingham Company, 1909.

————. *Four Years in Rebel Capitals: An Inside View of Life in the Southern Confederacy from Birth to Death*. Mobile, Ala.: Gossip Printing Co., 1890.

Denney, Robert E. *The Civil War Years: A Day-by-Day Chronicle of the Life of a Nation*. New York: Sterling Publishing Co., 1992.

Dictionary of American Biography. Edited by Allen Johnson et al. New York: Scribner, 1946–1958.

Foster, A. J. *Early James River History in and around Hopewell, Virginia*. Falls Church, Va.: 1965.

Dillard, Anthony W. "William Loundes Yancey: The Sincere and Unfaltering Advocate of Southern Rights." *Southern Historical Society Papers* 21 (1893): 151–59.

Dodd, William E. *Statesmen of the Old South, or, From Radicalism to Conservative Revolt.* New York: Macmillan Company, 1911.

Donovan, J. W. *Modern Jury Trials and Advocates.* New York: Banks & Brothers, 1881.

Doubleday, Abner. *Reminiscences of Forts Sumter and Moultrie in 1860–'61.* 1876. Reprint. Spartanburg, S.C.: Reprint Company Publishers, 1976.

DuBose, John Witherspoon. *The Life and Times of William Loundes Yancey.* 2 vols. 1892. Reprint. New York: Peter Smith, 1942.

Eaton, Clement. *The Waning of the Old South Civilization, 1860–1880's.* Athens: University of Georgia Press, 1968.

———. "Henry A. Wise and the Virginia Fire Eaters of 1856." *Mississippi Valley Historical Review* 21 (March 1935): 495–512.

Eckenrode, H. J. "Negroes in Richmond in 1864." *Virginia Magazine of History and Biography* 46 (July 1938): 193–200.

Edmondston, Catherine Ann Devereux. *"Journal of a Secesh Lady": The Diary of Catherine Ann Devereux Edmondston.* Edited by Beth G. Crabtree and James W. Patton. Raleigh: North Carolina Division of Archives and History, 1979.

Eggleston, George Cary. *A Rebel's Recollections.* 1959. Reprint. New York: Kraus Reprint Co., 1969.

Eichner, Alfred S. *The Emergence of Oligopoly: Sugar Refining as a Case Study.* Baltimore: Johns Hopkins University Press, 1969.

Elder, Thomas Claybrook. Papers. Virginia Historical Society Library, Richmond, Va.

Elmore, Grace Brown. *A Heritage of Woe: The Civil War Diary of Grace Brown Elmore, 1861–1868.* Edited by Marli F. Weiner. Athens: University of Georgia Press, 1997.

Eno, Clara B. "Activities of the Women of Arkansas during the War between the States." *Arkansas Historical Quarterly* 3 (Spring 1944): 5–27.

Epes, T. P. "Roger Atkinson Pryor, LL.D." *Kaleidoscope* 11 (1902): 9–17.

Eppes, Susan Bradford. *Through Some Eventful Years.* 1926. Reprint. Gainesville: University of Florida Press, 1968.

Erwin, Margaret Johnson. *Like Some Green Laurel: Letters of Margaret Johnson Erwin, 1821–1863.* Edited by John Seymour Erwin. Baton Rouge: Louisiana State University Press, 1981.

Evans, Augusta Jane. *Macaria; or Altars of Sacrifice.* Edited by Drew Gilpin Faust. Baton Rouge: Louisiana State University Press, 1992.

Faust, Drew Gilpin. *Mothers of Invention: Women of the Slaveholding South in the American Civil War.* New York: Vintage Books, 1997.

———. "Altars of Sacrifice: Confederate Women and the Narratives of War." *Journal of American History* 76 (March 1990): 1200–28.

Fidler, William Perry. *Augusta Evans Wilson, 1835–1909: A Biography.* University, Ala.: University of Alabama Press, 1951.

Fitts, Albert N. "The Confederate Convention." *Alabama Review* 2 (April 1949): 83–101; (July 1949): 189–210.

Fletcher, Miss A., *Within Fort Sumter; or, a View of Major Anderson's Garrison Family for One Hundred and Ten Days.* New York: N. Tibbals & Company, 1861.

Forney, John W. *Anecdotes of Public Men.* 2 vols. New York: Harper & Brothers, 1873.

"Fort-La-Fayette Life," 1863–64 in Extracts from the "Right Flanker." London: Simpkin, Marshall & Co.; / Liverpool: Edward Howell, 1865.

Fox, Richard Wightman. *Trials of Intimacy: Love and Loss in the Beecher-Tilton Scandal.* Chicago: University of Chicago Press, 1999.

Fox, Tryphena Blanche Holder. *A Northern Woman in the Plantation South: Letters of Tryphena Blanche Holder Fox, 1856–1876.* Edited by Wilma King. Columbia: University of South Carolina Press, 1993.

Frank Leslie's Illustrated Newspaper.

Freeman, Douglas Southall. *Lee's Lieutenants.* 3 vols. New York: Charles Scribner's Sons, 1942.

Fremantle, Arthur J. L. *Three Months in the Southern States, April–June 1863.* 1864. Reprint. Westport Conn.: Negro Universities Press, 1970.

Frobel, Anne S. *The Civil War Diary of Anne S. Frobel.* Edited by Mary H. and Dallas M. Lancaster. 1986. Reprint. McLean, Va.: EPM Publications, 1992.

Furgurson, Ernest B. *Ashes of Glory: Richmond at War.* New York: Alfred A. Knopf, 1996.

Gallagher, Gary W., ed. *Antietam: Essays on the 1862 Maryland Campaign.* Kent, Ohio: Kent State University Press, 1989.

Garner, James Wilford. *Reconstruction in Mississippi.* New York: Macmillan Company, 1901.

Gavin, William Gilfillan. *Campaigning with the Roundheads: The History of the Hundredth Pennsylvania Veteran Volunteer Infantry Regiment in the American Civil War, 1861–1865.* Dayton, Ohio: Morningside House, 1989.

Gay, Constance Mary. "The Campaign of 1855 in Virginia and the Fall of the Know-Nothing Party." *Richmond College Historical Papers* 1 (June 1916): 309–35.

Gay, Mary A. H. *Life in Dixie during the War.* 1897. Reprint. Atlanta: Darby Printing Company, 1979.

Genealogies of Virginia Families: From the "Virginia Magazine of History and Biography." Vol. 4. Baltimore: Genealogical Publishing Co., 1981.

Gerson, Armand J. "The Inception of the Montgomery Convention." In *Annual Report of the American Historical Association for the Year 1810.* Washington, D.C.: 1912.

Glass, Paul, and Louis C. Singer. *Singing Soldiers: A History of the Civil War in Song.* 1968. Reprint. New York: Da Capo Press, 1975.

Glenn, John F. "Brave Defence of the Cockade City." *Southern Historical Society Papers* 35 (1907): 1–24

Golden, James L. "The Southern Unionists, 1850–1860." In *Oratory in the Old South, 1828–1860*. Edited by Waldo W. Braden. Baton Rouge: Louisiana State University Press, 1970.

Goode, John. "The Confederate Congress." *Conservative Review* 4 (September 1900): 97–112.

Gorgas, Josiah. *The Civil War Diary of General Josiah Gorgas.* Edited by Frank E. Vandiver. University: University of Alabama Press, 1947.

Graves, Thomas Thatcher. "The Fall of Richmond: The Occupation." In *Battles and Leaders of the Civil War*. Vol. 4. Edited by Robert Underwood Johnson and Clarence Clough Buel. 1887. Reprint. Secaucus, N.J.: Castle, n. d.

Gray, Virginia Davis. "Life in Confederate Arkansas: The Diary of Virginia Davis Gray, 1863–1865, Part I." Edited by Carl H. Moneyhon. *Arkansas Historical Quarterly* 42 (Spring 1983): 47–85.

Green, Anna Maria. *The Journal of a Milledgeville Girl, 1861–1867.* Edited by James C. Bonner. Athens: University of Georgia Press, 1964.

Gregory Family. Papers. Virginia Historical Society Library, Richmond, Va.

Guernsey, Alfred H., and Henry M. Alden. *Harper's Pictorial History of the Civil War*. 1866. Reprint. New York: Fairfax Press, n.d.

Habersham, Josephine Clay. *Ebb Tide: As Seen through the Diary of Josephine Clay Habersham, 1863*. Edited by Spencer B. King Jr. Athens: University of Georgia Press, 1958.

Hague, Parthenia Antoinette. *A Blockaded Family: Life in Southern Alabama during the Civil War*. Boston: Houghton Mifflin & Company, 1888.

Hallum, John. *The Diary of an Old Lawyer: Scenes behind the Curtain*. Nashville, Tenn.: Southwestern Publishing House, 1895.

Halsey, Ashley, Jr. "South Carolina Began Preparing for War in 1851." *Civil War Times Illustrated* 1 (April 1962): 8–10, 12–13.

Halstead, Murat. *Three against Lincoln*. Edited by William B. Hesseltine. Baton Rouge: Louisiana State University Press, 1960.

Hambleton, James P. *A Biographical Sketch of Henry A. Wise, with a History of the Political Campaign in Virginia in 1855*. Richmond, Va.: J. W. Randolph, 1856.

Hankinson, Alan. *Man of Wars: William Howard Russell of "The Times."* London: Heinemann Educational Books, 1982.

Hanrahan, Allan C. "The Portsmouth Grays: From 'Mutiny' to Glory." *Virginia Cavalcade* 24 (Autumn 1974): 88–95.

Hardin, Elizabeth Pendleton. *The Private War of Lizzie Hardin: A Kentucky Girl's Diary of the Civil War in Kentucky, Virginia, Tennessee, Alabama, and Georgia*. Edited by G. Glenn Clift. Frankfort: Kentucky Historical Society, 1963.

Hardy, W. H. "The Homespun Dress." *Confederate Veteran* 9 (May 1901): 213–14.

Harper, Annie. *Annie Harper's Journal: A Southern Mother's Legacy*. Edited by Jeannie Marie Deen. Denton, Miss.: Flower Mound Writing Company, 1983.

Harper, Robert S. *Lincoln and the Press*. New York: McGraw-Hill Book Company, 1951.

Harper's Weekly.

Harris, Alexander. *A Review of the Political Conflict in America*. 1919. Reprint. Westport, Conn.: Negro Universities Press, 1970.

Harris, Emily Lyles. "Emily Lyles Harris: A Piedmont Farmer during the Civil War." Edited by Philip N. Racine. *South Atlantic Quarterly* 79 (Autumn 1980): 386–97.

Harrison, Constance Cary. *Recollections Grave and Gay*. New York: Charles Scribner's Sons, 1911.

———. "A Virginia Girl in the First Year of the War." *Century Magazine* 30 (August 1885): 606–14.

———. "Virginia Scenes in '61." In *Battles and Leaders in the Civil War*. Vol. 1. Edited by Robert Underwood Johnson and Clarence Clough Buel. Secaucus, N.J.: Castle, n.d.

Harrison, M. Clifford. "Petersburg's Ninth of June." *Virginia Cavalcade* 8 (Summer 1958): 10–15.

Hastings, Earl C., Jr., and David S. Hastings. *A Pitiless Rain: The Battle of Williamsburg, 1862.* Shippensburg, Pa.: White Maine Publishing Co., 1997.

Hazelton, Gerry W. "The Chicago Convention of 1860 and the Man It Nominated." In *War Papers* read before the Commandery of the State of Wisconsin, MOLLUS. Vol. 4. 1914. Reprint. Wilmington, N.C.: Broadfoot Publishing Company, 1993.

Headley, John W. *Confederate Operations in Canada and New York.* New York: Neale Publishing Company, 1906.

Heidler, David S. *Pulling the Temple Down: The Fire-Eaters and the Destruction of the Union.* Mechanicsburg, Pa.: Stackpole Books, 1994.

Henderson, William D. *Petersburg in the Civil War: War at the Door.* Lynchburg, Va.: H. E. Howard, 1998.

———. *The Unredeemed City: Reconstruction in Petersburg, Virginia, 1865–1864.* Washington, D.C.: University Press of America, 1977.

Hendrick, Burton J. *Statesmen of the Lost Cause: Jefferson Davis and His Cabinet.* Boston: Little, Brown & Company, 1939.

Hennessey, John J. *Return to Bull Run: The Campaign and Battle of Second Manassas.* New York: Simon & Schuster, 1993.

Herd, Elmer Don, Jr., ed. "Lawrence M. Keitt's Letters from the Provisional Congress of the Confederacy, 1861." *South Carolina Historical Magazine* 61 (January 1960): 19–25.

Hesseltine, William B. "The Pryor-Potter Duel." *Wisconsin Magazine of History* 27 (June 1944): 400–9.

Heyward, Pauline DeCaradeuc. *A Confederate Lady Comes of Age: The Journal of Pauline DeCaradeuc Heyward.* Edited by Mary D. Robertson. Columbia: University of South Carolina Press, 1992.

Hickerson, Thomas Felix. *Echoes of Happy Valley: Letters and Di-*

aries, Family Life in the South, Civil War History. Chapel Hill, N.C.: Bull's Head Bookshop, 1962.

Hoehling, A. A., and Mary Hoehling. *The Last Days of the Confederacy.* 1981. Originally titled *The Day Richmond Died.* New York: Fairfax Press, 1986.

Holmes, Emma. *The Diary of Miss Emma Holmes, 1861–1866.* Edited by John F. Marszalek. Baton Rouge: Louisiana State University Press, 1994.

Holzman, Robert S. *Adapt or Perish: The Life of General Roger A. Pryor, C. S. A.* Hamden, Conn.: Archon Books, 1976.

———. *Stormy Ben Butler.* New York: Macmillan Company, 1954. *Home Talk.*

Hopley, Catherine C. *Life in the South; from the Commencement of the War. By a Blockaded British Subject.* 2 vols. London: Chapman & Hall, 1863.

House, Ellen Renshaw. *A Very Violent Rebel: The Civil War Diary of Ellen Renshaw House.* Edited by Daniel E. Sutherland. Knoxville: University of Tennessee Press, 1996.

Houston, Henry Clarence. *The Thirty-second Maine Regiment of Infantry Volunteers: An Historical Sketch.* Portland, Maine: Press of Southworth Brothers, 1903.

Howard, Francis K. *Fourteen Months in American Bastiles.* Baltimore: Kelly, Hedean & Piet, 1863.

Howard, Wiley C. *Sketch of Cobb Legion Cavalry.* Prepared and read under appointment of Atlanta camp 159, U. C. V, August 19, 1901.

Howe, Thomas J. *Wasted Valor: The Petersburg Campaign, June 15–18, 1864.* Lynchburg, Va.: H. E. Howard, 1988.

Huckaby, Elizabeth Paisley, and Ethel C. Simpson, eds. *Tulip Evermore: Emma Butler and William Paisley, Their lives in Letters, 1857–1887.* Fayetteville: University of Arkansas Press, 1985.

Hudson, Frederick. *Journalism in the United States.* New York: Harper & Brothers, 1873.

Hurst, Marshall B. *History of the Fourteenth Regiment Alabama Volunteers.* Edited by William Stanley Hoole. Richmond: Confederate Publishing Company, 1982.

"In Memoriam." United Confederate Veteran Collection, New York Camp. Eleanor S. Brockenbrough Library, Museum of the Confederacy, Richmond, Va.

Jackson, Walter M. *The Story of Selma.* Birmingham, Ala.: Birmingham Printing Company, 1954.

James, Edward T., Janet Wilson James, and Paul S. Boyer, eds. *Notable American Women, 1607–1950: A Biographical Dictionary.* 3 vols. Cambridge, Mass.: Belknap Press of Harvard University, 1980.

Jervey, Susan R., and Charlotte St. J. Ravenel. *Two Diaries from Middle St. John's Berkeley, South Carolina, February–May 1865.* Pinopolis, S.C.: St. John's Hunting Club, 1921.

Johannsen, Robert W. *Stephen A. Douglas.* New York: Oxford University Press, 1973.

Johnson, Andrew. *The Papers of Andrew Johnson.* Edited by Paul H. Bergeron. Vol. 9. Knoxville: University of Tennessee Press, 1991.

Johnson, Ludwell H. "Fort Sumter and Confederate Diplomacy." *Journal of Southern History* 26 (November 1960): 441–77.

Johnson, Robert Underwood, and Clarence Clough Buel, eds. *Battles and Leaders of the Civil War.* 4 vols. 1887. Reprint. Secaucus, N.J.: Castle, n.d.

Jones, James P., and William Warren Rogers, eds. "Montgomery as the Confederate Capital: View of a New Nation." *Alabama Historical Quarterly* 26 (spring 1964): 1–125.

Jones, John B. *A Rebel War Clerk's Diary.* Edited by Earl Schenck Miers. New York: Sagamore Press, 1958.

Jones, Katherine M., ed. *Heroines of Dixie: Confederate Women Tell Their Story of the War.* 1955. Reprint. New York: Konecky & Konecky, 1995.

————. *Ladies of Richmond, Confederate Capital.* Indianapolis: Bobbs-Merrill Company, 1962.

————. *When Sherman Came: Southern Women and the "Great March."* Indianapolis: Bobbs-Merrill Company, 1964.

Jones, Mary Sharpe, and Mary Jones Mallard. *Yankees A'Coming: One Month's Experience during the Invasion of Liberty County, Georgia, 1864–1865.* Edited by Haskell Monroe. Tuscaloosa, Ala: Confederate Publishing Company, 1959.

Kean, Robert Garlick Hill. *Inside the Confederate Government: The Diary of Robert Garlick Hill Kean.* Edited by Edward Younger. New York: Oxford University Press, 1957.

Keiley, Anthony M. *Prisoner of War, or Five Months among the Yankees.* Richmond, Va.: West & Johnston, 1865.

Keitt, Sue Sparks. "Sue Sparks Keitt, to a Northern Friend, March 4, 1861." Edited by Elmer Don Herd Jr. *South Carolina Historical Magazine* 62 (April 1961): 82–87.

Kelly, Alfred H., and Winfred A. Harbison. *The American Constitution: Its Origins and Development,* 3rd edition. New York: W. W. Norton & Company, 1963.

Kimball, William J., ed. *Richmond in Time of War.* New York: Houghton Mifflin Company, 1960.

————. "The Bread Riot in Richmond." *Civil War History* 7 (June 1961): 149–54.

Kirwan, Albert D., ed. *The Confederacy.* New York: Meridian Books, 1959.

Krick, Robert K. "The Army of Northern Virginia in September 1862: Its Circumstances, Its Opportunities, and Why It Should Not Have Been at Sharpsburg." In *Antietam: Essays on the 1862 Maryland Campaign.* Edited by Gary W. Gallagher. Kent, Ohio: Kent State University Press, 1989.

Kunkle, Camille. "'It Is What It Does to the Souls': Women's Views on the Civil War." *Atlanta History* 33 (Summer 1989): 56–70.

Lamon, Ward Hill. *Recollections of Abraham Lincoln.* Edited by

Dorothy Lamon Teillard. 1911. Reprint. Lincoln: University of Nebraska Press, 1994.

Largent, Robert L. "Virginia Takes the Road to Secession." *West Virginia History* 3 (January 1942): 120–46.

Lebsock, Suzanne. *The Free Women of Petersburg: Status and Culture in a Southern Town, 1784–1860.* New York: W. W. Norton, 1984.

LeConte, Emma. *When the World Ended: The Diary of Emma LeConte.* Edited by Earl Schenck Miers. New York: Oxford University Press, 1957.

LeConte, Joseph. *'Ware Sherman: A Journal of Three Months' Personal Experience in the Last Days of the Confederacy.* 1937. Reprint. Baton Rouge: Louisiana State University Press, 1999.

Lee, Charles Robert. *The Confederate Constitutions.* Chapel Hill: University of North Carolina Press, 1963.

Lee, Robert E. "Secession Is Nothing but Revolution: A Letter of R. E. Lee to His Son 'Rooney'." Edited by William M. E. Rachal. *Virginia Magazine of History and Biography* 69 (January 1961): 3–6.

Lee, Stephen D. "The First Step in the War." In *Battles and Leaders of the Civil War.* Vol. 1. Edited by Robert Underwood Johnson and Clarence Clough Buel. 1887. Reprint. Secaucus, N.J.: Castle, n.d.

Leech, John W. T. "The Battle of Frazier's Farm." *Southern Historical Society Papers* 21 (1893): 160–65.

Le Grand, Julia. *The Journal of Julia Le Grand, New Orleans, 1862–1863.* Edited by Kate Mason Rowland and Agnes E. Croxall. Richmond: Everett Waddey Co., 1911.

Leland, Isabella Middleton, ed. "Middleton Correspondence, 1861–1865." *South Carolina Historical Magazine* 63 (January 1962): 33–41; 64 (April 1963): 95–104; 65 (April 1964): 98–109.

Leyburn, John. "The Fall of Richmond." *Harper's New Monthly Magazine* 33 (June 1866): 92–96.

Lightfoot, Mrs. William B. "The Evacuation of Richmond." *Virginia Magazine of History and Biography* 41 (July 1933): 215–22.

Lincoln, Abraham. *The Collected Works of Abraham Lincoln*. 8 vols. Edited by Roy P. Basler. New Brunswick, N.J.: Rutgers University Press, 1953.

Livingston, E. A. (Bud). *President Lincoln's Third Largest City: Brooklyn & the Civil War*. New York: Privately printed, 1994.

Logan, Kate Virginia Cox. *My Confederate Girlhood: The Memoirs of Kate Virginia Cox Logan*. Edited by Lily Logan Morrill. Richmond: Garrett and Massie, 1932.

Long, A. L. *Memoirs of Robert E. Lee*. 1886. Reprint. Secaucus, N.J.: Blue & Grey Press, 1983.

Long, E. B., with Barbara Long. *The Civil War Day by Day: An Almanac, 1861–1865*. Garden City, N.Y.: Doubleday & Company, 1971.

Lunt, Dolly Sumner. *A Woman's Wartime Journal: An Account of the Passage over a Georgia Plantation of Sherman's Army on the March to the Sea, as Recorded in the Diary of Dolly Sumner Lunt*. Edited by Julian Street. New York: Century Co., 1918.

Lynch, Denis Tilden. *"Boss" Tweed: The Story of a Grim Generation*. New York: Boni and Liveright, 1927.

McAdam, David, et al., eds. *History of the Bench and Bar of New York*. 2 vols. New York: New York History Company, 1897.

McCabe, James D., Jr. *The Grayjackets: And How They Lived, Fought, and Died, for Dixie. By a Confederate*. Richmond, Va.: Jones Brothers & Co., 1867.

McClatchey, Minerva Leah Rowles. "A Georgia Woman's Civil War Diary: The Journal of Minerva Rowles McClatchey, 1864–'65." Edited by T. Conn Bryan. *Georgia Historical Quarterly* 51 (June 1967): 197–216.

McClellan, George B. *McClellan's Own Story*. Edited by William C. Prime. New York: Charles L. Webster & Company, 1887.

McClure, Alexander K. *Colonel Alexander K. McClure's Recollections of Half a Century*. Salem, Mass.: Salem Press Company, 1902.

McCrady, Edward, Jr. *Formation, Organization, Discipline, and Characteristics of the Army of Northern Virginia: An Address before Association Army of Northern Virginia, 21 Oct 1886.* Richmond, Va.: W. Ellis Jones, Book & Job Printer, 1886.

McDonald, Cornelia Peake. *A Diary with Reminiscences of the War and Refugee Life in the Shenandoah Valley, 1860–1865.* Edited by Hunter McDonald. Nashville, Tenn.: Cullom & Ghertner Co., 1935.

McGuire, Judith B. *Diary of a Southern Refugee during the War.* 1867. Reprint. Harrisonburg, Va.: Sprinkle Publications, 1996.

McLean, Margaret Sumner. "A Northern Woman in the Confederacy." *Harper's Monthly Magazine* 128 (February 1914): 440–51.

———. "When the States Seceded." *Harper's Monthly Magazine* 128 (January 1914): 282–88.

McWillie, William. Notebooks. Mississippi Department of Archives and History, Jackson, Miss.

Magill, Mary Tucker. *Women, or Chronicles of the Late War.* Baltimore: Turnbull Brothers, 1871.

Manarin, Louis H., ed. *Richmond at War: The Minutes of the City Council, 1861–1865.* Chapel Hill: University of North Carolina Press, 1966.

Manly, Basil. "The Diary of Dr. Basil Manly, 1858–1867." Edited by W. Stanley Hoole. *Alabama Review* 4 (April 1951): 127–49.

Markens, Isaac. Papers. Virginia Historical Society Library, Richmond, Va.

———. *President Lincoln and the Case of John Yates Beall.* New York: Privately printed, 1911.

Massey, Mary Elizabeth. *Ersatz in the Confederacy.* Columbia: University of South Carolina Press, 1952.

———. *Refugee Life in the Confederacy.* Baton Rouge: Louisiana State University Press, 1964.

———. *Women in the Civil War.* 1966 (as *Bonnet Brigades*). Reprint. Lincoln: University of Nebraska Press, 1994.

Maury, Betty Herndon. Diary, 1861–63. Manuscript Division, Library of Congress, Washington, D.C.

Mayer, Grace M. *Once upon a City.* New York: Macmillan Company, 1958.

Miller, Alphonse B. *Thaddeus Stevens.* New York: Harper & Brothers, 1939.

Miller, Robert H. "Letters of Lieutenant Robert H. Miller to His Family, 1861–1862." Edited by Forrest P. Connor. *Virginia Magazine of History and Biography* 70 (January 1962): 62–91.

Mitchell, Betty L. *Edmund Ruffin: A Biography.* Bloomington: Indiana University Press, 1981.

Molineux, Will. "The Battle of Williamsburg: 'A Most Sanguinary Engagement.'" *William and Mary Alumni Gazette* 51 (Summer 1983): 30–36.

Monteiro, Margaret Kean. "The Presidential Election of 1860 in Virginia." *Richmond College Historical Papers* 1 (June 1916): 222–58.

Moore, Frank, ed. *The Rebellion Record: A Diary of American Events.* 12 vols. 1861–1868. Reprint. New York: Arno Press, 1977.

Mordecai, Emma. Diary. Typescript. Virginia Historical Society Library, Richmond, Va.

Morrissette, Kate H. "Social Life in the First Confederate Capital." *Montgomery Journal*, 13 March 1907. Typescript copy. State of Alabama Department of Archives and History, Montgomery, Ala.

Mott, Frank Luther. *A History of American Magazines, 1865–1885.* Cambridge: Harvard University Press, 1938.

Murry, Ellen N. *The Code of Honor: Dueling in America.* Washington, Tex.: Star of the Republic Museum, 1984.

Myers, Robert Manson. *The Children of Pride: Selected Letters of the Family of The Rev. Dr. Charles Colcock Jones, 1860–1868.* New, abridged edition. New Haven, Conn.: Yale University Press, 1984.

Nevins, Allan. *The Emergence of Lincoln.* 2 vols. New York: Charles Scribner's Sons, 1950.

New York Evening Post.

New York Herald.

New York Law Journal.

New York Sun.

New York Times.

New York World.

Nichols, Roy Franklin. *The Disruption of American Democracy.* New York: Macmillan Company, 1948.

————. *Franklin Pierce: Young Hickory of the Granite Hills.* Philadelphia: University of Pennsylvania Press, 1958.

Nicolay, John G. *The Outbreak of the Rebellion.* 1881. Reprint. Wilmington N.C.: Broadfoot Publishing Company, 1989.

———— and John Hay. *Abraham Lincoln: A History.* 10 vols. New York: Century Co., 1914.

Niles, Blair. *The James: From Iron Gate to the Sea.* New York: Farrar & Rinehart, 1945.

Overdyke, W. Darrell. *The Know-Nothing Party in the South.* Baton Rouge: Louisiana State University Press, 1950.

Page, Charles A. *Letters of a War Correspondent.* Edited by James R. Gilmore. Boston: L. C. Page & Company, 1898.

Patrick, Rembert W. *The Fall of Richmond.* Baton Rouge: Louisiana State University Press, 1960.

Patterson, A. W. *The Code Duello, with Special Reference to the State of Virginia.* Richmond, Va.: Richmond Press, 1927.

Pearson, Alden B., Jr. "A Middle-Class Border-State Family during the Civil War." *Civil War History* 22 (December 1976): 318–36.

Pember, Phoebe Yates. *A Southern Woman's Story: Life in Confederate Richmond.* Edited by Bell Irvin Wiley. 1959. Reprint. Wilmington, N.C.: Broadfoot Publishing Company, 1991.

Perritt, H. Hardy. "The Fire-Eaters." In *Oratory in the Old South, 1828–1860.* Edited by Waldo W. Braden. Baton Rouge: Louisiana State University Press, 1970.

Peterson, Owen. "Speaking in the Southern Commercial Conventions." In *Oratory in the Old South, 1828–1860.* Edited by Waldo W. Braden. Baton Rouge: Louisiana State University Press, 1970.

Peyton, John Lewis. *The American Crisis; or, Pages from the Note-*

Book of a State Agent during the Civil War. London: Saunders, Otley, & Co., 1867.

Pfanz, Donald C. *Abraham Lincoln at City Point, March 20–April 9, 1865.* Lynchburg, Va.: H. E. Howard, 1989.

Phillips, Ulrich B. "The Correspondence of Robert Toombs, Alexander H. Stephens, and Howell Cobb." *Annual Report of the American Historical Association for the Year 1911.* Vol. 2. Washington, D.C.: 1913.

Pickett, LaSalle Corbell. *Across My Path: Memories of People I Have Known.* New York: Brentano's, 1916.

Polk, James K. *Polk: The Diary of a President, 1845–1849.* Edited by Allan Nevins. New York: Longmans, Green & Co., 1929.

Pollard, Edward A. *The Lost Cause: A New Southern History of the War of the Confederates.* 1867. Reprint. New York: Bonanza Books, n.d.

———. "The Confederate Congress." *Galaxy* 6 (December 1868): 749–58.

Poore, Benjamin Perley. *Perley's Reminiscences of Sixty Years in the National Metropolis.* 2 vols. in 1. Philadelphia: Hubbard Brothers, 1886.

Porcher, Francis Peyre. *Resources of the Southern Fields and Forests.* 1863. Reprint. New York: Arno & The New York Times, 1970.

Porter, David Dixon. *Incidents and Anecdotes of the Civil War.* New York: D. Appleton & Company, 1885.

Porter, Horace. *Campaigning with Grant.* New York: Konecky & Konecky, 1992.

Potter, David M. *The Impending Crisis, 1848–1861.* Completed and edited by Don E. Fehrenbacher. New York: Harper & Row, 1976.

Potts, Frank. *The Death of the Confederacy: The Last Week of the Army of Northern Virginia as Set Forth in a Letter of April 1865.* Edited by Douglas Southall Freeman. Richmond, Va.: Privately printed, 1928.

Preston, Margaret Junkin. *Beechenbrook: A Rhyme of the War.* Baltimore: Kelly & Piet, 1866.

"Proceedings of First Confederate Congress—First Session." *Southern Historical Society Papers* 44 (June 1923): 3–206.

"——— ——. Third Session." *Southern Historical Society Papers* 48 (September 1941): 1–329.

Pryor, Anne Campbell. "Incidents in the Life of a Civil War Child." Typescript. Anne Campbell Pryor Papers, Virginia State Library, Richmond, Va.

———. "Recollections Concerning Dr. Theodorick Bland Pryor." Typescript. Anne Campbell Pryor Papers, Virginia State Library, Richmond, Va.

Pryor, Roger Atkinson. "The Bar and Forensic Oratory." In *Essays and Addresses with Explanatory Notes*. New York: Neale Publishing Company, 1912.

———. *Essays and Addresses with Explanatory Notes*. New York: Neale Publishing Company, 1912.

———. *The Foundation of Professional Success*. Chicago: La Salle Extension University, 1911.

———. *Independence of the South: Speech by Roger A. Pryor, of Virginia*. Washington, D.C.: Henry Polkinhorn, 1861.

———. Letter, Miscellaneous Manuscripts Collection, Manuscript Division, Library of Congress, Washington, D.C.

———. *Speech of Hon. Roger A. Pryor, of Virginia, on the Principles and Policy of the Black Republican Party; Delivered in the House of Representatives, December 29, 1859*. Washington, D.C.: Printed at the Congressional Globe Office, 1859.

———. "Virginia's Part in American History." In *Modern Eloquence*. Vol. 3. Edited by Thomas B. Reed, Justin McCarthy, Rossiter Johnson, and Albert Ellery Bergh. Philadelphia, Pa.: John D. Morris & Company, 1900.

Pryor, Roger Atkinson, Jr. *The Capture of Gen. Roger A. Pryor*. New York: 1889.

Pryor, Sara Rice. *My Day: Reminiscences of a Long Life*. New York: Macmillan Company, 1909.

————. *Reminiscences of Peace and War.* New York: Macmillan Company, 1904.

Pulliam, Samuel Harper. Letter. Virginia Historical Society Library, Richmond, Va.

Putnam, Sallie Brock. *Richmond during the War: Four Years of Personal Observation.* 1867. Reprint. Lincoln: University of Nebraska Press, 1996.

Quattlebaum, Isabel. "Twelve Women in the First Days of the Confederacy." *Civil War History* 7 (December 1961): 370–85.

Rable, George C. *Civil Wars: Women and the Crisis of Southern Nationalism.* Urbana: University of Illinois Press, 1989.

Ramsdell, Charles W. *Behind the Lines in the Southern Confederacy.* Edited by Wendell H. Stephenson. Baton Rouge: Louisiana State University Press, 1944.

Randall, James G., and David Donald. *The Civil War and Reconstruction.* 2nd edition. Boston: Little, Brown, 1969.

Reagan, John H. *Memoirs with Special Reference to Secession and the Civil War.* Edited by Walter Flavius McCaleb. New York: Neale Publishing Company, 1906.

Richmond Record.

Reniers, Perceval. *Springs of Virginia: Life, Love, and Death at the Waters, 1775–1900.* Chapel Hill: University of North Carolina Press, 1941.

Rhett, Robert Barnwell. *A Fire-Eater Remembers: The Confederate Memoir of Robert Barnwell Rhett.* Edited by William C. Davis. Columbia: University of South Carolina Press, 2000.

————. "The Confederate Government at Montgomery." In *Battles and Leaders of the Civil War.* Vol. 1. Edited by William Underwood Johnson and Clarence Clough Buel. 1887. Reprint. Secaucus, N.J.: Castle, n.d.

Rhodes, James Ford. *History of the United States from the Compromise of 1850 to the McKinley-Bryan Campaign of 1896.* 8 vols. 1892–1919. Reprint. Port Washington, N.Y.: Kennikat Press, 1967.

Rice, Marie Gordon Pryor. "Sarah Agnes Pryor." In *Library of Southern Literature*. Vol. 10. Edited by Edward Anderson Alderman and Joel Chandler Harris. Atlanta: Martin and Hoyt Company, 1909.

Rice, Philip Morrison. "The Know-Nothing Party in Virginia, 1854–1856." *Virginia Magazine of History and Biography* 55 (January 1947): 61–75 (April 1947): 159–67.

Richmond Examiner.

Richmond News Leader.

Richmond Sentinel.

Richmond Times-Dispatch.

Riley, Ben A. "The Pryor-Potter Affair: Nineteenth Century Conflict as Percursor to Civil War." *Journal of the West Virginia Historical Association* 8 (Spring 1984): 29–40.

Robertson, William G. *The Battle of Old Men and Young Boys, June 9, 1864.* Lynchburg, Va.: H. E. Howard, 1989.

Roland, Charles P. *The Confederacy.* Chicago: University of Chicago Press, 1960.

Roman, Alfred. *The Military Operations of General Beauregard.* 2 vols. New York: Harper & Brothers, 1884.

Rowland, Dunbar, ed. *Jefferson Davis, Constitutionalist: His Letters, Papers, and Speeches.* Jackson, Miss.: J. J. Little & Ives Company for the Mississippi Department of Archives and History, 1923.

Ruffin, Edmund. *The Diary of Edmund Ruffin.* Edited by William K. Scarborough. 3 vols. Baton Rouge: Louisiana State University Press, 1972.

Russell, William Howard. *My Diary North and South.* Boston: T. O. H. P. Burnham, 1863.

———. *Pictures of Southern Life, Social, Political, and Military.* New York: James G. Gregory, 1861.

Sabine, Lorenzo. *Notes on Duels and Duelling.* Boston: Crosby, Nichols, & Company, 1855.

Sandburg, Carl. *Abraham Lincoln: The War Years.* 4 vols. Sangamon Edition. New York: Charles Scribner's Sons, 1943.

Sangston, Lawrence. *Bastiles of the North, by a Member of the Maryland Legislature.* Baltimore: Kelly, Hedian & Piet, 1863.

Saxon, Elizabeth Lyle. *A Southern Woman's War-Time Reminiscences.* Memphis, Tenn.: Pilcher Printing Co., 1905.

Scales, Cordelia. "The Civil War Letters of Cordelia Scales." Edited by Percy L. Rainwater. *Journal of Mississippi History* 1 (July 1939): 169–81.

Schlesinger, Arthur M., Jr., ed. *History of U.S. Political Parties.* Vol. 1. New York: Chelsea House Publishers in Association with R. R. Bowker Company, 1973.

Schurz, Carl. *The Reminiscences of Carl Schurz.* 3 vols. New York: S. S. McClure Company, 1907–08.

———. *Speeches, Correspondence, and Political Papers of Carl Schurz.* Edited by Frederic Bancroft. 6 vols. 1913. Reprint. New York: Negro Universities Press, 1969.

Scott Family. Correspondence. Virginia Historical Society Library, Richmond, Va.

"Secret Societies—The Know Nothings." *Putnam's Monthly* 5 (January 1855): 88–97.

Scott, James G., and Edward A. Wyatt IV. *Petersburg's Story: A History.* Petersburg, Va.: Titmus Optical Co., 1960.

Sears, Stephen W. *Landscape Turned Red: The Battle of Antietam.* New Haven, Conn.: Ticknor & Fields, 1983.

———. *To the Gates of Richmond: The Peninsula Campaign.* New York: Ticknor & Fields, 1992.

"Second Presbyterian Church of Petersburg, Virginia." Typescript. Second Presbyterian Church, Petersburg, Va.

Shanks, Henry T. *The Secession Movement in Virginia, 1847–1861.* Richmond, Va.: Garrett and Massie, 1934.

Sherman, John. *Recollections of Forty Years in the House, Senate, and Cabinet.* 2 vols. Chicago: Werner Company, 1895.

Shofner, Jerrell H., and William Warren Rogers. "Montgomery to Richmond: The Confederacy Selects a Capital." *Civil War History* 10 (June 1964): 155–66.

Simkins, Francis Butler, and James Welch Patton. *The Women of the Confederacy.* Richmond, Va.: Garrett & Massie, 1936.

Smith, Charles H. *Bill Arp, So Called: A Side Show of the Southern Side of the War.* New York: Metropolitan Record Office, 1866.

Smith, William Ernest. *The Francis Preston Blair Family in Politics.* 2 vols, New York: Macmillan Company, 1933.

Solomon, Clara. *The Civil War Diary of Clara Solomon: Growing up in New Orleans, 1861–1862.* Edited by Elliott Ashkenazi. Baton Rouge: Louisiana State University Press, 1995.

Sommers, Richard J. *Richmond Redeemed: The Siege at Petersburg.* Garden City, N.Y.: Doubleday & Company, 1981.

Speer, Lonnie P. *Portals to Hell: Military Prisons of the Civil War.* Mechanicsburg, Pa.: Stackpole Books, 1997.

Spencer, Warren F. "A French View of the Fall of Richmond: Alfred Paul's Report to Drouyn de Lhuys, April 11, 1865." *Virginia Magazine of History and Biography* 73 (April 1965): 178–88.

Sperry, Kate. "Kate Sperry's Diary, 1861–1866." Edited by Christine Andreae. *Virginia Country's Civil War* 1 (1983): 43–75.

Stephenson, Nathaniel W. *The Day of the Confederacy: A Chronicle of the Embattled South.* New Haven, Conn.: Yale University Press, 1919.

Sterkx, H. E. *Partners in Rebellion: Alabama Women in the Civil War.* Rutherford, N.J.: Fairleigh Dickinson University Press, 1970.

Stiles, Henry R., ed. *The Civil, Political, Professional, and Ecclesiastical History and Commercial and Industrial Record of the County of Kings and the City of Brooklyn, NY.* New York: W. W. Munsell & Co., 1884.

Stone, Kate. *Brokenburn: The Journal of Kate Stone, 1861–1868.* Edited by John Q. Anderson. Baton Rouge: Louisiana State University Press, 1955.

Stowe, Steven M. *Intimacy and Power in the Old South: Ritual in the Lives of the Planters.* Baltimore: Johns Hopkins University Press, 1987.

Sulivane, Clement. "The Fall of Richmond: The Evacuation." In *Battles and Leaders of the Civil War.* Vol. 4. Edited by William Underwood Johnson and Clarence Clough Buel. 1887. Reprint. Secaucus, N.J.: Castle, n.d.

Sullivan, Walter, ed. *The War the Women Lived: Female Voices from the Confederate South.* Nashville, Tenn.: J. S. Sanders & Company, 1995.

Suplée, Thomas D. *The Life of Theodorick Bland Pryor: First Mathematical-Fellow of Princeton College.* San Francisco, Calif.: Bacon & Company, 1879.

Supplement to the Official Records of the Union and Confederate Armies. Pt. 1—Reports. 12 vols. Edited by Janet B. Hewett, Noah Andre Trudeau, and Bryce A. Suderow. Wilmington, N.C.: Broadfoot Publishing Company, 1994–1998.

Sutherland, Daniel E. *The Confederate Carpetbaggers.* Baton Rouge: Louisiana State University Press, 1988.

Taliaferro, Harriotte Lee. "Memoir of Mrs. Harriotte Lee Taliaferro Concerning Events in Virginia, April 11–21, 1861." Introduction and Notes by Ludwell Lee Montague. *Virginia Magazine of History and Biography* 57 (October 1949): 416–20.

Tapp, Hettie Wisdom. "Hettie Wisdom Tapp's Memoirs." Edited by Emma Inman Williams. *West Tennessee Historical Society Papers* 36 (October 1982): 117–23.

Taylor, George Braxton. *Virginia Baptist Ministers.* 3rd series. Lynchburg, Va.: J. P. Bell Company, 1912.

Taylor, Mrs. Thomas, and Mrs. A. T. Smythe, Mrs. August Kohn, Miss Mary B. Poppenheim, and Miss Martha B. Washington, eds. *South Carolina Women in the Confederacy.* Vol. 1. Columbia, S.C.: State Company, 1903.

Thomas, Anna Hasell. "The Diary of Anna Hasell Thomas, July 1864–May 1865." Edited by Charles E. Thomas. *South Carolina Historical Magazine* 74 (July 1973): 128–43.

Thomas, Ella Gertrude Clanton. *The Secret Eye: The Journal of Ella Gertrude Clanton Thomas, 1848–1889.* Edited by Virginia

Ingraham Burr. Chapel Hill: University of North Carolina Press, 1990.

Thomas, Emory M. *The Confederate Nation, 1861–1865*. New York: Harper & Row, 1979.

———. *The Confederate State of Richmond: A Biography of the Capital*. Austin: University of Texas Press, 1971.

———. "The Richmond Bread Riot of 1863." *Virginia Cavalcade* 18 (Summer 1968): 41–47.

Thompson, Holland, ed. *The Photographic History of the Civil War in Ten Volumes*. Vol. 7. New York: Review of Reviews Co., 1912.

Thompson, John. "Eye Witness to Fort Sumter: The Letters of Private John Thompson." Edited by Ron Chepesiuk. *South Carolina Historical Magazine* 85 (October 1984): 271–79.

Thompson, William E. "First in War, Foremost in Peace: Roger Atkinson Pryor, H-S 1846." *Museum* (spring 1993): 7–20.

Tice, Douglas O. "Bread or Blood!: The Richmond Bread Riot." *Civil War Times Illustrated* 12 (February 1974): 12–19.

Time-Life Books. *Echoes of Glory: Illustrated Atlas of the Civil War*. Alexandria, Va.: Time-Life Books, 1991.

Timrod, Henry. "The Two Armies." In *Poems of Henry Timrod, with Memoir and Portrait*. Richmond, Va.: B. F. Johnson Publishing Company, 1901.

Tomkins, Ellen Wilkins. "The Colonel's Lady: Some Letters of Ellen Wilkins Tomkins, July–December 1861." Edited by Ellen Wilkins Tomkins. *Virginia Magazine of History and Biography* 69 (October 1861): 387–419.

Tompkins, Christopher Q. "The Occupation of Richmond, April 1865: The Memorandum of Events of Colonel Christopher Q. Tompkins." Edited by William M. E. Rachal. *Virginia Magazine of History and Biography* 73 (April 1965): 189–98.

Towsend, George Alfred. *Rustics in Rebellion: A Yankee Reporter on the Road to Richmond, 1861–1865*. Chapel Hill: University of North Carolina Press, 1950.

Trietsch, James H. *The Printer and the Prince: A Study of the Influence of Horace Greeley upon Abraham Lincoln as Candidate and President*. New York: Exposition Press, 1955.

Truman, Ben C. *Duelling in America*. San Diego, Ca.: Joseph Tabler Books, 1992.

Tucker, Dallas. "The Fall of Richmond." *Southern Historical Society Papers* 29 (1901): 152–63.

Turner, Charles W., ed. *Civil War Letters of Arabella Speaiers and William Beverley Pettit of Fluvanna County, Virginia, March 1862–March 1865*. 2 vols. Roanoke: Virginia Lithography & Graphics, 1988–1989.

Turner, W. R. *Old Homes and Families in Nottoway*. Blackstone, Va.: Nottoway Publishing Co., 1932.

———. "Some Early Nottoway County History." *Virginia Magazine of History and Biography* 45 (July 1937): 260–72.

Tyler, Lyon Gardiner, ed. *Encyclopedia of Virginia Biography*. 5 vols. New York: Lewis Historical Publishing Company, 1915.

Underwood, J. L. *The Women of the Confederacy*. New York: Neale Publishing Company, 1906.

U.S. War Department. *The War of the Rebellion: A Compilation of the Official Records of the Union and Confederate Armies*. 70 volumes in 128 parts. 1880–1901. Reprint. Harrisburg, Pa.: Historical Times, 1985.

Van Duesen, John G. *The Ante-Bellum Southern Commercial Conventions*. Historical Papers published by the Trinity College Historical Society, ser. 16. 1926. Reprint. New York: AMS Press, 1970.

Van Lew, Elizabeth. *A Yankee Spy in Richmond: The Civil War Diary of 'Crazy Bet' Van Lew*. Edited by David D. Ryan. Mechanicsburg, Pa.: Stackpole Books, 1996.

Wait, Horatio L. "Reminiscences of Fort Sumter." In *Military Essays and Recollections*. Papers read before the Commandery of the State of Illinois, MOLLUS. Vol. 1. 1891. Reprint. Wilmington, N.C.: Broadfoot Publishing Company, 1992.

Walker, Eliza J. Kendrick (Lewis). "Other Days: An Account of Plantation Life on Chunnennuggee Ridge before the War between the States." *Alabama Historical Quarterly* 5 (spring 1943): 71–97; (summer 1943): 209–33.

Walker, Georgiana Gholson. *The Private Journal of Georgiana Gholson Walker, 1862–1865*. Edited by Dwight Franklin Henderson. Tuscaloosa, Ala.: Confederate Publishing Company, 1963.

Wallace, Elizabeth Curtis. *Glencoe Diary: The War-Time Journal of Elizabeth Curtis Wallace*. Edited by Eleanor P. Cross and Charles B. Cross Jr. Chesapeake, Va.: Norfolk Historical Society of Chesapeake, Virginia, 1968.

Wallace, Lee A., Jr. *3rd Virginia Infantry*. The Virginia Regimental History Series. 2nd ed. Lynchburg, Va.: H. E. Howard, 1986.

Walmsley, James E., ed. "The Change of Secession Sentiment in Virginia in 1861." *American Historical Review* 31 (October 1925): 82–101.

Walthall, Ernest Taylor. *Hidden Things Brought to Light*. 1908. Reprint. Richmond, Va.: Dietz Printing Co., 1933.

Warner, Ezra J. *Generals in Blue: Lives of the Union Commanders*. Baton Rouge: Louisiana State University Press, 1992.

———. *Generals in Gray: Lives of the Confederate Commanders*. Baton Rouge: Louisiana State University Press, 1987.

———, and W. Buck Yearns. *Biographical Register of the Confederate Congress*. Baton Rouge: Louisiana State University Press, 1975.

"Washington City." *Atlantic Monthly* 7 (January 1861): 1–8.

Washington, Ella. "'An Army of Devils': The Diary of Ella Washington." Edited by Ames O. Hall. *Civil War Times Illustrated* 16 (February 1978): 18–25.

Watertown (Wisconsin) *Democrat*.

Watson, Walter A. "Notes on Southside Virginia." Edited by Mrs. Walter A. Watson. *Bulletin of the Virginia State Library* 15 (September 1925).

———. Papers. Virginia Historical Society Library, Richmond, Va.

Waugh, Charles G., and Martin H. Greenberg, eds. *The Women's War in the South: Recollections and Reflections of the American Civil War.* Nashville, Tenn.: Cumberland House, 1999.

Webster, Clyde C. "John Minor Botts, Anti-Secessionist." *Richmond College Historical Papers* 1 (June 1915): 9–37.

Weddell, Elizabeth Wright. *St. Paul's Church, Richmond, Virginia: Its Historic Years and Memorials.* 2 vols. Richmond, Va.: William Byrd Press, 1931.

Weitzel, Godfrey. *Richmond Occupied.* Edited with an introduction by Louis H. Manarin. Richmond, Va.: Civil War Centennial Committee, 1965.

Welton, J. Michael, ed. *"My Heart Is So Rebellious": The Caldwell Letters, 1861–1865.* Warrenton, Va.: Fauquier National Bank, 1991.

Wender, Herbert. *Southern Commercial Conventions, 1837–1859.* Johns Hopkins University Studies in Historical and Political Science, ser. 48, no. 4. Baltimore: Johns Hopkins Press, 1930.

"When the Band First Played 'Dixie.'" *Confederate Veteran* 34 (June 1926): 234.

"Who Fired the First Gun at Sumter?" *Southern Historical Society Papers* 11 (1883): 501–4.

Wiley, Bell Irvin. *Confederate Women.* Westport, Conn.: Greenwood Press, 1975.

———. *The Plain People of the Confederacy.* Baton Rouge: Louisiana State University Press, 1943.

———, ed. *Letters of Warren Akin, Confederate Congressman.* Athens: University of Georgia Press, 1959.

Wilkinson, Warren. *Mother, May You Never See the Sights I Have Seen: The Fifty-seventh Massachusetts Veteran Volunteers in the Army of the Potomac, 1864–1865.* New York: Harper & Row, 1990.

Willcox, Louise Collier. "A Light Is Out!" *Harper's Weekly,* 24 February 1912.

Williams, Jack K. *Dueling in the Old South: Vignettes of Social History.* College Station: Texas A & M University Press, 1980.

Wilstach, Paul. *Tidewater, Virginia.* New York: Blue Ribbon Books, 1929.

Wise, Barton H. *The Life of Henry A. Wise of Virginia, 1806–1876.* New York: Macmillan Company, 1899.

Wise, John S. *The End of an Era.* Edited by Curtis Carroll Davis. New York: Thomas Yoseloff, 1965.

————. "The Fire-Eaters." *Saturday Evening Post* 178 (23 June 1906): 8–9, 24.

Wish, Harvey. *George Fitzhugh: Propagandist of the Old South.* 1943. Reprint. Gloucester, Mass.: Peter Smith, 1962.

Wright, Mrs. D. Giraud. *A Southern Girl in '61: The War-Time Memories of a Confederate Senator's Daughter.* New York: Doubleday, Page & Company, 1905.

Wriston, Henry Merritt. *Executive Agents in American Foreign Relations.* 1929. Reprint. Gloucester, Mass.: Peter Smith, 1967.

Wyatt, Edward A., IV, ed. *Preliminary Checklist for Petersburg, 1786–1876.* Richmond: Virginia State Library, 1949.

Yearns, Wilfred Buck. *The Confederate Congress.* Athens: University of Georgia Press, 1960.

Yoder, Paton. "Private Hospitality in the South, 1775–1850." *Mississippi Valley Historical Review* 47 (December 1960): 419–33.

Young, John Russell. *Men and Memories: Personal Reminiscences.* Edited by May D. Russell Young. 2 vols. New York: F. Tennyson Neely, 1901.

Zacharias, Donald W. "The Know-Nothing Party and the Oratory of Nativism." In *Oratory in the Old South, 1828–1880.* Edited by Waldo W. Braden. Baton Rouge: Louisiana State University Press, 1970.

Index